Sicily

From the Italy Experts

Touring Club of Italy

NOT TO BE MISSED IN

SICILY

The Touring Club of Italy has chosen what it considers to be the ten highlights of Sicily – musts for even the most hurried visitor. Descriptions of these sights can be found on the pages indicated.

3 *Bust of Eleanor of Aragon, Galleria Regionale della Sicilia, Palermo (p.39)*

A. Garozzo

2 *The Norman church of San Giovanni degli Eremiti, Palermo (p. 30)*

Monreale **1**

2 Palermo
3

4 Segesta

Agrigento
5

H. S. Huber/Marka

4 *The Doric temple of Segesta, still intact after 2,400 years (p. 83)*

W. Leon...

5 *Greek vase, Museo Archeologico Regionale, Agrigento (p. 91)*

M. Mazzola/Marka

6 *A mosaic in the Roman Villa of Casale, Piazza Armerina (p. 199)*

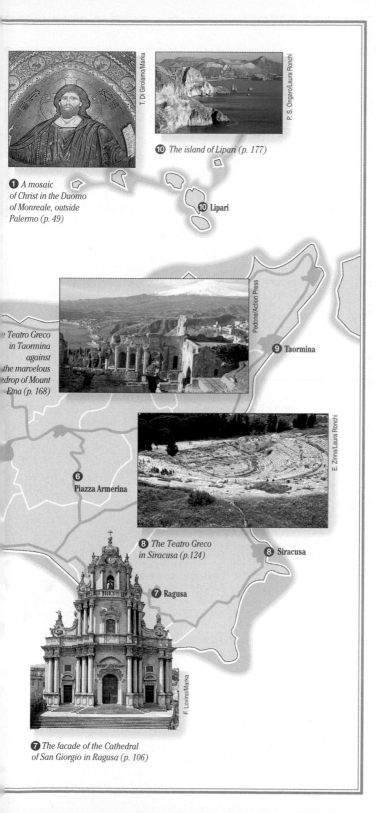

1 *A mosaic of Christ in the Duomo of Monreale, outside Palermo (p. 49)*

T. Di Girolamo/Marka

10 *The island of Lipari (p. 177)*

P. S. Ongaro/Laura Ronchi

10 Lipari

The Teatro Greco in Taormina against the marvelous backdrop of Mount Etna (p. 168)

Pedone/Action Press

9 Taormina

6 Piazza Armerina

E. Zinna/Laura Ronchi

8 *The Teatro Greco in Siracusa (p.124)*

8 Siracusa

7 Ragusa

F. Lovino/Marka

7 *The facade of the Cathedral of San Giorgio in Ragusa (p. 106)*

Touring Club of Italy
President and Chairman: *Roberto Ruozi*
Chief Executive Officer: *Guido Venturini*

Touring Editore
Chief Executive Officer: *Guido Venturini*
Managing Director: *Alfieri Lorenzon*
Editorial Director: *Michele D'Innella*
Series Editor and Editorial Co-ordinator: *Anna Ferrari-Bravo*

Authors: *Ilario Principe* (Sicily: the environmental picture); *Letteria Tripodo* (Sicily: the characteristics of settlement; chapters 4, 8, 9, 10); *Elena Del Savio* (chapters 1, 2); *Francesco Tranchida* (chapter 3); *Maria Pia Di Gaetano* (chapter 6); *Maurizio Mannanici* (chapters 5, 7).
Translation: *Antony Shugaar*
Editing and layout: *Voltapagina Associati*
Copy Editor: *Abigail Asher*
Jacket layout: *Federica Neeff*, with *Mara Rold*
Map design: *Cartographic Division - Touring Club of Italy*
Drawings: *Antonello* and *Chiara Vincenti*
Production: *Vittorio Sironi*

Picture credits: *Action Press*: M. Pedone 171; *Archivi Alinari*: 21; *Archivio Ketto Cattaneo*: 18; *Barbagallo*: 40, 98, 108, 117, 118, 122, 143, 144, 179, 180; *M. Casiraghi*: 115; *Controluce*: 68, 70, 86; *Controluce / C. Fusco*: 91; *E. Dati*: 125, 136, 172, 189; *A. Garozzo*: 20, 27, 30, 39, 45, 54, 79, 81, 85, 101; *Image Bank: G. Colliva* 106, 165, *F. Fontana* 169, *Mahaux* 196, *G.A. Rossi* 25, 53, 102; *W. Leonardi*: 15, 16, 74, 82, 87, 90, 132; *G. Leone*: 51, 63; *M. Lo Verde*: 138; *Marka*: L. Fioroni 160, F. Giaccone 121, 127, 159, *L. Marioni* 193, M. Mazzola 181; *P.S. Ongaro*: 11, 37, 42; *Laura Ronchi*: P. Negri 3; *P.S. Ongaro* 12, 48, 56, 59, 140, 200, E. Zinna 130; *Santini*: 76.
Cover: Temple of the Dioscuri, Agrigento (*Image Bank: G. Colliva*).
Pictures pp. 4-5: *Vases at the Museo Eoliano, Lipari* (Barbagallo); *Façade of Syracuse Cathedral* (M. Lo Verde); *Local folk at S. Biagio Platani, Agrigento* (W. Leonardi).

Colour separation: *Emmegi Multimedia - Milano*
Printed by: *New Litho - Milano*

Touring Club of Italy
Corso Italia 10
20122 Milano
www.touringclub.it

© 2002 Touring Editore s.r.l. - Milano
Code L2GAA
ISBN 88-365-27477
Printed in October 2002

Foreword

The detailed tour of Sicily proposed by this guidebook, part of "The Heritage Guide" series, takes us through one of Italy's most resourceful and captivating regions, a region that offers an extraordinary wealth of history and art, all set amid a countryside of breathtaking intensity and variety. The largest island in the Mediterranean, Sicily has been a vital focus of all the ancient civilizations that navigated this ancient sea.

The portrait of the island's geography and long history is followed by a guide to its cities and sights, divided into 10 chapters, with 29 different excursions that cover the entire island, starting from the capital, Palermo, the subject of the first chapter. From here we travel down the west coast and round to Agrigento, then on toward Ragusa at the southernmost tip of the island. The return trip brings us up to the Tyrrhenian coast (with a visit to the outlying islands), leaving for last our exploration of the island's fascinating interior. All these itineraries and excursions are illustrated with street and road maps, and plans of archaeological sites, together with a host of illustrations and drawings. On the way we discover the legacies of the Phoenician, Greek, and Roman occupations of the island, which were followed in more recent historical times by a succession of Muslim, Norman, Swabian, Angevin, and Aragonese domination. Each culture left its mark on the territory and on the towns and cities, though perhaps the most memorable aspect of Sicily's architecture is the lively. Baroque style that pervades the entire island. The

Temple of the Dioscuri (Agrigento)

guide concludes with a section of travel tips and useful addresses, with lists of hotels and restaurants, places to shop, cafés and pastry shops, as well as the main art galleries, museums, and archaeological sites.

Contents

Introductory chapters

Excursions

Information for Travelers and Index of places and monuments

Excursion key map
and index of maps and plans

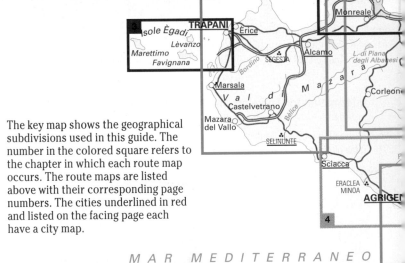

The key map shows the geographical subdivisions used in this guide. The number in the colored square refers to the chapter in which each route map occurs. The route maps are listed above with their corresponding page numbers. The cities underlined in red and listed on the facing page each have a city map.

6

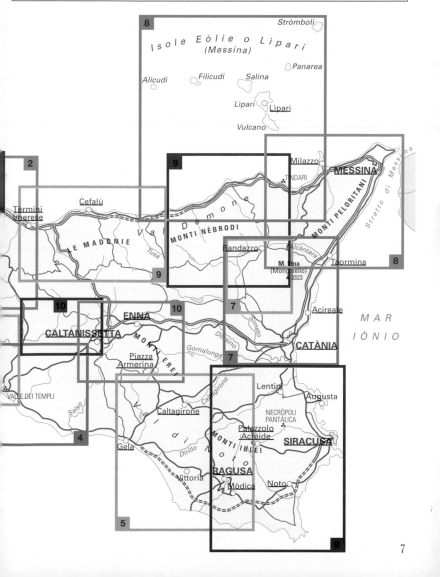

How to use this guidebook

■ We have attempted to use the original Italian names of all places, monuments, buildings, and other references where possible. This is for a number of reasons: the traveler is thus made more comfortable with the names as he or she is likely to encounter them in Italy, on signs and printed matter. Note also that maps in this book for the most part carry the Italian version of all names. Thus, we refer to Piazza Pretoria and Parco dell'Etna rather than to Pretoria Square and Etna Park. On first mention, we have tried to indicate both the Italian and the English equivalent; we have renewed this dual citation when it is the first mention in a specific section of text. In Italian names, one of the most common abbreviations found is "S." for "saint" (and "Ss." for "saints"). Note that "S." may actually be an abbreviation for four different forms of the word "saint"

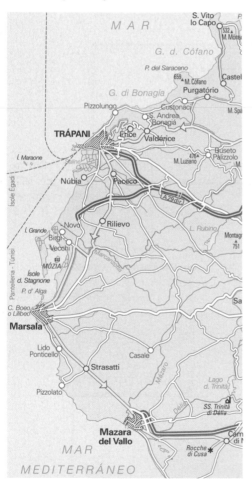

– "San," "Sant'," "Santo," and "Santa." Many other terms, while generally explained, should be familiar: "cattedrale" or "duomo" is a cathedral, "chiesa" is a church, "cappella" is a chapel, "chiostro" is a cloister, "oratorio" is an oratory, "via" is a street, "ponte" is a bridge, "museo" is a museum, "biblioteca" is a library, "torre" is a tower, "campanile" is a bell tower, "giardino" is a garden, "parco" is a park, "pinacoteca" is an art gallery, "teatro" is a theatre, "piazza" is a square, "ospedale" is a hospital, "porta" is either a door or a city gate, "sala" or "salone" is a hall or a room.

Maps and plans

The itineraries and excursions described in this guide are accompanied by *route maps*, in which the suggested route is traced in yellow, with an arrow denoting the direction followed by the description in the text. All the main towns and cities have an accompanying *city map*; here the suggested itinerary is marked in blue. A key to the symbols used can be found on page 10. The principal monuments and museums and other public facilities are marked directly on the maps, and are followed by a reference to their location on the map or street plan (e. g., I, A3, meaning map I, square A3). The notation "off map" indicates that the monument or location mentioned lies outside the areas shown on the maps. Floor plans of museums are marked with letters or numbers for identification, and correspondingly linked to the descriptions in the text. The guidebook also includes the plans of some monuments and archeological sites.

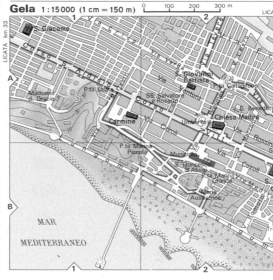

The places to visit

Each entry opens with a description of the place, and most towns are given a short historical profile as well. In all descriptions of monuments or landmarks, differences in typography (names shown in **bold** or in *italics*), larger or smaller type size, and one or two asterisks (*) indicate the importance of each monument, museum, or other site. Written descriptions are illustrated with drawings and photos that help the reader to visualize works of art or architecture which he or she should not miss. Opening hours are indicated in italics immediately after the name of the monument or museum they refer to. Such information is updated to the publication date of this guidebook; however, changes many occur at any moment after this date.

Information for travelers

A compendium of useful addresses of hotels and restaurants suggests a selection of the hospitality facilities. Specific symbols and criteria are described on page 206. We provide information which is up-to-date as of the writing of this book. The reader should be aware that some subsequent changes may have occurred in hours or schedules. Hotels and restaurants are classified in conformity with the Italian laws on tourism.

The Valley of the Temples, with the town of Agrigento in the background

Conventional Signs Used in the Maps

City maps

Lines of communications

	Highways
	Highways and throughfares
	Main roads
	Other roads
	Pedestrian ramps
	Secondary roads
	Trails
	Roads under construction
	Railroad lines and stations
NOTARBARTOLO	Subway lines stations
	Cableways
	Chairlifts
	Cable cars

Monuments and buildings

	of exceptional interest
	quite interesting
	interesting

Other indications

	Public offices
	Churches
	Hospitals
	Tourist information offices
	Principal parking areas
	Gardens and parks
	Contour map showing elevation and grade
	Arcades

Excursion maps

Lines of communications

	Excursion, with direction followed
	Detour from the route
A1	Highway, with route number
	Main roads
	Other roads
	Shipping lines

Towns and cities

o	Places to see along the excursion
	Urban area
o	Other places

Symbols

	Churches
	Castles
	Ruins
	Caves
*	Waterfalls, natural curiosities
	Mountain huts
	Mountain passes
.	Mountain peaks
347	Elevations
	Airports
	Borders of countries

Sicily: the environmental picture

Extending over 25,708 square kilometers, Sicily is the largest and the most populous island in the Mediterranean Sea, and it is the southernmost and the largest region of Italy; it comprises 8.5 percent of the total surface area of the country. With a population of roughly 5,200,000, Sicily is the home to nearly 9 percent of the national population.

The distinctive shape of the island – an isosceles triangle – resulted, early on, in its being called Trinacria, or island of three promontories; this was the name of the island in antiquity. The modern name of Sicily comes from the tribes of the Siculi or the Sicani, two of the earliest populations of the island (the third ancient tribe residing here was that of the Elimi), and the name of Sicily appears as early as the Homeric sagas. Until the 20th century, the island was divided into 7 provinces, of which only one lay inland, a division which dated

Sicilian puppets, one of the symbols of the island

back to King Ferdinand I's decree of 1817. In 1927 the island was re-divided into 9 provinces (Agrigento, Caltanissetta, Catania, Enna, Messina, Palermo, Ragusa, Siracusa, and Trapani), a division that remains in place today.

The islands and the coast

The insular nature of Sicily is mitigated by the closeness of the mainland at Calabria, which lies at a distance of only 3 km across the Stretto di Messina (Strait of Messina), and by an array of islands and islets lying at various distances off the long sides of the island's perimeter. The group of the Eolie (Aeolian Islands), which lies in the province of Messina in administrative terms, is the most numerous island group, and includes 7 major islands: the three largest are Vulcano, Lipari, and Salina, aligned along the meridian and clustered close together, and then there are two pairs of islands, Alicudi and Filicudi to the west and Panarea and Stromboli to the north, as well as a certain number of rocks and shoals of smaller size. Of these, the loveliest are Strombolicchio and Basiluzzo. Much farther off is the other island along the northern coast: this is Ùstica, which has a surface area of 8.6 square kilometers, and which forms part of the province of Palermo, from which it lies at a distance of 57 km. To the west of Sicily lies the small island group of the Egadi, near the coast of Trapani, to which they belong in administrative terms. This group features the three larger islands of Favignana, Levanzo, and Marettimo, and the smaller land-masses of Maraone and Formica, while the islands of Stagnone and Mozia can be considered, in morphological terms, as continuations of the salt marshes of the larger island, from which they are separated only by a narrow channel. Also part of the province of Trapani is the relatively distant island of Pantelleria, which lies at roughly one hundred km from Cape Granitola, midway between Mazara del Vallo and Selinunte, and just 70 km from Cape Mustafà in Tunisia. The small Pelagie island group, part of the province of Agrigento, is scattered even further out in the central Mediterranean Sea: Lampedusa, the largest in the group, is no less than 205 km from the Sicilian coastline (while it lies just 113 km from Tunisia and 150 km from Malta); Linosa is set roughly forty km north of Lampedusa, and to the west is the uninhabited shoal of Lampione, which has nothing but a lighthouse.

The coastal perimeter of Sicily extends for 1039 km, but that distance increases to 1500 km if we include all of the smaller islands that surround it: beginning with the three capes – Peloro above Messina, Lilibeo at Marsala, and Passero at the southwestern extremity – the Tyrrhenian coastline extends 440 km, the coastlines along the Mediterranean Sea toward Africa extend 312 km, and the Ionian coast stretches for 287 km. These coasts are not perfectly linear, though there are no major marked variations in their structure. The northern coast, lying perfectly along the parallel and running counterclockwise from Messina, presents first the narrow peninsula of Milazzo extended toward Vulcano, followed by the minor outgrowths of Cape Calavà and Cape Orlando; the coast then runs straight, except for the curve of the gulf of Termini Imerese, nearly all the way to the valley of Palermo, guarded by Cape Zafferano to the east and by Cape Gallo to the northwest. The gulf of Castellammare is far more pronounced and deeper than all of the other gulfs in Sicily, and it is bounded to the west by the high and steep promontory of Cape San Vito. The coast remains tall and dramatic all the way to Trapani where, with the salt flats characterizing the landscape, we see the beginning of the low-lying tableland that runs along the more properly Mediterranean coast-land: between Marsala and Cape Passero there are virtually no noteworthy geographic features, and the few short promontories or the slight sandy bluffs do little to interrupt the sense of sameness that is so typical of this part of Sicily. Between Messina and Cape Passero the coast once again runs straight and rather high as far as Catania, and then opens out on a line with the only real plain in Sicily, at the mouth of the river Simeto. The marked promontory of Augusta gives its name to the gulf of Augusta, with another promontory looming to the south, terminating in Ortigia; the gulf is marked at its center by the peninsula of Magnisi, just as, to the south of Ortigia, Cape Murro di Porco and other frequent features dotting the coastline interrupt the line, creating micro-environments of considerable charm.

The morphological nature of the territory: land-forms and volcanoes

While its form is clear and its coasts are linear, it remains quite difficult to describe the overall morphology of Sicily in simple terms. First of all, 61 percent of the territory is classified as hilly (as against the national average of 42 percent), while 25 percent of the ter-

A farm in the countryside near Trapani, where high-quality wines are produced

ritory is covered by mountains (in Italy as a whole, the figure is 35 percent), and only 14 percent is occupied by the few plains available (as opposed to 23 percent of Italy). The only genuine alluvial plain is the Piana di Catania and, perhaps to lesser degree, the coastal fringe of low sand dunes arching southeast of Gela. The rest of the plains are a few open areas set in the limestone of the main promontories, as is the case with the Conca d'Oro of Palermo and the neighboring rolling plains of Carini and Alcamo; or they are the areas of debris near relatively high outcroppings, such as is the case at Milazzo or in the area around Trapani; or they are the high and slightly sloping plains which, in the area facing Africa, crumble into limestone breccia, or tufa stone in the area between Trapani and Castelvetrano and the Iblei, or else spread out into the broad sand dunes of the area around Agrigento.

There are four major mountain groups in Sicily. The most noteworthy of these groups is represented by the alignment of the northern chain, which – in its basic structure – continues the chain of the Calabrian Apennines; this is not a homogeneous chain, however, and in it we can distinguish at least three sections: the Peloritani, entirely similar to the Calabrian chain, which never rises above an elevation of 1300 m; the Nèbrodi, or better yet, to use the local term, the Caronie, which rise to an altitude of 1800 m and which are generally marked by bare summits; and lastly the Madonìe, which rise to an altitude of nearly 2000 m, and are characterized by handsome oak forests and, higher up, by beech groves. The mountains of western Sicily, on the other hand, sometimes appear as irregularly-grouped massifs, isolated in some places; and where they are, they're quite large because they're nearly disconnected from the surrounding features, and in certain cases, they stand as full-fledged islands, as is the case in the Egadi. There are no clearly distinguishable alignments or ranges, save in the case of the link with the Madonìe, which in some sense connect with the morphology of the Palermo area (through the Rocca Busambra, 1615 m). The "sulphur-bearing" highland ("altopiano solfifero"), which occupies the central and the southern part of the island, sloping slightly down toward the sea, can almost be considered an area of debris from two major geographic features with a more sharply defined identity. Toward Enna, the sulphur-bearing highland comes together into another system of limestone ledges and saddles, suited to serve as a watershed between the two southern slopes of the island; these are the Monti Erei, linked in turn to the system of long tablelands, the Iblei, that are so distinctively characteristic of the area around Siracusa and the entire southern expanse of Sicily. The landscape here looks flattened, and even the highest elevation – Monte Lauro, 986 m, near Buccheri – only just rises from the surrounding territory, which seems to constitute one vast stretch of land embracing the sea. These white limestone tablelands, tending toward the golden yellow that is so typical of

the Sicilian Baroque buildings common in the Val di Noto, are crisscrossed by watercourses running in long, narrow cuts, often with vertical walls: the remains of the *quarries* that in the past housed remarkable prehistoric and protohistoric civilizations.

But the volcanoes are what most unmistakably distinguishes the island of Sicily, and in particular, Mount Etna. Visible from incredible distances, this imposing and perennially smoking cone is not only a feature of the landscape and the morphology; with its great remarkable silhouette and its distinctive personality, it suggests an idea of Sicily that does not fit into any of the environmental categories of the Mediterranean region. Mount Etna is the largest active volcano in Europe, and its elevation varies, as is the case with all volcanoes; nowadays it is roughly 3323 m. Despite the impression that the volcano may give when observed from a distance, this is not a uniform cone, nor are the craters at the summit the active ones. The other two active volcanoes of

Sicily, Stromboli (924 m) and Vulcano (500 m), are roughly comparable with Etna in size, but their roots are 2000 m below sea level, so only their summits are visible. Particularly noteworthy is the summit of Stromboli, with its incessantly active cone emerging directly from the water.

Lakes and rivers

Sicily may be rich in fire, but it is considered poor in water, and not because there is any real lack of rainfall (roughly 60 cm of precipitation a year, on average), but rather because that rainfall is poorly distributed and is soon lost from soil that is generally not permeable; the effects are disastrous at times, destroying crops and villages. To forestall these unfortunate occurrences, manmade reservoirs and lakes have been built; the only natural lake is the Lago di Pergusa, unless we count the "bivieri," or ponds behind the dunes, which nowadays can be found only along the littoral strip of the southern coast. The line of mountains to the north, overlooking the Tyrrhenian coast, allows only numerous short rivers like like those found in the Calabrian area (there is roughly one every 5-6 km of coastline) from exceedingly limited watersheds; all the same, the waters of these streams manage to nourish flourishing citrus groves and other fine crops. The river beds spread out and the basins of water become more extensive for the watercourses that empty into the Mediterranean Sea, but the actual flow of the streams tends to become much smaller due to the lower amount of rainfall in this area; that flow also becomes intermittent because of the impermeable nature of the ground, which reduces flow in the summer practically to nothing. The Salso or the Imera Meridionale, which is 144 km long and has a basin 2000 square kilometers wide, is the most important of the rivers of Sicily, and the Platani, which empties into the sea near Eraclea Minoa, is 110 km long and has 1785 square kilometers of basin area and is the third largest; the other streams along this area of the Sicilian coast – the Belice, the Gela, the Acate or Dirillo, and so on – present rather extensive basins but small flows of water. This is not the case for the eastern slope, where we find the largest river system on the island, formed by the Simeto-Dittaino-Gornalunga, with a main stream running some 113 km and a feeder basin extending over nearly 4300 square kilometers, including that rich source of water that is Mount Etna, covered as it is with abundant snow for much of the year. To the north of Etna, on the other hand, is the Alcantara, gathering the waters of the mountains, while the Monti Peloritani empty numerous torrents into the Ionian Sea.

Climatic conditions and vegetation

If Sicily is not endowed with much water, it does have a remarkable abundance of sunlight: there is an average of 133 beautiful sunny days in Siracusa, 130 in Taormina, 125 in Catania, 110 in Messina, and 98 in Palermo. Catania holds the European record for sunshine, with an average of 2518 hours a year, while Palermo has an average of 2200 hours. But these statistics give only a partial idea of how much light there is in the sky, and because of the location of the island, that means an unparalleled amount of light, more than anywhere else in Italy or continental Europe. The mildness of the climate along the coasts, with an annual average temperature ranging between 17 and 19 degrees Celsius, drops considerably, however, toward the mountains and plateaus of the interior, where the Mediterranean influence fades and there are much sharper variations in temperature, with chilly winters and more frequent precipitation – even snowfall.In the summer, however, and especially in August, it is not rare for there to be very high temperatures, and it was the highest temperature ever recorded in Italy was in fact in Sicily in August 1885 – 49.6 degrees Celsius. The hot sirocco wind is typical of Sicily; it generally blows humid on the eastern coast and dry on the western coast, and blows for three days running from the south, often bringing with it dust and sand from Africa.

Forests, even the tall trees high on the mountain ridges, must have greatly suffered from the historical events to which the island has been theater and witness; in any case these forests have generally been fought back to a few fragmentary patches, found most often along the northern range and around the splendid slopes of Mount Etna, which is to say in the areas that are furthest from crowding and overuse, or at any rate, most difficult to reach and to deforest. In those areas where deforestation has taken place on a large scale, as for example on the slopes of Mount Etna, often the vanished forests are replaced with magnificent chestnut groves. It comes as no surprise, then that the plants that are now found in Sicily do not come at all from the island itself, but were imported in the more-or-less recent past: grapevines and olive trees as well as almond, pistachio, pomegranate, and other fruit trees came in antiquity from the Near East; the hazelnut tree came from Campania; the carob, the palm tree, and the mulberry, and cotton, sugar cane, lemon, and bitter oranges were all introduced by the Moors. The sweet orange, still called "arancio portogallo" in Sicily, was in fact brought by the Portuguese in the 16th c. from China; the tangerine was brought from the islands of the Sunda Strait, and it was introduced no longer ago than two hundred years back; and the prickly pear and the agave arrived in the 17th c. from Central America.

Agriculture and other economic activities

The last great crop is wheat, and ever since the time of the ancient Romans, when Sicily was considered the breadbasket of the empire, Sicily has literally always built its economy and its society on a foundation of wheat. Now things are a little different, because alongside the traditional latifundium planted in grains – partly undercut by the agricultural reform of the 1950s, indeed probably a little less profitable, since grains do not require the little patches of land that the reform attempted to foist off on the Sicilian working class – a substantial and variegated sector of specialized intensive crops has developed in the wake of the considerable array of public works designed to improve irrigation. These crops are grown both in the fields and in greenhouses, especially located along the coastal areas and in the better-protected and more-fertile interior valleys. Extensive zones were then converted to the cultivation of specialty shrub and bush crops, as well as olive and almond trees, and particularly grapevines, which have largely and widely substituted the old grain crops with their three-year rotations, especially in the Bèlice area in the wake of the emergency assistance that came in the aftermath of the earthquake (and not always bringing the best of results).

The ambivalence found in agriculture, which remains the locomotive of the Sicilian economy and here employs twice the Italian average, is found as well in the industrial sector. Here – even though many of the most notable Italian crafts traditions have managed to save themselves because they are such a deep-rooted part of the local culture – new enterprises suffered. Ceramics, the industrial projects of the 19th c. linked to the production of wine, shipyards, the conservation of fish, without even mentioning the mining of sulphur, which, in what we might call its "heroic" phase, had a very short run of no more than two decades – all these new enterprises were soon mired in crisis because they were unsuccessful in meeting the demands of the market; and the capital-

The Pelagie Islands are an uncontaminated natural environment with a wealth of marine and land fauna

intensive investments in industrialization, so rich in money and poor in employees, failed to get past the short-sighted objectives of a number of well-funded multinationals, both from Italy and from the outside world. The discovery of oil in Gela and the Ragusa area, or Ragusano, at the end of the 1950s authorized in some way or other the construction of major refineries and elephantine chemical plants; off the waters of Gela and especially in the seaways of Augusta, or Rada di Augusta, there are seabeds particularly suited for super-tankers; instead of docking to load up with crude oil, they bring the petroleum need-

ed to run the plants, because the size of the oilfields was far less than had been predict-
ed, and oil exploration had to be extended out to the continental shelf off the areas being developed. Instead of integrated industrial development, which had been the objec-
tive of the state funding, there was a terrible and irreversible imbalance created in the territory, which led to the massive destruction of irreplaceable resources, and, to a social
mechanism of the encouragement – but not the satisfaction – of expectations, and to
promises broken, the kind of broken promises that have loomed so large so often in the
history of Sicily and its contacts with the outside world. All this eventually resulted in damage to the environment and civil and moral breakdown that undercut the great institutional
advantage given to Sicily on 15 May 1946, when it was given a special statute and semi-
independent status even before the constitution of the Italian Republic entered into force
(1948).

Mediterranean faces and colors permeate the whole island

The character of the island and its inhabitants

This breakdown appears to most people nowadays to be a distinctive characteristic of
Sicily, partly because it has not remained trapped in its territory, but rather has emerged,
exploring the outside world with a vigor and an audacity that had not been expected of
the Sicilian people. We should not indulge in facile stereotypes, however, and the development of Sicilian history and culture can teach us much in this regard. Deep local tradition, in fact, reveals the powerful and distinctive presence in all Sicilian towns and villages of customs, traditions, and habits that manage to express not only a personality of
great scope and a quality of life that is translated into literary and artistic forms of national
and international renown, but in particular a discrete and profound social fabric, casu-
ally dialectic and open to the stimuli and influences of civil society, wherever they may
come from. We are not talking merely of the folkways and the colorful Sicilian traditions
that, in some sense, complete the image of the island of sunshine that has been assigned
to Sicily. It is true that the Sicilian cart has been banished from the streets by noise and
violence, and that the puppet theater is present only as a relic, and perhaps a spurious
relic, simply because of the good efforts of a few generous fans; but processions, religious
festivals, family celebrations, mystery plays, and so on, survive in considerable numbers
to tell of a history that even today lives on in the humblest layers of society. It is from this
history that we must begin if we wish to have anything other than a false and cheerful image of this surprising island.

Sicily: the characteristics of settlement

Sicily nowadays is considered to be a polycentric region, a place of several cities, because in Sicily an equilibrium has developed among the roles – and of course the ranks – of three major cities: Palermo, in the western corner, and Catania and Messina, on the eastern shore. Perhaps it would be more accurate to say of Sicily that it is a place with two centers. For if Palermo is the regional capital and has been the capital of the island for more than a millennium now, Catania is, after Naples, the most thriving center of industrial manufacturing in the Italian south, or Mezzogiorno d'Italia; Messina, although it is a vital "landgate" between Italy and Sicily, plays no other real role, aside from that service. For more than a century now, Catania has contended with its rival Palermo, trying to replace it as the leading city in the island's economy. Moreover, if we consider the infrastructure of the island's highway system, we may note that while one highway, on the east coast, runs from Messina to Catania and another highway through the interior provides a direct link between Catania and Palermo, in comparison, the highway on the Tyrrhenian coast between Messina and Palermo has remained unfinished.

But the prosperity of Catania and its powerful role on the island have recent origins. In the 18th c., it was still Messina and Siracusa that determined the fate of the eastern coast, and with Palermo, they composed the system of cities that ran Sicily.

Historical Sicily

It is difficult to set forth a sufficiently clear chart of Sicilian historical development through the birth and development of its systems of settlements. For too long, the island has been treated as a territorial and administrative entity all of its own, and too often the role played in political history by Sicily has been incorrectly analyzed, when it was recognized at all. A crucial issue in any evaluation is the question of historical and cultural unity. One historian suggested at the turn of the 20th c. that Sicily had received from Greek rule a character that vitally affected all subsequent development, and not only of its own history, but of the history of all Italy, and even that of Europe. In more recent years, there has been a revival of interest among scholars in the philo-Islamic aspects of Sicilian culture. Everything, or nearly everything, in Sicily is seen as a derivation of Arabic culture: from etymologies and inflections in the language to social behavior, sweets, and ornamental plants. Whether it was from the Greeks or the Moors that the prime influence on the formation of Sicilian culture came, the problem remains the same: in order to understand Sicilian history, it is necessary to divide it up into periods marked by various occupations, right up to the unification of Italy.

Greek and Roman domination

The earliest inhabitants were Sicani, Elimi, and Siculi, of unknown origin, but certainly not aboriginal. The first signs of organized life on the island date back to the 8th/7th millennium B.C., while in the 5th millennium there was development and proliferation of the Aeolian towns linked to trade in obsidian. Interestingly, there are also finds – again from the Aeolian islands – that indicate that as early as the 16th c. B.C. there was intense trade with the Aegean Cretan-Mycenaean cultures.

It is common belief that the Phoenician presence on the island was only due to trading requirements, and that it was limited, especially after the arrival of the Greeks, to the western regions. Here, aside from the Phoenicians, the Greek colonists found Sicani and Elimi and, to the east, Siculi, who were well organized in a dense network of cities, built for the most part, on highlands overlooking extensive territories. On the east coast, the first colonies began to flourish: Naxos in 735 B.C., Syracusai in 734, Leontinoi and Katane in 729, Megara Iblaea in 728, Zancle and Selinunte in 628, Mylai and Gela in 689, Akragas in 581, and Lipara in 576. Some of these towns were new foundations, while others simply were settled on the site of an existing indigenous village; but the innovation, which clearly points to Hellenic influence, was the partial or total reorganization of urban space, in accordance with orthogonal schemes of distribution of the various zones.

The Phoenicians took up residence in the western corner of the island, as did the Carthaginians, and laid the foundations for the formation of a solid system of cities that were capable of withstanding the Greek advance. The cities founded and reinforced in the 7th

c. B.C. under Punic and Phoenician influence are Mozia, Palermo, and Solunto.
The 6th c. witnessed an almost total Hellenization of the indigenous towns, partly because tyrannies were established in all of the "poleis" in the island. Hippocrates in Gela, Theron (one of the fiercest opponents of the Carthaginians) in Akragas and Himera, and in Gelon in Syracuse: under their rule, the early Sicilian cities grew considerably, from the 5th c. on, in accordance with the plans developed by the architect and urbanist Hippodamus of Miletus: an orthogonal network of main roads (plateiai) and secondary roads, which cut out standard-sized city blocks, leaving ample space in the central areas for public functions. In the 5th c. B.C., following the attempted revolt of the Siculi, there was a general consolidation of Greek control and supremacy, over the cities in the interior as well, but by the end of the same century, the Carthaginians had destroyed the system formed by Selinunte, Imera, Gela, and Kamarina. Syracuse held out, and under the tyranny of Dionysius, at the end of the 5th and the beginning of the 4th c. B.C., reached the peak of its power. Aside from the ensuing urban expansion, Syracuse extended its spheres of influence and staked the preservation of its power on its control over the Strait of Messina through the creation of a triangle of cities guarding this exceedingly important stretch of sea. Messina on the cape or Capo Peloro, Taormina on the Ionian Sea, and Tindari on the Tyrrhenian – these were all possessions of Dionysius I and it is interesting to note that this tyrant had a thorough and complete knowledge of the geography, not only of the island, but indeed of all of southern Italy and the surrounding waters. The reinforcement of the coastal strongholds was accompanied by a renewed interest in the towns of the interior, now that the Carthaginians were out of the run-

ning after their defeat of 386 B.C. The Greeks regained control of Henna, along with Akragas, Selinunte, and Gela. In the second half of the 4th c. B.C., these cities once again became free "poleis," and Timoleon, the Greek general who restored democracy in Sicily, undertook an intense project of urban renewal.
During the reign of Hieron II of Syracuse, which is to say at the beginning of the 3rd c. B.C., there was a development of residential quarters featuring aristocratic homes richly decorated with mosaics and murals. Between the end of the fourth and the beginning of the 2nd c. B.C. there was a consolidation of the form of the theater, which was directly imported from the motherland; the theaters of Syracuse, Eraclea Minoa, Segesta, Solunto, and Morgantina all survive in their original

Archimedes was born in Syracuse in the 3rd c. B.C.

form; while the theaters of Tindari, Taormina, and Catania were transformed through the adaptation of the orchestra to an arena for gladiatorial fights. With the end of the second Punic War and the conquest of Syracuse in 212 B.C. by Marcellus, Sicily passed into Roman hands. In the early empire there was an agricultural rebirth, a result of renewed interest in the countryside. Many "vici" and "pagi" were formed: these were small villages with a purely agrarian economy. The Piana di Gela, as it is settled now, preserves this organizational structure of the "borghi" practically unaltered. With the Romans, the primary transportation routes that been traced for many millennia by the succession of peoples that had lived here were improved, as were the territorial infrastructure such as aqueducts, irrigation and other canals, ports, and fortifications.
In the late empire, the development of the latifundium, an administrative structure that was of enormous importance to the economic history of the island, went hand in glove with the construction at the center of each latifundium of sumptuous villas: one remarkable example is the villa of Piazza Armerina. With an overall policy of intensive exploitation of the land, the island became a major site for the production of wheat and other foodstuffs to feed the empire, to the point that it won itself the nickname of "breadbasket of Rome." In the 3rd c. A.D., Diocletian, in his effort to reorganize the provinces of the empire, attributed new importance to the role of Sicily, making it a "regio suburbicaris," a direct dependency of Rome, in other words. Through a system of granting privileges and the generous distribution of funds, immense landholdings, or latifundia, were formed, which were to become the foundation for the administration of the region for centuries to come.

Early Christian Sicily

An important role was played by the Eastern monks who, with their monasteries located on the outskirts of towns and villages, formed active communities, encouraging the spread of the Greek rite in Sicily, and reinforcing the dependency of the Sicilian clergy upon the patriarch of Constantinople. So while the larger cities were being routinely plundered by corrupt Byzantine administrators, leading to the popular power of major towns and cities, a dense network was forming in the rural areas: small inter-related villages, communicating one with another along the roads that had served for millennia for the migration of sheep (these were later called "trazzere," a term that is probably of Moorish origin). Dating back to this crucial point in history was the subdivision of Sicily into three sub-regions, which were named, under the Moors, Val Demone, Val di Noto, and Val di Mazara. The first extends from the northern course of the river Imera to that of the river Simeto; the second lies between the Simeto and the southern Imera; the third is located in the remaining western area, with Palermo as the chief town.

Arab domination

The Moors, who arrived in Sicily in the first half of the 9th c., introduced a new system for the management of the territory, launching a full-fledged agrarian reform. They proceeded to break up the latifundia, assigning small lots of land to the direct care of the peasants, and encouraging the free exchange of the goods thus produced. They developed and perfected the best system of water supply that the island had ever had, based on the preservation of the wooded areas on the interior, so as to ensure the existence of a moist local microclimate, and on the safeguarding of large marshy areas alongside the main rivers. The Moors were skilled engineers, and they reinforced the bridges and aqueducts built by the Romans while also building new ones: it is still possible to see those Moorish structures, like the lovely bridge near Càccamo.

A Virgin Mary mosaic on the façade of Palermo Cathedral

The adoption of Arabic culture in Sicily, however, is also documented by the survival today in many of the island's cities of urban layouts with the irregular grid so typical of Moorish culture. One study of Islamic town planning has pointed out how unnecessary it would be to have orthogonal thoroughfares and blocks in an urban context made up of minarets and houses: the radial propagation of the voice of the muezzin suggested instead a city model made of concentric circles. The articulation of space into lanes and courtyards is particularly evident in the historical centers of nearly all those western cities that were not plagued by earthquakes. The locations of settlements and their urban fabric date from the Moorish period, but there are no longer traces of houses of worship, such as mosques. In this period, Sicily became an important base for the expansion of Islam toward the peninsula.

Palermo was chosen, in A.D. 831, as the capital of the Emirate; the city grew and was celebrated as one of the loveliest cities in the known world.

Norman Sicily

Norman Sicily in the 11th c., according to the descriptions of Edrisi, the Arabic geographer at the court of Roger, appeared to be a synthesis of two worlds – the typical world of the southeastern Mediterranean Sea, of Muslim influence, and another world that had been constructed in the high Middle Ages in western Europe. The deep mark that the Normans left on the Sicilian landscape included the efficient apparatus of military cities dotting the long "service roads" which run along the coasts and into the interior of the island. It would appear that the countless establishment and re-establishment of cities in this period were all prescribed by a territorial plan; we find them in various strategic locations. The "plan" must have called for the reinforcement of the port towns along the coasts, and, on the interior, the definitive paths of the "penetration" routes, with the formation of a system of cities all equidistant from one another, guarding the immense valleys.

The Normans brought Sicily back under the jurisdiction of the Church of Rome; they restored the feudal system, assigning the control of the latifundia, or large landholdings, not only to lay barons, but also directly to monasteries and convents. The Norman policy of settlement, moreover, was distinguished by the custom of spending on the construction or restoration of a church, which often constituted the nucleus for a new quarter or a new city, settlements that were often encouraged to grow by the establishment of a colony of Lombards. In the large cities, such as Palermo, which became the capital of the kingdom,

Our Lady of the Annunciation by Antonello da Messina, at Palazzo Abatellis in Palermo

the expansion was often accompanied by massive projects of urban reconstruction, with the building of churches and official palazzi, and not without a reinforcement of the defensive structures of the place.

From Frederick II to the end of Spanish domination

Frederick II continued the project of reinforcing defenses, especially for the cities of Catania, Enna, and Siracusa. In the meanwhile, the enormous privileges bestowed upon the barons led to the formation of a landed aristocracy that exercised unfettered power, first in the province and later in the city. In the 14th and 15th c. two families shared all power in western Sicily: the Chiaromonte and the Ventimiglia families. They took advantage of the Prammatica di Re Martino, which was decreed in Catania in 1406 and then extended to the other cities; this law ensured that a private citi-

zen who wished to build a home had the right to expropriate the lands bordering his property, in order to increase the beauty of the city). One family filled the towns of the Belice and the hinterland of the Agrigento area with Chiaromonte architecture, or "architetture chiaromontane," and the Ventimiglia filled the towns of the Madonìe and the Monti dei Nèbrodi with their towers. Often these buildings were erected to redound to the power of the lord, but it is not rare to encounter examples of great compositional elegance, as is the case with the "Palazzo Steripinto" of Sciacca.

In 1415 the Spanish government sent the first viceroy to Sicily. There began a long period of subjugation, ending only in 1712. But the island at the heart of the Mediterranean Sea was an important possession for Charles V, who spared no effort to defend it from Turkish invasion, with massive fortified works around the most important coastal cities. The 16th c. was also was the time of the refeudalization of the countryside and of the program of extensive farming launched by the crown. In the vast areas of the interior, new farming towns developed, with regular checker-board plans, which were to attract the populations of the larger cities, such as Enna and Caltanissetta.

During the Counter Reformation, in the 17th c., the cities were already solidly laid out along the lines suggested by the main monastery structures and complexes. Perspective demanded the use of straight thoroughfares, ending scenically in a monumental building or a city gate, as in Carlentini, a city-fortress with broad streets lined with elegant buildings, striding in succession toward one of the monumental gates of the city. The "piazza" took on great importance in Sicilian Baroque urban planning, as a logical solution to the other fundamental element, the "croce di strade," or road intersections. An eloquent example can be seen in the Quattro Canti di Città in Palermo. For the layouts of new cities, there was a tendency to use the feudal models of the form of the cross and the eagle; these were respectively the symbols of the Roman Catholic Church and the Holy Roman Empire. An exception to this rule is Ragusa, with its remarkable fish-shaped plan.

From the 18th to the 20th centuries

In 1713, the treaty of Utrecht decreed the end of Spanish domination, and Sicily passed to the house of Savoy. In the Val di Noto work was begun on the reconstruction of the cities destroyed by the earthquake of 1693, rebuilding in 17th-c. Baroque style but also in accordance with modern city design, while in other cities the strict late-Baroque was opened up, and there began to be parks and public promenades.

With the admission of Naples to the kingdom in 1735, Palermo lost its ancient standing as the capital of a kingdom. In 1812 Ferdinand IV conceded the Constitution and feudal privileges were abolished. Finally, with the unification of Italy the south, which was still governed by medieval laws, came up against the capitalist economy of industrialized nations. The great enterprise of extracting sulphur from the mines of central Sicily began. The export of the mineral led to the growth of some of the port cities in contact with the mining towns, such as Catania. In the same century great public works were undertaken, fundamental structures for the bourgeois city. The chaotic form with which the first industrial experiments started off caused inevitable damage to the cities. The solution was found with a first set of general regulatory plans, at the end of the 19th c. and the start of the 20th c., but the First World War made the efforts of the planners quite useless. The island had to wait for the 1960s before there was a concrete response to the problem of the reorganization of the architecture of the cities of Sicily.

The Mafia

The imposition and the exercise of power by a rigidly – even "militarily" – organized group with the purpose of controlling the economic activities of a town and its surrounding territories: these could certainly be considered as the essential components of the phenomenon of the Mafia. The Mafia, which originated as a tool of economic and political power, was itself transformed over time into an economic and political power. The Mafia originated in the earliest decades of the 19th c. after feudal power was abolished in 1812. From this date on, the barons began to hire their own personal troops of soldiers, the "compagnie d'armi," with which they were able to preserve the privileges that they had enjoyed until that moment. These "armed companies," composed of unscrupulous lowlifes and criminals, defended the property of the barons, using the weapons of abuse, intimidation, and violence. The members of these companies enjoyed more than just economic rewards; they also got the baron to protect them politically form from the authorities, who might pursue them for their crimes. The Mafia, therefore, became a sort of counterpower, or perhaps we should say, a power that was parallel to that of the State. The absence of any serious repression from the state, and the fierce vendettas against those who were unwilling to submit to the uncontrolled power of the Mafia, allowed the growth and reinforcement of the much lamented culture of "omertà," which has so much to do with the definition of "mafiosità" offered by many serious historians. At the end of the 19th and the beginning of the 20th c., the Mafia underwent considerable changes. Its interests expanded so that from the countryside it came to take over the cities; it established close ties with politicians; it dabbled in politics directly, supporting its own members for elected office (seethe Commissione d'Inchiesta Franchetti-Sonnino 1876, from M. Pantaleone, *Mafia e Droga*); and it became international, establishing ever closer ties with the American Mafia. Under Fascism, the Mafia was apparently on the ropes for a time, but during the Allied Occupation and during the years directly following WWII it found new vitality, playing a major role in the issue of Sicilian separatism.

The phenomenon of the Mafia in all its forms is certainly the least appealing aspect of Sicily now. Especially recently the Mafia, with its massacres and its frontal attack on institutions, has become regular front-page news. Despite this, the most encouraging aspect – aside from a greater commitment of the state – appears to be the Sicilians' wider awareness that the Mafia must be attacked and fought day by day, freeing the island from all that the culture of "omertà" has imposed for too many long years.

Sicily: tips for travelers

Transportation

Sicily's two main airports are Palermo Punta Raisi and Catania Fontanarossa, the former serving western Sicily and the latter eastern Sicily. They offer frequent links with other major Italian airports, and with some European ones, especially during summer. The small airports on the islands of Lampedusa and Pantelleria offer flights to and from Palermo and the airport called Trapani Birgi.

The Ferrovia dello Stato (Italian Railways) network in Sicily is well distributed. Timetables and routes can be consulted and reservations can be made online at www.fs-on-line.com. Many travel agents can also dispense tickets and help you plan your journey. Many of the express trains require reservations at least one day in advance. Local trains (classified as "Espresso," "Diretto" or "Locale") require a simple ticket, but express Eurocity and Intercity trains require a supplementary ticket ("supplemento"). Almost all of them carry both first- and second-class cars. Only a few ("Locale") usually are second-class only. All tickets must be time-stamped before boarding: there are numerous time-stamping machines in every station (failure to do so will result in a moderate fine). On those trains that do not require a reservation, tickets can also be purchased on board from the conductor (a surcharge is included).

Sicily is linked with the rest of Italy by an efficient maritime network. The port of Palermo is the major one and is linked to Genoa, Livorno (Leghorn) and Naples. Service crossing the Strait of Messina is offered 24 hours a day on ferryboats for the transport of both cars and trains. Many shipping lines link the many little islands which surround Sicily.

Taxis are a convenient but expensive way to travel in Italian cities. There are taxi stands scattered throughout major cities. You cannot hail taxis on the street in Italy, but you can reserve taxis by phone in advance or at the moment: consult the yellow pages for the number or ask your hotel reception desk or concierge to call for you. Taxi drivers have the right to charge you a supplementary fee for every piece of luggage they transport, as well as evening surcharges.

Hotels

In Italy it is common practice (and Sicily is no exception) for the reception desk to register your passport, and only registered guests are allowed to use the rooms. This is mere routine, done for security reasons, and there is no need for concern. Room rates are based on whether they are for single ("camera singola") or double ("camera doppia") occupancy. In every room you will find a list of the hotel rates (generally on the back of the door). While 4- and 5-star hotels have double beds, most hotels have only single beds. Should you want a double bed, you have to ask for a "letto matrimoniale."

All hotels have rooms with bathrooms; only 1-star establishments usually have shared bathrooms only. Most hotel rates include breakfast ("prima colazione"), but you can request no breakfast, thus reducing the rate. Breakfast is generally served in a communal room and comprises a buffet with pastries, bread with butter and jam, cold cereals, fruit, yogurt, coffee, and fruit juice. Some hotels regularly frequented by foreign tourists will also serve other items such as eggs for their American and British guests. The hotels for families and in tourist localities also offer "mezza pensione," or half board, in which breakfast and dinner are included in the price.

Eating and drinking

The Italian "bar" is a multi-faceted, all-purpose establishment for drinking, eating and socializing, where you can order an espresso, have breakfast, and enjoy a quick sandwich for lunch or even a hot meal. You can often buy various items here (sometimes even stamps, cigarettes, phone cards, etc.). Bear in mind that table service ("servizio a tavola") includes a surcharge. Lunch at bars will include, but is not limited to, "panini," sandwiches with crusty bread, usually with cured meats such as "prosciutto" (salt-cured ham), "prosciutto cotto" (cooked ham), and cheeses such as mozzarella topped with tomato and basil. Often the "panini" and other savory sandwiches (like stuffed flatbread or "focaccia") are heated before being served. Some bars also include a "tavola calda." If you see this sign in a bar window, it means that hot dishes like pasta and even entrées are served. In Sicily, as in Italy, coffee is never served with savory dishes or sandwiches, and cappuccino is seldom drunk outside of breakfast (although the bars are happy to serve it at any time).

Whether at an "osteria" (a tavern), a "trattoria" (a home-style restaurant), or a "ristorante" (a proper restaurant), the service of lunch and dinner generally consists of – but is not limited to – the following: "antipasti" or appetizers; a "primo piatto" or first course, i.e., pasta, rice, or soup; "secondo piatto" or main course, i.e., meat or seafood; "contorno" or side-dish, served with the main course, i.e., vegetables or salad; "formaggi," "frutta," and "dolci," i.e., cheeses, fruit, and dessert; caffè or espresso coffee. Wine is generally served at mealtime, and while finer restaurants have excellent wine lists (some including vintage wines), ordering the house table wine generally brings good results. Mineral water is also commonly served at meals and can be "gassata" (sparkling) or "naturale" (still). The most sublime culinary experience in Italy is achieved by matching the local foods with the appropriate local wines: wisdom dictates that a friendly waiter will be flattered by your request for his recommendation on what to eat and drink.

The pizzeria is in general one of the most economical, democratic, and satisfying culinary experiences in Italy. Everyone eats at the pizzeria: young people, families, couples, locals and tourists alike. The acid test of any pizzeria is the Margherita, topped simply with cheese and tomato sauce. Beer, sparkling or still water, and Coca Cola are the beverages commonly served with pizza. Some restaurants include a pizza menu, but most establishments do not serve pizza at lunchtime.

Communications

Nearly everyone in Italy owns a cellular phone. Although public phones are still available, they seem to be ever fewer and farther between. If you wish to use public phones, you will find them in bars, along the street, and phone centers generally located in the city center. Pre-paid phone cards can be purchased at most newsstands and tobacco shops, and can also be acquired at automated tellers. For European travelers, activating personal cellular coverage is relatively simple, as it is in most cases for American and Australian travelers as well. Contact your mobile service provider for details. Cellular phones can also be rented in Italy from TIM, the Italian national phone company. For information, visit its website at www.tim.it. When traveling by car through the countryside, a cellular phone can really come in handy. Note that when dialing in Italy, you must always dial the prefix (e.g., 02 for Milan, 06 for Rome) even when making a local call. When calling to cellular phones, however, the initial zero is always dropped.

Everyday needs and general information

Tobacco is available in Italy only at state-licensed tobacco shops. This kind of vendor ("tabaccheria"), often incorporated in a bar, also sells stamps.

Medicines can be purchased only in a pharmacy ("farmacia"). Pharmacists are very knowledgeable about common ailments and can generally prescribe a treatment for you on the spot. Opening time is 8:30-12:30 and 3:30-7:30 p.m. but in any case there is always a pharmacy open 24 hours and during holidays.

Every locality offers tourists characteristic shops, markets with good bargains, and even boutiques featuring leading Italian fashion designers. Opening hours vary from region to region and from season to season. In general, shops are open from 9 to 1 and from 3 or 4 to 7 or 8 p.m., but in large cities they usually have no lunchtime break.

Banks are open from Monday to Friday, from 8:30 to 1:30 and then from 3 to 4. However, the afternoon business hours may vary.

Post offices are open from Monday to Saturday, from 8:30 to 1:30 (12:30 on Saturday). In the larger towns there are also some offices open in the afternoon.

Effective 1 January 2002, the currency used in all European Union countries is the euro. Coins are in denominations of 1, 2 and 5 cents and 1 and 2 euros; banknotes are in denominations of 5, 10, 20, 50, 100 and 200 euros, each with a different color.

Sicily, like the rest of Italy, is in the time zone which is six hours ahead of Eastern Standard Time in the USA. Daylight saving time is used from March to September, when watches and clocks are set an hour ahead of standard time.

When you sit down at a restaurant you are generally charged a "coperto" or cover charge ranging from 1.5 to 3 euros, for service and bread. Tipping is not customary in Italy. Beware of unscrupulous restaurateurs who add a space on their clients' credit card receipt for a tip, while it has already been included in the cover charge.

Italy: useful addresses

Citizens of Australia, Canada, New Zealand, and the United States can enter Italy with a valid passport, and stay for a period of not more than 90 days; citizens of Great Britain and Ireland, as members of the European Union, can travel either with valid passport or with a valid identification card. No vaccinations are necessary.

Foreign Embassies in Italy

Australia:
Corso Trieste 25, Rome, tel. 06852721

Canada:
Via G.B. de Rossi 27, Rome, tel. 06445981

New Zealand:
Via Zara 28, Rome, tel. 064402928

United States of America:
Via Vittorio Veneto 119/A, Palazzo Margherita, Rome, tel. 0646741

Great Britain:
Via XX Settembre 80/A, Rome, tel. 06 42200001

Ireland:
Piazza Campitelli 3, Rome, tel. 066979121

Foreign Consulates in Italy

Australia:
Via Borgogna 2, Milan, tel. 02777041/217

Canada:
Via Vittor Pisani 19, Milan, tel. 0267583420

New Zealand:
Via F. Sforza 48, Milan, tel. 0258314443

United States of America:
– Lungarno A.Vespucci 38, Florence, tel. 0552398276
– Via Principe Amedeo 2/10, Milan, tel. 02290351
– Piazza Repubblica, Naples, tel. 081 5838111
– Via Vaccarini 1, Palermo (consular agency), tel. 091305857

Great Britain:
– Via S. Paolo 7, Milan, tel. 02723001
– Via dei Mille 40, Naples, tel. 0814238911

Ireland:
Piazza San Pietro in Gessate 2, Milan, tel. 0255187641

Italian Embassies and Consulates Around the World

Australia:
12 Grey Street - Deakin, Canberra, tel. (06) 273-4223
Consulates at: Adelaide, Brisbane, Melbourne, Perth, Sydney

Canada:
275 Slater Street, 21st floor, Ottawa (Ontario), tel. (613) 2322401
Consulates at: Edmonton, Montreal, Toronto, Vancouver

New Zealand:
34 Grant Road, Wellington, tel. (4) 4735339
Consulates at: Auckland, Christchurch, Dunedin

United States of America:
3000 Whitehaven Street, NW, Washington DC, tel. (202) 612-4400
Consulates at: Boston, Chicago, Detroit, Houston, Los Angeles, Miami, New York, Newark, Philadelphia, San Francisco

Great Britain:
14, Three Kings' Yard, London, tel. (020) 73122200
Consulates at: London, Bedford, Edinburgh, Manchester

Ireland:
63, Northumberland Road, Dublin, tel. (01) 6601744

ENIT (Italian Tourist Board)

Canada:
Office National Italien du Tourisme / Italian Tourist Board, 175 Bloor Street, Suite 907 - South Tower, Toronto, Ontario M4W 3R8, tel. (416) 925-4882, fax (416) 925-4799

United States of America:
– Italian Tourist Board, 630 Fifth Avenue, Suite 1565, New York, N.Y. 10111, tel. (212) 245-4822, fax (212) 586-9249
– Italian Tourist Board, North Michigan Avenue, Suite 2240, Chicago, Illinois 60611, tel. (312) 644-0996, fax (312) 644-3019
– Italian Tourist Board, Wilshire Blvd., Suite 550, Los Angeles, CA 90025, 12400, tel. (310) 820-9807, fax (310) 820-6357

Great Britain:
Italian Tourist Board, 1 Princes Street, London W1B 2AY, tel. (020) 73993562

Emergency numbers

112 Carabinieri
113 Police Help
115 Fire Department
116 Road Assistance
118 Medical Emergencies
176 International inquiries
12   Phone directory assistance

1 Palermo and the Conca d'Oro

The traditional image of Palermo (elev. 14 m, pop. 683,794; city maps on pp. 28-29, 32-33), set amid the greenery of vast citrus groves at the foot of the distinctive promontory of Monte Pellegrino, celebrated by view painters and etchers of the 18th and 19th c., has collided with the conditions of the 20th c. It has collided too with the changes brought about by the considerable growth of the city, which has historically played the role of "capital," and even more serious, the speculative growth that – ever since the end of WWII – has played a fundamental role in the development of the modern city and the equilibrium of the entire territorial system. This, indeed, could be described as the latest act in a series of urban developments that, over the last five centuries, have profoundly altered the natural characteristics of the site where, in ancient times, the first settlement grew: a long, low-lying and extensive promontory, bathed on either side by rushing streams, the Papireto to the north and the Kemonia to the south, stretching out into the sea in the heart of a broad bay protected from the winds.

The historical center of Palermo with Cala, the city's original port, in the foreground

The phases of the settlement's growth clearly show three areas whose basic structure can be distinguished within the context of the present-day city: first, the once-walled city, within whose perimeters, established as early as the Islamic age, the history of the settlement developed from its origins all the way up to the 18th c. Second, the 19th-c. city, anchored by the two theaters, the Massimo and the Politeama, and jutting into the harbor; and third, the more recent city, lying along the axis of Viale della Libertà and reaching northward toward the plain known as the Piana dei Colli. The Pheonicians landed here in the 7th c. B.C. and, establishing themselves on the more elevated inland section of the promontory, started a trading post with the early Sicilian and Greek peoples then occupying this territory. The rapidity with which the settlement expanded, and the crucial considerations of safety and stability during the maturation of the city's structure, required the fortification by the 4th c. B.C. of the entire surface of the promontory, breaking it up into two walled areas. These were the Paleàpoli (Paleapolis), the earliest core, a sort of citadel walled as early as the 6th c. B.C., and the Neàpoli (Neapolis), the new city overlooking the harbor. The ease in dropping anchor and the remarkable structure of the harbor itself (originally some 500 m further inland than the present-day Cala) served to identify the settlement as Panormos, meaning "all harbor." A name taken from a Greek term although the city was never ruled by the Greeks; this shows not only the intensity of the ties with neighboring Greek colonies, but also the aspiration to assimilate the character of a more mature and refined culture.

Allied with Carthage following the war of Himera (480 B.C.), Palermo progressively took on a more important role in the political scene of the Mediterranean, becoming the chief Punic base in Sicily. Under the Romans, who conquered it in 254 B.C., the city saw its prestige decline, while the political and economic interests of Sicily shifted to the east-west axis that tied Siracusa (Syracuse), the capital of the province, to Lylibeo, headquarters of the propraetor. The harbor preserved its strategic importance, and the value that accrued to it from its position at the heart of the sea routes of the Mediterranean, while Palermo itself became a municipium, with a senate comprising 100 citizens, as well as the headquarters for a quaestor. Occupied by the Vandals and later by Odoacer, in A.D. 491 Palermo was conquered by Theodoric and in A.D. 535 was brought under Byzantine rule by the general Belisarius. The Arabs conquered the city in A.D. 831, during the earliest period of their occupation of the island. When, in A.D. 948, Sicily became an autonomous emirate, Palermo served as its capital, and, as part of the vast Islamic economic and cultural empire, it generated a complex urban organism that was clearly bound up with the social and political structure of Islam. The city expanded outside of its walled perimeter, along the banks of the two watercourses and along the progressively developing delta of the rivers Kemonia and Papireto. The ancient settlement became the privileged center of life in the city and the core of the city government, while new and larger districts developed around the port itself, a part that was further protected and fortified by a castle, near which a citadel was built in 937; in time this became the headquarters of the emir and the Muslim ruling class.

In the middle of the 11th c., while Islamic strength in the central Mediterranean was declining, Palermo revealed the complex features of a cosmopolitan metropolis, whose boundaries were to remain substantially unchanged right up to the modern era, and whose development was to condition the shape and future layout of the city. With the subsequent Norman conquest (1072) and the ensuing alliance between monarchy and clergy, solidified by the coronation of Ruggero II (Roger II) as King of Sicily (1130), the city became a giant construction site, intended to consolidate the authority of the crown and the episcopal cathedral by means of material structures. And with the contributions of Arabic, Byzantine, and Latin master craftsmen there developed that remarkable architectural synthesis that now survives in the glory of the Cappella Palatina (Palatine Chapel) and the Duomo (Cathedral) of Monreale.

In 1266, the city and its surrounding region passed from Swabian rule to that of the Anjou, but shortly afterward, the dramatic events that followed the revolt of the Vespro (Sicilian Vespers, 1282) led to the Aragonese, replacing the House of Anjou. The triumph of the great feudal families in this period offered Palermo a chance – now that it had been supplanted as capital by Naples – to enjoy a limited autonomy and to undertake ambitious construction programs and a general reorganziation of the urban layout, through the power of the ruling aristocracy.

The imposing palace-fortresses of the Sclàfani and the Chiaramonte families stand as the chief fulcrums of the new city layout; they are the prototypes of a remarkable architectural form that characterizes the civil and religious building of the 14th c.

Palermo's position of on the Mediterranean chessboard during the years of the greatest hostility between the Turkish and Spanish empires led to a radical restructuring of the city that profoundly modified its layout and overall appearance and image. Palermo's role as a stronghold, as well as the capital of a viceroyal province under Spain, brought the renovation of its public spaces and a different layout of its political and military headquarters. What ensued was the most substantial and spectacular urban reconstruction of Palermo, done during the 16th c., which, in close conjunction with the renewed fortifications, led to a profound reordering of the city's central area, creating an internal longitudinal axis of communications (a main artery that also served as a ceremonial and official avenue) along which lay the squares of the chief institutions of the city and the most prestigious buildings of the nobility and the religious orders.

From the Baroque experience to recent urban structures

The construction, in the early years of the 17th c., of Via Maqueda, perpendicular to the Càssaro, and the creation, at the center of their intersection, of Piazza Vigliena, actually gutted a broad swath of the city and, with the establishment of a second chief artery, triggered a total revolution in the existing structure of the city. The urban image that was thus created is symbolically summed up in terms of the politics of the period, and of the Catholic Counter Reformation, by the concave settings of the four Cantoni Centrali, or central corners. This marked the beginning of the Palermitan Baroque movement, when the city was profoundly transformed through a process of renovation that exalted the splendor of power over the two centuries of ecclesiastic and feudal rule. The many, often contradictory reforms that – under the pressure of the growing crisis of the old regime – characterized the rule of the House of Bourbon (Sicily, following the short rule of the Houses of Savoy and Austria, passed under Bourbon rule in 1734), launched a series of city-planning and cultural projects that aimed at more intelligent and responsible growth for the city.

The development of the economic and political bonds that linked Palermo to the rest of Europe at large in the first half of the 19th c. clarified the broad outlines of a program of construction and urban renovation that aimed at a complete implementation of the bourgeois model. In the "belle époque" marked by a lively growth of industrial manufacturing and a general increase in prosperity that culminated in the Esposizione Nazionale (National Exposition) of 1891, Palermo established its two major theaters, the Teatro Massimo and the Teatro

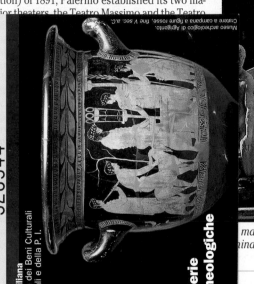

... magnificent fountain which ...inates Piazza Pretoria

...dieval city as well, when the foun-... of the Palazzo dei Normanni (Nor-...alace) and the Cattedrale (Cathe-...stablished the "Galca" (from the ...l-Halquah," the walls) as the the po-...tical and religious center.

...tablished a trading station by fortifying a square area that coincides, roughly, with the area that now lies between the Palazzo dei Normanni and the Cattedrale (or Cathedral; roughly corresponding to the present-day Piazza della Vittoria). The settlement grew rapidly, and the entire summit of the promontory was enclosed, in the 4th c. B.C., by a new set of walls that, while preserving the earlier settlement uphill (Paleàpoli), extended the new settlement (Neàpoli) down toward the port basin, which then ran deep and inland as far as what is now Via Roma.

The sudden expansion that came in the wake of the Islamic invasion and the foundation, around the length of the old walls, of populous and new districts, confirmed this area known as the "Càssaro" (from the Arab "al-Qasr," the castle) as the heart of the city of Palermo. It remained the heart of

From the complex of Piazza della Vittoria-Piazza del Parlamento, which extends before the Palazzo dei Normanni, the itinerary follows the narrow roads that cut through the compact structural mass of the buildings of the Càssaro, reaching the Piazzetta S. Giovanni Decollato, with the Palazzo Sclàfani. Continuing along Via dei Biscottari it runs into Piazza Bologni, which is surrounded by handsome Baroque palazzi.

One climbs up to the left along Corso Vittorio Emanuele, central artery of the area and major "marble road" through the medieval city, straightened and widened in the 16th c. Past the Biblioteca Regionale (library), one emerges into Piazza della Cattedrale, set between the Cattedrale and the Palazzo Arcivescovile (archbishop's palace).

1 Palermo and the Conca d'Oro

Piazza della Vittoria (II, E-F3). This square lies at the center of the area occupied by the earliest fortified settlement. Originally bounded by the high ground of the Palazzo Reale, it took on its present-day layout around the middle of the 16th c.

The chief site of public events and official parades, and the location, in 1820, of the victorious insurrection of the people of Palermo against the local Bourbon garrison (commemorated in the present-day name), this square is almost entirely occupied by the palm gardens of *Villa Bonanno* (with ruins of Roman homes).

Palazzo dei Normanni* or Royal Palace (II, F3). Now the headquarters of the Assemblea Regionale Siciliana, or Sicilian parliament, this building is one of the most important monuments in the city of Palermo in terms of its historical and artistic importance. It was built by the Arabs in the 9th c., on the site of what was probably a Punic and Roman fortress; the façade, which dates from the 17th c., shows features (the *Torre Pisana*, or Pisan tower) dating back to the Norman expansion, which transformed the original fortress into a sumptuous palace and the political and administrative headquarters of the state. Beginning in the middle of the 13th c., with the decline of the Swabian dynasty and the decay of Sicilian political life, the building so lost its former standing that by the middle of the 16th c. it lay abandoned and serious neglected, with the exception of the Cappella Palatina. In 1555, the Spanish viceroys decided to use it once again as their residence, and they made radical renovations. In 1921, work began on the project of uncovering traces of the original buildings, which were thought to have been entirely destroyed, with the exception of the Torre Pisana, the Cappella Palatina, and the hall known as the Sala di Ruggero in the Gioaria. The surprising result, to the contrary, was the rediscovery of nearly all of the rooms recorded by history, as well as others whose existence was previously unknown. In the *Torre Pisana* the chamber of treasures, or *Stanza dei Tesori*, was discovered with a double entry door, surrounded by battlements topped by majestic vaults, illuminated by narrow windows with double splaying. The four large urns that are sealed into the floor could contain hundreds of millions of golden coins.

On the second story is the entrance to the **Cappella Palatina**** (*open 9-11:45 and 3-4:45; Sat., morn. only ; Sun., 9-9:45 and 12-*

Palermo/I 1 : 80 000 (1 cm = 800 m)

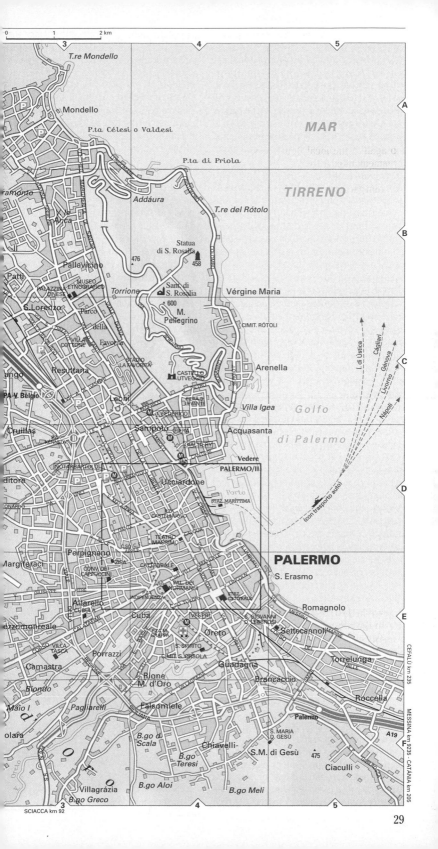

MAR

TIRRENO

A

B

C

D

E

F

3

4

5

0   1   2 km

T.re Mondello

Mondello

P.ta Célesi o Valdesi

P.ta di Priola

Addáura

T.re del Rótolo

Statua
di S. Rosalia

476   458

Pallavicino

MUSEO
PALAZZINA ETNOGRAFICO
CINESE

Torrione

Sant
S. Rosalia

Vérgine Maria

S.Lorenzo

Parco

della

600

M.
Pellegrino

CIMIT. RÓTOLI

CIVILI
COTTONE

Favorita

STADIO
LA FAVORITA

Arenella

Resuttana

CASTELLO
UTVEGGIO

PA-V. Belgio

FIERA
DI LEVANTE

P.za
FEDERICO

Villa Igea

Golfo

Leoni

Cruillas

P.za
KENNEDY

Sampolo

FIERA

Acquasanta

di Palermo

GALLERY

NOTARBARTOLO

ditora

Vedere
PALERMO/II

I. di Ùstica

Cagliari

Livorno

Genova

Napoli

(con trasporto auto)

Ucciardone

P.za
CASTELNUOVO

Porto

STAZ. MARÍTTIMA

Perpignano

TEATRO
MASSIMO

C.so
ZISA

CANCRO

ZISA

CONV. DEI
CAPPUCCINI

CATTEDRALE

S. Erasmo

PALERMO

Margiferaci

PAL. DEI
NORMANNI

Altarello

CUBULA

P.za
INDIPENDENZA

Cuba

VESPRI

STAZ.
CENTRALE

Romagnolo

ezzomonreale

CALATAFIMI

P.za M.
GRAPPA

Oreto

S. GIOVANNI
D. LEBBROSI

Settecannoli

Torrelunga

Porrazzi

S. SPIRITO

CIMIT. S. ORSOLA

Camastra

Guadagna

Bíondo

Rione
M. d'Oro

Brancaccio

Roccella

Máio I

Pagliarelli

Falsomiele

Palermo

A19

olara

B.go di
Scala

B.go
Teresi

Chiavelli-

S. MARIA
D. GESÙ

S.M. di Gesù

475

Villagrázia

B.go Aloi

B.go Meli

Ciaculli

B.go Greco

CEFALÙ km 235

MESSINA km 9235 - CATANIA km 205

12:45), a splendid monument from Norman times, founded by Ruggero II in 1130. The **interior** stands as one of the best known instances of the integration of architecture and the figurative arts: basilican in form, it features a nave and two aisles divided by subtle oval arches; in the raised sanctuary with three apses, the central square is bounded by mosaic transennas and topped by a hemispheric dome set on corner niches.

The floor is in mosaic; the walls have marble facing. The nave has a magnificent wooden caisson ceiling (circa 1143) and "muqarnas" painted with Kufic figures and inscriptions; the small side aisles have pitch roofs with painted beams. Altogether, this is the largest cycle of Islamic paintings to survive to the present day. At the beginning of the nave is the vast *royal throne*, encrusted with mosaics; near the sanctuary, on the right, is a rich mosaic *ambo*, supported by striated columns, and a splendid *Paschal candelabrum* (4.5 m tall), carved with acanthus leaves, figures, and animals: all these date from the 12th c., and they combine Romanesque, Arabic, and Byzantine elements. The wooden choir is modern.

Mosaics** cover the upper sections of the walls of the aisles and the sanctuary, glittering with a golden background. The oldest ones are those in the sanctuary, which date back to 1143: in the dome, *Christ Pantokrator in the Act of Blessing*, amidst angels, archangels, prophets, saints, and evangelists; on the arches of the presbytery, the *Annunciation* and the *Presentation to the Temple*. In the vault of the apse, note the *Christ in the Act of Blessing*. Dating from a slightly later period (circa 1154-66) are the mosaics with Latin inscriptions in the central nave, depicting *Stories from the Old Testament*; still later are the mosaics of the little side aisles.

On the upper floor are the **royal apartments** (*guided tours only; Mon., Fri., Sat., 9-12*). Of special interest is the *Salone d'Ercole* or *Sala del Parlamento*, built in 1560-70 and decorated in 1799 with frescoes by Giuseppe Velasquez: currently, it is used for sessions of the Assemblea Regionale Siciliana, or Sicilian parliament. Forming part of the royal apartments is the *Sala dei Viceré*, a hall featuring portraits of the viceroys and lieutenants of Sicily, a *dining room* that was once an open atrium, with high oval arcades supported by corner columns and, adjoining this room, the hall, or *Sala di Re Ruggero**, with its magnificent mosaics depicting hunting scenes (circa 1170) that cover the upper sections of the walls, the eaves of the arches, and the vaults. These refined decorations with animals and plants show the pictorial influence of the Persian Middle East.

On the upper story is the observatory, or *Osservatorio Astronomico* (*closed for restoration*), set in the top section of the Torre Pisana. It was founded in 1786 at the behest of the Bourbon government by Giuseppe Piazzi, who was its first director.

Porta Nuova (II, E-F3). This massive gate done in the Mannerist style features a single broad fornix, or aperture, surmounted by a small loggia, and topped by a cusped majolica roof. It was built in 1583 along the straight avenue of the Càssaro, in place of an existing 15th-c. gate, to commemorate the entrance of Charles V into the city, upon his return in 1535 from his victory in Tunis. The lower section of the outer front, where there are four telamons, was badly damaged and it was rebuilt in 1669.

S. Giovanni degli Eremiti** (II, F3). One of the best-known monuments from the Norman period of Palermo's history, it was rebuilt at the behest of Ruggero II (Roger II) in 1136 on the site of an earlier Gregorian monastery. Considering the distinctive and essentially Arab architecture, the construction should be attributed to Islamic craftsmen.

The *interior* has a single nave divided into two bays and surmounted by a dome. The presbytery, with apses and topped by a small cupola, is flanked by two square rooms, also with apses. Rising over the left-hand apse is the bell tower; from the right-

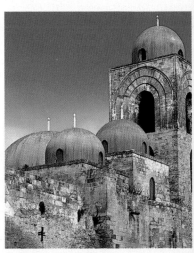

S. Giovanni degli Eremiti

hand apse, with a dome, one steps into the structure of an existing building, erected between the 10th and 11th c. (perhaps a mosque). This building comprises a rectangular hall, originally featuring two aisles divided by five pillars (on the left wall, note the remains of *Virgin with Child and Saints*, a fresco dating from the 12th c.), a Moorish portico with five arches, since destroyed, and a square open courtyard, once the cemetery for courtiers.

In the handsome garden, note the remains of a Moorish cistern and a small cloister from the late Norman era which belonged to the original Benedictine convent.

Palazzo Sclàfani (II, E-F3). Imposing and massive, with a square plan and a large central atrium, this building, now housing the Comandi Militari, or military offices, was built by Matteo Sclàfani in 1330, and was erected according to tradition in just one year. The dynamic interweaving of arches with intarsias in black tufa stone encloses a series of elegant twin-light mullioned windows in the first order, while below that, in the compact curtain wall, originally without apertures (the windows were built at the end of the 19th c.), is a very fine portal with a pediment topped by an aedicule and an eagle.

With the decline of the family of the Sclàfani the palazzo, which had become Spanish property, was transformed in 1435 into a hospital. By the middle of the 15th c., the atrium was decorated with a cycle of frescoes featuring a Triumph of Death; detached following WWII, the cycle is now in the Galleria Regionale della Sicilia (art gallery of the region of Sicily).

Palazzo Speciale (II, E4). Built by the praetor of the city in 1468 and largely rebuilt during the 17th and 18th c. by the Valguarnera family, and later by the Raffadali family, who had become the owners of the building. Its façade preserves the mullioned windows and the moldings of the original, Catalonian-style façade. Into this façade, in the second half of the 17th c., was built the large portal that leads into the inner atrium.

Piazza Bologni (II, E4). This vast rectangular plaza opening out onto the Càssaro, built in 1566 by the Bologna family, which had built its palazzo here, established a powerful Baroque unity with the later construction of the surrounding palazzi. These are *Palazzo Ugo* (to the south), built in the early years of the 18th c., with a loggia over the entrance and marble statues from the school of the Gagini; *Palazzo Villafranca* (to the west), built in the 17th c. in place of the demolished home of the Bologna family, with a broad façade rebuilt around the middle of the 18th c. offering two symmetrical portals and large decorative heraldic crests in stucco; *Palazzo Belmonte-Riso* (to the north, on Corso Vittorio Emanuele), built to plans by Venanzio Marvuglia in 1784, with the heraldic crest of Ignazio Marabitti.

Collegio Massimo dei Gesuiti (II, E4). This institute of higher education was an expression of the cultural domination by the Jesuit Order, a virtual monopoly from the middle of the 16th c. until 1767. Transformed in 1778 into a public library, it now serves as the site of the library of the region of Sicily, or *Biblioteca Regionale Siciliana*; one enters through the portal of the former church of S. Maria della Grotta (1615).

The palazzo, badly damaged during WWII, has been subjected to radical restoration. A broad staircase, built at the expense of the interior of the church, leads up to the library, or Biblioteca, and its archive of some 400,000 volumes, including collections of hand-written texts, collections of correspondence, illuminated codices, and incunabula.

Cattedrale** or Cathedral (II, E3). This major architectural monument reflects a great part of the history o the city because of the stratification of styles produced during the numerous renovations. Built in 1184 by the archbishop Gualtiero Offamilio on the site of an existing basilica, transformed by the Arabs into a mosque and then restored by the Normans to a place of Christian worship, it stands on the square of the same name (Piazza della Cattedrale). The piazza was built in the 15th c. and surrounded by balustrades adorned with statues during the following century. From the 14th to the 16th c., it underwent continual alterations and additions which did nothing to fundamentally alter the ancient structures; between 1781 and 1801 it was subjected to a radical transformation which resulted in the changing of the basilican plan to a Latin-cross plan, with the addition of the side-aisles and the wings of the transept, and the construction n of the cupola.

The **main façade** overlooking Via Matteo Bonello preserves the appearance developed between the 14th and 15th c., with two tall and slender towers with mullioned

A29 km 15

VIALE DELLA REGIONE SICILIANA

V. G. Sciuti

Via L. Ariosto

Via L. Leopardi

Fondazione Mormino

Ass. Reg. d'Turismo

P.za Gentile

Via Duca d. Verdura

Via E. Notarbartolo

Staz. Notarbartolo F.S.

Via Da Vinci

Via D. Costantino

Via Terra Santa

Via Marchese

Giardino Inglese

Villa Gallidoro

Villa Bordonaro

Villa Gonzaga

Via Della Libertà

Via delle Croci

Cavr. E. Albanese

Via Maraspina

Villa Trabia

Via Farini

Via Prino

P.za F. Crispi

P.za Mordini

Viale della Libertà

Via E. Amari

Via Archimede

Via Catania

Via Siracusa

Via XX Settembre

P.za Mazzini

Nas

Via Q. Sella

Via G. Aurispa

Via G. Cusmano

Via Gen. Cantore

P.za D. Siculo

P.za Busacca

Via Maraspina

Via G. Marconi

Via Messina

Via Villareale

Galleria Arte mode

Politeama

P.za Ruggero Settimo

P.za Castelnuovo

Via Dante

P.za Virgilio

Staz. Lolli F.S.

Via Latini

Via Dante

V. Paternostro

P.za S. Oliva

S. Francesco di Paola

Quattro di Campa

Via Regina Margherita

Villa Malfitano

Via Dante

P.za Amendola

V. Cluverio

S. Francesco di Paola

Via Goethe

Via Juvara

Villa Filippina

Via N. Turrisi

Pignatelli D'Aragona

Teatro Massimo

P.za

Via Re Federico

Via Volturno

P.za Principe di Campofiore

Corso Finocchiaro Aprile

Via Veneziano

P.za Vitt. Eman. Orlando

P.ta Carini

P.za Stig

Cantieri Culturali alle Zisa

V. Guglielmo il Buono

V. Cantù

Zisa

P.za Zisa

Via Alberto

P.ta Cuccia

Pal. Concezione di Giustizia

Via S. Agostino

P.za a Aragones

Mc di F

V. Contessa Giuditta

Via C. Lascaris

P.za Noviziato

P.za Beati Paoli

Via Zisa

Via d'Ossuna

Corso Alberto Amedeo

Via Papireto

P.za Beati Paoli

P.za Ingastone

Via d'Ossuna

P.za Peranni

Papireto

Cattedrale

P.za An

Via Cipressi

Via Mosca

Via G. Imera

Via Colonna

Pal. arcivescovile (Museo diocesano)

Cattedra

Pal Sclaf

Convento d. Cappuccini

Piazza Danisinni

Via Rotta

Corso Vitt. Emanuele

Villa Bonanno

Via G. Mosca

P.ta Nuova

Pal. d. Normanni

P.za d. Vittoria

P.za del Parlamento

P.ta di Castro

Dec

Via Cappuccini

Cappella Palatina

P.za Indipendenza

P.ta d. Pinta

P.za di Castro

S. Giov. d. Eremiti

P.za Vann

Mong

Albergo delle Povere

Corso Calatafimi

Corso Pisani

Pal. Orleans (Residenza Regione Siciliana)

Parco d'Orleans

Corso Re Ruggero

P.ta tu Montalto

Via Pindemonte

Via Benedetti

4
5
6

Piazza
Giachery

Carri

E. Albanese
P.za
Ucciardone

P.za
Strazzen

Archimede

Ximenes

Scina

Via

Banchina Puntone

Banchina Francesco Crispi

Banchina Quattroventi

Pontile S. Lucia

Pontile Piave

Molo
Nord

Molo Martello

Diga

foranea

A

B

P O R T O

Approdo aliscafi per Ústica
Pontile Vitt. Véneto

A.A.
Staz. Marittima

Traghetti per Cagliari, Genova,
Napoli, Tunisi

Capitaneria
di Porto

Banchina Sammuzzo

P.za
ella Ximenes

Via

Via

Amari

Via Francesco Crispi

Principe

Stabile

Belmonte

Mariano

Storta

Via

Roma

Via

Cavour

P.ta
S. Giorgio

P.za XIII
Vittime

P.za
S. Giorgio

Via
F
a
t
t
i

Castello a Mare
(resti)

Banchina trapezoidale

Molo
Sud

MAR

TIRRENO

C

Via
Cavour
Prefettura

Museo archeologico

P.za
Olivella

Ch

P.za
S. Olivella

Verdi

ueda

rino
Via
S. Agostino
Madonna
d. Soccorso

Via Bandiera

Pal Termine
Pietratagliate

Posta
e T.

Oratorio
di S. Cita

Oratorio
d. Rosario

Via
Mati

S. M.
la Nuova

S.
Eulalia
d. Catalani

P.za
S. Domenico

S. Domenico

S. Cita

S. Giorgio
d. Genovesi

Mercato
ittico

P.ta
Carbone

S. Maria di
Porto Salvo

Via Cala

Via
Emanuele

Istituto
Nautico

Archivio
di Stato

S. Maria
d. Catena

Loggiato di
S. Bartolomeo

P.ta
Felice

S. Spirito

Museo d.
Marionette

la Cala

D

Via Napoli

S. Antonio

Garraffello

Oratorio
di S. Lorenzo

Piazza
Giardino
Garibaldi
Marina

Pal.
Chiaramonte

Villa
a Mare

S. Ninfa
d. Crociferi

Iso

S. Matteo

P.za
Cassa di
Risparmio

S. Francesco
d'Assisi

Palazzo
Mirto

S. Maria
d. Miracoli

la Gancia

Pal
Abatellis
(Galleria reg.)

La Pietà

P.za d.
Kalsa

S. Teresa

BAGHERIA

Via Allori

Via Spasimo

Quattro Canti

S. Giuseppe
d. Teatini

bioteca
reg.

Fontana
Pretoria

P.za
Bologni

S.
Caterina

Munic.

Martorana

S. Cataldo

S. Anna

P.za
Croce
o. Vespri

P.za
d. Rivoluzione

Piazza
S. Euno

S. Maria
d. Spasimo

P.ta
Reale

Via
Lincoln

Ingresso

Ingresso

Villa
Giulia

Salvatore

Palazzo
Speciale

S. Chiara

Università

Biblioteca
comunale

P.za
Casa
Professa

Gesù

Pal-Comitini
(ex Prefettura)

S. Nicolò
da Tolentino

Via

Via

Roma

Garibaldi

Chris

la Magione

P.za
Magione

Pal.
Ajutamicristo

Orto
botanico

scoltan

Pal
S. Croce

Via Milano

P.ta
Castrofilippo

Giardino Tropicale

Via

Archirafi

rna di Castro

S. Nicolò
d. Albergheria

nditore

Albergheria

Carmine

P.ta d.
Carmine

V. Torino

P.za

Tel.

P.ta Garibaldi

Corso
dei

Mille

P.ta
S. Antonino

S. Agata

S. Antonino

Corso Tukóry

Giulio Cesare

V. Pisacane

Staz. Centrale
F.S.

Corso Tukóry

Via
Marino

Via

F

windows and slender columns, lightly sketched blind arches, and multiple oval arches with slender columns set in the corner ribbings. The central portal, dating from the first half of the 15th c., is surmounted by a twin-light mullioned window; on the keystones of the interior it also features the heraldic crests of the House of Aragon and of the Senate of Palermo; in the aedicule is a 15th-c. *Madonna*.

The 18th-c. wooden doors have been replaced by modern bronze doors, with *Episodes from the Old and the New Testaments* and from local history (Filippo Sgarlata, 1961). Two tall oval arches link the façade to the *bell tower* that faces it across Via Bonello, whose massive lower volume is medieval. Set in the *left-hand façade* of the church – the most extensively reworked side – is a portico in the Gagini style dating from the middle of the 16th c. that was included in the late-18th-c. reconstruction; on its elevation can be seen the portal from 1659. At the beginning of the *right-hand façade* overlooking the square, a broad portico is set between little towers, a magnificent example of Catalonian-style flamboyant Gothic, built in 1429-30 by Antonio Gambara, with three tall oval arches. (In the first column on the left, probably already part of the church when it was converted into a mosque, is a carving of a passage from the Koran.) The pediment, adorned with Gothic motifs, is opened by an elaborate, broad portal (1426) with handsome wooden doors (1432). The *absidal façade*, enclosed by little corner towers similar to those of the façade, curves around three apses carved with a motif of intertwined arches and covered with an intarsia decoration. This is the section of the building that most faithfully preserves the original 12th-c. forms.

The **interior**, completely transformed from 1781 to 1801, has a Latin-cross plan, with a nave and two aisles divided by pillars, each of which includes four slender granite columns originally part of the previous basilican church.

The interior is rich in works of art, notably the sculptural elements of a dismantled Gagini tribune, now set in the presbytery and the transept, and statues by Francesco Laurana and Antonello Gagini.

At the foot of the right-hand aisle are the famous **Tombe Imperiali e Reali**** (royal and imperial tombs), majestic in their simplicity: the *sarcophagus* (Roman, with hunting scenes) *of Costanza d'Aragona*, or Constance of Aragon, wife of Federico II (Frederick II, d. 1222); the *tomb of Enrico VI* (Henry VI, d. 1197); the *tomb of Federico II* (Frederick II, d. 1250; the urn also contains the remains of Pietro II d'Aragona, or Peter II of Aragon, d. 1342); the *sarcophagus of Guglielmo*, or William, the duke of Athens (d. 1338), son of Federico II d'Aragona, or Frederick II of Aragon; the *tomb of Ruggero II* (Roger II, d. 1154); the *tomb of the empress Costanza*, or Constance, his daughter (d. 1198).

In the presbytery are a rich carved wooden *choir* of the Catalonian Gothic school (1466), an *episcopal throne*, reassembled in part with mosaic fragments from the 12th c., and a *Paschal candelabrum* from the same period, with mosaics. Above the altar of the left transept, note the wooden *Crucifix* from the early 14th c., an exceptional piece of work in the Gothic of the Rhine style, taken from the since-demolished church of S. Nicolò la Kalsa. The *crypt* is divided by granite columns into two transverse aisles with cross vaults (12th c.). The front aisle is partly occupied by the base of the church's apse. To the right of the presbytery, the chapel of S. Rosalia conserves the remains of the city's patron saint in an ornate silver urn.

The complex mass of Palermo Cathedral, surmounted by a late 18th-century dome

Palazzo Arcivescovile, or archbishop's palace (II, E3). Founded by the archbishop Simone di Bologna, this building features the remains of the original 15th-c. medieval construction, in the façade overlooking Piazza della Cattedrale, rebuilt in the 18th c. Those remains are an elegant Catalonian Gothic triple-light mullioned window, in the corner on the left, and the geometric basket-arch portal with the coat of arms of the Beccadelli-Bologna family.

From the second courtyard on the left, one can enter the **Museo Diocesano** (*cur-rently closed for renovation*), or museum of the diocese, created in 1927 and expanded in 1952. This museum features marblework from the Cathedral; paintings and statues from churches that had been suppressed in the Napoleonic period or destroyed by collapses and fires (among them are triptychs and panels from the Sicilian and Tuscan schools of the 12th to 15th c.); and lovely decorations in the form of sculptures, friezes, and figured capitals dating from the periods of Sicilian Renaissance and Baroque, originally from the Cathedral.

1.2 The medieval districts and the Quattro Canti

This itinerary plunges into the compact and slightly chaotic fabric of the walled city, bounded to the south by the train station, or Stazione Centrale, and to the north by the Teatro Massimo. This close-knit system of roads was over laid, during the 16th and 17th c., with the crossroads of Corso Vittorio Emanuele and Via Maqueda, built to improve traffic within the city, but also with the idea of giving Palermo a new monumental image and a new administrative structure (the city was broken into four parts), culminating in the construction of the Quattro Canti (literally, Four Corners). From Via S. Agostino, with the 13th-c. church of S. Agostino, one crosses Via Maqueda and, following Via Bandiera, reaches Piazza di S. Domenico and the church of S. Domenico. From here, the route continues along Via dei Bambinai (the name refers to the craftsmen here who shaped wax figures), with the Oratorio del Rosario di S. Domenico, and Via Squarcialupo, with the church and the Oratory of S. Cita, and finally reaches the late-Renaissance church of S. Giorgio dei Genovesi. Along a labyrinth of little streets whose names recall the presence of various craftspeople (Via Argenteria Vecchia, for silversmiths; Via dei Chiavettari, for locksmiths; Via dei Materassai, for mattress-makers; Via dei Maccheronai, for pastamakers), and which are enlivened by the nearby market known as the Vucciria, the oldest in Palermo, one reaches Corso Vittorio Emanuele. After crossing this major artery, you continue along Via Paternostro (formerly Via dei Pisani), one of the most important thoroughfares of the medieval city, along which you will see the 13th-c. church of S. Francesco d'Assisi and the Oratory of S. Lorenzo. As you head down the Corso toward the sea, you will reach the Renaissance churches of S. Maria di Porto Salvo and S. Maria della Catena, which adjoin the harbor area overlooking the Cala, where in centuries gone by merchants from Genoa, Pisa, Amalfi, and Naples kept their fondaci, or storehouses. Not far away is the 14th-c. Steri, the palazzo of the powerful Chiaramonte family. In Via Alloro, a major residential street of late-medieval Palermo, now in ruins, stand the church of the Gancia, from the 15th c., and, from the same period, the adjoining Palazzo Abatellis, which now houses the Galleria Regionale della Sicilia, or regional gallery of Sicily, a rich collection of art from Sicily and elsewhere. Take Via Torremuzza to reach the church of S. Teresa della Kalsa, in the heart of a district that bears the same name, as well as a fortified citadel built by the Moors in A.D. 937 for the emir and his viziers; then you will continue until you reach the southern boundary of the medieval city, marked by the broad Via Lincoln, built in the 18th c. along the perimeter of the walls. From here you can enter the botanical gardens, or Orto Botanico, and the adjoining gardens of Villa Giulia, which – taken together – form the largest green space in the city. Along Via Garibaldi, where the Renaissance Palazzo Ajutamicristo stands, one heads back into the medieval city, and after passing the straight avenues of Via Roma first and then Via Maqueda, one heads along Via del Bosco, flanked by lordly homes from the 16th to the 18th c., finally reaching the church of the Carmine. After passing through the church of the Gesù, one reaches Piazza Bellini – set near the Baroque crossroads, or Croce di Strade – the city center of medieval Palermo, with the monumental churches of the Martorana and S. Cataldo, and the adjoining Piazza Pretoria. Piazza Vigliena – better known as the Quattro Canti – is the point of departure for the tour of Baroque Palermo where the four arms of the cross (Corso Vittorio Emanuele and Via Maqueda), with their array of 17th-/18th-c. façades display the most remarkable products of that period.

S. Agostino (II, D4). The façade, constructed in the early years of the 14th c., has a stern Gothic portal with a niched pediment and an exquisite rose window. The side portal dates from the 15th c. and has been attributed to Domenico Gagini (the lunette dates from the 16th c.); in the vestibule there is a late-Roman sarcophagus and a 16th-c. holy-water stoup. The *interior*, completely redone in 1671, has a single nave and walls punctuated with pillars, as well as a rich decorative array of stuccoes by Giacomo Serpotta (1711-1729); among other things there is a panel by Simone di Wobreck (mid 16th c.) and a 14th-c. panel and Crucifix.

Palazzo Termine-Pietratagliata. At n. 14 of Via Bandiera, this palace was built in 1573 in the Catalan-Gothic style. In the 18th c. a new structure was added which includes a great hall frescoed by Vito D'Anna. In the 1920s Ernesto Basile worked here.

S. Domenico (II, D4-5). This church is one of the most noteworthy Baroque monuments in all of Palermo, adorned with stucco statues and flanked by two tall belltowers. It overlooks Piazza di S. Domenico, which was designed in 1724. The church was erected in 1640, from plans by Andrea Cirincione, on the structure of an existing church, founded along with the convent in 1300, and rebuilt to a larger scale in 1458; the façade was added in 1726. In the vast *interior*, built on a Latin-cross plan, with a nave and two side-aisles divided by stout columns, has the tombs and cenotaphs of noted Sicilians, making this the Pantheon of the city of Palermo (among others, one-time Italian prime minister Francesco Crispi is buried here). Note the handsome marblework by Antonello Gagini and the Gagini school.

Oratorio del Rosario di S. Domenico* (II, D5; *open 9-1 and 2-5:30; Sat, 9-1; closed Sun.*). In order to tour this oratory, contact the custodian, at n. 16 in Via dei Bambinai. The interior is a masterpiece of elegance, with the exquisite **stuccoes*** by Giacomo Serpotta, who created a spectacular array of putti, reliefs and allegorical statues (depicted on the column of the second figure

on the right, representing Strength, is the lizard, or in Sicilian dialect, the "sirpuzza," emblem of the artist); above the altar is a little cupola, from the cornice of which ladies, knights, and boys look down. On the walls, note the *Mysteries* painted by Pietro Novelli, Giacomo Lo Verde, Matthias Stomer, and Luca Giordano; in the vault, note the *Coronation of the Virgin Mary* by Pietro Novelli. On the altar, note the *Madonna del Rosario**, or Virgin of the Rosary, with St. Dominick and the patron saints of Palermo, a magnificent canvas by van Dyck, commissioned in Palermo at the start of 1624, and completed by him in Genoa in 1628.

S. Cita or **S. Zita** (II, D4-5). Although this church is known by these two variants on the same saint's name, it is actually dedicated to S. Mamiliano, or St. Mamilian, and was founded in 1369, rebuilt in 1586-1603, and completed with its façade in 1781; it was badly damaged by bombing in WWII, and has since been restored. The interior, built on a Latin-cross plan, contains works of sculpture from the original church, including a number of masterpieces by Antonello Gagini.

Oratorio di S. Cita (II, D4, *open 8-12; Sat., 9-1; closed Sun.*). This oratory is famous for the stuccoes that adorn the interior (if you find it closed, ask at the nearby church). From the small door, set high on a flight of steps, you cross through a late-16th-c. loggia with a double order, and you enter the rectangular interior completely covered with magnificent **stuccoes*** by Giacomo Serpotta. Created in several stages between 1688 and 1718, these stuccoes depict allegorical statues, spectacular flights of putti, and little representations of the Mysteries of the Rosary. On the entrance wall, note the *Battle of Lepanto*, with two putti, on either side of a tropaeum of arms. Along the walls, there are benches with mother-of-pearl intarsias for the brothers of the order.

S. Giorgio dei Genovesi (II, C5; *usually closed; the church, which has been deconsecrated, is periodically the site of temporary exhibitions*). This church was built by the colony of Genoans in Palermo in 1576-81; the simple and unassuming façade has two orders, and is divided into three parts by pilaster strips, with a crowning element formed of large decorated cornices. The *interior*, an elegant layout with a Latin-cross plan, has a nave and two side-aisles with pillars formed of bundles of marble columns, with a high cupola at the intersection of the arms of the cross. Handsome sepulchral plaques, largely from the

16th and 17th c. (one dates from 1756), cover much of the floor.

S. Francesco d'Assisi* (II, E5). A significant marker of the presence of the Franciscan mendicant Order in this neighborhood of merchants, beyond Corso Vittorio Emanuele, this church was built for the third time between 1255 and 1277. Over the centuries it was subjected to a variety of modifications: in the 14th and 15th c., the side chapels were added, in 1533 the wooden roofing was replaced with a cross vault, and in 1589 the presbytery was elongated. Decorated and frescoed in the 17th c., it was further embellished in 1723 by Giacomo Serpotta with very fine stuccoes. It was damaged in the earthquake of 1823, and restored in the Neoclassical style. Damaged again by bombing in 1943, it then had a radical restoration which restored the original appearance of the 13th c. The *façade*, restored toward the end of the 19th c., has a remarkable flamboyant Gothic portal, built in 1302, with a small loggia in the pediment, frescoed at the turn of the 20th c., surmounted by a lavish rose window rebuilt to the model of the rose window of the church of S. Agostino. The side portals date from the end of the 16th c. Along the right side and outside of the apses it is possible to glimpse several elements belonging to the earliest structure. The **interior** features a nave and two aisles set on cylindrical pillars with broad Gothic arches. In the central nave, note the allegorical statues by Giacomo Serpotta (1723); in the side aisles are Gothic and Renaissance chapels. Among the artworks to be seen here, should be mentioned major sculptures by Antonello, Antonio, and Giacomo Gagini, Pietro de Bonitate, and Francesco Laurana (the last two are probably responsible for the portal of the 4th chapel on the left), in the presbytery, and a handsome carved wooden *choir* from the 16th c. The church possesses a considerable treasure archive, with religious canvases and furnishings dating back from the 15th to the 19th c.

Oratorio di S. Lorenzo* (II, E5; *open Mon.-Fri., 9-1*). This oratory, built after 1569 by the Compagnia di S. Francesco, contains magnificent **stucco decoration***, a masterpiece from Giacomo Serpotta's late period (1698-1710). The vivid and magnificent interior, full of grace and elegance, comprises ten symbolic statues, including figures of *Charity and Almsgiving*, eight smaller stories full of lively details (*Scenes from the Lives of Saint Lawrence and Saint Francis*), a large panel

with a *Martyrdom of Saint Lawrence* in the far wall; a spectacular array of festive putti flies everywhere, and higher up are a number of male figures.

S. Maria di Porto Salvo (II, D5). This church was built in 1526, perhaps to plans by Antonello Gagini, and it served as the back-

The oratory of S. Cita with stucco work by Giacomo Serpotta

drop to the straightaway formed by the Càssaro Nuovo (now Corso Vittorio Emanuele). The *interior* features pointed arches and is covered with a cross-vault (note the magnificent star-studded vault arching over the old presbytery). It also contains noteworthy late-Gothic sculpture and paintings, including a wooden 15th-c. *Crucifix* and a triptych with the *Virgin with Child and Saints* from the 16th c.

Piazza Marina (II, D5). This large square features the gardens created in 1863 by G.B. Basile with an imposing Ficus magnolioides. It is surrounded by buildings of many periods, including the 16th-c. *Palazzo Denti-Fatta* to the west, and the Renaissance church of *S. Maria dei Miracoli* at the southern end. At the eastern corner is the bulk of Palazzo Chiaramonte (see below). Note also *Palazzo Galletti*.

Palazzo Mirto (*open 9-7; holidays, 9-1*). Behind the church of S. Maria dei Miracoli, with an entrance at n. 2 in Via Merlo, the palace was built in the late 18th c. on previous structures from the 15th-16th c. Inherited by the Regione Siciliana, it is a marvellous example of a 20th-c. dwelling for the nobility, and it still houses the original furniture from the 18th and 19th c.

Palazzo Chiaramonte* (II, D6; *open for exhibitions only*). This palazzo is also known as *Steri* – from the Latin term "Hosterium," meaning fortified palace – and it is a clear indication of the prestige of the most powerful feudal family of Sicily in the 14th c. The building has a square plan and a central atrium; and it was begun by Manfredi Chiaramonte in 1307, and was completed with its decorations in 1380. Although it has been extensively altered, the exterior's front and sides still show the forbidding lines of the original, three-story construction: the massive first floor closed, and the other two open, with broad double-light and triple-light mullioned windows, elegantly decorated with intarsias done in lava stone. The last member of the Chiaramonte family, Andrea, was beheaded in front of the palazzo in 1396 for his rebellion against King Martino I of Aragon. In the middle of the 15th c., the Steri became the headquarters of the viceroys of Sicily, and in 1601 it became the headquarters of the Tribunale del S. Offizio (the church courts; in the *Carceri Filippine*, a long area split up by pointed arches set on columns, which can be reached from an inner courtyard, are drawings, paintings, and writings of the nameless victims of the Inquisition); it was occupied by various tribunals from 1799 to 1960, the year in which the offices were transferred to the new hall of justice, or Palazzo di Giustizia. Once it became the site of the new Rettorato Universitario, or university administration, it was subjected to extensive restoration, but is not open to the public. The large hall on the second story has a wooden ceiling painted with decorative motifs that hearken back to the Muslim tradition and with Bible stories and stories of knighthood by Simone da Corleone, Cecco di Naro, and Darenu da Palermo (1377-80). In the loggia, set on pointed-arch columns, which runs around the inner courtyard, note the two handsome twin-light mullioned windows (one of which has been damaged) with unusual ashlars.

S. Maria della Catena* (II, D6). This church is named for a chain, or "catena," that was used to close off the city's old port, and was built in the early years of the 16th c. It is a splendid example of the Catalonian Gothic style, with Renaissance elements mixed in, and some have attributed it, though without documentation, to Matteo Carnalivari. It sits high atop a stairway, and before it

stands a portico with three basket arches. Beneath the portico are three portals with bas-reliefs by Vincenzo Gagini leading into the interior. On the left side, with single mullioned windows and pillars, is a Gagini portal. The *interior* has a nave and two aisles divided by slender Renaissance columns; the nave has ribbed vaults and side barrel vaults; it has a raised presbytery and three apses. In the chapels, note the reliefs and statues of the Gagini school.

Museo Internazionale delle Marionette (II, D6). This international museum of marionettes and puppets is housed in the Associazione per la Conservazione delle Tradizioni Popolari in Via Butera 1. It holds more than two thousand items, including hand-puppets, puppets, marionettes, shadow puppets, backdrops, and stages: there are puppets from Palermo, Trapani, and Naples; marionettes and puppets from various countries; Indian, Greek, Turkish, Malaysian, Balinese, Thai, and Cambodian shadow puppets; and stick puppets from Java and Mali.

Porta Felice (II, D6). This majestic structure, a city gate, stands at the mouth of Corso Vittorio Emanuele. It was named after the wife of the viceroy Marcantonio Colonna who ordered it built in order to commemorate the completion of the last section of the Corso. It is formed of two huge decorated pillars which act as true side scenes to the entrance. The different styles reveal its two building phases, 1584 and 1603.

Foro Italico (II, D-E6). The former Passeggiata alla Marina, established in 1582 upon commission of the viceroy Marcantonio Colonna, was one of the favorite promenades of 17th-/18th-c. nobility. Disregarded for many decades, it has been now renovated and brought back to its original splendor. The Palchetto della Musica (for summer performances) and the Scuderie (horse stables) of Palazzo De Seta have also been restored.

S. Maria degli Angeli, known as **La Gancia** (II, E6). Built at the turn of the 16th c., this church was a hospice for Franciscan monks. The façade, in undressed square ashlars, is pierced by a Gothic portal with a delicate bas-relief on the arch. The *interior*, radically transformed in the second half of the 17th c., has a single nave with a lacunar ceiling and is lined with chapels. Over the main entryway is an organ dating back to 1620, probably the oldest organ in Palermo, built by

Raffaele La Valle. Among the works of art are the *Virgin with Saints Catherine and Agatha* (Madonna of Monserrat) by Antonello da Palermo (1528).

Palazzo Abatellis* (II, E6). This sumptuous residence was begun in 1490 by Matteo Carnelivari and was completed five years later for the Maestro Portolano del Regno and the praetor of Palermo, Francesco Abatellis. It is a compact structure with undressed stone ashlars set on a square plan; the style is Catalonian late-Gothic, with various Renaissance details. The *façade* is embellished on the main floor with elegant three-light mullioned windows, and it rises on either side into towers with rich Gothic decoration; the broad portal contains a bundled motif of staffs and batons braided with cabling, and is surmounted by three heraldic crests. It was very badly damaged during WWII, and was restored and adapted by Carlo Scarpa in 1954 as the site of the **Galleria Regionale della Sicilia*** (art gallery of the region of Sicily; *open 9-1:30; Tue. and Thu., also 3-7:30; holidays, 9-1; closed Mon.*) This high quality museum installation features works of sculpture and painting, especially dating from the 14th to 16th c. In the atrium and in the courtyard, with their portico and loggia, are rows of sculptures, dating from before the Romanesque all the way up to the 16th c. Following this, in the halls on the ground floor, there are wooden sculptures from the 12th to the 16th c. and stone statuary from the 14th and 15th c., including the renowned **bust of Eleonora of Aragon****, a masterpiece by Francesco Laurana (ca. 1471). Among the paintings,

note the **Triumph of Death****, a spectacular fresco from the Palazzo Sclàfani, done around 1450, with a depiction of Death on horseback, shooting his arrows at a group of festive young people. In the rooms on the first floor, there are numerous paintings of various Italian schools on wooden panels from the 14th and 15th c., among these is the small and very famous panel of the **Annunziata**** (Our Lady of the Annunciation) by Antonello da Messina. Also held here are various works by Flemish artists; among them the renowned **Malvagna triptych**** by Jan Gossaert (1510) merits particular attention. The last sections are dedicated to painting from the 16th, 17th, and 18th c.

S. Teresa (II, E6). This church is one of the most noteworthy works of Palermo Baroque, and was built by Giacomo Amato between 1686 and 1706. The immense façade dominates Piazza della Kalsa; in the luminous interior, are wonderful decorative stuccoes by Giuseppe and Procopio Serpotta.

Complex of S. Maria dello Spasimo (II, E6). The church and the convent were built in 1506. Here Raphael painted a canvas depicting Jesus Falling Beneath the Cross, known as the *Spasimo di Sicilia*, now in the Prado in Madrid.

Villa Giulia* (II, E-F6; *open 8-8 p.m.*). This magnificent Italian-style garden was designed in 1778 by Nicolò Palma, and was enlarged and decorated in 1866; it takes its name from Donna Giulia, wife of the Spanish viceroy Guevara. The first public green space in the city, it is based on a geometric design of concentric rays on a square plan; in the central square, there are four Neoclassical exedrae with niches, and, in the fountain in the center, a dodecahedron upheld by a putto. In the broad walkways, note the busts of illustrious Palermitans.

Orto Botanico (II, E-F6), or botanical garden. Set next to Villa Giulia, and designed to integrate that large park, this botanical garden was established in 1785. The square building in the middle with Neoclassical pronaoi on the two opposite façades is known as the *Ginnasio* and contains the herbarium. The most interesting feature is the actual garden, encompassing roughly 10 hectares, or 25 acres, with an abundant array of specimens from every climate and type of vegetation to be found on earth.

The famous bust of Eleonora of Aragon

A specimen of ficus in the botanical garden

Magione (II, E5). Founded in 1191 by Matteo d'Ajello on behalf of the Cistercian monks, this church was given by the Holy Roman Emperor Henry VI in 1197 to the Teutonici Order, who held it until their expulsion, in 1492, by command of Pope Innocent VIII. One enters the church through a Baroque portal that opens, on the left, onto the street of the same name (Via della Magione). The *interior*, with a nave and two aisles divided by marble columns and pointed arches, features a vast transept and three apses; there is an open-beam ceiling (rebuilt). In the flooring (rebuilt), note the large funereal slabs of Teutonic knights. At the far end of the right aisle, note the marble triptych dating from the 16th c.; in the left apse, note the small Renaissance portal. On the left of the church, are interesting remains of a 12th-c. *cloister* with small pointed double-lintel arches set on small twin columns with very elegant capitals, built prior to the cloister of Monreale by the same craftsmen.

Palazzo Ajutamicristo (II, E5). Built by Matteo Carnelivari in 1490-95 at the behest of Guglielmo Ajutamicristo, a century later it became the property of the Moncada di Paternò, who planted a magnificent garden there. The architecture of the building, in bare stone ashlars, reveals a Renaissance influence in the shape of late Catalonian Gothic. Entering through the portal at n. 23 in Via Garibaldi, you will cross a first courtyard, and then you will enter a courtyard on the left with a magnificent portico, of basket arches set on columns and a pointed-arch loggia adorned with tondos and rhomboids set in the pendentives of the arches. Beneath the portico, note the round- and pointed-arch portals, and traces of twin-light mullioned windows.

Carmine (II, F4). Rebuilt from 1626 from plans by Vincenzo La Barbera and Mariano

Smiriglio, this church displays an unusual cupola, completed in 1681, with a very ornate drum (telamons set between columns) andan interior sheathed in polychrome majolica. There are statues by the Gagini, stuccoes by Giuseppe and Giacomo Serpotta, and paintings by Tommaso de Vigilia (15th c.). Behind the main altar is a small late-Gothic chapel with a cross vault, and frescoes between the ribbings. From the left aisle you can enter the *cloister* with three sides featuring 14th-c. arches set on Renaissance columns.

Gesù * (II, E4). This is the first church built by the Jesuits in Sicily, where they arrived in 1549, and where they quickly gained influence. This church was begun in 1564, and was considerably enlarged with the addition of the side chapels (1591-1633) and a new cupola in the middle of the 17th c. The *interior*, built to a Latin-cross plan with a nave and two aisles, has deep intercommunicating chapels, transept, and apsed presbytery as well as a cupola, and constitutes a magnificent example of Sicilian Baroque art. Every corner is sheathed in polychrome intarsia, marble adornments, and stucco reliefs, with a great profusion of sculpture and paintings, works done by a small army of artists over the course of two centuries; among the most respected supervisors of this spectacular "coating of decorations," should be mentioned the Jesuits Lorenzo Cipri and Angelo Italia. All that survives of the original pictorial decoration are the frescoes in the first bay of the vault of the nave signed by Filippo Randazzo (1743), and those in the vault of the presbytery (the others are replacements, done by Federico Spoltore in 1954-56). The exceedingly lavish original decoration is preserved in the presbytery and in the apse; the sculptures by Gioacchino Vitaliano stand out. The chapel to the left of the main chapel, the Cappella di S. Anna, is entirely sheathed in marble decorations.

To the right of the church stands the western front of the **Casa Professa**, with a portal dating from 1685 and a cloister from the 17th c., through which you can reach the *Biblioteca Comunale*, or city library, founded in 1760 and moved here in 1775, eight years after the expulsion of the Jesuits from the kingdom.

Martorana ** (II, E4). This Norman church was built in 1143 by Giorgio d'Antiochia (George of Antioch), admiral of King Roger II, and is also known as *S. Maria dell'Ammiraglio*; it overlooks Piazza Bellini with a Baroque façade that resulted from reconstruction in the 16th c. Entrusted to the Greek clergy in 1221, in 1433 it was given by King Alphonse of Aragon to the nearby Benedictine monastery founded by Eloisa Martorana in 1194; it took her name. Over the centuries, it suffered both destruction and additions, and modern restorations have freed it from some of those additions. Parts of the original structure can be seen from the square: the campanile and, beyond the façade, the rough-hewn body of the church, topped by a small hemispheric cupola, set on a polygonal drum, and inset architectural decoration on the exterior. Since 1937, the church has been the co-cathedral of the diocese of Piana degli Albanesi, and services are conducted in accordance with Greco-Byzantine rites. Take a stairway up to the base of the **campanile**** dating from the 12th c., square in plan, open at the base with a pointed-arch arcade and corner columns. Further up there are three orders of large twin-light mullioned windows, beneath which one enters the **interior*** of the church. The interior was originally made up of a square structure divided into a Greek cross by four columns supporting a cupola, with three apses; it was connected to the campanile by a portico, which was replaced in

The church of S. Cataldo and the Martorana

the 17th c. by a series of bays. The church proper, which once had marble sheathing along the lower sections of the walls, is decorated on the higher areas of the walls almost entirely in **mosaics****; together with the mosaics of the Cappella Palatina, this is the oldest series of mosaics in all of Sicily. The iconographic scheme and the distribution of the mosaics correspond to the most orthodox of Byzantine canons; despite the numerous different artists who worked here, the style too hearkens back to the purest tradition of the middle Byzantine period. They depict *Christ Pantokrator* surrounded by *archangels*, *Prophets*, *Evange-*

lists; *Apostles*; the *Nativity of Jesus* and the *Death of the Virgin Mary*; *Annunciation* and the *Presentation in the Temple*. There are mosaic chancels before the apses; the restored flooring is original. In the first portal on the right, dating from the 9th c. and set here in 1599, note the interesting carved wooden doors, an excellent piece of Moorish craftsmanship (12th c.).

S. Cataldo* (II, E4). This is another church from the Norman period, built around 1160 by the admiral, or Ammiraglio, Majone di Bari; it preserves the clean square forms of the original architecture with blind arches, the cornice with parapets and the three little hemispherical domes raised above the drum. In the tripartite façade are single-light windows. The **interior**, with its remarkable bare walls which were never coated with mosaics, is a rectangle (10 x 7 m), divided into three aisles by six columns taken from ancient buildings, with varied capitals supporting Moorish-style arches, and with three apsidioles. The nave is topped by three little cupolas set on corner niches. The mosaic is original: so too is the altar, upon which is carved a cross, a lamb, and the symbols of the Evangelists. The church is the headquarters of the Order of the Knights of the Holy Sepulcher, or Ordine dei Cavalieri del S. Sepolcro.

S. Caterina (II, E4). Adjoining an enormous Dominican monastery which was founded in 1310, this building stands opposite the Martorana across Piazza Bellini. Built between 1580 and 1596, it has a late-Renaissance façade with two orders dominated by a large cupola built in the middle of the 18th c. The *interior* features a single nave, with three chapels per side, a cupola and a transept. Spectacular decoration sheaths the entire surface in a marvelous fusion of polychrome marble inlay, frescoes, sculptures, and altarpieces.

Piazza Pretoria (II, E4). This monumental square, leveled and built up in the 16th c., is almost entirely occupied by the immense fountain known as the **Fontana Pretoria***, a creation of the Florentine sculptor Francesco Camilliani (1554-55); the fountain is adorned with statues of deities, allegories, heads of animals, and herms. On the southern side of the square, straddling Piazza Bellini, stands the *Palazzo Senatorio*, or Palazzo del Municipio, also known as the Palazzo delle Aquile after the marble eagle that stands above the portal. Built in 1463 with a square plan, and made of stone ashlars, it originally turned its main façade toward the Piano di S. Cataldo. In the façade is a niche with a statue of Saint Rosalia (1661), patron saint of Palermo.

Quattro Canti (II, E4). Via Maqueda, which the viceroy Maqueda built in 1600 by brutally ripping through the ancient structure of the city, crosses the Càssaro at a right angle (at the time, it was known as Via Toledo; now it is Corso Vittorio Emanuele). At the center of the large crossroads that identifies the Baroque section of Palermo is the spectacular *Piazza Vigliena*, also known as the Ottangolo (Octangle), Teatro del Sole (Theater of the Sun), and, more commonly, the Quattro Canti (Four Corners). The symbolic apparatus of this ceremoni-

this crossroads. Begun in 1612, construction was completed in 1645, and decoration was undertaken from the middle of the 17th c. and throughout the 18th c. The church is topped by a soaring cupola, with a drum decorated with twinned columns; the interior of the cupola is covered with majolica. The *interior* is spectacular, and is built to a Latin-cross plan with three aisles divided by 14 monolithic marble columns, with a central cupola set on eight colossal twinned columns, which are also monolithic, and small cupolas along the lesser side-aisles. There is lavish decoration on the vault over the nave, with stucco ornamentation by Paolo Corso and frescoes by Filippo Tancredi, largely damaged during the war but lovingly restored since. The

One of the stalls at the local Vuccirìa market, an explosion of color and tradition

al square – which reproduces, in the decorations of the corners, the four-part division of the city itself – concealed the reformist intent of a project of great urban renewal. The four façades of the corners, adorned with balconies, cornices, windows, and niches set in three orders, were designed in 1608 by Giulio Lasso and completed in 1620. In the first order, there are four fountains with statues of the Seasons; in the niches of the second order, there are statues of the Spanish kings Charles V and Philip II, III, and IV; in the niches of the third order, there are statues of patron saints of the city; in the crowning element, note imperial and royal crests.

S. Giuseppe dei Teatini (II, E4). This church is set on the southern corner of Piazza Vigliena with its side elevation on Piazza Pretoria, and occupies a privileged position in the new urban center that was created by

vault of the cupola is frescoed by Guglielmo Borremans, and the pendentives are done by Giuseppe Velasquez. The plastic decoration of the vault of the transept is by Giuseppe Serpotta, while the frescoes are attributed to Guglielmo Borremans. Beneath the church, as if it were a crypt, is the church of the *Madonna della Provvidenza* (there is an entrance to the left of the main entrance).

Corso Vittorio Emanuele (II, E4). In the western section, running toward the Cattedrale (Cathedral), is a line of Baroque palazzi that have been heavily renovated. In the eastern section, facing the 16th-c. elevation of the monastery of S. Caterina, stands the church of **S. Matteo**, built between 1633 and 1647 with a powerful Baroque façade, three orders in grey marble adorned with statues. The interior is splendidly decorated with marble work, with statues in stucco by Giacomo Serpotta and frescoes by Vito D'Anna in the cupola. The main altar is rich in gilt bronzes and precious stones, agate, and lapis lazuli.

Via Maqueda (II, D-E4, F5). From the Quattro Canti you walk first through the northern section of this street. You will immediately see the *Palazzo Merendino* (n. 217), built by Venanzio Marvuglia in 1785-88 around a stern colonnaded atrium. On the other side of the street, following the impressive late-18th-c. façade of *Palazzo Rudinì*, stands the former *Casa dei Crociferi* (with fragments of a cloister on the interior) and the church of **S. Ninfa dei Crociferi**, dating from the first half of the 17th c., in the Roman late-Renaissance style; on the interior is a dramatic stucco group of the *Crucifixion* by Giuseppe Serpotta. Further along, the 17th-c. *Palazzo Branciforti* (n. 323), clustered around a porticoed courtyard, features handsome decorated and frescoed halls on the interior; then comes the church of the *Madonna del Soccorso*, built in 1603 with a Gagini portal.

Along the southern section of this street, just after Piazza Pretoria and – directly across from Piazza Bellini stands the *former convent of the Teatini*, dating from the early years of the 17th c., which was radically renovated at the turn of the 19th c. to house

the University of Palermo (a handsome cloister dates from the same period). Just past the intersection with *Via dei Calderai*, a working-class market street selling metal crafts, stands the 17th-c. church of **S. Nicolò da Tolentino**: it contains a number of structures dating from the Renaissance (baptismal font and two tabernacles) and canvases by Pietro Novelli (17th c.). Further along is the church of *S. Orsola*, with a Mannerist façade from the first half of the 17th c.: on the interior are stuccoes by Giacomo Serpotta and paintings by Pietro Novelli. Adjoining it is the sumptuous *Palazzo Comitini*, built around the middle of the 18th c., with handsome frescoed halls. On the opposite side of the street stands the *Palazzo S. Croce-S. Elia*, one of the loveliest pieces of Baroque architecture in Palermo, likewise dating from the middle of the 18th c., with large pedimented windows, wrought-iron balconies, and sumptuous frescoed halls, with majolica floors. Further along stretches the three-portal façade of the *Palazzo Filangeri di Cutò*, built in the first half of the 18th c. Beyond the *Porta Vicari*, a gate that stood in the southern wall of the city, marking the end of the Via Maqueda, is the church of *S. Antonino*: it contains the last Crucifix done by Fra' Umile da Petralìa, left unfinished upon the death of the artist, who is buried here.

1.3 The modern section of the city

This itinerary, running from the central train station, or Stazione Centrale (Piazza Giulio Cesare) to Piazza Vittorio Veneto along Via Roma, Via Cavour, Via Ruggero Settimo, and Viale della Libertà, follows the thoroughfares that marked the growth of the modern city and pioneered the expansion that, starting from the middle of the 19th c., was to shift the center of Palermo out of the walled city. Already as early as the middle of the 16th c., on the occasion of the construction of the new seaport, there was a proposal for the enlargement of the urban perimeter through the development of a vast area next to the northern city walls. But it was not until 1778 that the plan for the "addition" proposed by the Pretore Regalmici, drawn up in accordance with the cross-intersection grid that had already been tested in the old town, established the bridgehead of later urban development with the extension to the north of Via Maqueda. The construction of Viale della Libertà, undertaken by the new city government that arose fol-

lowing the revolutionary disturbances of 1848, confirmed this direction for the growth of the city, and led to a radical redesign of the city's structure, and a new, middle-class approach to city space. The new road, along with Via Ruggero Settimo, Via Maqueda, and Via Oreto, form a straightaway extending for over 6 km, and it took on the role of thoroughfare for future residential expansion, though in a context that was still primarily suburban. The construction, beginning in the 1860s, of the Teatro Massimo and the Teatro Politeama with their respective squares, set as hinges between the new and the old city, served to accelerate the processes of urbanization that tended to class this part of Palermo as the new, or modern city. The transfer of the population to the new districts was encouraged by the urban "renewal" of the second half of the 19th c. (Via Roma, which cuts brutally through the medieval structure of Palermo, dates from 1865). With the construction of other new thoroughfares in the historic center of town, reduced the center to a traffic passageway. From the central train station, or Stazione Centrale, built in the distinctive "Umbertino" style between 1879 and 1886, this route runs along the straight Via Roma, a "modern" commercial thoroughfare that was completed in 1922. Lined with Neoclassical and Art-Nouveau ("Liberty") buildings, Via Roma runs parallel with Via Maqueda. Following the intersection with Corso Vittorio Emanuele, Via Roma runs along the massive building of the former Convento dei Padri Filippini, which now houses the important Museo Regionale Archeologico, and then intersects with Via Cavour, the northern boundary of the walled city, which ends on the right at the seaport (Porto) and to the left runs into Piazza Verdi. The elegant Via Ruggero Settimo, heart of modern Palermo, which runs from here to the piazza of the same name, links the two largest theaters in Palermo – the Teatro Massimo, in Piazza Verdi, and the Teatro Politeama, in Piazza Ruggero Settimo – and then continues along in Viale della Libertà, symbol of the modern city. This road ends in the circular Piazza Vittorio Veneto, near the entrance to the Parco della Favorita.

Museo Archeologico Regionale** (II, D4; *open Mon.-Sat., 8:30-1:30; Thu.-Fri., also 3-6:30; holidays, 9-1*). This regional archeological museum is one of the most important of its kind in all of Italy because of the vastness and the quality of the collections, and especially the complex of Siceliot sculpture from Selinunte; it was founded at the turn of the 19th c. as the Museo dell'Università (university museum), and moved to its present site in 1866. The collections – divided into sections in accordance with typological criteria and according to site of provenance – occupy numerous halls distributed over the three stories of the building. On the *ground floor* are halls of underwater archeology (containing, among other things, the most complete collection of ancient anchors on earth), the halls of Oriental-style sculpture (Phoenician, Greek, Egyptian) and classical sculpture (including epigraphs, architectural fragments, and sarcophagi). Note in particular the twin steles from Selinunte depicting couples of deities, plastic creations by local artists with clear Punic and Hellenistic influence; also note the architectural fragments from the temples of Selinunte, in stone and painted terracotta, and the lion's-head rain gutters from the temple of the Victory of Imera (5th c. B.C.). The most important items in this section

are the larger **sculptures**** from the temples of Selinunte, a remarkable series of great importance, not only for their beauty but also for the light they cast on Siceliot sculpture at large: there are *three splendid metopes from Temple C, four superb metopes from Temple E*, and, in the center of the hall, a 5th-c. B.C. bronze statue known as the **Ephebe of Selinunte***. The Etruscan collection, from Chiusi, includes funereal cippi with relief decorations, numerous funerary urns in stone, terracotta, and alabaster with a depiction of the deceased on the cover, sarcophagi, cinerary urns, and vases in terracotta and bucchero.

On the *first floor*, there are other collections of varied material from numerous different sites; from Marsala, Selinunte, Mozia, Segesta, Tèrmini Imerese, Imera, Randazzo, and Sòlunto: oil lamps, *votive terracottas*, funerary aedicules. The *collections of bronzes* are divided into small pieces (statuettes of Greek, Etruscan, and Roman heroes; mirrors; votive objects) and larger items: among the latter is the *ram** from Syracuse (3rd c. B.C.), a work of remarkable realistic power, and the group depicting *Hercules as he kills a stag*, from Pompeii (Roman era). Two halls are dedicated to *Greek and Roman sculpture*, and there are many small halls devoted to *goldsmithery and numismatics*. On the *second floor* are the *prehistoric collections, collections of Greek ceramics* (from the proto-Corinthian and the Corinthian to the Attic), *Roman mosaics and frescoes*, and *Italic ceramics*.

Porto (II, B-C5) or port. This was a fundamental piece of infrastructure for 19th-c. Palermo, and the chief point of departure, in the 20th c., for Sicilian emigration to North and South America; the port of Palermo, the largest in Sicily, with its naval shipyards (Cantieri Navali) represents an essential nexus in the economic structure of the city. It is protected by moles and an offshore breakwater rebuilt after the disastrous sea storm of 1973. The northern mole dates back to 1567, when it became evident that the old natural basin of the Cala was no longer adequate for military security in the Mediterranean Sea, and it was necessary to move the port further north, with a project that was widely considered grandiose and too expensive. Partially destroyed by bombing in WWII, it was rebuilt and improved with the trapezoidal mole, where the ruins of the first defensive fortress, the Castello a Mare, have recently been brought to light (*open by request, tel. 0916961319*).

Teatro Massimo (II, D3-4; *open 10-3:30; closed during rehearsals and Mon.*). Situated in Piazza Giuseppe Verdi, which was rebuilt to suit the theater at the end of the 19th c., in the wake of massive demolition, this is the main opera house in Palermo and one of the largest theaters in Europe (7730 square meters of surface area). The masterpiece of Giovanni Battista Filippo Basile, it was begun in 1875 and completed by his son Ernesto in 1897. The building presents a broad elevation, pushing outward in the center with a Corinthian hexastyle pronaos set on a high staircase, and a cupola set on a high tambour. On the *interior* is a splendid hall with five rows of boxes and a gallery, seating a total of 3200.

Teatro Politeama (II, C3). This theater was built by Giuseppe Damiani Almeyda between 1867 and 1874 in classical forms of Pompeiian inspiration; it dominates Piazza Ruggero Settimo. The front has a jutting structure reminiscent of a triumphal arch, and is adorned with a vast relief crowned by a quadriga (chariot) and spirits on horseback.

The Teatro Politeama

The halls on the top floor contain a modern art gallery, the **Civica Galleria d'Arte Moderna Empedocle Restivo** (*open 9-8; holidays, 9-1; closed Mon.*), a major collection that was installed in this setting in 1910. The works exhibited here present a fine panorama of modern and contemporary Italian art, especially in the Sicilian setting, and continue of the array of art exhibited in the regional art gallery, or Galleria Regionale di Palazzo Abatellis (in which there are artworks from the Middle Ages throughout the 18th c.). There are sculptural works by Domenico Trentacoste, Stefano De Lisi, Benedetto Civiletti, and Ettore Ximenes; among the important painters represented are let us mention Antonio Mancini, Giovanni Boldini, Carlo Carrà, Renato Guttuso, Felice Casorati, Gino Severini, Mario Sironi, Massimo Campigli, Remo Brindisi, Corrado Cagli, Domenico Purificato, and Fausto Pirandello.

Fondazione Mormino (II, A2). This foundation, the cultural institution of the Banco di Sicilia, is housed in the 19th-c. Villa Zito, in Viale della Libertà 52. Here is the *Museo d'Arte e Archeologia Ignazio Mormino* (*open Mon.-Fri., 9-1 and 3-5*), with the interesting collections owned by the great Sicilian bank. Aside from the major collection of Greek ceramics, most of which come from archeological digs financed by the Banco di Sicilia, there is also a numismatic collection, documenting the history of Sicilian coinage from the times of the House of Aragon to the reign of the House of Bourbon, a group of majolica, and a stamp collection including those of the Kingdom of Sicily (Regno di Sicilia) engraved by Tommaso Aloisio Juvara, and others from the kingdom of Naples (Regno di Napoli). Also of interest is the collection of prints and engravings with Sicilian subjects.

1.4 The Conca d'Oro and Ùstica

The broad area of territory that is known as the Conca d'Oro (route map on p. 47) comprises the land immediately surrounding Palermo; it extends from the slopes of Monte Gallo in the west all the way to the promontory of Monte Catalfano in the east. It is bounded inland by the massifs of Monte Castellaccio, Monte Cuccio, Monte Caputo, Monte Grifone, and Monte Porcara; all but the last of these peaks stand between 800 and 1000 m high. The morphology and the settlement history make it possible to divide the Conca d'Oro into three areas. The area to the northwest consists essentially of the Piana dei Colli, an area of considerable urban development in the 19th c. following the construction of Viale della Libertà: this territory was marked by peasant villages, and in the 17th and 18th c. it was covered with spectacular residences built by the nobility of Palermo, attracted by the fine climate and eager to vacation amidst the lush greenery of parks and gardens. The construction in 1799 of the large royal park of the Favorita, which became a public park following the unification of Italy, laid the foundation for a final set-aside of this area of the Conca d'Oro as an area for leisure time and enjoyment, reinforced by the reclamation of the marsh of Mondello and the construction, at the turn of the century, of a garden-town that was to serve as a beach resort for the well-to-do. The great appeal of this area pushed the expansion of Palermo ever northward, and in the last few decades the city has invaded the entire plain with a dense and extensive residential area.

The central area of the Conca d'Oro is a territory that has been inhabited ever since antiquity, an area with which the city has woven an intense though fragmentary relationship over the course of its history. In the 9th c., the Moors transformed this plain, so rich and well-irrigated, into a vast and flourishing garden dotted with farms and agrarian compounds, and built spectacular residences. This was primarily a vacation spot, and the Normans unified it in the 12th c. into a single royal landholding, establishing a system of parks including the Parco Vecchio in the southeastern area of the Conca d'Oro, centered around the Castello della Favara, and the larger Parco del Genoardo, which contains the castles of the Zisa, the Scibene, the Cuba, the Cuba Soprana and the Castello del Parco at the south end. The Benedictines, who were present at S. Martino delle Scale as early as the 6th c., founded the monasteries of Monreale, Castellaccio, and Baida on the mountain slopes; in the 15th c., the Minori Osservanti established themselves on the slopes of the Monte Grifone. Over the course of the 16th c. the territory once again became a place of leisure and entertainment for the city aristocracy, which transformed many agricultural buildings into seasonal vacation homes and built many sumptuous villas in the centuries that followed. At the end of the 16th c. the construction of the great thoroughfare, the "Stradone di Mezzomonreale" (now Corso Calatafimi) at first pushed urban expansion outside of the city walls in a southwesterly direction; expansion then moved definitively, in the 19th c., in the direction marked out by Viale della Libertà.

The eastern strip of the Conca d'Oro is a fertile valley, watered by the river Eleutero and closed off to the east by the Monte Catalfano; on the slopes of the mountain overlooking the sea, the settlement of Sòlunto developed in Roman and Punic times.

The broad plain, heavily farmed, was crossed by the old consular road, or Via Consolare, which linked the capital of Sicily with the cities along the northern coast; in 1658 the prince, or Principe di Butera, built his new residence on a little hill here, quickly triggering a mass return of the other well-to-do families of the Palermo aristocracy, who, in the course of fifty years, built the most spectacular Baroque villas of the Conca d'Oro in the surrounding area. Around the middle of the 18th c., the rebuilding of Villa Butera and the construction of two straight thoroughfares led to the foundation of the town of Bagherìa, whose feverish and uncontrolled development soon reached the surrounding residences, destroying the great parks and even damaging the homes themselves.

In the period following the second World War, massive residential tourism has covered the coastline, resulting in a dense network of seasonal homes, blighting large areas of considerable environmental importance.

The northwestern strip of the Conca d'Oro

Parco della Favorita*

This is a vast public park at the foot of Monte Pellegrino; its array of woodlands and forests is a fundamental treasure of greenery wedged between the city and the beach resort of Mondello. The usual entrance to the Parco della Favorita (I, C3-4) is through the gate, or Porta Leoni, which opens onto Piazza Leoni. Established by Ferdinand III of Bourbon in 1799, when, ejected from Naples by the armies of Napoleon, the king and his court took refuge in Palermo, the park covers a surface of some 400 hectares. It was originally created as a hunting and fishing preserve and as a botanical garden for agricultural experimentation, of which the king was particularly fond. Today, there are a number of notable sports facilities here. Running lengthwise, the park is crossed by two long boulevards, known as Viale di Diana and Viale di Ercole; the latter boulevard terminates at the fountain, or *Fontana di Ercole*, a round basin at the center of which stands a massive Doric column surmounted by a statue, a copy of the Farnese Hercules (Ercole Farnese), now in the Museo Nazionale in Naples.

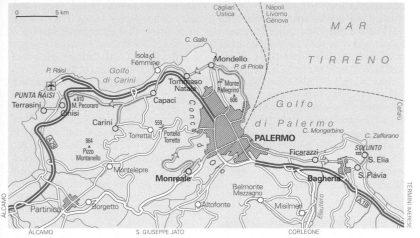

Villa Cottone di Castelnuovo

At n. 66-70 of Viale del Fante, which flanks the perimeter of the Favorita, is this 18th-century villa. Its park houses the *Teatro di Verdura*, a theater where the summer performances of the Teatro Massimo are held, decorated with a scultural allegory of Music by Ignazio Marabitti (1777). The park also includes one of the three historical orange groves of Palermo. The other two are in the Riserva Naturale di Monte Pellegrino and in the Parco di Ciaculli.

Palazzina Cinese

Built in 1799 by Venanzio Marvuglia at the behest of Ferdinand III of Bourbon, the Palazzina Cinese (I, B-C3; *closed to the public*), or Chinese pavilion, is a picturesque interpretation in the Neoclassical style of various Chinese motifs. It is not presently open to visitors. This was the favorite residence of the king and of his consort Maria Carolina during their forced stay in Sicily, and it was also home to Admiral Nelson and Lady Hamilton. This building is a singular product of the end-of-the-century taste for "chinoiseries," interesting also because it presents bizarre juxtapositions of disparate stylistic elements, such as the Gothic-arch porticoes on the ground floor, the classical-style vestibule, and the columned terraces, and the turrets with open spiral staircases built by Giuseppe Patricolo.

Museo Etnografico Siciliano Pitrè*

Founded by the Palermitan ethnologist Giuseppe Pitrè in 1909, and later enlarged and reorganized in this space (1934-35) by Giuseppe Cocchiara, the ethnographic museum, or Museo Etnografico Siciliano Pitrè (I, B-C3; *open 8:30-7:30; closed Fri. and holidays*), one of the most interesting museums

of its sort in all Europe, occupies the halls adjoining the Palazzina Cinese. The objects that make up the rich collection documenting the lifestyles, customs, and folkways of the Sicilian people, are classified according to the various activities to which they belong, and are displayed in the rooms originally occupied by the servants, arranged around a cross-shaped courtyard. A great variety of regional and traditional activities are shown here: hunting, fishing, spinning and weaving (linen and embroidery done by women of the Rione Kalsa, costumes and other garb of Sicilian peasants, carpets from Èrice, costumes worn by the Sicilian-Albanian women), shepherding and farming, ceramics produced by Sicilian craftsmen, games and toys and musical instruments. Also on display are carriages and sedan chairs, Sicilian carts, cribs, votive offerings, and a working puppet theater.

Monte Pellegrino

The ancient Heirkte, called "Gebel Grin" by the Moors and described by Goethe as "the loveliest promontory on earth," is now Monte Pellegrino (I, B-C3-4), a distinctive limestone mountain standing 606 m tall, closing off the gulf, or Golfo di Palermo, to the north. Craggy on every side, it is covered with patchy vegetation, and here and there reforested with pines, especially on the southwestern slope.
On its slopes, are grottoes of geological and prehistoric interest.

Santuario di S. Rosalia

This sanctuary (I, B4; *open 7-7 p.m.*) dates back to 1625 and comprises a grotto that has been transformed into a chapel of the convent with a 17th-c. façade built into the

47

rock; in an aedicule to the left is a marble 18th-c. statue of S. Rosalia. The saint, born in 1130 and traditionally said to have been the daughter of the duke, or Duca Sinibaldo, lord of Quisquina, and nephew of William II, lived here in penitence for many years, until she died in 1166. Her bones were uncovered on 15 July 1624 after a miraculous apparition; they were transported to Palermo, where they were thought to have caused a halt in the outbreak of the plague; it was for this reputed miracle that she was proclaimed patron saint of the city. On 4 September, there is a popular pilgrimage to the grotto, with a procession.

Mondello

Extending along the curve of the little bay that lies between Monte Gallo and Monte Pellegrino, Mondello (elev. 11 m) is the "lido," or beachfront of Palermo (which lies some 10 km away) as well as one of the best-known beach resorts in Sicily. The oldest core of the resort is comprised of a fishing village that lies at the northern extremity of the inlet, around an old tonnara that was still in operation at the turn of the 20th c.; all that remains of it is a cylindrical 15th-c. tower absorbed into the fabric of the village (another cylindrical watch tower, also dating from the 15th c., stands isolated on the rocky spit that stretches around to encircle the bay). The surrounding countryside, which was marshy and unhealthy until the 19th c., was reclaimed between 1892 and 1910 and leased to the Belgian company "Le Tramways de Palerme," which developed a garden-city here. In the climate of the Belle Époque, the first homes were built, incorporating stylistic concepts and architectural features of the late-Floral style (the *Kursaal-by-the-Sea*), as early as the First World War; but it was

between the two wars that the little town developed and grew, taking on a strongly elitist flavor. This elitist sense has been vanishing since the Second World War under the crush of mass bathing and vacationing and the pressure of the new buildings that have sprung up in the surrounding greenery.

The *grottoes of Addàura* ("laurel") are set above the nearby beach of the Addàura, in the spur of the Monte Pellegrino which runs down to the Punta di Priola, half-hidden amid the greenery. These are caves of considerable speleological and above all paleontological interest; note the human and animal figures carved into the walls, dating back to the upper Paleolithic.

From Mondello, continue along the state road toward the airport of Punta Raisi, and you will reach the intersection (176 km) for **Carini** (elev. 170 m, pop. 25,029). This little town, built on the slopes on the site of a Moorish settlement from the 10th c., took its name from Hyccara, which must once have existed in the vicinity, and which was destroyed in 415 B.C. by the Athenian statesman Nicias. The *castle* adjoining a fortified village probably dates back to Norman times, but was rebuilt in its present form in the 16th c. The castle, along with the fief of Carini, probably belonged to the Chiaramonte, Moncada, and La Grua Talemanca families. The church of *Matrice* (Assunta) has a late-18th-c. façade. The interior is decorated with Neoclassical stuccoes and frescoes (1795), and features an *Adoration of the Shepherds* by Alessandro Allori (1578).

If you head back down to the state road and drive another 12 km past the jutting form of Punta Raisi you will reach **Terrasini** (elev. 33 m, pop. 11,024), a fishing and farming town, where you will find an interesting civic museum, or *Museo Civico*, broken into three sections: natural history, archeology, and ethno-anthropology. The ethno-anthropological section includes the museum of Sicilian carts, or *Museo del Carretto Siciliano*.

The Mondello beach, one of the most famous seaside resorts in Sicily

The central area of the Conca d'Oro

Zisa**

This is one of the best examples of the Fatimid architecture of the Norman period; it was begun under William I and was completed under William II around the years 1165-67. The Zisa (II, D-E1; *open 9-7; holidays, 9-1*) (from the Arabic "aziz," splendid) is a high, compact building with a rectangular plan; the hermetic cubic shape of the structure, broken on the short sides by two slender square towers, is interrupted by three orders of slight blind arches, which originally enclosed little twinlight mullioned windows, and ends at the top in a cornice with an Arabic epigraph, removed in the 16th c. and replaced by battlements. It became private property, and over time the owners made numerous transformations and adaptations; after a period of neglect, it was purchased by the Sicilian region, or Regione Siciliana, which undertook its restoration. This was the seasonal residence of the Norman kings, once surrounded by an immense park and overlooking a body of water in which it was mirrored. The building has an exceedingly complex interior composed of public rooms and private suites; the latter tend to stretch over numerous floors.

Convento dei Cappuccini

Built in 1621, the Convento dei Cappuccini (II, E-F1) stands on the site of an earlier building complex. The church, which was renovated and enlarged in 1934, still houses wooden altars dating back to the 18th or 19th c. as well as other fine furniture and artworks, including a wooden *Crucifix* from the late Middle Ages. Note the funerary monuments on the entrance wall, erected by Ignazio Marabitti between 1753 and 1764. The monastery is known especially for its *catacombs*, mentioned by Ippolito Pindemonte in his work, the "Sepolcri." This is a vast subterranean cemetery where, beginning in the 17th c. and continuing until 1881, wealthy Palermitans were buried in long corridors. There are roughly 8000 bodies, a few of them mummified but most of them in a skeletal state; many are standing, others are seated, others still are contained in caskets or crystal urns.

Cuba*

Another splendid piece of Fatimid architecture in the Norman park of the Genoardo (now part of a barracks), built by William II in 1180, the Cuba (II, F1; *open 9-7; holidays, 9-* 1) is, like the Zisa, a tall building with a rectangular plan. This one too is compact and squared off, with flat avant-corps at the center of each front. Blind arcades extend the height of the masonry surface and enclose stacked blind windows and elongated niches; at the top, a band with an Arabic epigraph bears the name of the king and the foundation date. In the 14th c. Giovanni Boccaccio made this the setting for a novella in the "Decameron" (Day V, 6). It was purchased by private citizens; in the 16th c. it became a leper colony, and under the reign of the Bourbons it was incorporated into a cavalry barracks. This hermetic structure originally stood at the center of a manmade pond, surrounded by a garden, and was a pleasure pavilion. Inside, beyond a vestibule, there was a large square hall rising the height of the building with a central atrium.

Monreale*

This busy little city lies 8 km from Palermo, and is set on a spur looking out over both the valley of the river Oreto and the Conca d'Oro. Monreale (elev. 310 m, pop. 29,493; city map on p. 50) is the leading tourist attraction in the area around Palermo; it is renowned for its beautiful views and, first and foremost, for its superb Cathedral, or Duomo. It developed beginning in the 13th c., clustering around the Benedictine abbey that was made into an archbishop's see (1183); it was one of the largest and wealthiest such archbishoprics in Sicily. Subsequent growth was consolidated in the 16th c. with the settlement here of numerous religious Orders, followed by the construction, during the 17th and 18th c., of many churches, convents, and educational institutes; all of them give the little town a distinct Baroque identity.

Duomo**

(B3), or Cathedral. This architectural masterpiece from the Norman period, in which expressions of Muslim, Byzantine, and Romanesque culture combine to create one of the greatest creations of the Italian Middle Ages, stands in Piazza Vittorio Emanuele, the center of the village. It was founded by William II in 1174 and was rapidly completed, along with the abbey, the Palazzo Reale, and the Palazzo Arcivescovile, with which it formed a single organic complex. The *façade* in Piazza Guglielmo II Normanno, set between two enormous square towers, is fronted by an 18th-c. portico with three arches set on columns in the Doric style, crowned by balustrades; beneath it is a magnificent centered pointed-arch portal, adorned with carvings and mosaic strips. The bronze doors*, a creation by Bonanno Pisano (1186), are divided into 42 panels with Biblical scenes in relief, accompanied by explanatory legends in the vernacular (as opposed to Latin). The entrance is through a simple portal with bronze doors dating from 1179, opening under the portico on the left side. The **interior*** is immense (102 x 40 m), with a nave and two aisles divided by columns, most of which are ancient, with ancient and lovely capitals with clipei (shields) of deities set amidst cornucopias, supporting Moorish pointed arches. The cross vault is of the Byzantine type, with a square plan (bounded by four broad pointed arches and enclosed at the front by 19th-c. mosaic transennas) without a cupola and with three apses, decorated on the exterior by intertwined arches set on small columns. The mosaic flooring, with porphyry and granite disks, features marble bands interwoven in broken lines, and is the original pavement, completed in the 16th c. Of particular interest are the **mosaics**** with gold background, which cover over 6,340 sq. m the walls of the aisles, the sanctuary, the apses, and the area above the high socle of

marble slabs. These mosaics were done between the end of the 12th c. and the middle of the 13th c.; they were made partly by local craftsmen, who studied under Byzantine mosaicists, and partly by Venetian master mosaicists. They depict the stories of the Old and New Testaments, with legends written in Latin and Greek. In the central apse, high in the vault, there is a colossal half-figure of *Christ Giving Benediction*, with the Greek legend "Pantokrator" (all-powerful); beneath it is the *Virgin with the Christ Child Enthroned*, and the legend "Panacrontas" (all-chaste), flanked by angels and apostles; below are saints.

To the right of the façade of the Cathedral, or Duomo, is the entrance to the **cloister**** of the very old Benedictine monastery, or Convento dei Benedettini (*open 9-7; holidays, 9-1*); it too was founded during the reign of William II (last quarter of the 12th c.). It is a square measuring 47 x 47 m The pointed arches of the portico, with a double arch lintel and a distinctive large torus in the intrados (this is a particularly Islamic feature), are supported by 228 twinned columns with a rich variety of ornamentation, many of them with mosaic in-

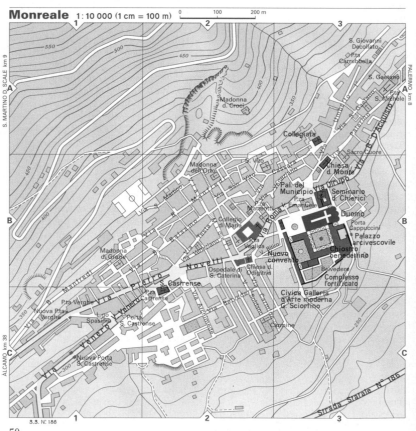

Monreale 1 : 10 000 (1 cm = 100 m)

tarsias, and others carved with arabesques. In the southern corner is a square enclosure* with three arches on each side and a little fountain in the center; the jet of water spurts up from a small column in the shape of a stylized palm tree. High above the side of the cloister opposite to the church rises the strong wall of the old *Benedictine monastery*, punctuated by blind, pointed arches; the interior, now open to the sky, is divided into three aisles by pillars; in the facing wall are twin and single-light windows.

The Duomo of Monreale: detail of cloister column

Collegiata (A3). This church presents 17th-c. architecture, which was altered in the two ensuing centuries; in its apse is a *Crucifix* done on majolica tiles from the 17th c.; inside, in the three aisles with columns decorated in stucco by Giacomo Serpotta (1723), are noteworthy canvases from the 17th and 18th c.

At a distance of 5.3 km from Monreale are the ruins of the imposing bulk of the **Castellaccio**, which features seven towers. Built in the 12th c. on the summit of the Monte Caputo as a fortress and a sanitorium for the Benedictine monks of Monreale, it was abandoned at the end of the 16th c. Restored in 1898, it became the property of the Club Alpino Siciliano, which adapted it for use as a mountain hut, establishing the Stazione Alpina Castellaccio and undertaking the reforestation of the summit.

S. Martino delle Scale*
At a distance of 9.5 km from Monreale, S. Martino delle Scale (elev. 589 m) is a popular hillside resort set amongst extensive pine forests dotted with vacation accommodations. On the large plaza that overlooks the valley stands the **Benedictine abbey** (*open 9-6; holidays, 9:30-11:30 and 5-7*) founded, according to tradition, by St. Gregory the Great in the 6th c., and destroyed by the Moors in 820. It was rebuilt in 1346 and enlarged in several stages between the 16th and 17th c.; it was completed in 1770 by G. Venanzio Marvuglia. The enormous construction, articulated around various courtyards and porticoed cloisters with arched loggias, was at one time a major center of culture, and is now occupied in part by the Benedictines, who officiate at the church services, and in part by the disciples, who run a large charitable institution. The 16th-c. church has an interior with a single vast white nave, side aisles set between large pillars, a deep transept, and a cupola. One should note the monumental 16th-c. carved wooden choir and numerous paintings by the Palermitan painter Giuseppe Salerno, known as the Zoppo di Gangi. In the monastery part you will find the cloister of St. Benedict (Chiostro di S. Benedetto), with columns and arches, dating back to 1612.

Roughly 15 km to the north of the town is the monastery, or **Convento di Baida**, set on a secluded promontory. It was founded in 1388 by Manfredi Chiaramonte for the Cistercians. The church preserves its original double-pitch façade, fronted by a portico with three pointed arches; beneath the portico, note the marble Renaissance portal, by Antonio Vanelli (1507). The interior has a single nave, with a whitewashed 18th-c. architectural face.

The eastern strip of the Conca d'Oro

S. Spirito.* In the southern part of the town, near the hospital, is the cemetery, or *Cimitero di S. Orsola* (I, E4), or *di S. Spirito*, founded by the viceroy Caracciolo in 1782, with monuments and chapels of fine 19th-/20th-c. architecture. Within the enclosure, at the far end on the left, is the Norman church of S. Spirito or Chiesa del Vespro, in front of which, on 31 March 1282, in the late afternoon (or Vespro), the people of Palermo rose against the Angevins. Founded by the archbishop Gualtiero Offamilio in 1178, it has a solid masonry structure bounded along the right side and in the transept by pointed arches, which intertwine in the apsidal area, vividly adorned with volcanic-stone inlay, with ashlar windows, screened by transennas. The *interior (if it is closed, contact the custodian of the cemetery)* is austere, with a nave and two aisles divided by pillars made of square-hewn blocks of stone, a higher and broader presbytery, and three apses. Behind the main altar is a *Crucifix* on a shaped panel from the 15th c.; on the sides of the presbytery, sarcophagi from the 16th c.

S. Maria di Gesù*

The church of S. Maria di Gesù (I, F5) stands on the southeastern outskirts of Palermo, on the lower slopes of Monte Grifone. You will enter a small terraced garden, now a cemetery. Up high on the right is the church (1426), behind by a little square with a 17th-c. fountain. In the façade, note the marble portal with figures of the *Apostles* (1495); on the left side is a pointed-arch portal, topped by an aedicule with the Virgin Mary in relief, dating from the 16th c. On the left, note the elegant Catalonian Gothic portal (15th c.) of the chapel, or Cappella La Grua-Talemanca. The *interior* has a single nave, with a raised presbytery, pierced by a Gothic arch; it contains 16th-c. sarcophagi, including that of Antonio Alliata, by Antonello Gagini (1512). In the apse are 15th-c. frescoes. To the right of the church, there are relics of the 15th-c. *cenobium*, or religious community, with a *cloister* featuring stout columns with the original capitals.

S. Giovanni dei Lebbrosi

In Corso dei Mille (eastern outskirts of Palermo), the church of S. Giovanni dei Lebbrosi (I, E4) is one of the earliest churches of the Norman period, founded by Roger I in 1071 and completed in the following century, when a leper hospital was added (1150). The church, which is thought to have been the work of Moorish craftsmen, stands at the center of a palm garden, and before its façade stands a little portico, topped by a campanile, built in 1934 as a part of a very drastic restoration project. The *interior*, which is basilican, has a nave and two aisles supported by pillars, as well as a hemispheric cupola set on niched pendentives above the raised transept, and three apses. Above the altar is a *Crucifix* on a shaped panel, dating from the 15th c. To the right of the church are the scanty ruins of a Moorish building, the Castello di Iehia (John), to which the church was once joined.

Bagherìa

A populous trading town set on gentle slopes amidst green expanses of citrus groves, medlar trees, and olive groves, overlooking the sea and Monte Catalfano, Bagherìa (elev. 78 m, pop. 54,035) lies 14.3 km from Palermo brings together in its territory a number of the loveliest Baroque villas in the Palermitan countryside. The town grew up around the structure of the Villa Butera, built by the Principe Giuseppe Branciforte, who retired to the country in the 17th c. and began to cultivate the surrounding land. Other villas rose in the surrounding area, and a century later, in 1769, Salvatore Branciforti rebuilt the old residence and created a thoroughfare on a straight line running due north toward the Mare di Aspra (Corso Butera), intersecting at a right angle with another thoroughfare terminating at the Chiesa Madre (Corso Umberto); these established the layout of the later development of the town. Along the two thoroughfares, the spread of cement and development has been ineluctable, over the past century filling in the greenery of the surviving parks and growing up around the villas.

Villa Cattolica (*open 10-8, closed Mon.*) was completed in 1736; its rigid mass – enlivened by two exedrae, one of which contains a great staircase – stand at the center of a cruciform courtyard surrounded by the low structures of the secondary buildings. This is the town's modern art gallery, or *Galleria Comunale d'Arte Moderna e Contemporanea*, established in 1973 around a considerable collection donated by Renato Guttuso, and subsequently enriched by other artworks. Aside from numerous paintings by Guttuso and various watercolors by the painter's father, Gioacchino, there are artworks by Mirko Basaldella, Robert Carrol, Mario Schifano, Domenico Quattrociocchi, Ernesto Treccani, and Carlo Levi.

Villa Butera (*closed to the public*), built in 1658 by Giuseppe Branciforte, has a newer façade added by Salvatore Branciforti in 1769. To the left of the 18th-c. façade, which has a balcony across the second story, and the heraldic crest of the family in the attic, above the clock, you will enter a courtyard. Here the elevation of the construction dates back to 1658; a staircase, covered with climbing plants, leads up to the entrance of the first floor, surrounded by festoons and draperies made of stucco, held up by two putti who flank the marble bust of the founder.

Villa Valguarnera in Bagherìa

A strip of coastline near Bagherìa with Capo Zafferana in the background

Villa Palagonia (*open 9-1 and 4-7*), built in 1715 by Tommaso Maria Napoli (and later continued by Agatino Daidone) at the behest of Ferdinando Francesco Gravina, prince of Palagonia and Pretore of Palermo, is the most renowned of the villas of Bagherìa; described by Jean-Pierre Houel (1776) and lauded by Giovanni Meli, it made a strong impression on Goethe. It has vivid architecture, which becomes spectacular and theatrical in the façade of the little central mansion, with its lively staircase and ribbing of yellow tufa stone against white plaster. On the first floor there is an elliptical vestibule, frescoed with the *Labors of Hercules*; the adjoining hall has walls encrusted with marble-work and has a pavillion ceiling covered with mirrors. The four-sided enclosure in the midst of which the little mansion ("palazzina") stands, presents a great variety of perspectives and is crowned by a celebrated and choreographic procession of grotesque depictions, mostly monstrous, clumsily sculpted beginning in 1747 as a product of the whimsy of the grandson of the founder also named Ferdinando Gravina Alliata. Sadly, even this creation of 18th-c. forerunners of the surrealists has been spoiled by modern construction, which emerges beyond the fence and clusters in on every side. Even the very long boulevard punctuated by exedrae (now Via Palagonia), which began on a line with Corso Butera (where the entrance portal still stands, isolated, between two monstrous figures) has been absorbed into the chaotic expansion of the city.

Villa Valguarnera* (*closed to the public*). Built in 1721 to plans by Tommaso Maria Napoli, this is the most sumptuous of all the villas, and it enjoys the best location, in the midst of a park framed by terraces and balustrades. Before it lies a broad square; it has a concave façade, to accommodate the staircase that leads up to the first story; the rear façade, facing the sea, is rectilinear, and the attics of both façades feature statues by Ignazio Marabitti.

Sòlunto*

Situated on the southeastern slopes of the Monte Catalfano, at a distance of about 3 km from Bagherìa, the ruins of Sòlunto (elev. 235 m) constitute a major built document of Punic civilization in Sicily. Soloeis or Solus was, with Mozia and Palermo, one of the three chief Punic cities in western Sicily. The town was founded toward the middle of the 4th c. B.C., and it remained under Carthaginian rule until it was conquered by the Romans around 250 B.C. At the end of the 2nd c. A.D. it was abandoned, perhaps voluntarily, by its inhabitants. In the ruins (it was destroyed by the Saracens) there is a prevalence of Hellenistic and Roman shapes.

The excavation of "Soluntum" began in 1826; it was begun again several more times; major sectors of the settlement have yet to be unearthed. The relics from the digs are largely in the archeological museum, or Museo Archeologico, of Palermo. At the entrance of the ruins is the Antiquarium (*open 9-6; holidays, 9-1:30*), which holds capitals, statues, casts of coins from the local mint, and all sorts of material from the most recent excavations; cartographic documentation of the ancient city explains various aspects of it.

The city, which appears in its Hippodamean urban layout, had a regular plan: the main street, or Decumano Maggiore, is crossed at right angles by narrow passageways for the drainage of rainwater, and by the trans-

One of the many finds unearthed in Ùstica

verse streets flanked by "insulae," or blocks of houses. The most interesting is the so-called **Ginnasio**, a Hellenistic-Roman house with an atrium and Doric columns surrounding the portico. The cobblestone paving is pretty well preserved; the terracotta paving of the main street is typical. It is interesting to note the quantity (one per house) and variety of cisterns, some of them with complex systems for gathering water, ensuring an adequate water supply in a city without natural springs.

On the slope of the hill, to the west of the *agora*, stands the Roman-Hellenistic *theater* (you climb up to the left after the exedrae), of which you can clearly see the few remaining fragments of the steps of the cavea and the scaena. Alongside it is a small, semicircular, very well preserved, building with steps, probably an "odéion" (for dances) or a "bouleutèrion" (for public assemblies).

The island of Ùstica

Linked to the port of Palermo by a regular service of ferryboats and hydrofoils, and located 52 km to the north of cape or Capo Gallo, Ùstica is the emerging tip of a great, extinct underwater volcano; its geological structure is similar to that of the Aeolian Islands (Eolie), and it has a surface area of 8.6

sq. km. A small ridge of hills, which culminates in the point or Punta Maggiore (also known as the Punta di Guardia di Mezzo), elev. 244 m, crosses the island transversely. The island, with a mild though decidedly maritime climate, has fertile plains, intensely cultivated with vineyards, wheat, figs, prickly pears, and legumes; hemp willow and the occasional olive tree also grow. The traditional income sources linked to agriculture and fishing have been joined by a flourishing tourist industry. Thanks to its exceedingly jagged and generally steep coasts, the island is a famed sea resort particularly attractive for divers.

The first marine natural reserve was created here in 1986, followed, in 1997, by the *Riserva Naturale Isola di Ùstica*, for the protection of the natural and artistic environment of the island, which has been inhabited since prehistory. Archeological finds attest to the successive presence of prehistoric populations (2nd millennium B.C.), Phoenicians, and Romans. From the 8th c. to the 11th c., Ùstica was ruled by the Saracens; here, the Normans built the church of S. Maria and the convent or Convento dei Benedettini which the Saracens destroyed when they took over the island again in the 14th c., exterminating and scattering the population. Various efforts to occupy and populate the island made thereafter by the Spanish government were unsuccessful. It was not until 1763, the year following the last Saracen raid, that the island was colonized by the Bourbons, with roughly a hundred families from the islands of the Eolie and a garrison of 250 soldiers. Natives of the Eolie, the population of Ùstica still preserves the customs, garb, and dialects of those islands.

From the *Cala S. Maria*, which is equipped with landing piers, a road made of three ramps runs up to the town of Ùstica (elev. 49 m, pop. 1373), set on a tufa ledge between two inlets, in the shadow of Capo Falconara, on the summit of which stands a *Bourbon fortress*. The town was founded in 1763 in accordance with an orderly plan of straight streets and rectangular blocks. To the south of the little town, in the *Torre di S. Maria*, there is a *Museo Archeologico* (*open by request*), with finds from the island. At Punta Spalmatore is the Aquarium, with 13 basins (*open summer, 10-1 and 3-6; winter, 10-1*). A car road runs all the way around the island, while several tracks and paths allow hikers to take interesting strolls. The *Grotta Azzurra* and *Grotta Pastizza* are interesting sights.

2 The territory to the south of Palermo

The territory under consideration (route map on p. 57) is bounded on the west by the valleys of the rivers Iato and Bèlice, to the south by the massif of the Monti Sicani, with the high summits of Monte Cammarata (elev. 1578 m) and the Monte delle Rose (elev. 1436 m), and to the east by the rivers San Leonardo and Plàtani. The route (a total of 164 km) originates in Palermo and – after passing Altofonte, the residence and hunting preserve of king Roger the Norman (King Peter II of Aragon was born in the Palazzo Reale), immediately after a turnoff on the right to San Giuseppe Jato and San Cipirello – after 23 km the route arrives in Piana degli Albanesi, the most important of the four colonies of Albanians in Sicily (the other three are Palazzo Adriano, Contessa Entellina, and Mezzojuso). You then head south, amidst rolling hill country, covered with fields, and after skirting the great woods, or Bosco della Ficuzza, extending out at the foot of the Rocca Busambra, you will get onto the state road 118, which links Palermo and Agrigento; head toward Agrigento, and some 34 km later you will reach Corleone, a major farming town. After a turnoff that takes you through Bisacquino, Chiusa Sclàfani, Giuliana, and Palazzo Adriano, you will continue toward Prizzi. The route as far as Lercara Friddi, a town that was founded in the 17th c., includes one more detour: to Castronuovo di Sicilia. You will then head back to Palermo with a stretch of 61 km along state road 121, which skirts, one after the other Mezzojuso, Cefalà Diana (with the old Moorish thermal Baths), and Misilmeri; by this point you are on the eastern outskirts of Palermo.

To Piana degli Albanesi, to Corleone, and to Lercara Friddi

If the northern section of this area may rightly be described as the Palermo region, or Palermitano, the southern part is far more difficult to categorize, at least in any way that is more specific than a historical, artistic, or even simply morphological "membership" in a recognizable tradition. This subdivision is accentuated as well by the diverse character of the two areas; the northern one is fertile, rich in water. The other is harsher, with scattered and isolated villages, linked by a fragile network of communications, and marked by extensive cultivations featuring crops.

San Giuseppe Jato

This town (elev. 467 m, pop. 8969) was founded on a feudal landholding acquired in 1779 by Giuseppe Beccadelli di Bologna e Gravina on a site once occupied by a hamlet and a little Jesuit church; the Jesuits had once controlled this fief. The town has an orthogonal grid like the nearby **San Cipirello** (elev. 394 m, pop. 5027), which lies next to it without any real break in the urban fabric. An agricultural center, San Cipriello developed after a terrible landslide from the Monte Iato which destroyed, in 1838, two-thirds of the town of San Giuseppe. Located there is a little *Museo Civico*, in Via Roma n. 320 (*open 9-1; Sun., 9-12:15 and 4-6:15*), featuring materials found in excavations of the ancient Ietas.

On the southern slope of Monte Iato, to the east of San Giuseppe Jato, excavations are uncovering the ancient city of **Ietas**. Inhabited by the Elimi from mid-6th c. B.C., it developed in the 4th c. The main urban monuments are now visible in the *Parco Archeologico (open 9-1)*: the *theater*, which could accommodate 4500 spectators; the *agora*, 50 X 40 m in size; the *bouleutèrion*, a small council hall; a *sanctuary* dedicated to Aphrodite, and a *Hellenistic peristyle house*. Ietas came under Roman rule in 250 B.C., declined in the 1st c. A.D., and was abandoned after the 6th c. A.D.

Piana degli Albanesi: S. Demetrio

*Orthodox ceremony in the church of
S. Giorgio at Piana degli Albanesi*

Piana degli Albanesi

The town (elev. 720, pop. 6305) is the most important of the five Albanian colonies to the south of Palermo. Given the difficult morphology of the terrain (a slope that runs down toward the river Bèlice), the town has an irregular plan, crossed by the straight thoroughfare of Corso Giorgio Kastriota (an Albanian national hero). The church of **S. Giorgio**, transformed in 1759, is the oldest in town. Its presbytery is closed off by an iconostasis adorned with recent icons by the Greek painter Stefano Ermacolas; in a niche on the left wall is a St. George, a wooden equestrian statue by Nicolò Bagnasco. The Chiesa Madre of **S. Demetrio**, or Cathedral, is a Greek rite church, begun in 1590; it has been partially modified by recent restorations. The interior, built to a Greek-cross, with a nave and aisles, is decorated with frescoes by Pietro Novelli (17th c.). Albanian costumes, traditional objects, and ethnographic material is on exhibit in the antropoligical museum, or *Museo Antropologico (open 9-1; Tue., Thu., Sat., Sun. also 3-7; closed Mon.)* at n. 213 in Corso Kastriota.

To the south of the town, at an elevation of about 600 m above sea level, is the lake, or *Lago di Piana degli Albanesi*. It is the oldest artificial lake in Sicily, created by the construction of a dam (1921-23) on the upper right stretch of the river Bèlice, for the production of electricity, drinking water, and irrigation. The lake is now a WWF protected area where many ducks and wading birds live.

Bosco della Ficuzza

The wood area of the Ficuzza is part of the *Riserva Naturale Bosco della Ficuzza, Rocca Busambra, Bosco del Cappelliere* and *Gorgo del Drago*. You can visit this forest which is an exceptional green expanse, (4000 hectares of deciduous forest, largely comprising oak trees) covering the northern slope of the Rocca Busambra. In 1910 the adjoining forest of Godrano was added to the Ficuzza. A road runs from the town of *Ficuzza*, to the left of the square on which the Casino di Caccia stands, and goes into the woods, from where many tracks start. The *Casino di Caccia*, or hunting lodge, built in 1803 by the architect G. Venanzio Marvuglia at the behest of King Ferdinand III, stands out against a background of greyish limestone walls. Today it houses the Corpo Forestale (forest guards). On its left is the *Centro Regionale per il Recupero della Fauna Selvatica*, an institution for the assistance to wild animals in difficulty. Visitors to the park can apply to it for any information *(open 9-1 and 3-6)*.

Corleone

This inland farming town has a vast and well-watered territory; Corleone (elev. 550 m, pop. 11,202) is set in a valley surrounded to the east and the south by limestone and sandstone mountains, which erosion has modelled into bastions and tower: particularly distinctive is the "Castello Soprano" (elev. 661 m), to the east, topped by a *Torre Saracena*, or watch tower, and the "Castello Sottano," an enormous boulder that stands, alone, on the right bank of the river that runs through the town to the south.

Corleone probably existed in Byzantine times, and it was of considerable economic and military importance during the Moorish occupation. It was conquered around 1080 by the Normans, and in 1095 it was ceded by Count Roger to the diocese of Palermo, and in 1176 it was assigned to the abbot of Monreale. In 1418 a major landslide damaged the upper part of the city, near the castle, or Castello Soprano, destroying the church of S. Giuliano and badly damaging the district of the same name; similar landslides (in some cases aggravated by violent flooding), due to the clayey nature of the ground upon which the structure stands and the presence of underground and surface water, have repeatedly caused serious damage to the interior of the city and especially to the eastern and southern outskirts, closest to the river bed. The general impoverishment of the economy and of the island's resources during the 17th c. had particularly serious consequences in Corleone, forced not once but twice to pay heavy ransoms lest the town be sold by the king; there was a slow process of social and economic decay, which seriously conditioned the history of this town right up to recent times.

The **Chiesa Madre**, or Cathedral, dedicated to St. Martin (S. Martino), was built in 1382, probably on the site of an existing church, enlarged in the first half of the 15th c., and completed with its cupola in 1663; it acquired its present-day appearance primarily in the 18th c., when it was further enlarged and decorated with frescoes in the cupola. The immense interior, with a nave and two aisles, contains numerous artworks, including a number that were rescued from other churches in the city; among them are handsome wooden sculptures from the 16th and 17th c. Not far is the church of *S. Rosalia*, built in the 17th c., which contains artworks

of various origin, including a canvas of the *Nativity*, attributed to Vito D'Anna; *St. John the Evangelist on the Island of Patmos*, by Giuseppe Velasquez; *St. Benedict* by Pietro Novelli; wooden 15th-c. *Crucifix*, known as the Crocifisso della Catena.

Bisacquino

Situated in a panoramic position overlooking the southwest slope of the Monte Triona (elev. 1215 m), Bisacquino (elev. 744 m, pop. 5148) takes its origin from the Moorish hamlet of "Busackuin" (named for the great abundance of water to be found in this site). The present-day settlement is characterized by the complexity of the urban fabric, where it is still possible to see signs of its Islamic origins. The **Chiesa Madre** (dedicat-

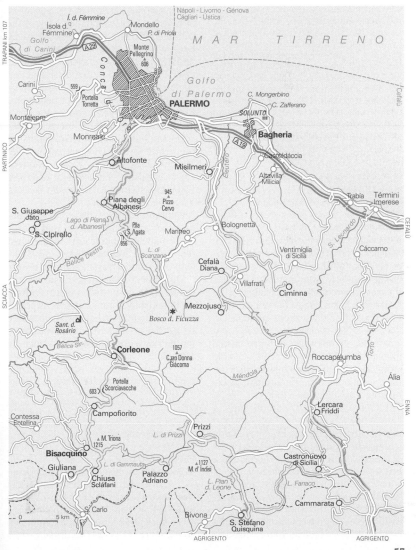

ed to St. John the Baptist) was built in 1713 by the Cardinal Francesco Giudice on the same site as the 16th-c. Chiesa Matrice; all that remains of the previous structure is the bell tower. The former monastery, or Convento dei Cappuccini, located in one of the oldest districts of the town, houses the *Museo Civico*, which focuses on ethnography and anthropology, archeological finds, and historical-artistic pieces, and thus offering an interesting cross-section of the history of the territory.

At 2 km from the town, is the sanctuary of the *Madonna del Balzo* (1664-79). A spectacular view of the valley can be enjoyed from the square opening out in front of it.
Roughly 7 km to the west of Bisacquino is all that survives of the immense abbey, or **Abbazia di S. Maria del Bosco di Calatamauro**. There is documentation of the existence of a hermitage on this site as early as the 13th c.: in the 14th c., the hermits subscribed to the Benedictine rule, and in 1401 the abbey was established; at the end of the 15th c. the abbey was ceded to the Order of the Olivetani, who remained there until 1784. This impressive complex was built between 1583 and 1646; around the two large *cloisters* stand the immense structures of the abbey, which open out to a scenic view of a vast expanse of western Sicily. Adjoining the monastery is the monumental *church*, irreparably damaged by the earthquake of 1968 and by later collapses: all that stands of it today is the façade and the campanile.
The abbey is included in the *Riserva Naturale Monte Genuardo e Santa Maria del Bosco*, a protected area rich in wildlife and plants.

Chiusa Sclàfani

A town of medieval origins, lying on a slope and closed off to the southeast by the Serra dell'Omo Morto, Chiusa Sclàfani (elev. 658 m, pop. 3425) was founded in 1320 by the count Matteo Sclafani, probably on the site of an existing hamlet. Since the 16th c., with the arrival of numerous religious Orders, the urban layout began to evolve, and is still largely recognizable today; in the middle of the 17th c. a very bad landslide swept away much of the central area of the town, creating a fracture in the urban structure that can still be seen today.
The *Chiesa Madre* (S. Nicolò di Bari), a church that was founded in the 14th c. and rebuilt between 1772 and 1813, has a large interior with a cupola. Not far is the complex of the Badia, with a Baroque portal and a bell tower. The well-preserved Via Greco, which runs through the oldest and most charming section of the town, is characterized by numerous lanes and courtyards with interesting pavement, leads to the enormous Piazza Castello; here, flanked by

a cusped campanile, stands the church of *S. Sebastiano*, with a single nave; the interior is particularly rich in decoration, featuring frescoes and stuccoes of the school of Serpotta.

Giuliana

Set on an isolated basalt crag, high above the valley of the river Malotempo, Giuliana (elev. 710 m, pop. 2384) already existed during the Moorish occupation. During the 14th c., at the behest of Frederick II of Aragon, this town was fortified with a long enclosure wall and an imposing castle, probably rebuilt on the site of an existing fortress. During the long feudal period, the center of town was enclosed within the old walled perimeter (which was demolished in the 19th c.), strongly marked by a complex medieval layout, and characterized by a great number of religious buildings, dating back to the 16th and 17th c., by the numerous monastic Orders that settled here.
At the top of the town stands the castle, or *Castello*, constituted by two structures that contain the ceremonial and living quarters, and by a massive tower with a pentagonal base. Inside the perimeter of the walls stands the complex of the *monastery of the Santissima Trinità*, built toward the middle of the 17th c. by the Olivetan monks of S. Maria del Bosco; the *church*, rebuilt on the site of an existing church (dedicated to St. Catherine), has a single nave, with frescoes dating back to the 17th c.
Set on a vast clearing to the north of the castle is the Cathedral, or **Chiesa Madre**; originally built in the 14th c., after subsequent renovations, it was demolished in 1935-38, with the present-day building in a Neo-Gothic style. On the southern side, a late-Gothic portal was installed, originally from the church of S. Antonio; numerous panels in carved stone from the old cathedral were set along the retaining wall to the north. On the interior is a marble baptismal font from 1593.

Before reaching Palazzo Adriano, to the right of the road 188, is the artificial lake, or *Lago di Gammauta*. The basin is surrounded by a wood which is part of the *Riserva Naturale Monti di Palazzo Adriano e Valle del Sòsio*, one of Sicily best protected areas.

Palazzo Adriano

Situated on a slight incline, on the slopes of the Cozzo Braduscia, in the high valley of the river Sòsio, the present-day Palazzo Adriano (elev. 696 m, pop. 2610) was built in the second half of the 15th c. by a colony of Greco-Albanian refugees. The urban plan is characterized by a radial/concentric lay-out, which has its point of confluence in the central square, or *Piazza Umberto I*, up-on which both of the principal churches face. The Greek-rite church (on the right as you reach the square), is dedicated to the Virgin (*S. Maria Assunta*; Our Lady of the Assumption), and was built at the end of the 15th c.; facing it is the church of *S. Maria del Lume*, of the Latin rite, built in the 18th c. Particularly noteworthy is the northern section of the town, which constitutes the earliest core; in a concentric array, the blocks wind over the little hill, around the ruins of the old *castle* and of the first church dedicated to St. Nicholas (15th c.).

was held by Giovanni Caltagirone; in this period, probably, there already existed the earliest core of the present-day town. From that original nucleus, which probably was consolidated around the present-day Chiesa Matrice, or Cathedral, the town continued to develop from the 16th c., in an expansion that can still be recognized in the regular lay-out of the long rectangular city blocks.

In *Piazza Castello*, raised and characterized by a stone fountain dating from the 18th c.,

Piazza Umberto I, central square of Palazzo Adriano

Prizzi

Lying on the southern slope of the mountain of the same name, Prizzi (elev. 966 m, pop. 5919) has a vast scenic view of the valleys of the rivers Sòsio and Vicaria. The origins of the town are linked to the old settlement of Hyppana, situated on the mountain, or Montagna dei Cavalli, where abundant archeological material has been found, from various periods of history. The present settlement began to develop, beginning in the 12th c.; according to the description of the Arabic geographer al-Idrisi, Prizzi is a small fortified "borgo," or village, abounding in water and surrounded by vast areas covered with fields of wheat. The earliest inhabited town, which clustered around the castle, occupies the higher part of the mount, and is markedly characterized by a medieval layout, with a dense grid of roads and lanes, in some cases so steep that they have steps. The **Chiesa Madre**, which stands on an elevated location, was built in the 16th c. on the site of the earlier church of S. Giorgio; the interior contains a statue of *St. Michael Archangel*, by Antonello Gagini. From the Largo Matrice, if you continue in a westerly direction, you reach the ruins of the *castle*, built at the turn of the 12th c. and rebuilt by the Chiaramonte; today, the few pieces left are incorporated in a number of homes.

Santo Stefano Quisquina

Situated on a gentle slope of the Serra Quisquina, Santo Stefano Quisquina (elev. 730 m, pop. 5579), surrounded by fertile farmlands, was inhabited during the Moorish period. During the reign of Frederick II of Aragon (1296-1337) the fief of Santo Stefano

stands the 18th-c. *Palazzo Baronale*. The *Chiesa Madre*, founded in the 16th c. by Federico Chiaramonte, is dedicated to S. Nicolò di Bari (St. Nicholas of Bari).

Castronuovo di Sicilia

This small town which originated in the Middle Ages stands on the left bank of the river Plàtani; Castronuovo di Sicilia (elev. 660 m, pop. 3470) is situated upon a slight slope, dropping down to the southeast, in the shadow of the Monte Kassar. Numerous traces of constructions on the vast highland that extends on the summit of the mountain, testify to the existence of an ancient settlement of proto-historical origins, later Hellenized. Situated in a place that has fine natural defences, this settlement was of considerable strategic importance, especially during the wars between the Greeks and the Carthaginians. Following the destruction of this fortified town (probably during Roman times), the inhabitants gathered on the steep crag of S. Vitale (to the west of the present-day town), where it is still possible to see ruins of buildings from the Byzantine period and from later periods. Between the 9th and the 11th c., on the eastern high plain, downhill from the fortified crag, near abundant springs, there developed two small villages ("borghi"), originally located outside of the town precincts; in the 13th c. the Borgo Rabat, closer to the crag, was enclosed within the perimeter walls (no longer in existence) which protected the original nucleus of the present-day town. The settlement of the Padri Carmelitani and the Padri Conventuali di S. Francesco to the east of the city walls (middle of the 14th c.) and the construction of the new church of the Madre della Santissima Trinità (1404) marked the progressive abandonment of the settlement set on the highland of S. Vitale and the rapid development of the town downstream, which soon grew beyond the boundaries of the town walls. The *Chiesa Madre* preserves, of the original construction (1404) the side portal and a number of pointed-arch windows; the interior, with a single nave and side chapels, renovated many times, contains numerous works of artistic interest, partly from other churches that no longer exist (including a statue of the *Madonna della Catena* by Gagini, a canvas from the school of Rubens depicting the *Flagellation of Christ*; a painted 14th-c. *Cross*; a marble statue of *St. Peter Enthroned*, by Domenico Gagini). From Piazza Duomo, if you head west, through the complex urban layout, articulated into lanes and courtyards, you will reach the church of *S. Caterina* (16th c.): the interior, adorned with precious marble altars and stucco work by Antonio Messina, contains a number of canvases from the 18th c. A little further along is the fountain, or *Fontana del Rabato*, rebuilt in 1531.

Lercara Friddi

Lying along the slopes of the peak, or Pizzo Lanzone (elev. 917 m) on the interior of the broad hilly area that separates the basin of the river Torto from that of the river Plàtani, Lercara Friddi (elev. 660 m, pop. 7565) was founded in the fief of Friddi by the Spanish aristocrat D. Baldassarre Gomez de Amescua, in 1605. The new foundation stood not far from an existing "fondaco" (Arabic term, for a stopping place and trading market), located along the royal way, or Regia Trazzera that linked Palermo and Agrigento. Of fundamental importance in the economic history of this town, at the turn of the 19th c., was the mining of sulphur from the rich and numerous mines; Lercara then gradually became the most important town in the northern sulphur-bearing basin of the island, which included the groups of the Colle Croce, the Colle Madore, and the Colle Serio. All the same, by the end of the Second World War, the development of this industry was hindered by a series of problems which culminated in the closure of the mines. The mining work is documented in the *Parco Archeologico Industriale della Zolfara* (*guided tours, tel. 338313843*). The urban layout of Lercara is characterized by an orthogonal road grid, which has its fulcrum in the main square, Piazza Duomo, on the east side of which stands the Cathedral, or Chiesa Madre.

Mezzojuso

Set on the slopes of the wooded hill, or Colle la Brigna, whose walls serve as a backdrop to the town, dominated by the campaniles of the two Cathedrals, or Chiese Madri, Mezzojuso (elev. 534 m, pop. 3092) takes its name from "Manzil Jusuf," meaning "village of Joseph," a Moorish hamlet that stood here before. In the 15th c., it became an Albanian town, after refugees fled here from the onslaught of the invading Turks. In the main square there are two *Chiese Madri*: atop one staircase is the church of the *Annunziata*, founded by the Normans and of Latin rite; lower down is the church of *S. Nicolò*, built in the 16th c., and of the Greek rite; both have undergone Baroque renovations. On the interior of the second church are six late-Byzantine panels, from an iconostasis that has since been dismantled; on the main altar, dating back to the 18th c., in polychrome marble, there is an ivory *Crucifix*, on a 17th-c. ebony cross. At the northwestern extremity of the town is the church of *S. Maria delle Grazie*, with a monastery. Built in 1501, it was officiated from 1650 on by Basilian monks of the Greek rite. It was modified around the middle of the 18th c.: on

Lercara Friddi. a "solfatara", or place where sulfurous gases are emitted

the interior, there is an iconostasis with Byzantine panels dating back to the 15th c.; on the walls, note the frescoed medallions, with the Doctors of the Greek church. The monastery has housed, since 1968, a workshop for the restoration of old books.

Cefalà Diana

The foundation of the town of Cefalà Diana (elev. 563 m, pop. 977) dates back to the second half of the 18th c. The name, of uncertain origin, may derive from the head-shaped rock spur upon which stands the castle. The fortress was part of a system of fortresses strategically arranged along the route that leads to Palermo. The town stands on a slope behind the castle, and has a layout based on an orthogonal grid, revolving around the central square. The houses that date back to the foundation generally are built to a plan with a single room divided up into two or three sectors, a common typology in towns of this period. The *castle*, which may be of Moorish origin, is in ruins.

Ciminna

Situated in a hollow to the south of the Pizzo S. Ananìa, Ciminna (elev. 530 m, pop. 4,251) may correspond to the Moorish hamlet of "Has," which the Arab geographer Idrisi described as rich in crops. Punic and Roman finds uncovered in the surrounding countryside confirms the existence of earlier forms of settlement. In the Norman era, the "borgo" must have clustered around a castle, of which not a trace survives. You will enter the town along the straight thoroughfare of Corso Umberto I and, before entering Piazza Umberto I, you will come to the church of *S. Domenico*, which contains two works by Antonello Gagini: a statue of the Virgin Mary (1532) and a ciborium (1521). In Piazza Umberto I stands the church of the *Purgatorio*, which contains a 16th-c. polyptych depicting the Virgin Mary and Saints. The church of *S. Francesco* preserves, in various locations, parts of a dismantled marble polyptych of the Gagini school, and a papier-mâché Crucifix (1521). The **Chiesa Madre** (S. Maria Maddalena), which was founded in the 16th c. on a highland, atop another, earlier structure, has undergone considerable renovations, from the 17th c. on, and preserves, of the earlier structures, a Gothic rose window and a massive campanile (1519). In the Baroque interior, which has a nave and two aisles, divided by pillars, there are stucco decorations, and a 16th-c. wooden ceiling; the carved wooden choir dates back to 1619. In the chapel of the right aisle, closed by a

stone arch that was placed here in 1531, is a copy of the *Spasm of Sicily* by Raphael, by Simeon of Wobreck. The church of *S. Giovanni Battista* is the largest in the town, after the Chiesa Matrice; it was built, to plans by Paolo Amato (17th c.), on an ancient oratory of the Confraternita del Santissimo Crocifisso, a brotherhood that venerated the 16th-c. *Crucifix* now behind a grate, just past the main altar.

Just a short distance to the north of the town are the Baths, or **Bagni di Cefalà***, *(open weekdays 9-1; holidays, also 4-7)* comprising a rectangular building, with exterior walls of irregular stone, and a band in tufa stone, with traces of writing in a Kufic character. Tradition would have it that this building dates back to the Arab period, but another hypothesis has been developed, based on historical considerations and methods of construction, which holds that the original layout dates back to the Romans (exterior walls, 2.5 m tall and 1.6 m thick); under the Normans, the vault was built on that, with Arab craftsmanship. After a partial collapse, they were entirely reconstructed in the 15th c. The Baths are included in the *Riserva Naturale Bagni di Cefalà e Chiarastella*.

Misilmeri

Misilmeri (elev. 129 m, pop. 23,533), a farming town, grew up on the site of a Moorish hamlet, the "Manzil al-Amir" (Hamlet of the Emir), around the ruins of a Norman-Moorish castle, which dominated a long stretch of the valley of the river Eleutero, an obligatory passage between Palermo and the hinterland. In the 16th c. Misilmeri was refounded and repopulated: a previous settlement from the Norman period, which clustered around the Arab castle can be recognized in the higher section of Misilmeri, where the houses are clustered in a circle around the ruins of the castle. The town was shifted downhill, and in 1553 the main church, or Chiesa Madre was built. It was upon the site of that church, and along the royal way, or Trazzera Tegia, that the new settlement with a geometric structure was laid out. The ruins of the *castle* dominate the large settlement: ruins of walls and polygonal towers belong to the reconstruction done by the Chiaramonte family (14th c.) and a further expansion done in 1487 by Matteo Carnelivari. The **Chiesa Madre** (S. Giovanni Battista) possesses an altarpiece with *The Immaculate Conception*, by Vito D'Anna (1768), who also did a Via Crucis on slate (1767), and various 18th-c. wooden *statues*, including one of *The Immaculate Conception*, by Pietro Marabitti (1734).

3 Western Sicily

At the western extremity of the island, contact with other civilizations had considerable influence in terms of historic formation and in the development of human occupation. Relationships with the material and political cultures that flourished in the western Mediterranean Sea – and more specifically with the cultures of Africa and the Iberian peninsula – counterbalanced by the peripheral effect of other civilizations, more common in the eastern areas – such as Greek civilization, or that of the Italian peninsula – exerted enormous influence in this area.

With the abandonment or destruction of the settlements of classical antiquity, what remained was the excellent network of Roman roads, serving as the skeleton of a new layout and organization of the territory in the High Middle Ages. The Arabs in particular between the 9th and the 11th c. undertook to reorganize the structures of settlement, production, and administration, establishing an influence that was to affect the history of the island right up to modern times, especially in this part of Sicily, where Islamic penetration was much deeper and where the damage done by feudalism was more serious; with the Norman conquest and the spread of the "latifundium," or large landed estate, the relationship between city and countryside altered irrevocably, causing an irreversible crisis in the last few centuries of the Middle Ages.

A geographic revolution in the settlement of the island was created, beginning in the middle of the 16th c. by the baronial class with the repopulation of immense uncultivated feuds, though there was also an element of political and economic consideration involved. This immense drive to construct and build led to a radical change in the structures of the territory and in the general system of communications; hence the Sicilian settlement grouped into large compact centers, which serve as counterpoint to the virtually empty countryside, which are dotted at most with infrequent farms.

Following the unification of Italy, there was a progressive and increasingly acute isolation of the western territories of Sicily, which had become peripheral to the areas undergoing development; this peripheral status – except for the few towns with considerable capacity for production, such as Marsala and Mazara del Vallo – translated into a general social and economic impoverishment.

3.1 Trapani, Èrice, and the Salinas

Trapani (elev. 3 m, pop. 69,453; city map on pp. 64-65) was a major seaport and an important industrial center until relatively recent times. The closure of the historic seaport of Lilibeo in the Stagnone, the splendid lagoon that extends to the north of Marsala, in the late 16th c., shifted the maritime traffic of the western Mediterranean Sea to the port of Trapani, which prospered greatly in the 18th and 19th c. thanks to the fish-salting industries and the shipyards, which took the place of the coral working that once flourished here. The city of Trapani established major salinas (salt pits and works) along the coast of the Mediterranean Sea, in Africa and in Asia, that lasted until the earliest decades of the 20th c., and crews and officers from this area long manned the great tuna-fishing boats. Nowadays, Trapani is a city of service industries.

The original village of Drapano became Drepanon under the Greeks and, as an emporium and a strategic seaport under the Phoenicians, grew in importance when it became a naval base and the keystone of the Punic system of defenses in Sicily. Beginning with the Roman conquest of the city, however, and despite the increase of population thanks to the transfer of the Ericines, a slow decline began which extended into the Byzantine Age.

The Moorish invasion of the island succeeded in giving Trapani a new period of prosperity from the 9th c. on; and it was precisely with the arrival of the Arabs that the city was rebuilt, with numerous features typical of Islamic town planning. This period of prosperity continued even after the Norman conquest, with the development of maritime trade accompanied by the skilled local manufacture of coral and gold jewelry.

The consequent growth in population led James II of Aragon (1286) to enlarge the town, organizing new residential areas with the reclamation of peripheral land surrounding the old city walls. During the same period, construction began on the new system of defenses, which included areas of expansion, with a new fortress erected to the northeast (Castello di Terra).

As is common in the history of this area, the building-in of unoccupied lots happened between the 14th and 15th c., with the establishment in the city grid of the large convent buildings. In the 16th c., a plan of modernization fostered by Charles V led to the construction of powerful bastions as city walls; isolating the city from the mainland by means of a navigable channel, which linked the inlet of the port with the inlet of the walls, known as the Tramontana; this channel has since been filled in, and is now Via XXX Gennaio.

With the demolition of the city walls in 1862 a new phase of expansion of the city began, justified by the need to find residential areas inland; it coalesced along the main thoroughfare of Via G.B. Fardella, which nowadays extends to the slopes of Monte Èrice. The reconstruction that followed the bombing of 1940-43, accompanied by the demands of the new city, led to a definitive shift of the center city outside of the historic center, with a remarkable revolution of the territorial layout of modern-day Trapani.

The tour begins from the "peripheral" Sanctuary of the Annunziata, which, with the adjoining Museo Pepoli, is one of the most interesting aspects of a tour of the city. Beyond the 19th-c. Piazza Vittorio Emanuele, one of the narrow lanes that runs off from Via Garibaldi takes one on a stroll through the medieval districts, where ancient churches stand alongside the Jewish ghetto, while Corso Vittorio Emanuele leads past 17th-c. palazzi to the "punta dell'insenatura," or point of the bay. It is pleasant, in the summer evenings, to mingle with the people of Trapani in Piazza Garibaldi and Piazza Lucatelli sitting in one of the many ice cream shops, enjoying the cool sea breezes.

Not far from the city, one obligatory stop is nearby Èrice, which looks out over the surrounding territory from its mountain perch (there is daily bus service from the train station of Trapani, a recommended alternative to using cars), and, along the road to Marsala, the Salinas and the remarkable museum of salt, or Museo del Sale.

South of Trapani, the landscape is characterized by salinas

Santuario dell'Annunziata* (A6). This sanctuary is the leading monument of the city, and was built between 1315 and 1332, but the interior was radically redone in 1760, with the older division into three spaces transformed, by Giovanni Biagio Amico, into a single nave. The original façade remains, with an immense rose window and the Norman Gothic portal from the early 15th c.; the massive Baroque campanile that stands beside it, a symbol of the continual reconstruction of the complex, dates from 1650. **Inside**, note the chapel of fishermen, or *Cappella dei Pescatori* (on the right) and the chapel of sailors, or *Cappella dei Marinai* (on the left), both of which date back to the 16th c. and built in tufa stone: the former has a square plan topped by a cupo-

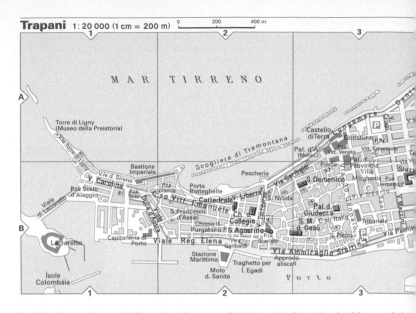

la (the decorative seashell motifs refer to those to whom this chapel is dedicated); the latter stands out for the remarkable monochrome punctuation of its architecture given by the distinctive yellow color of the tufa stone, typical of so many buildings in this part of Sicily. On the other hand, the chapel of the Virgin, or *Cappella della Madonna* (the sanctuary proper, which can be reached from behind the high altar) dates back to 1530, and has remarkable polychrome marble decorations on the walls and floors: the large marble arch, adorned with exquisite reliefs (*God the Father with Prophets*), is by Antonino and Giacomo Gagini (1531-37), while the *Virgin with Child**, known as the "Madonna di Trapani," on the altar is by Nino Pisano or by his workshop.

Museo Regionale Agostino Pepoli* (A6; *open 9-1:30; Tue. and Thu., also 3-6:30; Sun. and holidays, 9-12:30*). This regional museum is housed in the former *monastery of the Carmelite Fathers of Trapani*, an imposing building from the 17th c., though it was originally founded in the 14th c. along with the Santuario dell'Annunziata. The museum has undergone numerous changes over the years, and it displays important collections of applied arts: corals, gold and silverware, crèches, liturgical furnishing, church furniture and a rich series of majolicas. Among the sculpture, we should mention the *St. James the Greater** by Antonello Gagini (1522) and a holy-water stoup dating from 1486. The art gallery includes paintings dating from the 14th to the 18th c., and among them we should note a *Virgin Crowning St.*

Catherine with Saints by the Master of the Polyptych of Trapani; a *Pietà** by Roberto di Oderisio; a triptych by Antonio Massaro, and a *St. Francis with Stigmata** by Titian. The archeological section (room XXIII) is made up of finds from Èrice, Selinunte, and Lilibeo. Among the masterpieces of the *local applied arts* (rooms XII-XXII) are fine sculptures in wood, papier-mâché, ivory, seashells, semiprecious stones, and creations in coral, silver, and ceramics. Above all, what is noteworthy here is the unrivalled skill of Trapani's artists in the working of coral. The objects of this particular profession were born from the imagination and the skill of a Franciscan monk, Fra' Matteo Bavera, who executed several of the pieces displayed here: a large gilt bronze *lamp*, with coral and enamel (1633), a coral *Crucifix*, set on a cross made of ebony, tortoise-shell, and mother-of-pearl. Note also the fine *crèches* set made of coral, ivory, alabaster and other sea materials.

Piazza Vittorio Emanuele (A3). This square marks the western extremity of *Via G.B. Fardella*, a thoroughfare built during the 19th-c. expansion. It features an *equestrian statue of Vittorio Emanuele* (1882) and the fountain of the triton, or *Fontana del Tritone* (1951). Next to it is *Villa Margherita*, the city's public park, dating from the 19th c.

To one side of Viale Regina Margherita are the ruins of the *Castello di Terra*, the castle built from 1186. Overlooking Piazza Vittorio Veneto is the *Palazzo d'Alì* (1904), which is the Town Hall, and the Art Nouveau *Palazzo delle Poste e Telegrafi* (post office and telegraph office, 1924).

64

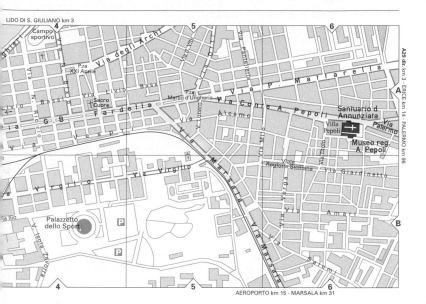

Via Garibaldi (B2-3). The former Rua Nova is a remarkable setting, lined with Baroque palazzi and churches that overlook it; one should examine the magnificent façade of *S. Maria dell'Itria*, built in 1621 and later enlarged (inside, it is possible to admire 17th-c. sculpture and paintings) and, at the end of the road, the church of *Maria Santissima del Soccorso*, founded in the 15th c. and partly rebuilt in 1874, featuring handsome Baroque choir lofts.

S. Domenico (B3). Rebuilt between the 17th and the 18th c., this church has some elements of the original 14th-c. construction: the rose window in the façade and traces of the original structure in the apse, where the *sarcophagus of Manfredi* (1318), son of Frederick III of Aragon, is preserved. The chapel or Cappella Pepoli behind the apse contains considerable fragments of the original frescoes, dating from the 14th c. (*Crucifixion*) and the 15th c. (*St. Catherine and other Saints*; dating from the same period is the *Virgin with Child* to the right of the entrance); the exquisite Baroque chapel with polychrome marble decorations, which Giovanni Biagio Amico built along the left wall, features on its altar a rare wooden *Crucifix** in the Iberian style known as dolorous-Gothic (13th/14th c.).

The church of *S. Nicolò Mirense* (B2), which can be reached from S. Domenico by taking Via Carreca, is the second-oldest church in the city (it was built in A.D. 536) and it boasts the title of basilica; in 1749 the plan of the church was modified to plans by Giovanni Biagio Amico. The marble *triptych* of *Christ between Sts. Peter and Paul*, in the apse, is of the Gagini school; the *baptismal font* is a gift from Charles V.

Palazzo Senatorio (B2). This Senate Palace was built between 1696 and 1702 on the site of the former Loggia dei Giurati and is one of the finest examples of Baroque civil architecture, with its framework with two orders of free-standing columns set against a façade adorned with statues linked above by a console-balcony which overlooks the Corso Vittorio Emanuele. Adjoining the palazzo is the clock tower or *Torre dell'Orologio*, one of the five towers depicted in the city's heraldic crest.

Corso Vittorio Emanuele (B2). Formerly the Rua Grande, this broad, long thoroughfare dates back to the development of the city in the 13th c., and the beauty and size of the public and private buildings that line it make it into the drawing room of the city.

Church of the Collegio (B2). Begun in the 17th c. and dedicated to the Immaculate Conception, this church is the work of Natale Masuccio. It presents a sumptuous Mannerist-Baroque façade, rich in marble decorations, which joins sleekness to a certain magnificent splendor, thanks to the elegant columns and the two statues of women standing in the place of caryatids. The *interior* features a nave and two aisles, with stucco panels (*Bible Scenes*) highlighted in gold; in the apse is the *icon* of the church of the *Immacolata*, carved in half-re-

65

lief in white marble, a masterpiece by Ignazio Marabitti.

Adjacent to the church is the Baroque building of the former Collegio dei Gesuiti, with a portal flanked by columns beneath a balcony.

Cattedrale (B2) or Cathedral. Dedicated to St. Lawrence (S. Lorenzo), this church was built in 1635 on the site of an existing church built in the 14th c., while the elegant Baroque façade, with portico, dates back to 1740 and was built to plans by Giovanni Biagio Amico. Inside there are a nave and two aisles set on columns, with decorations in the early Baroque style; there is also a 17th-c. *Crucifixion* attributed to the Trapanese painter Giacomo Lo Verde.

Directly across from the façade of the Cattedrale, or Cathedral, take Via Generale Domenico Giglio to reach the church of the **Purgatorio** (B2) built in 1683 with an elegant and lively façade with two orders (Giovanni Biagio Amico, 1712) decorated with statues of the Apostles. Inside are the 20 sculptural groups of the *Mysteries*, elements of a procession which is one of the most important sacred events held in Trapani. It traces its origins back to the determination of the Church, at the turn of the 16th c., to impose order and composure on the less easily controlled living groups who portrayed the Passion and death of Jesus; the 20 wooden groups, completed in the 17th-c. and made of wood, cloth, and glue depict this moment in the life of Christ with nearly life-size characters.

Torre di Ligny (A1). This tower was erected in 1671 in honor of the arrival in Trapani of the viceroy Claudio Lamoraldo, prince of Ligny, at the northwestern end of the breakwater of the port; it now houses the museum of prehistory, or *Museo della Preistoria* (*open 9:30-12:30 and 4:30-7*).

Isole Colombaia (B1). These islands, set opposite the fishing port and surrounded by shallow waters (you can see the seabed from the sidewalks along Viale Regina Elena), were the site of the construction in the 14th c. of an octagonal tower, which in the following century was put to use as a fortress. In the 17th c. it was converted into a judiciary prison; it no longer serves that function, and it now awaits restoration.

S. Agostino (B2). This church is actually dedicated to St. John the Baptist, and not to St. Augustine; it was built in the 15th c. near the hospice of the Knights Templar (Cavalieri Templari; this is also known as the church of the Templars, or Chiesa dei

Trapani: Palazzo della Giudecca

Templari), and was entrusted during the reign of Frederick III to the Augustines, who established a monastery there. It was later used by the city senate as a site for official, religious, and civil ceremonies. It was seriously damaged by bombing in 1942; of its original structure, what survives is the single, foreshortened hall, and in the façade both the magnificent *rose window**, with little intertwined arches and alternating fretwork, and a Gothic archivolt portal.

The square that contains the church features a fountain of Saturn, or **Fontana di Saturno**, built in 1342 by the Chiaramontani family, lords of the city, in commemoration of the aqueduct which they also had ordered built.

The **Biblioteca Fardelliana** (B2-3), a library that occupies the 18th-c. former church of S. Giacomo Maggiore (it is reached by following Via S. Agostino and Via dei Biscottai), was founded in 1830 by G.B. Fardella di Torrearsa; it contains approximately 118,000 volumes, a number of valuable incunabula and 851 manuscripts; of particular interest are the 15 illuminated codices dating from the 14th and 15th c. and an exceedingly fine collection of engravings (historical views of the Trapani area) from the 17th and 18th c.

S. Maria del Gesù (B2-3). Dating back to the first half of the 16th c. it was built at the behest of Charles V, along with the convent that was destroyed during the Second World War, on a plan similar to that of the Duomo di Monreale. This church has a façade with Gothic/Renaissance features and a handsome portal with decorations in the Catalonian style. In the *interior*, with its nave and two aisles which were originally divided by pointed arches, ribbed vaulting of the left apse and the presbytery has been uncovered, with small late-Gothic columns; the chapel or Cappella Staiti (to the right of the presbytery) contains an exquisite marble *baldachin* by Antonello Gagini (1521) above the *Madonna degli Angeli**, a fine glazed terracotta statue by Andrea della Robbia.

Palazzo della Giudecca (B3). This building (also called the "Spedaletto" or Casa Ciambra) is one of the most important relics of Jewish heritage in Sicily. It was built at the behest of the aristocratic family of the Ciambra (hence the other name by which it is still known) inside the area of the ghetto. The building has been renovated extensively over the course of the centuries: all that survives from the turn of the 16th c. testifies to the "stile plateresco," an exuberant and fanciful manner architectural style that spread in Spain at the end of the 15th c. and through the last few years of the 16th c., and ranged widely throughout Sicily. Damaged by the brutal events of history (the entire left side was demolished in the 19th c.), the building still boasts a rusticated tower, a large portal, and, in the wing that was spared demolition, apertures with lavish cornices and columns.

Èrice*

This little town (elev. 751 m, pop. 31,026; city map below) is set high on an isolated mountain at the western edge of Sicily: Monte San Giuliano, which was long the only point of visual reference for sailors on the other side of the nearby Ègadi Islands. It is a magnificent medieval village that has survived intact to the present day, and from which, on particularly clear days, it is possible to see the summit of the majestic cone of Mount Etna at the other end of the island. Èrice is a remarkable synthesis of mythology and history, art and culture, landscape and environment, fantasy and reality. It is said it was founded by the mythical Èrice, son of Venus and Bute, who became king of the Elimi, an ancient tribe that settled here, extending as far as neighboring Segesta. A Punic stronghold since 260 B.C., the town lost importance in Roman times, only to develop again, first under Moorish rule, and then under the Normans. The latter built the walls and castle on the site of the former sanctuary. In the 13th-14th c. the main civic and religious buildings were erected inside a triangular perimeter. With its cobblestone streets and its remarkable urban layout, Èrice met the requirements of a population that lived on a limited amount of land: the considerable steep climbs explain the twisting nature of the lanes and streets, which also had to be

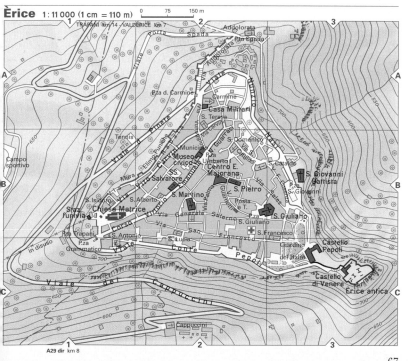

Èrice   1 : 11 000 (1 cm = 110 m)

The Castello Pepoli in Èrice

sheltered from strong winds, and that of the narrow "vanelle," passageways so narrow that only a single person can get through at a time. Aside from the streets, the most typical and best-known aspect is the town's little courtyards.

Besides being the headquarters of a scientific institute, the Centro di Cultura Scientifica "Ettore Majorana," Èrice hosts major cultural events through the course of the year, such as the international week of medieval and Renaissance music (Settimana Internazionale di Musica Medievale e Rinascimentale). Of particular interest is the Mystery Procession (Processione dei Misteri) on Good Friday.

If you enter through the gate or *Porta Trapani* (B-C1), one of the three entrances in the enormous *enclosure walls* (the lower part of which dates back to the 8th-/7th c. B.C., with Roman reconstruction; the upper section dates back to the Norman period), you will find yourself on the *Corso Vittorio Emanuele*, once the "royal way," or Via Regia, along which stood between the 13th and 14th c. the main civil and religious buildings. Among the handsome Baroque buildings along the "corso" we should mention the *Palazzo La Porta* and the *Palazzo Platamone* (B1-2), behind which lies the square that contains the **Chiesa Matrice*** (B1). This church is dedicated to Our Lady of the Assumption, and was erected in 1314 and then renovated (especially the interior) in 1865. The façade facing the town walls is fronted by a 15th-c. pronaos, beneath which stands a handsome Gothic portal. Facing it is an isolated campanile, with Gothic twin-

light mullioned windows in the Chiaramonte style, possibly built at the behest of Frederick of Aragon as a watch tower (1312).

The "corso" forks into Via Albertina degli Abbati, which skirts the church of *S. Martino* (B2), rebuilt in the 17th-18th c., and then reaches the pink church of *S. Giuliano* (B2-3), rebuilt in the 18th c., but founded by the Normans. Also dating from this era is the church of *S. Cataldo* (B2-3), beneath which, on the brink of a great cliff, the church of *S. Giovanni Battista* (B3) was built in the 12th c. and rebuilt in 1436 and again in 1631. It features a side portal from the 13th c., and fine statues of *St. John the Evangelist* and *St. John the Baptist* by Antonello and Antonino Gagini respectively.

If you climb up toward the southwest tip of the triangular walls, you will reach the 19th-c. garden or *Giardino del Balio* beyond which was the platea of the ancient acropolis. Here stands the castle, or *Castello Pepoli* (C3), formerly the site of the "baiulo" (governor's palace) and converted into a villa in the 19th c. (closed to the public). On the isolated crag of the acropolis, in the 12th and 13th c. ancient materials were used in part to build the castle of Venus or **Castello di Venere** (C3) crowned with parapets; inside, scholars have identified the site of the temple of the Venus of Èrice (Venere Ericina).

From the fork in the road, the Corso Vittorio Emanuele continues uphill; on the left, dating from the late-13th or the early-14th c., is the *Palazzo Chiaromonte* (B2), which belonged at one point to an Order of Benedictine nuns. At the end of the "corso" stands the centrally located *Piazza Umberto I* (B2), a 19th-c. version of the venerable town "loggia." Located in the municipal complex is the civic museum, or **Museo Civico A. Cordici** (*open 8-2; Mon. and Thu., also 2:30-5:30; holidays, 9-1*), which houses, among other things, archeological finds from the necropolis of Èrice, including a *Head of Aphrodite* dating from the 4th c. B.C. The tour can end with a trip down to the historical center of the town, i.e., the medieval crossroads where the church of *S. Pietro* (B2) stands; it was built in the late 14th c. and was rebuilt in 1745 to plans by Giovanni Biagio Amico. Nowadays, the former monastery houses one set of offices of the Centro Culturale "Ettore Majorana."

The Salinas

Among the most notable of the Sicilian saltworks, these salinas have until quite recently been a major feature in the urban landscape of Trapani and the entire coastal area as far as Marsala. Described by the Arab geographer al-Idrisi, they enjoyed great prosperity under the House of Aragon, and from the 18th c. until the end of the 19th c. there were roughly forty of them, and their product was exported to Norway, where it was used in the processing of cod. Nowadays, this traditional industry is in crisis, and few of the plants remain active. The distinctive landscape of the salinas to the south of the city can be observed by driving along the coast road to Marsala and then turning off every so often down toward the coast. It is advisable to walk between the basins where the salt is left to dry. Since 1995, Trapani salinas are included in

the *Riserva Naturale Saline di Trapani e Paceco (open Oct.-Mar., 9-5; Apr.-Sep., 9-6)*, a WWF protected area which preserves one of the most interesting coastal wetlands of Europe. The territory is the natural habitat for a series of local and migratory birds. The "Centro Visite" organizes a guided tour called "Via del Sale," during which it is possible to admire the ancient windmills.
A stop in the *Contrada Nubia* (elev. 7 m), where you arrive after a short detour from the coast road to Marsala, will allow you to reach the interesting salt museum, or *Museo del Sale (open 9-1; closed Sat. and holidays)* installed in an old salt-grinding mill, restored by its owners.

3.2 The Ègadi Islands and Pantellerìa

Set in the transparent sea off the coast of Trapani and Marsala, the Ègadi Islands (route map below) are what is left of a Sicily that once reached farther into the Mediterranean. In the middle of the stretch of sea between Italy and Africa is the island of Pantelleria, where the architecture testifies to Moorish influence.
Trapani is a point of departure for boat service to the Ègadi Islands it has frequent connections by ship and by hydrofoil. With the exception of Favignana, which is the largest island and which has a good system of roads, we recommend against bringing cars. To reach Pantellerìa, too, the best point of departure is Trapani, and you can simply call the same shipping companies that serve the Ègadi Islands. This island is also equipped with an airport that has daily flights from and to Rome, with intermediate stops at Palermo and Trapani.

ments of the tip of a long-ago triangular Sicily. Composed of limestone and sandstone, the little island of Lèvanzo, the rocky and secluded Maréttimo, and especially the largest island, Favignana, have been enjoying great popularity in recent years, a popularity that only seems to grow; the recent establishment of a nature preserve – or *Area Marina Protetta Isole Ègadi* – is an attempt to put a halt to reckless development in the interests of preserving the natural environment.
Inhabited back in prehistoric times (there are important graffiti in the cave or Grotta del Genovese on Lèvanzo) and once the site of a Phoenician-Punic settlement, these islands became Roman in 241 B.C.; there is further historical mention of them in the middle of the 16th c., when the Spanish crown sold them to the Pallavicino-Rusconi family of Genoa.

The Ègadi Islands
In the sea to the west of Trapani and Marsala lie the Ègadi Islands (pop. 4410), frag-

Favignana. Capital of the Ègadi, it is the southernmost island in the group (19 sq. km); it rises to an elevation of 314 m.

It has been an island-fortress and a tuna-fishing station, as well as an island-prison (the Spanish, the Austrians, and the House of Bourbon all used it for ordinary criminals and for political prisoners). The archaeological digs are of particular interest, with the famous *Bagni delle donne romane* (Roman Women's Baths). Among the many interesting buildings is the *Villino Florio* (now Town Hall) from 1876.

The quarries of fine-grained quaternary seashell tufa stone, excellent as a building material, have long served as a major resource here: from grottoes as immense and as intricate as great cities came the "cantuna," or tufa blocks, with which entire towns were built in Sicily, in Tunisia, and in Libya. But the main resource here has always been the sea. This dry, arid, and fascinating island, exposed to winds and salt air, forms a barrier to the progress of schools of tuna as they make their way around Sicily; along with the islet of Formica and the shoal of Maraone, it serves as a huge turning buoy for the migrations of tuna, which at the end of the spring come close to the coasts to breed, and which are caught in the "tonnare."

The stations were divided into "tonnare di corso" situated on the northern and western littorals with the aim of catching the fish during their migrations toward their breeding areas, and "tonnare di ritorno," located on the southeastern coast, along the routes followed by the tuna following their breeding season.
The stations in the sea ("impianti a mare") were basically nothing more than a system of nets and floating buoys, which halted the fish and directed them toward a series of rectangular chambers ending with the "chamber of death," using fine and very strong netting. Here the tuna that had been caught were killed off in a ceremony – the "mattanza" – that is cruel but packed with cultural and anthropological significance.
The stations on the land ("impianti a terra") were also a complex of great historic and economic importance; they served as support plants to the fishing boats, storing nets, boats, and harpoons, but above all they contained the fish-processing and fish-packing plants.
These were very large complexes arranged around a large esplanade near the sea ("marfaraggio").
Of the roughly 50 "tonnare" or tuna-fishing stations that once existed in Sicily, only the one in Favignana (which has always been the largest) still operates with any degree of continuity, processing each year from 1000 to 1500 metric tons

Lèvanzo. The smallest island of the Ègadi is worth a visit for its enchanting coasts and sea, and for the **Grotta del Genovese*** alone, famous for its prehistoric graffiti. This cave penetrates the mountain on the western coast: you can reach it by following a mule track, but it is also very charming to take a boat. The enormous dark grotto – 8.5 m in width, 12 m in depth, and 4 m tall – bears "messages" on its left wall left some five to ten thousand years ago, when Lèvanzo and Favignana were still joined to Sicily and were inhabited by Mesolithic and, later, Neolithic tribes. One can see a *series of animals*, graffiti with exceedingly light lines and remarkable naturalistic perfection, and four *human figures* shown in a ritual dance.

Maréttimo. The westernmost of the Ègadi, this island is a world unto itself and has nothing in common with the two other islands. Here there is no group fishing, no ceremony of the "mattanza": here the fisherman works alone and faces the boundless sea, on tiny boats marked with an odd flour

The "mattanza" of the tuna, a tradition which continues to this very day in Favignana

The evocative village of Maréttimo, on the eastern coast of the island

ish on the bowsprit, strangely reminiscent of Viking craft. No hotels have been allowed on Maréttimo, but the inhabitants provide accommodations in their own homes.

Pantellerìa

After Malta, this is the largest of the islands surrounding Sicily (map below), with a surface area of 83 sq. km and a population of 7436 inhabitants. Set in the middle of the Canale di Sicilia, it is a prime attraction for those who love the sea in all its wild beauty, with coastlines abounding in inlets and points, coves and grottoes set amid sheer rocks. For those who love fishing or underwater photography, this is the place. Transport links with Sicily, which is further away than the African coast, are good: there are daily flights and boat services, which do much to reduce the island's isolation and to encourage tourism.

Pantellerìa clearly bears signs of its birth from the sea (the most recent eruption was in October 1891): the Montagna Grande, which rises to an elevation of 836 m, is a relic of a volcanic cone, and the "cuddie," 24 highlands that stand around that cone, are also ancient craters. A number of examples of secondary volcanism are also visible: the "favare," huge geysers of watery steam (circa 100 degrees Celsius), expelled thunderously from crevices in the boulders; the dry Baths, or "stufe," natural grottoes with steam vents that are used as a treatment for rheumatism; the "caldarelle," hot springs that bubble forth at temperatures ranging up to 70 degrees Celsius; the "mofette," with fumes of carbon dioxide; and the "buvire," wells of brackish water.

For those seeking something more than the charms of the sea, Pantellerìa offers relics and curiosities that cannot elsewhere be found all on the same island. The "dammusi," cubic houses of Moorish origin; the gardens and the "sesi."

The story of the "sesi" is an enigmatic chapter in the history of Pantellerìa. A mysterious people from the Neolithic age, who may have arrived here from the coasts of Libya, took refuge along the harsh and hostile coast that looks out toward Africa, in the area of Mursia. This tribe of hunters, fishermen, and gatherers had no writing; and yet it succeeded in leaving traces of its existence in a cyclopean enclosure wall, erected for the village's defense, and in the funerary monuments called "sesi." They are great cairns (tumuli) of rough stone in regular hemispherical blocks of considerable size, inside which were one or two cellae. There were more than 500 of these remarkable prehistoric monuments, which are not unlike the "nuraghi" of Sardinia; nowadays, only a few dozen survive (one in particular good condition is the *Sese del Re* or Sese Gigante, the largest of them all), for over the course of the centuries the stone of the "sesi" were used in the construction of the distinctive houses of Pantellerìa, the "dammusi."

It was the Moors, who ruled the island for 400 years (the name Pantellerìa derives from "Bent el-Rhia," daughter of the wind),

who transformed its appearance by cultivating every square inch of soil. They were responsible for the introduction of the cultivation of the "zibibbo," a sort of muscatel grape, which still grows here alongside plantations of capers and lentils and they live on in the place names, in the dialect, and in the distinctive houses and gardens.

The "dammusi" have thick walls and a cupola roof, which serves both to collect rain water and to keep the interior cool in the summer and warm in the winter. They were originally used as summer homes, and in the vineyards as tool sheds, and are now reused as tourist accommodations.

3.3 The southwest coast and the Valle del Bèlice

There are many faces to the territory around Trapani (route map on the facing page), and those faces are geographic as well as economic and cultural. The coastal area that bounds the Canale di Sicilia alternates gulfs with promontories, opening out over the sea with spectacular scenic views (splendid view from Selinunte); there are expanses of vineyards in the area just slightly inland (the area around Trapani is the home of the finest Sicilian wines).

The central area of the basin of the river Bèlice is known as the Valle del Bèlice, a land apart ever since the violent earthquake in 1968. The exasperating slowness of the reconstruction made the provisional settlements, built in the emergency reconstruction, practically permanent. The passing visitor can hardly help but notice, alongside the eloquent ruins of the towns, the shantytowns, now largely abandoned, and the ghost villages that are perhaps even sadder than the ruins themselves.

This is also the area where you are most likely to find "bagli" (the name comes from the Arabic word "bahal," or courtyard), built as early as the 17th c. (though some trace them back to the Middle Ages) for the organization of life in the "latifundium," or large landholdings. These were buildings, often several stories tall, enclosed by a defensive wall made of stone, with a few small windows and a large central courtyard (the "baglio" proper) paved with slabs of stone and cobbles arranged in elegant geometric patterns; they were built so as to contain the residence of the owner (usually on the first floor), the stables and other housing for the animals, the wine cellars, storehouses, storage areas for farming tools, and – quite often – a chapel as well. It was necessary to create, at the center of every feudal holding, large and efficient farm structures, which when needed could also serve as fortified structures (in some of them, which are closer in appearance to castles than to country homes, there are turrets, enclosure walls, and loophole windows), and this coincided with the common practice of extensive farmlands (especially grain) and livestock breeding and grazing.

The Tyrrhenian coast has been heavily marred by the development (often illegal) of the vacation homes along the splendid coast.

This route, which runs in a great circle extending a total of 174.8 km, heads south at first, along the state road 115, Sud-Occidentale Sicula, from which it is possible to see the islands of the Stagnone beyond the Ègadi (the ruins of Phoenician Mozia are worth a detour). After a distance of 31.4 km you will reach Marsala, the largest Sicilian wine-producing town and the home of the celebrated Marsala wine. After the fishing port of Mazara del Vallo, the route runs inland to Castelvetrano, set at 73 km along the route. From this town, another 12.2 km of driving takes you to Selinunte, one of the most important ancient-Greek archeological sites in the entire Mediterranean Sea.

After you leave the coast, you will drive along the sadly famous Valle del Bèlice along the state road 119/Gibellina, reaching the new site of the town of Gibellina, designed and rebuilt from scratch following the earthquake of 1968; after taking the state road 188A, you will arrive at Salemi. From here, you can continue to Calatafimi, renowned for the decisive battle of the expedition headed by Giuseppe Garibaldi. At 114.6 km) is Segesta, another archeological site, which is particularly important and interesting due to the ancient origins of the settlement and the size of the temple; then you will reach Àlcamo, a large farming town and the main industrial center in the district.

It is just a few kilometers from Àlcamo to the gulf, or Golfo di Castellammare, following the coast road of the inlet westward. On your right, you will pass the turnoffs to the *Riserva Naturale Regionale dello Zingaro* and the area around the Monte Còfano (from the little bay of San Vito lo Capo you can admire the other slope of the nature reserve) and then you will return to Trapani.

Mozia*

To the south of Trapani, the sea forms a lagoon called Stagnone flanked on the west by an island, the Isola Longa, and on the east by the Sicilian coast; from this body of water emerge not only the verdant crests of the Isola Longa but also the islets of Santa Maria and San Pantaleo. These were the precise features typically sought out by the ancient Phoenicians for a settlement: a small island near the coast, surrounded by shallow water, to ensure adequate defense against enemy attack and a safe anchorage for ships, on shores swept by the prevailing winds. And it was here, in fact, on the island of San Pantaleo, that the Carthaginians founded the city of Mozia at the end of the 8th c. B.C.; it is possible to take a boat to the ruins from a little pier on the Sicilian coast.

Thanks to ideal location, close to Africa and at an obligatory point of passage along the main trade routes to Spain, Sardinia, and central Italy, the island Punic housed one of the most prosperous Punic (i.e., Carthaginian) colonies in the Mediterranean Sea. The presence of the Greeks in Sicily – with whom the Phoenicians sometimes traded and sometimes engaged in hostilities – led to a series of wars, with first one then the other prevailing; in the end, Mozia was destroyed at the behest of Dionysis II of Syracuse in 397 B.C.; the survivors moved over to the Sicilian coast, founding the city of Lilibeo, present-day Marsala.

Mozia was fortified by a massive perimeter of *enclosure walls*, punctuated by watch towers and with *gates* at the four points of the compass (two are still in good condition). When the fortifications were built,

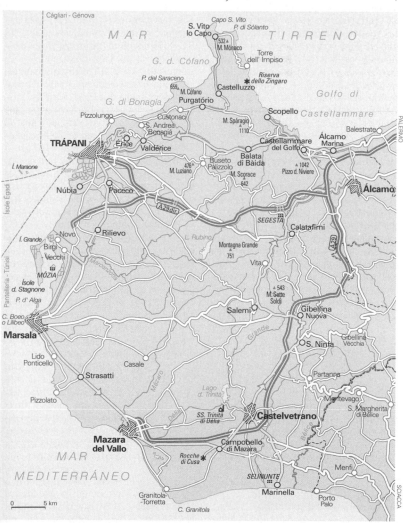

around the middle of the 6th c. B.C., the archaic *necropolis* that had been used to bury the dead since the very foundation of the city fell out of use because it was cut off by the wall; from that point onward the people of Mozia buried their dead on the mainland, in a coastal settlement now known as Birgi.

The necropolis is part of an archeological area which lies near Mozia and was brought to light during the digs by the Englishman Joseph Whitaker, one of the first foreign lovers of the island and its first archeologist. Whitaker moved to Sicily for purposes of business, and undertook the excavation of the ancient settlement. One can tour the digs by following the coastal road to the left of the city, toward south-west.

First you reach the *Casa dei Mosaici*, or Mosaic House, a Greek dwelling from 397 B.C., with a mosaic pavement in white and black cobbles featuring real and imaginary animals. Next is the *Casermetta*, a military building, and then the remains of the *South Gate* (whose present-day structure dates back to the 5th c. B.C.), adjacent to the ancient "*cothon*," a careening basin used in the maintenance and repair of ships, which with the larger one in Carthage, is the only one that has been found in the western Mediterranean Sea. Among the sacred areas that have been discovered, the *tophet* is unquestionably the most interesting one: it consists of an open-air sanctuary, inside of which is a burial ground with the remains of the human sacrifices made to the god Baal Hammon, in vases. The Phoenician religion, in fact, demanded that every firstborn male should be sacrificed to the gods; every human deposit, so to speak, was marked by a stele carved with symbolic or anthropomorphic depictions in a number of techniques (from graffito to engraving, and from high relief to full, in the round relief) or else painted (this latter sort of stele showed Egyptian and indigenous cultural influences as well as Phoenician ones).

In Mozia, a wing of Whitaker's villa houses a **Museum** (*open 9-1 and 3-6*), founded by the archeologist to exhibit the roughly 10,000 items that he found during his explorations. These were joined by pieces from later digs, and recently rearranged after the restoration of the building. They include a magnificent **Young Man dressed with a Tunic***, made of marble from Asia Minor (this is almost certainly a Greek original from the 5th c. B.C., probably taken as plunder of war), an eloquent piece of evidence of the continuity of ties between western Sicily and the eastern Mediterranean Sea.

Marsala

The survivors of Mozia, which was destroyed by Dionysius II of Syracuse in 397 B.C., took refuge on the nearby promontory of Lilibeo (now Capo Boeo) and, in conjunction with the Elimi and Sicane, early Sicilian tribes that lived here, founded a new settlement, named Lilibeo. With the passage of time it became the most important Punic base in Sicily, to the point that it was finally their last enclave on the island. The surviving inhabitants wanted it to be – as Mozia had been – wealthy and practically impregnable: expanding across an area of roughly 100 hectares, the city was washed on two sides by the waters of the sea and girt strongly, to the landward side, with walls as wide as 7 m, and by a broad moat (a network of underground passages made it possible to dart out sudden sorties against besiegers). Sadly, all that survives of these massive defensive works are descriptions by Polybius and Diodorus, because nothing, or practically nothing, remains of the original settlement.

The city remained impregnable until 241 B.C., when the Romans, following their victorious battle of the Ègadi against the Carthaginians, conquered Mozia and made it their chief naval base in the central Mediterranean Sea, as well as a stronghold along the routes to Africa.

After a period of decline, which was followed by a conquest by the Moors (830), the city once again became the chief port on

A clay mask unearthed in the sacred tophet area in Mozia

the African routes and the gateway for Muslim immigration to the island; use of the city's port, which was named "Marsa Alì" or "Marsa Allah" (hence, Marsala), encouraged renewed growth, with a renovation of the existing layout in accordance with Islamic patterns of settlement.

Between the 12th and the 14th c., the city returned to the Latin sphere of influence, consolidating its medieval layout and reorganizing its urban fabric with the construction of numerous churches, monasteries, and convents for the mendicant Orders. The city sided with the House of Aragon and against the Angevins, and the Aragonese – once they seized power – favored Marsala, making it even more important as a trading town. Aside from its importance as a port town, Marsala based its prosperity upon the production of a fertile hinterland, which produced wheat and sugar in particular. The flourishing economy also encouraged a general urban rebirth linked to the city's growing military might: the city became one of the leading strong-

holds in Sicily, and was enclosed within a perfectly square and symmetrical enclosure with bastions, inside of which a crossroads grid linked the four gates to the large central square, Piazza della Loggia. The city thus created an exemplary Renaissance model, which was in turn given a Baroque appearance with the construction and in some cases reconstruction in the 17th and 18th c. of the main civil and religious buildings.

Charles V made an extremely ill-advised decision, in 1575, to block up the port in an attempt to defend the city from pirate raids: from that point on, Marsala declined in importance as a great trading center. The little town reappeared in the center stage of history once again at the time of Garibaldi's great expedition, which began from a landing at this port on 11 May 1860.

Marsala (elev. 12 m, pop. 80,798; city map above) is nowadays a thriving farming and manufacturing town with a mental hospital of considerable quality, enclosed within a 16th-c. walled square, where many relics

75

survive. On the whole, the historic center is nicely preserved, maintaining a complex of fine homes and avoiding the sort of decay that blights other towns with concerted efforts to preserve and safeguard the town's important patrimony.

Part of Marsala's fame is linked to the fine fortified wine of the same name: it comes from a species of grape known as the Vitigno Grillo which, along with the Vitigno Catarratto, dominates the "alberello"-style grapevines that abound in the warm and colorful landscape. We should note that the success of Marsala wine was the product of the initiative of a number of British entrepreneurs who came here at the end of the 18th c.

One of the frequent sirocco tempests that hit the western shores of Sicily pushed John Woodhouse, in 1773, to seek haven in the port of Marsala. He tasted the local wine and was completely won over; he then shipped a considerable amount to England, adding a little brandy to preserve it during the voyage. His fellow Englishmen were so enthusiastic about the new wine that it immediately began to compete with the prestigious Spanish liquors that were already on the market; like those fortified wines, Marsala could be taken to sea for years without going bad, and it soon became standard fare in the warships of the Royal British Navy.

city, this building was erected beginning in 1576 and completed with broad arcades and a clock tower in the 18th c.

Duomo (B2), or Cathedral. The first stone of the Chiesa Madre, dedicated to St. Thomas of Canterbury, was laid in 1628 on an earlier (1176) Norman foundation, even though the imposing façade, adorned with statues and flanked by two small bell towers, was not completed until 1956; the interior, punctuated by tall columns, is adorned with works of art by the Gagini and their school. Behind the apsidal area of the Duomo is the tapestry museum, or *Museo degli Arazzi* (*open 8-1 and 4-6; closed Mon.*), containing eight magnificent Flemish *tapestries**, property of the church since they were a gift of the archbishop of Messina.

Florio's wine cellars with barrels of Marsala wine

Via XI Maggio (B2). This road runs along the ancient "càssaro," which may have been laid out as early as Carthaginian times, but which was straightened and realigned during the Baroque period. Among the many buildings (16th/18th c.) which line it, note, just past Piazza della Repubblica, the 16th-c. monastery, or *Monastero di S. Pietro*, which has a handsome tower with a majolica tip. It houses the *Museo Civico* (*open 8:30-1:30 and 3:30-8:30*), divided into three sections: one archeological, one devoted to Garibaldi and the Risorgimento, and one to folklore.

From Piazza Matteotti, the southeastern terminus of Via XI Maggio, by following the distinctive little lanes of Marsala, you can reach *S. Matteo* (B2-3), the first Chiesa Matrice of the town, founded in the 11th c. and later rebuilt.

Palazzo VII Aprile or Senatorio (B2). Overlooking *Piazza della Repubblica*, heart of the

Convento del Carmine (B2). This recently restored monastic complex houses the *Museo Nazionale di Pittura Contemporanea* (*open 10-1 and 6-8; closed Mon.*), with some hundred canvases of contemporary artists.

Museo Archeologico* (B1; *open 9-1:30; Fri.-Sun., also 4-7*), or archeological museum. Located in the Baglio Anselmi, it contains prehistoric materials from the area of Marsala and Mazara del Vallo, objects from Punic Mozia finds from the rich necropolises of Lilibeo, as well as artifacts from the early-Christian and the medieval city. The jewel of the museum is a **Punic ship*** (the sole example in the world of a "liburna," an agile warship roughly 35 m in length), discovered and salvaged by the submarine archeologist Honor Frost in 1979; it is thought that the ship formed part of the Carthaginian fleet which faced the Roman fleet in the battle of the Ègadi in 241 B.C.

Marsala: the Duomo and the city hall

The wreck is of particular importance because it has shown scholars the ship-building technique that was used in Carthage, apparently involving prefabricated units assembled in the shipyard.

Not far from the Baglio Anselmi – all alone – stands the church of *S. Giovanni Battista*, with a Baroque portal; through the interior, you can enter the so-called cave of the Sibyl of Lilibeo (*Antro della Sibilla Lilibea*); this Sibyl, according to legend, lived here and is buried here. Visits on request (tel. 0923714097).

Insula Romana* (A1; *open 9-1 and 3-an hour before sunset; closed Sun.*), or Roman block. In this area, accessible from Viale Vittorio Veneto, remains of a district of the ancient Roman city have been unearthed; the most substantial section of this area comprised a large *villa* from the 3rd c. A.D. with various rooms. Adjoining it are the remains of a *Bath building* with a polychrome mosaic floor. In the archeological area, storehouses, cisterns, and numerous tombs from an early-Christian necropolis have also been unearthed.

Mazara del Vallo
Set at the mouth of the river Màzaro and overlooking the Canale di Sicilia, this town (elev. 8 m, pop. 51,964) is the descendant of a Phoenician trading colony (about which we have accounts from Thucydides; further documentation is provided by the discovery of coins and tools), and a later trading colony that came from Selinunte. They continued to flourish under Roman rule, when the population became quite heterogeneous; that last quality is a constant in the history of this city forever the site of a wide range of exchanges and cohabitations, with the greatest mutual respect.

One of the happiest periods in the history of this town came under the Moors, who began their invasion of Sicily with a landing at Mazara, which they made the capital of one of the three administrative districts ("valli") into which they divided the island.

With the advent of the Normans, the city was made an episcopal see, and the fortified castle, or Castello – of which only the ruins of the portal still survive, following the demolition done after the unification of Italy to build the platform of a promenade near the sea – constituted the defensive bulwarks of the walls that form a square around the entire city. In each side of that square there is a gate: Porta Palermo, Porta Mokarta, Porta Salaria, and Porta Cartagine; in 1696 another gate was added, the Porta Salvatore. It was also during Norman domination that the Cathedral or Cattedrale, the church of S. Nicolò Regale, and the little church of S. Maria della Giummare (or Madonna dell'Alto) were all built.

The importance of the clergy in this city can be ganged from the continuous construction of ecclesiastical buildings tied to the various religious Orders. In the 17th and 18th c. these buildings forced a new equilibrium of the city layout with the Baroque reconstruction on the main squares, primarily among them Piazza Maggiore (now Piazza della Repubblica), while leaving perfectly visible the road grid of the Muslim layout of the town.

Mazara del Vallo is nowadays not only a major farming town; it is also one of the largest and best-equipped fishing ports in Italy; work related to that sector of the economy has caused the residential section of town to "explode," but the old center, happily, was spared; here, the labyrinth of lanes and little streets – which often take their names from ancient guilds or from the trades – of blind alleys, little arches, and courtyards is reminiscent of the general layout of the cities on the other side of the narrow channel. The geographic location of this town, so close to Africa, makes it an ideal gateway to that continent, as well as one of the liveliest and most bustling cities in all of Sicily.

Overlooking the Baroque *Piazza della Repubblica* (C2), is the *Seminario dei Chierici*, a porticoed structure with a broad loggia above (1710), housing the Diocesan Museum and an interesting library with 17th-c. texts, and the bishop's palace, or *Palazzo Vescovile*, built in 1596 but restructured at the beginning of the 18th c. Blocking off the eastern side of the square is the side of the Cathedral or **Cattedrale*** founded in 1093 and rebuilt in 1690-94; over the portal, note the relief depicting *Count Roger* (Conte Ruggero) *on horseback, trampling a Muslim* (1534). The presbytery contains a *Transfiguration** by Antonino Gagini (1537) amidst stuccoes by the Ferraro family.

Between the Cattedrale and the Lungomare Mazzini extends the park or *Giardino Pub-*

blico Jolanda (C-D2), on the site of the long-since destroyed Norman castle; all that survives of the castle is an *arch* overlooking the bustling *Piazza Mokarta*, backbone of the city's growth in the 19th and 20th c., at the southern edge of the ancient city.

From Piazza della Repubblica, Via XX Settembre leads to *Piazza del Plebiscito* (C1-2), with the church of *S. Egidio*, which is soon to become the seat of a new Museo Archeologico. The museum will house the precious **Dancing Satyr***, a bronze statue found by a fishing boat off the coast of Mazara. The adjoining *Collegio dei Gesuiti* contains the **Museo Civico** (*open Mon.-Fri., 9-1; Tue. and Thu., also 3:30-5:30*) with Roman archeological finds, fine medieval sculptures (*elephants bearing pillars* in the Muslim style of the 12th c., *little pillar-bearing lions*), sculptures and drawings by Pietro Consagra.

If you follow the *canal-port* (A-B1), constituted by the estuary of the river Màzaro, you will reach the little church of **S. Nicolò Regale** (B1), a Norman building dating back to 1124, with a square plan and three apses. You can then enter *Via Bagno* (B2), which was the main street of the Muslim city and the thoroughfare of the medieval trading district, serving as a link between countryside and port. Then you may take *Via dei Goti* (B2), in the heart of the working-class residential district, which is still strongly marked by Moorish urban features; go to the church of *S. Michele* (B-C2), adjoining the Benedictine convent. Founded in the 11th c. and rebuilt in 1637, it has a lavish interior decorated with marblework and stuccoes and with twenty allegorical statues by the school of Serpotta (1697). Via S. Michele leads to the church of *S. Veneranda* (C2), with a spectacular Baroque façade dating from 1714, set on a Norman plan. If you pass the *Casa Scuderi* (in Via Pino), with the remains of a cylindrical 15th-c. tower and a little portal in the "plateresco" style, you will reach *Via Garibaldi* (C2), the main business street of the historic center, along which you can return to Piazza della Repubblica.

Castelvetrano

This large farming town – specializing in olives and grapes – (elev. 187 m, pop. 30,045) originated with the ancient early Sicilian populace of "Legum" (in the area of Piazza Garibaldi a major necropolis from before the Greek period was uncovered in the 19th c. Later, the colonies of veterans from Selinunte were brought here to guard foodstuffs (hence the Latin name of "Castrum veteranorum"). The earliest information that we have concerning settlement in this area after the Greek period dates back only to the 12th c., when we have documentation concerning a large farmhouse built during the period of Moorish colonization. The grid of the historical center, with its complex and intricate urban structure, is indicative of the successive superimposition of two different urban models: one is radial, and dates back earlier, to the medieval formation of the inhabited center; the other has crisscrossing grids, with large square lots, cut by an endless array of blind alleys and courtyards, a clear indication of the Islamic urban tradition.

Of the monuments here (Castelvetrano had a considerable outpouring of art, especially in the 17th c.), several deserve mention: on the Piazza Garibaldi, in the heart of the little town, the *Chiesa Madre*, which was begun in 1520 and completed in 1579; the *Palazzo Pignatelli*, built in the 13th c. but considerably renovated over time; the church of the *Purgatorio*, built in 1642 on the site of an old religious building, and now housing the Auditorium "Lorenzo Perosi"; and the delightful fountain, or *Fontana della Ninfa* (Orazio Nigrone, 1615), which adorns Piazza Umberto I (facing the left side of the Chiesa Madre).

Along the straight thoroughfare of Via Garibaldi, which runs off to the south from the central square, you can follow Via Francesco la Croce to reach the civic museum, or **Museo Civico** (*open 9:30-1:30 and 3:30-7:30*) which contains archeological finds from Selinunte and paintings and sculpture from churches that are no longer in use (alabaster *statue of the Virgin with Child*, by the workshop of Francesco Laurana, 1467).

In Piazza Regina Margherita, which is reached, from Via Garibaldi, by Via Fra' Pantaleo, stands the church of *S. Domenico*, built beginning in 1470 but later renovated (inside, the presbytery and the choir are bedecked with lavish decorations in frescoed and stuccoed terracotta). Across from that church stands the church of *S. Giovanni Battista*, founded in 1589 and renovated heavily in 1797-1802 (in a niche in the presbytery, note the marble *statue of John the Baptist*, signed by Antonello Gagini and dated 1522).

It is worth taking a short detour (3.5 km) to the west to see the church of the **Santissima Trinità di Delia**, a beautiful piece of Norman-Moorish architecture, set in the pleasant greenery of a handsome park: dating back to the 12th c., the church is a square mass, crowned by a little red cupola in the Moorish style; around the windows, as the sole decorative motif, run smooth cornices.

Selinunte*

The name of this town comes from the name of the river that flows to the west of the ancient city, the "Selinon" (now the river Modione); this name in its turn comes from the Greek name for wild parsley ("selinon"), which grows abundantly on the site of this settlement, and which was a symbol of the city, as is shown by the ancient coins of Selinunte. Thucydides and Diodorus Siculus tell us that Selinunte was founded, under the leadership of Pammilos, by the colonists from Megara Hyblea (it is still uncertain whether that was in 628 or 650 B.C.), becoming the westernmost Greek colony in Sicily. Originally an ally of Carthage and, following the battle of Himera, of Syracuse, this town enjoyed sudden and vigorous growth that soon put it on a collision course with

Samuel Angell, who discovered the metopes that once decorated the temples, now housed in the archeological museum or Museo Archeologico of Palermo along with other notable finds.

The archeological complex of Selinunte, or *Parco Archeologico (plan on pag. 80; open 9-an hour before sunset)* is divided into four zones: the acropolis, the ancient city, the eastern temples, and the Sanctuary of Malophoros. Instead of beginning the tour from the southern edge of the acropolis – where the temples stand – we recommend climbing directly up to the immense fortifications that separate the acropolis from the site of the ancient city, and then going down to the Sanctuary of Malophoros and, lastly, visiting the majestic remains of the religious buildings.

One of the magnificent Selinunte temples, evidence of the city's great past

Segesta over disputes concerning territory and rivalries; in 409 B.C. it was defeated brutally and destroyed by Segesta, allied for this occasion with Carthage, in one of the most terrible massacres of the ancient world, a destruction which was completed, at the end of the first Punic war, by the Romans, who tore down the few houses that remained standing. In the Christian-Byzantine and Moorish era, small groups of people continued to live in the acropolis, but in the Middle Ages, even the name of Selinunte was lost, buried under the ruins after a terrible earthquake which wiped out the last few remaining structures.

It was only the middle of the 16th c. that the Dominican monk Fazello correctly identified the area of the old city; excavations did not begin until 1823, at the urging of two English archeologists, William Harris and

The ancient city (A1-2). Located on the hill of Manuzza, to the north of the acropolis, this section has only recently been the object of digging projects that have unearthed a road and the ruins of various homes; after the destruction in 409 B.C., much of the settlement must have been used as a necropolis by the survivors of Selinunte who still lived on the acropolis. Other necropolises are scattered in the area.

Acropoli* (B1-2), or acropolis. This acropolis stands on an irregularly shaped ledge sloping slightly down toward the sea, overlooking a long stretch of sea in one of the most alluring areas of all of the Mediterranean coast of Sicily. The enclosure walls that surround it, which we still see today though they have admittedly been renovated repeatedly, was built between the end of the 6th and the beginning of the 5th c. B.C., making use of materials from previous defensive works, systematically razed to the ground. The plateau is crossed by two thoroughfares that intersect at right angles, dividing the area enclosed within the walls into four districts. Aside from many public and religious buildings, this area contains five temples overlooking the river Gorgo di Cottone and the port – now filled in – which lay at the river's mouth. Well preserved, on the other hand, are a *gate* that has been sealed up, on the eastern side of the enclosure wall, and the *northern gate* at the end of the long road that cuts lengthwise across the center of the acropolis. Outside the gates, the Acropolis is still protected by huge fortifications, walls, towers and bastions partly belonging to the ancient city. To the south is the Tower, or Torre di Polluce, now housing the "Casa del viaggiatore", a sort of little museum of the site.

The *temple D*, built at the end of the 6th c. B.C. and possibly dedicated to Poseidon or to Aphrodite, had six columns on the short sides and thirteen columns on the longer sides, with the entrance facing east, as in all the other temples.

Not far away is *temple C*, the oldest temple (middle of the 6th c. B.C.) of those on the acropolis and, most probably dedicated to Apollo; in 1925-26 14 columns on the northern front were re-erected (it had 6 or 17 columns per side). This temple is now practically a symbol of Selinunte; a number of metopes from the trabeation and the colossal gorgon's mask from the pediment are now in the regional museum, or Museo Regionale di Palermo.

Next, heading south, you will find the little *temple B*, dating from the Hellenistic period, and possibly dedicated to Empedocles, the famous scientist and philosopher of Agrigento, who is thought to have overseen the project of draining the water from Selinunte.

The *temples A* and *O* – which are very close together and so similar in their hexastyle peripteros plan that it is thought that they were dedicated to Castor and Pollux – are more recent; they were built between 490 and 480 B.C.

If you head down from the westernmost extremity of the chief transverse street in the acropolis, to the river Modione, on the right bank of that river you can tour the less-than-spectactular, but very important ruins of the ancient **sanctuary of the Malophoros** (A-B1), dedicated to Demeter – goddess of fertility and harvests, and here described as a bearer of apples or pomegranates – and comprising a small altar, a large altar for sacrifices, and the temple. Well known in antiquity, this place of worship survived the decline of the city itself it was used first by the Carthaginians and later hosted Christian and Byzantine communities. The importance of this complex, which still poses many difficult problems, lies in the remarkable nature of the votive offerings that have been found here (little steles crowned with pairs of human heads, one beside the other) and the fact that a part of the population that coexisted here was not Greek.

The eastern temples* (A-B3). Probably surrounded by a single enclosure wall, these are the most imposing temples of Selinunte and they give some idea of the wealth and importance of this Greek settlement in the 6th c. B.C.

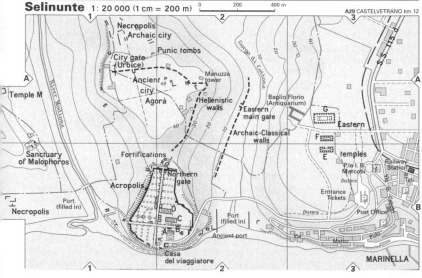

Selinunte 1: 20 000 (1 cm = 200 m)

Alberto Burri's "Labirinto" and the remains of a house devastated by earthquake

The *temple G**, commonly thought to be a temple of Zeus, is one of the largest temples of classical antiquity (110.36 X 50.1 m) and was never completed (its construction, undertaken around 550 B.C., was probably not complete at the time of the destruction of the city): we have evidence of this in the variations in style that occurred as it was being built (archaic in the eastern front, classical in the western front). From the enormous mass of ruins there now emerges only a single colossal column, restored in 1832, standing 16 m tall and measuring 3.5 m in diameter.

To the right of the road lie the ruins of the *temple F*, the smallest one (61.8 x 24.43 m) and the one that has been most severely plundered; it may have been dedicated to Athena and was built in the archaic style between 560 and 540 B.C. The nearby **temple E****, in a very pure Doric style (5th c. B.C.), was dedicated to Hera (Juno); this hexastyle peripteros (67.7 X 25.3 m) was rebuilt in the middle of the 1950s, and though the restoration is questionable, it now looms against the landscape of Selinunte creating a remarkable and striking effect.

Near Selinunte is a sandy stretch of coast which forms the *Riserva Naturale Foce del Fiume Bèlice e dune limitrofe*, a protected area which attracts many birds and sea turtles.

Gibellina

This town is a symbol of the tragedy of the Bèlice, destroyed by an earthquake in the night between 14 and 15 January 1968; Gibellina (elev. 227 m, pop. 4733) was rebuilt at a distance of 18 km from the rubble of the ancient town founded in the Middle Ages. The emblem of the new town is a *star*, a metal colossus gate built in 1980 by Pietro Consagra and set at the entrance to the new town. The new town of Gibellina was conceived as a city-cum-museum, in which works of contemporary art are displayed streetside, along a regular urban grid, serving to alleviate the desolation of the aftermath of the earthquake. Some of the leading contemporary artists were asked to contribute, among them many Sicilians (Consagra, Fausto Melotti, Giuseppe Uncini, Nino Franchina): each tried to offer a personal contribution to the difficult task of the recreation of a once lovely town. Other artworks by contemporary masters (Renato Guttuso, Fausto Pirandello, Antonio Sanfilippo, and Mario Schifano) are on exhibit in the *Museo Civico* (*open 9-1 and 4-7*) in Viale Segesta. In accordance with a project by Alberto Burri, the ruins of Gibellina have been progressively covered with a giant slab of white cement, apparently uniform but actually lacerated by a labyrinthine network of paths that correspond to the grid of roads of the little medieval village. The work by Alberto Burri is called **Cretto**, and is one of the most spectacular examples of landscape art. Each summer Gibellina now hosts the "Orestiadi," theatrical performances which sink their roots into the mythology of Mediterranean culture, a mythology which is represented through ancient, modern, and contemporary texts.

Salemi

The Elimi were the first inhabitants of this site, and the city built on these highlands is probably the town of Alicia, Diodorus Siculus wrote about (where the ruins of the apse of the Chiesa Matrice now stand, there once stood the acropolis on which was erected a temple to Venus). This was the theater of conflict between Selinunte and Segesta, and Salemi was allied with the latter beginning in the 8th c. B.C. The town flourished in particular under Moorish rule and it was the Moors who gave the town a new name: "Salem," place of delights. The reconstruction of the castle, or Castello (13th c.) and the settlement of mendicant Orders of monks here (12th-16th c.) encouraged the reorganization of the city's layout, culminating in the construction of the Jesuit college or Collegio Gesuitico and many other palazzi.

One first encounters Salemi (elev. 446 m, pop. 11,851) coming up from the Piano di S. Francesco, along the spiral climb up to the top of the hill. The finely calibrated Moorish layout, with remarkably complex blind alleys which lead into increasingly secluded little courtyards; steep staircases on the brink of very steep slopes; the monumental right-angled structure of the Jesuit complex, with its dense accompanying array of churches and patrician residences; the looming presence of the castle or Castello still seemingly jutting out to embrace the fragments of the city walls; the majestic ruins of what was once the Cathedral or Duomo until the earthquake devastated it; and from there the mind's eye ranges down to the silent wreckage of the district or Quartiere del Carmine on the slope behind the apse and the new area in which reconstruction was done, downhill from the old center of town: these are the features that characterize the old town, not entirely torn apart by the earthquake, thanks in part to the considerable work that has been put into restoration.

In the higher section of the little town, next to the presbytery of the Cathedral, or *Duomo* (rebuilt in 1615-1764 and destroyed by the earthquake), stands the castle or *Castello* dominated by the tall mass of the round tower, in which it is possible to make out the Swabian-Norman style (it was rebuilt, atop an existing structure, by Frederick II) and the traces of a long history of destruction and transformation. The college of the Jesuits or **Collegio dei Gesuiti** did abolish once and for all the continuity of the Muslim urban fabric (in order to build it in 1600 an entire medieval district had to be demolished) but gave the urban setting a strong dose of monumentality, which takes on a theatrical flavor in the façade of the church of the *Collegio*. The complex contains the civic museum or *Museo Civico di Arte Sacra* (*open 9-2 and 4-6; Sun. and holidays, 11-1 and 4-6*) with its artworks rescued from the rubble of shattered churches which collapsed in the earthquake, and the Museo dei Cimeli del Risorgimento (*open 9-2 and 4-6; Sun. and holidays, by request, tel. 0924982248*) a collection of souvenirs of the Risorgimento (1870).

Calatafimi

The name of this town (elev. 338 m, pop. 7328) is of Moorish origin (from "Qalat Fini"), though the Islamic village stood around a Byzantine fortress, the Castrum Phimes (castle of Euphymius). Populated by Berber peasants attracted by the richness of the surrounding farmlands, Calatafimi was conquered by the Norman army and became part of the royal estate; the House of Aragon was responsible for the reconstruction of the castle and the enclosure walls of the town. When it became a feudal landholding of the counts or Conti di Mòdica it grew, strengthened by the arrival of the mendicant Orders, flinging up new districts inside and around the walled area. Further development took place between the 15th and 16th c., when the chief thoroughfare (Via XV Maggio), which links the two monumental focal points that are the Chiesa Madre and the church of S. Michele, was extended in both directions along its axis: to the northeast, toward the sanctuary or Santuario della Madonna del Giubino, forming the

Splendid views may be enjoyed from the Greek theatre of Segesta

Rua Grande (Via Garibaldi); and to the southeast (Via Mazzini-Corso Vittorio Emanuele) along the axis linking it up with the territory of Bèlice. The earthquake of 1968 caused considerable damage here too, both to the architectural heritage and to lesser structures; the subsequent plan for the reconstruction and improvement of the historic center has not yet been fully implemented. The chief monuments of Calatafimi are the church of *S. Michele*, rebuilt in the 16th c.; the *Chiesa Madre*, founded in the 12th c. and enlarged in the 16th c.; the so-called *Pianto Romano*, a remarkable name (literally, "Roman weeping") for this ossuary-monument built just outside of the town in commemoration of the battle against the Bourbon army, resulting in Garibaldi's victory on 15 May 1860. But this little town is worth visiting especially for the Festa di Primavera or Festa del Crocifisso, which takes place on 3 May and is one of the most authentic Sicilian popular festivals, celebrated in commemoration of a number of miraculous events linked to an ancient Crucifix which occurred in 1657.

Segesta*

This was, along with present-day Èrice, one of the chief settlements of the Elimi, a people of uncertain origins (Thucydides said that they were the product of a mix of local populations with fugitives from Troy and Phocaea; Virgil wrote that Segesta was founded by the Trojan hero Aeneas). Of prehistoric origin, Segesta (or "Eghesta," according to the Greeks) extends over the slopes of the Monte Bàrbaro at an elevation of 304 m in a strategic location overlooking a vast territory. The main chapter of its history has to do with its conflicts with Selinunte over the border marked by the upper course of the river Màzaro; conflicts that, beginning in the 6th c. B.C., were ultimately fatal to Selinunte. Destroyed by the tyrant of Syracuse, Agathocles, as it was an ally of Carthage (end of the 4th c. B.C.), Segesta found new wealth and prosperity, thanks in part to the trading port of Castellammare, which was particularly important during Roman times; a slow decline ensued, ending with the city's devastation by Vandals and Saracens.

Some traces remain of the ancient town, which is still being excavated: the ruins of a number of square towers and of a gate from the old fortifications. On the other hand, the **temple**** is miraculously intact, a hexastyle peripteros (61.15 x 26.25 m) in the purest Doric style, which for the past 2400 years has stood, solemn and imposing,

on a hill to the west of the Monte Bàrbaro, in a dry and deserted landscape that emphasizes the grandeur of the structure. Scholars still debate the function that the temple was meant to serve (the only open-structure temple known in the ancient world) and why it seems to have been left unfinished: one of the hypotheses is that the Elimi built it with a view to making magnificent a sacred area in which indigenous religious rituals were performed, intentionally leaving it open to the elements; others believe that construction was interrupted because of the war that broke out with Selinunte in 416 B.C. (this is now the most widely held hypothesis), even though on the interior of the peristyle there is no trace of the cella in which the rites were celebrated. The **theater***, which dates back to roughly the middle of the 3rd c. B.C., stands right on the top of the mount, at an elevation of 400 m, in a location overlooking the city, and has one notable characteristic: unlike the other buildings of the same sort, it faces north, and this is probably so that it would offer an enchanting view of the hills and the distant sea. Little or nothing remains of the scaena, which must have been adorned with pillars and columns; under the scaena a number of excavations have unearthed the remains of existing constructions which date back to the 10th-9th c. B.C. In summer, classic dramas are performed in the theater.

Segesta gave its name to the hot springs, or *Terme Segestane*, which can be reached by turning off from the state road 113 in the direction of Àlcamo. The springs, which were already known in Moorish times, pour forth on both banks of the river Caldo, as well as inside a grotto which has formed a sort of natural sauna (the steam reaches a temperature of 38 degrees Celsius); the sulfurous waters (45 degrees Celsius) are used for baths, mudpacks, and inhalations.

Àlcamo

The old Arabic name, which is the origin of the modern name, was "Manzil Alqamah," which means "station of the lotus fruit." This large farming town (elev. 258 m, pop. 43,553, city map on p. 84) lies on one of the main roads linking Palermo with Trapani, in the heart of a broad valley abounding in vineyards, in a territory that – in Moorish times – boasted three large farm complexes corresponding to three fortified strongholds. Under the Normans, Àlcamo became part of a large feudal holding controlled first by the Peralta family and later by the Chiaramonte and the Ventimiglia families. The oldest core of the present-day town still has the original 14th-c. urban grid laid out by the latter family: an orderly plan of streets at right-angles and regular blocks with a crossroads; at the ends of those roads stood the main urban and architectural complexes of the 14th c.: the castle or Castello to the south, the market square or Piazza del Mercato to the north, the convent or Convento dei Francescani to the east, and the Chiesa Madre to the west.

The insertion into the urban fabric of numerous religious Orders (15th-17th c.) encouraged the development of the city, which is divided into districts and which extends, beyond the medieval enclosure walls, in a westerly direction along the extension of the chief thoroughfare (Corso VI Aprile). The center of the Baroque section, then, was the Piano Maggiore (now Piazza Ciullo), which serves almost as a hinge linking the old center and the new expansion; with the construction of the church of the Collegio it took on the function of city center that it still serves.

This city underwent a chaotic urban development that, while preserving the basic urban characteristics, in fact marked the slow decline of the historic city, with the creation of the new residential districts

that have spread the settlement all the way out to the slopes of Monte Bonifato.

The elongated *Piazza Ciullo* (B2), once known as the Piano Maggiore, is the center of life in this little town, opening onto the western section of the since-demolished 16th-c. walls. Here stands the church of *S. Oliva*, built in 1723 by Giovanni Biagio Amico on an existing structure dating from the 16th c. At the southern edge of this square in 1648 the church of the *Collegio* (B2) was built adjoining the complex of the Jesuits, with a harmonious façade with friezes, stuccoes, and sculptures. If you continue past the church along Via Mazzini, you will reach the enormous *Piazza della Repubblica* (B-C2), which has been turned into a garden. Closing it off to the north is the castle or **Castello dei Conti di Mòdica**, built in the higher section of the town during the 14th c. and recently restored (*open 9-12:30 and 4-8; Sat.-Sun., until 8.30 p.m.*). It has a rhomboid plan and cylindrical towers, with parallelepiped towers at the corners; on the northern elevation, there are traces of twin- and triple-light mullioned windows, in the Catalonian Gothic style, and a splendid rose window. The

The 14th-century castle in Àlcamo

castle will house a historic library and the ethnographical museum.

Beyond the square, you can cross the Piano S. Maria to the church of *S. Maria del Gesù* (C3), possibly founded in the 15th c., enlarged in 1507, and rebuilt in 1762.
From Piazza Castello, within the area of the walled "borgo," Via Navarra leads to the church of the *Badia Nuova* (B2-3) designed by Giovanni Biagio Amico; it contains allegorical statues by Giacomo Serpotta.

Passing Piazza Ciullo to the north is the *Corso VI Aprile* (B1-3), the ancient "strada imperiale" or "imperial road," a fundamental axis of the historical center marked by late-Baroque and Neoclassical architecture. If you follow the "corso" to the east, you will find the **Chiesa Madre** (B2) on Piazza IV Novembre, founded in the 14th c. and rebuilt in 1669; all that survives of the original structure is the campanile with mullioned windows and a handsome marble portal.
At the intersection with Via Rossotti, in the heart of the village, which was founded in the 14th-16th c., stands the church of *S. Angelo Custode* (B2), rebuilt to plans by Giovanni Biagio Amico. On Via Mariano De Ballis stands the *Casa De Ballis* (B2), a handsome Gothic building that preserves its 16th-c. tower adorned with triple-light mullioned windows, as well as a jutting set of bracketed parapets.
Further along on the "corso" we should mention on the left, the church of *S. Tommaso* (B2), a noteworthy example of 15th-c. architecture with a lavish Gothic portal; on the right, the Baroque church of the *Ss. Cosma e Damiano* (B2), adjoining the monastery of S. Chiara, built in 1721 to plans by Giuseppe Mariani.

Castellammare del Golfo

This town (elev. 26 m, pop. 13,981) was founded as a trading center for the two Elimi towns Segesta and Èrice; during the high Middle Ages, under Moorish rule, it became an impregnable stronghold, with a fortress perched on a promontory jutting over the sea. It was the Moors who gave the center its new role – dubbing it "Al-Madarig" (meaning the steps), possibly after a particularly steep street – as a major trading station at the confluence of routes leading inland, establishing cargo loading facilities and a tuna-fishing station ("tonnara"). This little town, which became prosperous under the rule of the House of Aragon (1281-1410) chiefly through trade in wheat, experienced further growth with the development, behind the castle or Castello, of an ancillary village, or "borgo": founded in 1560, it was enclosed by walls and a ditch and organized along a thoroughfare that ran lengthwise. The urban expansion that took place between 1600 and 1800 was also considerable; at first it was based on a crossroads system, and later on a system of streets and blocks that extended up to the slopes of the mountain.
The town, set in the lovely gulf or Golfo di Castellammare and at the foot of a high, harsh mountain rich with luxuriant vegetation, slopes gently down to the sea as far as the little peninsula where, between two magnificent sandy beaches, the **Castello** stands, renovated in Norman and Swabian times and then rebuilt entirely under the House of Aragon. Among the religious buildings here,

The entrance to the caves at Scurati

The splendid bay of Scopello with its old tuna-fishing station and rock stacks

we should mention the 18th-c. *Chiesa Madre* and the little church of the *Rosario*, widely known as the church of the "Madonna di l'Agnuni," with a handsome 16th-c. portal. From 19-21 August it holds the very popular festival of Maria Santissima del Soccorso, with an evocative sea procession.

Riserva Naturale dello Zingaro*

From Scopello to San Vito lo Capo there are a number of kilometers of coastline that still conceal uncontaminated nooks and crannies: coves, stack formations, coastal towers, and, above all, one of the last remaining areas of Mediterranean vegetation; here, thanks to a massive effort on the part of ecological organizations and the concerned public, in 1981, an area covering some 1600 hectares was set aside as a regional natural preserve or *Riserva Naturale Regionale*, a paradise for those who love nature and crags looming over the sea. The vegetation is that found in hot arid climes: lentisk bushes, carob plants, patches of euphorbia, broom, olive trees, and dwarf palms, which, despite their name, can grow to be as tall as two meters. In terms of the fauna, the existence of appropriate ecological niches has encouraged the presence of numerous animals, rabbits, porcupines, and foxes, and some forty species of birds (peregrine falcons, kestrels, and buzzards). The seabeds off the shores of the protected areas, which present interesting phytobentonic habitats, are of great biological value.

At the edge of the preserve is **Scopello** (elev. 106 m), a small peasant village which was built around an 18th-c. "baglio," on the site of an older Moorish hamlet, and

renowned for its tuna-fishing station, which is documented as far back as the turn of the 13th c., and was active until recent times. The development of the town as a beach resort has made Scopello a fashionable destination for vacationers, who crowd it during the summer, and for the people of Palermo during the weekends.

Monte Còfano

This dolomitic promontory looms far above the sea, and was for a long period a fundamental point along the route followed by Phoenician ships from the Ègadi Islands to Palermo. Human settlements around this promontory and the bay certainly date back, however, to the Paleolithic, as is shown by a number of shards, amphorae, and crockery found both on the seabed and in the cave dwellings of Grotta Mangiapane, at the foot of the mount, and at Scurati. The area of the Còfano was populated in Phoenician, early-Christian, and Norman-Moorish times, as is shown by the tower that overlooks the slope of Castelluzzo.

The landscape is truly African, with the occasional fig tree, carob, and lentisk tree, the only patches of greenery save for the distinctive dwarf palm trees; breaking up the enormous allure of the environment are the great cuts in the earth, made to extract the marble of Custonaci, especially on the slope facing Valderice.

The nearby town of **San Vito lo Capo** (elev. 6 m, pop. 3918), a lovely tourist attraction and beach resort, was, even in Roman times, an important maritime port; evidence is offered by the basins used for fish-farming, ruins of which can be seen near the "tonnara" of S. Vito.

4 Agrigento, its territory, and the Pelagie Islands

The charm of the landscape of southern Sicily consists of its colors, which are sharply drawn and made more brilliant by the intense light of the sun, which shapes these lands, differentiating them from the northern regions. The hills, which are an almost uniform green in the springtime, turn an array of colors in summer and fall that run from the golden yellow of ripe wheat to the dark brown of freshly turned soil, contrasting sharply with the blue of the sky.

Along the sea, the hilly cliffs, eroded by the wind, form a coastline with very few natural inlets, that is therefore poorly suited to the construction of ports. This was the main reason why the ancient Greeks waited so long before colonizing the area (the center of which was Agrigento), and were only driven to do so by the need to better monitor and control the ambitions of Carthage. And it was precisely, and paradoxically, the failure of the city to develop toward the coast – due to the lack of a structure so fundamental to transportation as a port – that allowed the preservation, in Agrigento, of Sicily's richest archeological treasure. Serving as a counterpoint to the only two major coastal towns – Sciacca, at the westernmost extremity of this area, and Licata, at the opposite extreme – are the many rural settlements in the hinterland, founded between the 15th and 17th c., high atop hills and mountains and in the center of vast feudal landholdings, dedicated to overseeing the cultivation of the interior and in certain cases to working the sulphur mines. While wheat was once the leading agricultural product, it is now an excellent table grape, known as the "Italia," which is allowed to ripen slowly until late winter, protected by heavy plastic sheets. Following the crisis brought about by the closure of the sulphur mines ("zolfatare") and by the drop in demand for wheat, the farming economy is slowly recovering, in part because of the establishment of cooperative associations. One common characteristic found throughout the territory, with the possible exception of Eraclea Minoa, is a wide array of reflections of Arab culture. We find these reflections in the very names of the towns, even those of recent foundation; in the structure of the lanes and the courtyards in the older districts, designed to

Greek vase on display at the Museo Archeologico Regionale

give shelter from the heat of the sun and the blast of the sirocco; in the techniques for irrigating fields, and even in the character of the popolation. And once again, we clearly see, in this entirely Sicilian area, a frontier between the Arab world and Europe.

4.1 Agrigento**

If you look at Agrigento (elev. 230 m, pop. 55,521; city maps on pp. 89, 93) from the Hill of the Temples (Collina dei Templi), the modern buildings that serve as a backdrop to the spaces between the columns almost seem to be a massive development in recent times, the logical continuation of the ancient magnificence of the city. But actually there is a sharp difference between the present-day city and the city of the past: the present-day city is distracted and listless, caught in a world that it would be kind to call provincial, cut off from the main Sicilian routes, and turned in on itself; the ancient city, preserved for our admiration as if by a mir-

acle, still imparts its vocation to open toward the outer world. But this gap in space and in time is also primarily in culture, the same gap described unhappily by Pirandello and denounced in anger by Sciascia. The Agrigentino or territory of Agrigento has been inhabited ever since prehistoric times, as is shown by the discoveries from an Aeneolithic site at Serraferlicchio, while the earliest signs of a Greek presence date back to the 7th c. B.C. (necropolis of Montelusa, on the coast, to the west of San Leone), although it was not until 581 B.C. that the people of Gela, together with a group of Greeks from the homeland, founded "Akragas" – this was one of the last Greek colonies in Sicily – locating it midway between Gela and Selinunte, controlling the coast that overlooked Africa, thus providing protection for the rest of Sicily against Carthaginian invasion. Between 570 and 555 B.C. Phalaris, the first tyrant of the city, built the first enclosure walls (much of which can still be seen), establishing the shape and size of the original urban core; the first years of settlement were marked by conflict with Carthage. Once the Carthaginians had been eliminated – albeit temporarily – in 480 B.C., in the battle of "Himera," one hundred years after its foundation "Akragas" was able to expand its dominion as far as the Tyrrhenian Sea; the territorial boundaries to the east and west were marked respectively by the course of the rivers Salso and Plàtani. In this period, documents record that the city had a population of roughly 200,000, including many illustrious thinkers, artists, and scientists (we need only mention Empedocles); the splendid temples on the southern hill were constructed, and the acropolis on the Rupe Atenea and on the northwestern heights was completed.

In 406 B.C. "Akragas" fell to yet another attack by the Carthaginians, who conquered it and held it until 310 B.C. In that year, the Corinthian statesman and general Timoleon, in his plan to liberate Sicily, moved on the town from Syracuse, retook it, and restored a regime of Greek democracy; the ruins of the so-called Hellenistic and Roman district are clear evidence of the economic and social rebirth that the city experienced after this.

The Romans, who settled here permanently in 210 B.C., renamed it "Agrigentum," and renewed the entire sector of farming and trade, laying the foundations for the major trading port that this town was later to become, during the Byzantine era. Toward the end of the 7th c., the inhabitants left their homes in the valley and moved up to the top of the acropolis, in a mass migratory process that scholars are still unable to explain fully. This settlement constituted the core around which the Moorish city was built, which as early as the 9th c. had been proclaimed capital of the Berbers in Sicily, with the name of "Gergenti." Aside from the name, which was slightly altered to Girgenti, the city preserved numerous place names into the 20th c. that originated during the Moorish occupation (Via Bac Bac, Porta Bibbiria, Quartiere del Rabato), as well as the twisting lanes and the charming courtyards.

The 11th c., with the arrival of the Normans – who did not hinder, and indeed encouraged trade with North Africa – was a time that witnessed the reaffirmation of the role of Girgenti in the interior of Sicily and in the control of the stretch of sea between Sicily and Africa. The ensuing growth of the "borgo," or village, was halted by the depopulation caused by the foundation of numerous farming towns in the hinterland, a project that was begun in the 15th c. and perpetuated until the 18th c., when the bishop Lorenzo Gioieni strenuously promoted a substantial social recovery that was to lead to a shift of the main thoroughfare of the city from Via Duomo to Via Atenea. In the first half of the 19th c., with the construction of the new avenue, or Viale della Vittoria, work began on the expansion that pushed outward from the Porta di Ponte, an ancient obstacle or stopping point on Via Atenea, which was then demolished and replaced with a sort of propylaeum. During that century, an initial phase of stagnation in new construction was followed by a period of chaotic development, of wildcat construction that did not end even in the aftermath of the great landslide of 1966, which tore away part of the old town as well as part of the new development, reminding the whole nation that there were serious problems in the south, and grave problems concerning the use which was being made of the south's environmental and cultural heritage.

A walking tour of Agrigento begins in the Valley of the Temples (Valle dei Templi), in which the succession from east to west of the religious buildings represents the most accurate analysis of them; they were in fact designed to turn their main front to the east. Alongside these there is the regional archeological museum or Museo Archeologico Regionale, and the Hellenistic-Roman district, which lie along the road that links the city to the coast, and the cliffside sanctuary of Demeter, located near the modern cemetery. Next comes the modern city, which has the church of S. Maria dei Greci and the Cathedral or Cattedrale has two major indications of its medieval prosperity; in the maritime satellite development of S. Leone, which you will need a car to reach, is a sadly eloquent example of chaotic urban development.

From the crag or Rupe Atenea, the spectacular view of the temples, with the sea in the distance, is one of the finest in Sicily; in this setting, unrivalled on earth and enriched by the early blooming of the almond trees in the valley, in the first ten days of February there

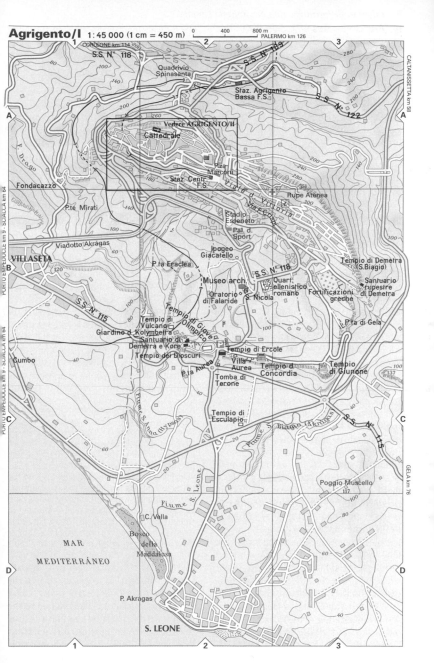

is the "Sagra del Mandorlo in Fiore" or festival of the almond blossoms, a ritual celebrating the arrival of spring.

Archeological area* (*open 9-9*). The ancient city – now declared a Heritage of Mankind site by UNESCO – extended over an area of more than 1800 hectares: included in it were, to the northwest, the hill of Girgenti (now occupied to the north by the Arabic center and to the south by the modern expansion) and the hill of the temples; it featured a Hippodamean layout, with long avenues running east-west, intersected at right-angles by smaller streets. The line of the fortifications, partly canceled by the modern expansion, first follows the ridge of the mountain crest, also enclosing the crag or Rupe Atenea, then runs along the course of the river "Akragas" (now the San Biagio), successively bending off to the west at a right angle (the line of the

Springtime in the valley of the temples, with the Tempio della Concordia

temples) and again to the north, along the river "Hypsas" (now the S. Leone) and its tributary, until it finally joins up – near the declivity or Avvallamento di Empèdocle – with the walls running out from the crag or Rupe Atenea; the old city, which the modern state road 118 cuts in two, was thus girt with walls and bastions toward the interior and by temples toward the sea.

The temples of Agrigento all belong to the Doric order and are entirely built of the local limestone with a deep yellow color; traces of white material on the surfaces lead scholars to think that the stone was covered with a plaster made of marble powder.

Before the Temple of Juno or **Tempio di Giunone Lacinia**** (I, C3) set on the summit of the Hill of the Temples stands a large altar for sacrifices; the temple was built in the middle of the 5th c. B.C. – just prior to the neighboring Temple of Concord (Tempio della Concordia) – with a hexastyle peripteric plan (at the stylobate, 38.15 m long and 16.9 m wide); of the 34 columns (6 on the short sides and 13 on the longer sides) no fewer than 25 are still standing, while the walls of the cella are completely ruined, due to a medieval earthquake.

A splendid example of the Doric style (middle of the 5th c. B.C.), the **Tempio della Concordia**** (I, C2), with a hexastyle peripteric plan (at the stylobate, 39.44 m long and 16.9 m wide) and with 34 columns, has been spared much of what happened to the previous temple; it now survives virtually intact, at least in its structural members, as a result of having been transformed (4th c. A.D.) into a basilica with a nave and aisles, which entailed the closure and the reinforcement of the intercolumniation, and the opening, in the walls of the cella, of round arches that can still be seen; the restoration of 1748 restored it to its original

form. It was Tommaso Fazello who gave the temple its name, and it is still unknown to what deity the temple was consecrated (maybe Castor and Pollux).

We do know to whom the *Tempio di Ercole* (I, C2) or Temple of Hercules is consecrated; it too is a hexastyle peripteros (at the stylobate, 67 x 25.34 m) but with 38 columns (6 on the short and 15 on the long sides); this is probably the oldest of the temples of Agrigento (end of the 6th c. B.C.).

Before you reach the Temple of Olympian Jove (see below) you can drive down toward the sea to the *tomb of Terone* (I, C2), which is also visible from the southern slope, close to the western edge of the Hill of the Temples. Set on a high podium is a little temple with a square base, with blind doors obtained by carving into the massive blocks of limestone; at the corners are Doric columns, with Ionic capitals and bases, supporting a Doric trabeation composed of smooth metopes and triglyphs. Across the state road 115, a trail leads to the ruins of the Temple of Aesculapius or *Tempio di Esculapio* (I, C2).

The temple of Olympian Jove, or **Tempio di Giove Olimpico*** (I, C2; *open 8-5*), of the hexastyle pseudo-peripteros type (112.6 x 56.3 m), has half columns attached to the outer walls that flank the long inner walls of the cella, and 6 full columns on each short side, and was built with the labor of prisoners caught on the field of the battle of "Himera;" it was, however, never completed. It was destroyed by earthquakes, but according to the plans of the tyrant Terone it was to become one of the largest temples of Greek architecture (it was smaller only than the Artemision of Ephesus and the Didimeon of Miletus). The columns, with fluting of deep enough for a man to stand in, stood some 17 m tall, and had a diameter of 4.20 m; colossal human figures (the so-called telamons) built of stone blocks, supported the weight of the interior trabeation like caryatids: in the regional archeological museum, or Museo Archeologico Regionale, one has been reassembled; a cast of it stands at the center of the cella of the temple.

The four surviving columns of the Temple of the Dioscuri or **Tempio dei Dioscuri** (I, C2; *open 8-5*) have become the symbol of Agrigento. Built toward the end of the 5th c. B.C., the temple, a hexastyle peripteros (38.69 X 16.63 m) with 34 columns, was badly damaged by the sack of the Carthaginian conquerors; it was restored in the Hellenistic style, and collapsed following one of the many earthquakes of the past (the present-day aspect was developed in the last century with the use of materials from other temples).

Near the temple there stands a complex of buildings that are believed to belong to the **Sanctuary of Demeter and Kore** (I, B2), explored in 1928-32 by Pirro Marconi, who reconstructed the development of the complex between the 6th and 5th c. B.C. At the northern end are the older structures which consist of two holy enclosures, with an altar on the interior, while in a second phase, probably sometime around the 6th c. B.C., other altars and three small temples were built. The valley set between the Temple of the Dioscuri and that of Vulcan is called the *Garden of the Kolymbetra (open Feb.-Apr., 9-6; May-Oct., 9-7; Nov.-Jan., 10-5; closed Mon.)*, a historic landscape recovered to its endemic vegetation by FAI, Fondo per l'Ambiente Italiano.

Museo Archeologico Regionale** (I, B2; *open 9-1:30; Tue.-Sat., also 2-6*). The archeological museum stands in an area of the old town that was dedicated to public functions, as is indicated by the quite visible ruins, on the esplanade adjoining the church of S. Nicola, of the "*ekklesiasterion*", a structure similar to a theater for popular assemblies, built in the 3rd c. B.C. with a semicircular cavea with 28 tiers; alongside it is the oratory or *Oratorio di Falaride*, a little 1st-c. B.C. temple, which was transformed into an oratory in the Middle Ages by the creation of pointed-arch windows. Inaugurated in 1967, the museum is located in a building comprising a recently built structure and the old church of *S. Nicola*, erected in the 13th c. by the Cistercians (in the 2nd chapel on the right, is a Roman *sarcophagus** with the myth of Phaedra, from the 2nd c. A.D.). The museum contains finds from excavations done in

"Akragas" and the prehistoric sites from the surrounding territory, and also works held up till 1966 in the Museo Diocesano (of the diocese) and the Museo Civico (civic museum); the material is displayed in accordance with chronological criteria.

In the first hall (I Sala) you may observe the archeological plan of ancient "Akragas;" this model is very useful in understanding the physical development of the city. The pre-historic material of the first and second millenia B.C. is visible in the hall II, while the hall III features a rich collection of ceramics, both black-figure and red-figure (among the red-figure ceramics, we should mention the *chalice krater*, dating from 490 B.C. – Deposition of a Warrior – originally from the necropolis or Necropoli Pezzino and a *krater* dating from 430 B.C. – Sacrifice to Apollo – from the necropolis or Necropoli di Poggio Giache); a splendid *dish with depictions of fish*, from the 4th c. B.C. and, at the far end of the same room, a marble fragment of a *statue of a warrior with shield* from the temple of Olympian Jove or Tempio di Giove Olimpico. (The position of the body, with the legs straight out on the ground, the torso erect, and the body inclined forward, is

Roman sarcophagus featuring the myth of Phaedra

typical of the sculptures that once adorned the triangular composition of the pediment). An original **telamon*** (7.75 m tall) from the temple mentioned above is located in the hall VI, where you can see the heads, set in niches, of three others. The hall VII is dedicated to artifacts from the Hellenistic-Roman district: among the works on exhibit, there is a particularly lovely mosaic depicting a *gazelle drinking from a spring*, dating from the 1st c. A.D., while the hall IX (*open to visitors with special permits*) features Greek, Roman, Byzantine, and Norman coins in silver, bronze, and gold. Among the Greco-Roman sculptures in the hall X, we should mention the famous **Ephebus*** dating back to 470 B.C., with remarkable, finely wrought hair. In hall XII and hall XIII, lastly, are finds dating back to prehistoric

times (from the Neolithic up to the time of
Greek colonization) originally from Sciacca,
Palma di Montechiaro, Montallegro, Milena,
Favara, and Sant'Angelo Muxaro.

Quartiere Ellenistico-Romano* (I, B2-3; *open 8:30-5*).

The term *Hellenistic-Roman dis-
trict* is used to indicate one of the best-pre-
served sections of ancient city structure in
all of Sicily. The area, which covers roughly a hectare, has been the object of archeological explorations ever since the 1950s
which have unearthed buildings and other
vertical structures, but also part of the grid
of roads, which, in accordance with the
prescriptions of Hippodameus of Miletus,
consists of regular grids of main streets
("plateiai") intersecting at right angles with
secondary streets ("stenopoi"). Over this
layout, which developed toward the end of
the 4th c. B.C., is juxtaposed the Roman
district, which re-uses part of the Hellenistic residential structures, embellishing them
with mosaic floors and wall decorations in
stucco and fresco. The presence of the peristyle distinguishes those buildings from
Roman buildings, which had an atrium and
an ambulatory overlooked by the rooms; also dating from the Roman era are the water
pipes and the heating pipes, as well as the
sewer facilities for the drainage of rainwater and human waste.

An interesting conclusion of the tour of the old
city is the rock-carved sanctuary of Demeter or
Santuario di Demetra (I, B3) located in the area
around the modern cemetery (you can reach it
from the central square, Piazza Marconi, by following Via Crispi and Via Demetra). A stone
building, jutting up against the mount, this marks
the presence of the earliest sanctuary of the
Agrigento area dedicated to the goddess, built in
the 7th c. B.C. (prior, that is, to the foundation of
"Akragas"); on the interior, comprising three
deep galleries carved into the living rock, the excavations of 1938 unearthed numerous statuettes depicting the goddess and her daughter
Kore (Persephone, or Proserpine; the name, in
ancient Greek, meant "maiden").
Not far from the sanctuary stands the little
church of *S. Biagio* (I, B3), built in the Norman period on the ruins of the *temple of Demeter and Kore*, an "in antis" building dating back to 480-460
B.C.; it is still possible to see, behind the semicircular apse, the structures of the pronaos of
this temple.

Via Atenea (II, B2-3). This is the main street
of Agrigento, as well as the entrance to the
historic city; its mouth off Piazzale Aldo
Moro is marked by the gate or *Porta di Ponte*,
a 19th-c. reconstruction of the medieval
Porta Atenea.

A monastery and a church make up the abbey, or
Abbazia di S. Spirito (II, B3;you arrive there from
Via Atenea , taking Via Porcello and the Salita S.
Spirito), founded in the 13th c. with contributions from the Contessa di Chiaromonte. The
church presents a composite tufa façade, largely
remodelled during the Baroque period, and enriched with a Gothic portal and the 14th-c. rose
window, which are off-center in the plane of the
façade; on the interior walls and in the presbytery are 18th-c. *stuccoes* attributed to Giacomo
Serpotta. The *monastery*, whose entrance is located on the continuation of the façade of the
church, has a lovely *cloister* and a pointed-arch
portal that leads into the chapter hall. It contains the *ethnographic and anthropological section*
of the *civic museum* or Museo Civico, with traditional objects (*open summer, 9-2; winter, 9-1; Tue.
and Thu. also 3:30-6:30; closed Sunday*).

San Domenico (II, B2). This church, on Piazza Pirandello at the end of Via Atenea, features an imposing Baroque façade. The ad-
jecent former monastery of the Dominican
Fathers, built in the 17th c. upon the structures of the Palazzo dei Principi di Lampedusa, now houses the town hall, or Municipio; opening out onto the courtyard is the
19th-c. town theater, the *Teatro Civico "Luigi Pirandello"*.

Museo Civico (II, B2; *closed for restoration*) or
civic museum. This museum is housed in
the convent building of the Augustinian Fathers, which was first built in the 16th c.; it
is normally called a "pinacoteca," or art
gallery, because it largely contains paintings, most from the Sicilian school of the
15th to 18th c., as well as the collection or
Collezione Sinatra of contemporary artists.

S. Maria dei Greci (II, A2). This church
stands on the site of a Doric temple from the
5th c. B.C.; you can still see remains of the
temple's columns on the interior and in the
gallery beneath the left aisle of the
church. The façade, surrounded by local
residential structures, presents a lovely
Chiaromonte Gothic portal with little carved
cornices in contrast with the smooth and
simple surface.

Cattedrale* (II, A2) or Cathedral. Named after Gerlando, the first bishop of Agrigento,
this Cathedral was founded around the end
of the 11th c. (some scholars say, on the
structure of an existing Greek temple) by the
Normans – who made it the headquarters of
the bishopric, as was the practice in other Sicilian cities. The church underwent various
transformations in the 14th, 16th, and 17th
c. The *façade*, surmounted by a double-pitch
pediment and punctuated by pilaster strips

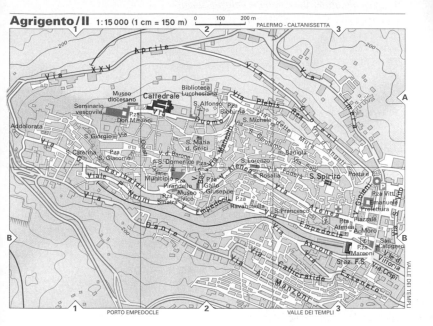

jutting from the surface, is fronted by a broad, tall staircase. The building is dominated by the *campanile*, with its square base, begun in the 15th c. and never completed, punctuated on the first two stories by two orders of blind Moorish-arched windows, on the third story by a balcony with rich brackets and a Gothic arcade decorated with zigzag motifs, and on the top story by a number of single-light mullioned windows with simple round arches, with a balustrade.

The **interior**, built to a Latin-cross plan, is divided into a nave and two aisles by high pillars with a polygonal base, supporting pointed arches; the ceiling over the two aisles features open beams painted with figures of saints and aristocratic heraldic crests dating from the 16th c.; the ceiling over the nave, in wooden lacunars, was completed in 1682. Note the remarkable tomb or *Arca di S. Gerlando* (in the chapel or Cappella di S. Gerlando, in the right wing of the transept), with a silver reliquary dating back to 1639; the Baroque *stuccoes* in the presbytery – where, due to a remarkable acoustic phenomenon, it is possible to hear

the slightest whisper at the entrance of the church, 85 m away – and, in the right apse, a *Virgin with Child*, a marble statue dating from 1495.

Museo Diocesano (II, A1; *closed for restoration*) or museum of the diocese. In a modern building, currently closed for renovation, this museum has ancient sculpture; 14th- and 15th-c. frescoes that were detached in 1951 from the walls of the Cathedral or Cattedrale in order to restore it to its original Norman Gothic appearance; and fine goldsmithery and sacred paraments. Adjoining it is a seminary or *Seminario Vescovile* originally built in the 16th c. but completed in 1611.

San Leone (elev. 2 m). This beach resort, some 7 km from the city, is a favorite with the people of Agrigento; this is the reason for the sudden explosion of second homes that began in the 1960s, and which completely transformed the old fishing village. In the nearby area is the *necropolis of Montelusa*, which dates back to the turn of the 6th c. B.C.

4.2 The eastern territory of Agrigento

The tour runs through territories that are characterized by the presence of rural villages founded by the Moors (the area now specializes in the cultivation of fine grapes), and by the permanent echo, in the place names and the structure of a number of

towns, of Arabic culture. This driving route (route map on p. 94), which leaves Agrigento in the direction of Caltanissetta, first winds along the state road 122 Agrigentina, reaching Favara, a little town of Islamic origin, from which it is possible to reach Arag-

93

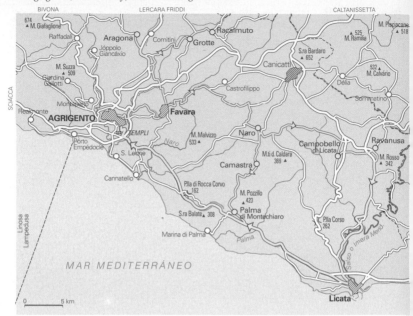

ona (note the little volcanoes or Vulcanelli of Macalube) and Racalmuto, which was also founded by the Moors. A good set of secondary roads then leads on to Naro (interesting for its Baroque appearance), Ravanusa (the immediate surrounding area features the major archeological site of Monte Saraceno), and Licata. The route covers roughly 80 km, to which you should add the 44 m of the coastal link to Agrigento along the state road 115 Sud Occidentale Sicula.

Favara
Observing the city (elev. 338 m, pop. 32,408) as a whole, as it extends over a rolling area in the immediate hilly hinterland of Agrigento (12.5 km away from the capital), what will strike you is the contrast between the massive new projects on the outskirts of town, in the foreground, and the structure of the old church of the *Rosario*, in the distance. Favara was a major sulphur-mining town until the turn of the 20th c.; nowadays it clearly shows signs of the mining crisis, even though lately the new cooperative approach to farming has brought about a slow and difficult recovery.

The name, of Moorish origin ("Fawar"), refers to the presence of spring water at the time of the Muslim conquest, when in this territory there was nothing but a hamlet guarding the farmlands. The site was fortified in the 13th c. with the construction of the castle or Castello dei Chiaramonte around which clustered the earliest settlement, which was then to grow, over all

of the 14th and 15th c., in accordance with the typical urban layout of the Middle Ages. In the 17th c., a great process of urban and architectural transformation began, starting with the renovation of the square that lay before the castle (the present-day Piazza Cavour), upon which the churches of the Rosario and the Purgatorio were built in the 17th-c., and, between the 18th and the 19th c., the Palazzo Fanara and the Palazzo Albergamo. The 19th c., finally, witnessed the final form of the present-day urban layout, with the creation of Corso Vittorio Emanuele perpendicular to Corso Umberto I.

Your visit can be limited to *Piazza Cavour*, an elegant piece of 18th-c. urban planning, with the compositional harmony of the structures and architectural rigor of the façades that rare in these towns of southern Sicily. Standing out from them all is the façade – sadly damaged – of the 14th-c. castle, or *Castello dei Chiaramonte*.

Aragona
This is a small farming town (elev. 400 m, pop. 10,181; 12 km from Favara), founded in 1606 by Count Baldassarre Naselli, who named it Aragona in honor of his mother. Overlooking the little Piazza Umberto I are the *Palazzo Feudale*, built in the 17th c. and renovated in the 19th c., now housing the Municipio, or town hall, and the Baroque church of the *Purgatorio*.
The interior, with a single nave, of the *Chiesa Madre* (17th c.) features a handsome wooden *crèche* from the 18th c. kept in a glass case, and beautiful stucco works.

Three km to the south of Aragona, along a turnoff from the road to Agrigento, is the **Riserva Naturale Macalube di Aragona*** (*guided tours, tel. 0922699210*), where are the so-called *Vulcanelli*, or little volcanoes. The lunar landscape that you will happen upon consists of a clayey expanse, shot through with fissures and openings which erupt – alternately – whitish slime and puffs of methane gas. It is one of the most striking and evocative demonstrations of a rare geological phenomenon known as "sedimentary vulcanism".

Racalmuto

This town (elev. 445 m, pop. 10,071) has become famous as the birthplace of one of the most illustrious contemporary writers, Leonardo Sciascia. Located on a sunny hill, the city was until the turn of the century a major sulphur-mining town and now thrives on agriculture and a limited industry based on the mining of rock-salt.

Like Favara (which lies some 21 km away), the town still preserves its Moorish name and the original medieval urban layout. On Piazza Umberto I are the *Chiesa Madre* housing five paintings by Pietro D'Asaro, and the *Castello* or castle with its massive corner towers.

The *Palazzo del Municipio* or town hall is in the former monastery of S. Chiara, overlooking the square of the same name. It now houses the Fondazione Sciascia. The palazzo was rebuilt in 1872, the year when the Roman *sarcophagus* (IV c. B.C.) depicting the *Rape of Proserpine* was placed in the atrium.

Naro*

In a position overlooking the center of the vast region to the east of Agrigento (which is about 30 km away), this little city (elev. 500 m, pop. 9364) – the origin of its name and the date of its first settlement are unknown – occupies one of the highest sites in the district, with a fine view of the valley of the river Naro; among the towns of this area, this is the one that best preserves its monumental Baroque appearance, one attraction that ensures an enjoyable visit.

Its territory, during the Greek era, fell under the sphere of influence of Agrigento, and the early-Christian necropolis of Contrada Canale offers evidence of Christianity as early as the 4th c. In the 14th c., on an existing Norman fortification, the castle or Castello Chiaramontano was built; around it developed the late-medieval expansion, which incorporated the restructured Norman buildings of the old Cathedral or Duomo Vecchio and of the church of S. Caterina; between the 15th and 17th c., the urban layout and the directions of the main thoroughfares were sharply conditioned and altered by the religious settlements of the Carmelites, the Dominicans, and the Jesuits, who encouraged the expansion of the city proper outside the enclosure walls.

The current image of the historical center is that of the city as it was renovated in the 18th c., with the expansions and the complete late-Baroque renovations of the religious buildings and the construction of the most representative palazzi of the middle class.

It is possible to see a good example of this as you walk through *Via Dante*, which crosses Naro from east to west, drawing a line between the high city and the low city, and along which you may note the Baroque church of the *Santissimo Salvatore*, the *Chiesa Madre* (1619), and the *Palazzo Destro*, from the same period. A staircase to the left of the church of the Santissimo Salvatore allows one to climb up to the medieval castle, **Castello**, adorned with a Chiaramonte portal with zigzag motifs, and to the old Cathedral, or *Duomo Vecchio*, which dates back to the 12th c. In the stretch of Corso Vittorio Emanuele beyond *Piazza Garibaldi*, flanked by elegant, late-19th-c. buildings, you can admire the façades of the *Palazzo Giacchetto*, laid out in the 15th c., and the 18th-c. *Palazzo Morillo*.

Toward the coast, at a distance of 15 km, is **Palma di Montechiaro** (elev. 165 m, pop. 24,518), which can be reached along state road 410.

A feudal landholding of the princes of Lampedusa until 1812, this is, according to experts on the book "Il Gattopardo" ("The Leopard") the villa of Donnafugata in the novel. Set on *Piazza S. Rosalia* is the superb Baroque façade of the **Chiesa Madre**, built between 1666 and 1703. In the interior, note the *tomb* of the astronomer Giovanni Battista Odierna (1597-1660), who played a role in the urban planning of the little town.

Palma di Montechiaro: the Chiesa Madre

Ravanusa

At a distance of 20 km from the previous stop, set in the fertile countryside of the Agrigento area, Ravanusa (elev. 320 m, pop. 14,559) blankets with buildings the southern slope of a hill/cliff overlooking the river Salso. This little town, which has grown considerably and which is based on an agricultural economy, was founded in the 17th c. by the duke or Duca di Montalbano owner of the fief. The duke also undertook the construction, on the present-day Piazza Umberto I, of the *Chiesa Madre*; the building features, on its main façade, a handsome carved *portal*, attributed to one of the Gagini.

At 1.5 km southeast of the town is the interesting early Sicilian/Greek archeological site of **Monte Saraceno***. The campaigns of digging undertaken so far have uncovered traces of a Greek city, founded by Gela in the 7th c. B.C., and later absorbed into the sphere of influence of Agrigento. The settlement was arranged at three consecutive levels: on the highest elevation stood the acropolis; on the middle elevation was the town itself (explorations have uncovered a layer of buildings that may be attributed to a previous Siculi settlement); on the lowest elevation there are traces of a sacred area.

Licata

Extending over the vast alluvial plain formed by the mouth of the river Salso and at the foot of the Colle Sant'Angelo, which the Greeks called "Eknomos," the city (24 km from Ravanusa) offers the frantic and fragmentary picture of an old town forced to adapt too quickly to the sudden developments of the contemporary world; endowed with a broad, safe port, whose construction was made possible by the favorable configuration of the coastline and the good seabed just offshore, this town has based its prosperity on that port, acquiring the distinctive features of a port town (elev. 8 m, pop. 41,269).

Artifacts dating back to the Paleolithic and traces of an archaic Greek settlement (6th c. B.C.) on the eastern slopes of the hill, or Colle "Eknomos," demonstrate that this site was frequented from the earliest times, even though the actual foundation of the city dates back only to the Hellenistic period, under Phintia, tyrant of Agrigento, who gave it the name of "Phintias;" in the 2nd c. B.C. the Romans improved the port structures, laying the foundations for a solid economic structure based on maritime trade.
The intensive agricultural exploitation of the fertile territory promoted by the Moors, along with its capacity to export products, led this town to become one of the most populous and dynamic centers of the southern Sicilian coast. Dating back to that period was the shift of the settlement from the slopes of the "Eknomos" to the plain below: this was the first, fortified nucleus of the modern city, destined to expand outside its walls continuously to the present day.

Between the 17th and the 18th c., a massive project of renovation of the religious and civil buildings here was undertaken, filling the empty spaces in the town and replacing the surviving medieval buildings, with a particular expansion along what are now Corso Vittorio Emanuele and Via S. Andrea. From the first half of the 19th c. to the early years of the 20th c., the city underwent rapid development, due to the export of sulphur and wheat through the port here; the old walls were knocked down and replaced with long blocks of buildings, which joined the old city and the new one together, through the usual type of construction, without taste or quality.

In the town of Licata, architectural and environmental motifs of various styles coexist, all merged together in a generalized expression of vitality. In the central square, *Piazza Progresso*, the nexus of the main thoroughfares, stands the floral-style town hall or *Palazzo del Municipio*, designed in 1935 by Ernesto Basile; in it, aside from fine artworks, are archeological finds from the ancient "Fintias." The civic archeological museum, or **Museo Civico Archeologico**, in Via Dante, comprises two sections: the prehistoric section contains materials that range from the Paleolithic to the Bronze Age, while the other section includes artifacts from the Greek period (note the interesting funerary furnishings from the archaic necropolises), and fine architectural mosaic floors from the Hellenistic era. One of the most noteworthy monumental relics of Licata's past is the church of the **Carmine**, part of the monastery of the same name, arranged along Corso Roma, which was built in the 13th c. and rebuilt in the 18th c.; it features a handsome Baroque façade and contains a lovely little cloister, overlooked by a number of twin-light mullioned windows and a portal, all adorned with Chiaromonte motifs. Along Corso Vittorio Emanuele, you will find the *Chiesa Matrice*, built in the 15th c. with a basilican plan, where the vault of the nave is decorated with 19th-c. frescoes.

It is also worth visiting the *Castel S. Angelo*, built on the summit of the Colle S. Angelo to plans by Camillo Camilliani between 1615 and 1640; from the square before it, you can enjoy a splendid panoramic view of the city and the coast as far as Gela.

4.3 The Agrigento coast, from Porto Empèdocle to Sciacca

The route (map above) covers the coastal strip stretching between Agrigento and Sciacca, from which this route (a total of 63 km) sometimes wanders to run through a landscape of rounded hills covered with orderly fields; the depressions between hills often offer a glimpse of the sea. Near sites that are of historic and artistic interest (suffice it to mention the lovely Eraclea Minoa), there are towns that appear uniformly dull to the traveler: rows of modern grey houses, apparently unfinished, and behind the row of buildings conceal behind are often-very-handsome urban cores, of much older origin. Once you have reached Porto Empèdocle, another seaside appendix of Agrigento and the point of departure for the Pelagie Islands, follow state road 115 Sud Occidentale Sicula to Siculiana, Eraclea Minoa, and Ribera (the two latter towns can be reached by taking short detours along secondary roads); from Sciacca, the last stop and an important hot-springs spa which preserves major ruins from antiquity, you may want to take a detour to the medieval town of Caltabellotta.

Home of Luigi Pirandello

If you head down from Agrigento toward Porto Empèdocle, just before Villaseta, you will reach the Contrada *Caos*, with the home in which Luigi Pirandello was born in 1867; the building, a typical example of a home in the Agrigento countryside, has been declared a national monument; several of its rooms have been converted into a *museum* (*open 8-2 and 4-6:30*) of souvenirs and memorabilia of Pirandello. In the garden, at the foot of an age-old cluster pine, there is an urn with the playwright's ashescemented into a limestone boulder.

Porto Empèdocle

The natural maritime complement to Agrigento, this town is the city's trading and shipping center, as well as the harbor for boats to the Pelagie Islands. The town (elev. 2 m, pop. 17,331) presents features that are quite typical of seaside settlements in this zone – a single main thoroughfare lined by private homes of no real interest – and bases its economy almost exclusively on sea trade and on a modest fishing industry.

With the name of Marina di Girgenti, this town was endowed in the 15th c. with one of the most important wheat-loading facilities in Sicily, a port structure that was indispensable to the export of Agrigento's main resource (on the wharf, you can still

97

The marvellous coast of Capo Bianco

see the 16th-c. *watch tower* built at the behest of Charles V). The first artificial jetty, which was built in part with stones from the Agrigento Temple of Olympian Jove or Tempio di Giove Olimpico, dates back to 1749, while a further improvement of the port facilities was made in the 19th c., to accommodate the export of sulphur, mined along the coast and in the inland regions, as far up as Caltanissetta. With the crisis that followed the closing of the sulphur mines, an economic decline began, for the port and for the city itself, that still persists.

There is an interesting archeological site in the area around the town; the *Villa di Durueli*, a Roman building dating back to the 1st c. B.C.: overlooking the sea, it features the ruins of a peristyle around which there are rooms with fine mosaic floors.

Siculiana

If you are coming from Agrigento (19 km away), this little town (elev. 129 m, pop. 4948) appears to lie behind the eastern slope of a hill, just above the roadway. The apparent skyward stacking of the buildings, the intertwining welter of lanes and courtyards, and the rapid growth of the city's construction which culminates in the two-tone cupola of the Baroque *Chiesa Matrice*, reveal the Moorish origins of the town, although historical documentation reveals its existence only from the 15th c. on, when it sprang up around the medieval castle or *Castello*.

The hill settlement corresponds to the coastal settlement of *Siculiana Marina* (elev. 12 m), which developed in recent years. The coast is a WWF protected area.

Eraclea Minoa*

At a distance of 15 km from Siculiana there is a turnoff that will take you (in another 3.6 km) to the ruins of this very ancient colony, possibly founded by the Myceneans. With its enchanting geographic location in a virtually unspoiled natural setting, this is one of the loveliest and most interesting archeological sites in Sicily; the cape or Capo Bianco on the summit (m 75) of which lies all that remains of the city, slopes westward toward the luxuriant valley of the river Plàtani; to the east, it turns a sheer wall of white rock over a splendid curve of beach surrounded by a dense blanket of vegetation, while to the south it directly overlooks the open sea.

A number of fragments found in the layers beneath the archaic necropolis, dating back to the 6th c. B.C., might lead us to date the origins of this settlement to the Neolithic, while the oldest coins testify to the presence of a Phoenician colony on this site. In documents, the city is cited by three different names: Macara, or city of "Makar," the Phoenician Hercules; Minoa, founded, according to legend, by the king of Crete, Minos, who had chased Daedalus to here; and finally, Eraclea, a Spartan colony named after the great demigod. After the Phoenicians and the Spartans, it became a subcolony of Selinunte in the 5th c. B.C., and, after reinforcing its fortifications, reached the apex of its urban development in Hellenistic times. Located at the border between Greek and Carthaginian spheres of influence, it passed repeatedly from one to the other, until, in 210 B.C., it was conquered by the Romans. In the 1st c. A.D., it was definitively abandoned, possibly due to a landslide that swept the southern part of the town and its enclosure walls into the sea.

Archeological exploration here began in 1907, unearthing a part of the *residential district* in which it is possible to distinguish two successive stratifications with traces of both the Hellenistic and the Roman city, the northern section of the enclosure walls, and a beautiful *theater*, with a proscaenium opening out toward the sea; from this theater come a number of sandstone blocks, used as seating, and now on exhibit in the *Antiquarium (open 9-an hour before sunset)*.

Ribera

Another short detour from the state road runs up (4.7 km) to Ribera (elev. 223 m, pop. 20,679), which occupies a verdant hilly bluff not far from the coast. Its traditional agrarian economy has, in recent years, been bolstered by considerable tourist traffic attracted by the excavations of Eraclea Minoa and by the beaches.

This town owes its foundation and its name to the de Ribera family, which founded it in the 17th c., and managed to absorb, in the 18th c., the feudal landholdings between the rivers Plàtani and Bèlice. Ribera nowadays presents the typical checkerboard urban layout of cities founded to rely upon agriculture and refeudalization, with a main thoroughfare (present-day *Corso Umberto*) from which the entire grid of the older section of town extends.

Sciacca*

Lying on a natural terrace formation sloping down toward the sea, Sciacca (elev. 60, pop. 41,019; city map below), terminus of the coastal route, looks toward Africa and is protected to the north by the limestone highlands of Monte San Calogero and to the west by the cape or Capo San Marco. The present-day name – discussion still rages about its meaning – was given by the Moors in the 9th c., but in ancient times the Greeks called it "Thermai Selinuntinai," and the Romans, "Thermae Selinuntinae." The city was founded in the sixth to fifth c.

B.C. as a hot-springs spa, a subject of the nearby and powerful Selinunte, whose fate it shared in the continual wars with Carthage; it was finally destroyed entirely by Carthage in 409 B.C. Beginning in the 2nd c. B.C., the Romans – aside from encouraging the use of the sulphurous hot springs of Monte Cronio – introduced a system of intensive cultivation which led to a sizable increase in population, making this city a major actor in the fields of culture and the economy along the axis linking Syracuse to Agrigento to Lilibeo. The remarkable urban configuration that still survives here is the product of the successive efforts of the Moors, who built their districts, bound with walls, above and below the main street, and of the Normans, who enlarged the enclosure walls, making it possible for the Greeks, Moors, and Franks to coexist within; these were the three chief ethnic groups to shape and characterize the urban spaces of the future city.

The 15th and 16th c. witnessed the replacement of the undistinguished civil architecture of the medieval period with the more sumptuous style of the palazzi of the landed aristocracy (Palazzo Steripinto), as

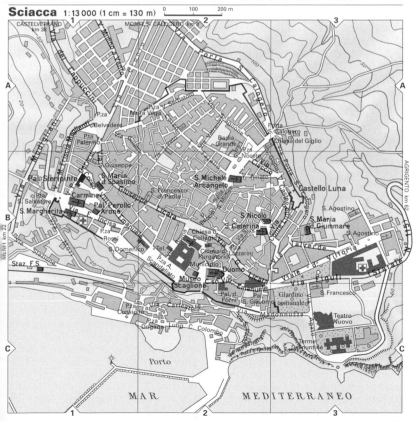

Sciacca 1:13 000 (1 cm = 130 m)

MAR MEDITERRANEO

well as the construction of the enclosure walls, with bastions, built at the behest of Charles V, while in the 17th c. there were radical restorations of churches and monasteries in the Baroque forms that we still see today. In the 1950s, the construction of the Grand Hotel delle Terme and the spa on Monte Cronio brought a new flow of tourists and spa-goers to the local economy.

The town, which you should tour on foot, has preserved its ancient division into districts, each lying spread out on one of the three planes of rock sloping down to the sea. The first of these, the largest, lies to the north of Via Licata, and is occupied by the medieval district known as "Terravecchia:" it is a welter of lanes and alleys, many of them with steps, bounded – also to the north – by an enclosure wall with bastions whose structure still survives in considerable stretches. The second district, a narrow strip of elegant religious and civil buildings, extends between the edge of the "Terravecchia" and the main road, present-day Corso Vittorio Emanuele. The third district lies immediately below the buildings along the "corso" and runs steeply down to the jetty; this is the district of sailors and ceramist/potters, and it still has its original urban function. On the promontory to the east, a splendid promenade lined with palm trees separates the Grand Hotel delle Terme from the precipice overlooking the sea, while to the west the coastline is adorned with a vast array of recent residential developments.

Even though most of the population earns its living from farming and fishing, much of the fortune of Sciacca is a result of the hot springs, excellent for the treatment of respiratory and rheumatic diseases; the craftsmanship here is quite impressive, especially the pottery, which is found in the older section of the town (art shops, murals).

Piazza Scandaliato (B2). This square is a splendid terrace overlooking the sea, and it is a meeting place for the whole town; embellishing it is the church of *S. Domenico*, an 18th-c. reconstruction of the church built here in 1534, and the *Collegio dei Gesuiti*, now the site of town hall or Municipio which, with the adjoining church of the *Collegio*, was begun in 1613.

Duomo (B2) or Cathedral. Built the first time in 1108 and rebuilt in 1656; of the original Norman structure, all that survives are the three apses, while the dark yellow color of the unfinished Baroque façade is en-

livened by the handsome Gagini marble *statues*, set in niches. The interior, built to a Latin-cross plan, was enlarged to nave and aisles during the Baroque period, and later adorned with frescoes and polychrome marble work.

S. Margherita (B1). The earliest construction of this church dates back to the 14th c., but all that survives from that period is the exquisite Gothic *portal** on the side of the church itself. The *statues* and the *bas-reliefs* that adorn it are attributed to Francesco Laurana and Pietro di Bonitade.

Palazzo Steripinto * (B1). Easily recognized by its diamond-point rustication, twin-light mullioned windows, and parapets, this is a remarkable building in the Catalonian Sicilian style dating back to 1501.

The **Castello Incantato** or enchanted castle (off map) is a singular art gallery in an olive grove, with hundreds of faces carved into the rock and on the trees by the peasant/artist Filippo Bentivegna.

Caltabellotta

A tortuous panoramic route of 20 km runs up to the high Dolomitic mount atop which stands the town (elev. 949 m, pop. 4709). The primarily military function that it has served since its foundation is clear from its image of compact strength that contrasts with the gentle slopes of the southern coast. And part of its reputation was won through its importance in war; a peace treaty was signed here, on 31 August 1302, between Charles of Valois and Frederick II of Aragon, putting an end to the bloody war of the Sicilian Vespers (Guerra dei Vespri Siciliani). Before acquiring the Arabic name of "Kal'at Ballut" (mountain of oaks), it was called "Triocala," which means "three nice things"; these three things, according to Diodorus Siculus, were its abundance of springwater, its fertile soil cultivated with vines and olive trees, and the natural protection of the impregnable crag.

It still enjoys these features, along with its exquisite medieval urban fabric, so to speak, typical of a mountain town of the Mediterranean region.

Among the monuments one should note the *Chiesa Madre*, founded by the Normans, and the hermitage or **Eremo di S. Pellegrino** whose architectural mass, set on the western edge of the mount, looms over the city. The sanctuary consists of a monastery and a chapel, which stand not far from the grotto where, according to an ancient legend, there lived a dragon that fed on the children of Caltabellotta until it was slain by the saint.

The *grotto necropolises* cut into the rocky wall (you can see them along the road lead-ing out of the town) and ruins of *fortifications*, not yet explored by archeologists, offer indications of an ancient human presence, about which much remains to be learned.

Part of Lampedusa's coastline: the island's natural environment has remained unspoilt

4.4 The Pelagie Islands

Scattered in the southernmost territorial waters of Italy (geographically closer to Africa than to Sicily), Lampedusa and Lampione to the south and Linosa to the north form the little island group with the somewhat tautological name of Pelagie (from the Greek "pelagos," meaning "sea"). The three islets present different geological characteristics: Lampedusa and Lampione are limestone in structure, while Linosa is volcanic in origin; moreover, while the first two belong to the African continental shelf, the third is considered part of the Sicilian continental shelf.

The islands (pop. 5624) maintain their original wild appearance, and constitute an unrivalled attraction, especially in their wealth of land and sea fauna: on the beaches of Lampedusa, the sea turtle burrows into the sand and lays its eggs; on the rocks, the monk seal splashes and suns itself; and on the crags high above, the Eleonora's falcon perches and observes.

There are regular flights from Palermo and ships running from Porto Empèdocle, so it is relatively easy to reach the little archipelago.

Lampedusa

Once known for its sponges, this island looks like a great inclined rock table rising out of the crystal-clear sea with sheer walls; the coastline is dotted with grottoes and shoals and little sandy inlets, and the waters abound in fish.

Although there are traces of the passage of Phoenicians, Greeks, Romans, and Arabs, the true colonization dates back to 1843, when Ferdinand II of the House of Bourbon established a colony there; until 1940 it was a place of political exile. The town is clustered to the southern extremity, in the Frazione *Lampedusa* (elev. 16 m). The recent establishment of regular flights from Palermo has encouraged the development of a limited tourist trade.

Lampione

Set to the northwest of Lampedusa, this uninhabited stack formation has only an automatic lighthouse or warning beacon.

Linosa

The summit of a volcanic cone that has been extinct for nearly 2,000 years, this island's slopes plunge down into the sea to a depth of roughly 100 m. The island has an almost perfectly circular form; the rocky seabeds are popular with scuba divers attracted by the abundance of fish; it is very nice to stop in the little village of Linosa (elev. 12 m) with its brightly colored houses.

5 Ragusa and its territory

The geographic context for this tour largely coincides with the Val di Noto, one of the three sections of Sicily as it was divided by the Moors. This is a territory that is varied and diverse, ranging from the plain to the north, the Piana di Catania, to the highlands of the Iblei to the east, from the coastline bathed by the Mar d'Africa or African Sea, to the Piana di Gela to the west, from the inland highlands to the territory of the Calatino; and it represents

The historical nucleus of Ragusa on the hill of Ibla, at the eastern end of the city

a complete microcosm of the finer characteristics of the island as well as its greater contradictions. The landscape is marked by the imbalances that have emerged in economic development. Once it became clear that there was no real possibility of industrializing the outlying areas, the farmers of the area around Gela relearned the finest old techniques of irrigating fields. That was not all: the dairy products of the Iblei – specifically the cheeses – became much sought-after in markets everywhere, proving much more lucrative than the phantom wealth from oil wells; indeed, the great landholdings – or "latifondi," from the Latin "latifundium" – of the Piana di Catania were broken up and cultivated, undermining the collective policies of the past. The only thing that seems to expand without signs of flagging is the multiplication of greenhouses – the product of a culture better known for pesticides and chemical fertilizers – which are now creeping up against the Mediterranean dunes, which remain pristine as of this writing. And it is this astonishing proliferation of greenhouse farming which characterizes the coastal landscape – so blighting a landscape that was once a harmonious patchwork of fields girded by dry-stone masonry walls; but this form of greenhouse agriculture brings so much money that any objections from environmentalists tend to fall on deaf ears.

5.1 Ragusa

Any proper analysis of Ragusa's chief features (elev. 502, pop. 69,631; city map on pp. 104-105) must focus on two important factors: the earthquake of 1693 and the city's relationship with the surrounding territory (and vice versa). The earthquake, because it triggered a two-part reconstruction of the city: "Ragusa supra," i.e., the city up on the highland, the one that developed into a city proper during the post-earthquake building, and "Ragusa iusu," i.e. Ibla, almost wholly rebuilt along the old medieval layout. The relationship between city and surrounding territory, on the other hand, allows one to glimpse the singular lives of the inhabitants, who are closely bound to the philosophy of the environment by peasant traditions which were particularly reinforced and emphasized from the 15th c. onward with the institution of emphyteusis, or perpetual lease.

From the earliest settlements to the twentieth century

Traces of settlement in the area around the hill of Ibla have been dated back to the 3rd millennium B.C., and settlement seems to have been much more continuous from the 9th to the 7th c. B.C. This favorable geographic location allowed the early Sicilians (the Siculi) to found a fortress here, defending the course of the river Irminio. The "Hibla Heraia" discussed in the early sources linked its development to the Greek colony of Kamarina, establishing economic and commercial ties that allowed them to preserve their independence from the Greek oppressors. Occupied first by the Romans and later by the Byzantines (4th c.), Ibla was fortified with a strong enclosure wall by the latter. Beginning in A.D. 848, under Moorish domination, the structure of the territory underwent a considerable transformation: the countryside was repopulated and new crops were planted, using new systems of cultivation. Under the rule of the Normans and then the families of the Chiaramonte and the Cabrera, the medieval city took shape. To the west, in the higher sections, stood the castle, the ancient Moorish "Kasr," and to the east the boundary was marked by what is now the Giardino Ibleo. The principal thoroughfare, running east-west, was the "piancata," which once crossed the Piazza d'Armi, now Piazza del Duomo (Cathedral Square). The city itself was occupied by numerous religious Orders. The concession of enphyteusis, beginning in 1452 at the behest of the Conte Cabrera was a major step forward in the transformation of the territory and the city. It was in fact through this economic revolution that a direct bond was established between the peasant and the land to be cultivated, subordinated only to a lease-rent to be paid to the count. In ensuring years, the territory was broken up and fenced in with distinctive dry-stone walls. From 1693 on, in the wake of the earthquake that devastated eastern Sicily, Ragusa and Ibla became the two historic centers of the same city, forced by geography and by politics to cohabit. The two cities grew necessarily one alongside the other, amid much bickering, until 1926, when they were "rejoined" with the single name of Ragusa.

The boundary between the two townships is set by the church of S. Maria delle Scale; the territory of Ibla includes the working-class districts that lie on the slopes of the upland. With the reconstruction of Ibla over the course of the 18th and 19th c., there arose a richer array of churches and aristocratic residences, an array that above all featured a more harmonious sort of lesser architecture. The new town center, on the other hand, which has fewer monumental features, extends over the highland. The growth of the past few decades, however, has resulted in the marginalization of Ibla, which is isolated from the economic processes of the rest of the city.

The itinerary of the tour

The route suggested here allows you to trace back the expansion of the city in accordance with successive phases of growth. If you begin from Piazza Libertà, you will then cross the bridge or Ponte Nuovo (1937), which, along with the Ponte dei Cappuccini (1835) and the Ponte Papa Giovanni XXIII (1964) spans the Cava di S. Domenica. You can continue along Via Roma and then Corso Italia, heading down toward the historic centers of the old city. After you cross Piazza S. Giovanni, with the Cathedral or Cattedrale, you can venture into the 18th-c. section of town, which cuts across a series of streets at right angles, until you reach the stairs that run down toward Ibla. At the end of Via XXIV Maggio, a continuation of Corso Italia, you will see a handsome panoramic view of Ibla. From here, if you walk down the 333 steps of the staircase, or if you follow Corso Mazzini, a linking road that was produced by demolition done during the Fascist era, you will find Piazza della Repubblica, the former Piazza degli Archi, which serves as a nexus connecting the various districts that climb sharply up toward the highland, and with the entrance to the medieval section of the city. From the square, you will continue along, concentrating on the route that is richest in historic and artistic elements, following the old main thoroughfare of the city as it was before the earthquake: Via del Mercato, Via XI Febbraio, Via S. Agnese, Via Tenente Di Stefano, and Via Capitano Bocchieri as far as Piazza del Duomo. (It is worth rounding off the tour by pushing into the ancient medieval routes, climbing and descending stairways in a labyrinth that makes it possible to discover little tucked-away jewels and urban settings with considerable charm). From the spectacular Piazza del Duomo, over which rises the

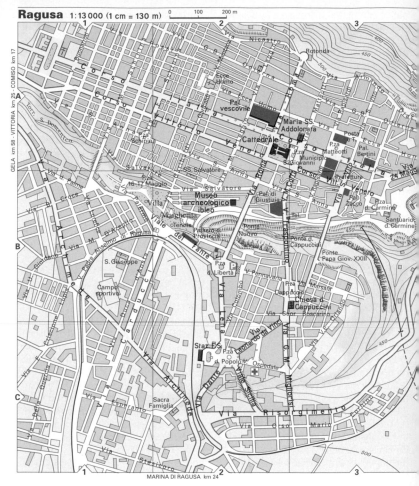

MARINA DI RAGUSA km 24

church of S. Giorgio (the Duomo or Cathedral), you will descend to Piazza Pola, along Corso XXV Aprile, and along the main thoroughfare, the backbone as it were of a 17th-c. "forma piscis" (fish shape). From Piazza Pola, which coincides in part with Piazza Maggiore of the medieval city, take a detour from Corso XXV Aprile (which runs down toward the Giardini Iblei), and continue along Via Orfanotrofio; after the church of S. Maria la Nova you will cross the ancient Jewish ghetto until you reach Largo Camarina; then take Via Chiaramonte to reach the Baroque church of S. Francesco all'Immacolata. From the church, along Via Tenente La Rocca and then Via Monte Ereo, you will return to Corso XXV Aprile, and then you will reach the park or Giardino Ibleo.

Piazza della Libertà (B2). Once known as Piazza Impero (Empire Square), this area was built during the Fascist era in accordance with the architecture of Marcello

Piacentini; it stands at the head of the *Ponte Nuovo*, a bridge that was built to encourage the city to grow past the Cava S. Domenica, in order to consolidate the 19th-c. district of the Cappuccini. The square stands as a major example of Fascist architecture, and is now a link between the "third," modern city of Ragusa and its older centers.

Museo Archeologico Ibleo (B2; *open 9-1:30, 4-7:30*). This archeological museum was established in the wake of the first systematic exploration of the territory of the Provincia di Ragusa in the years 1955-60, with emphasis on the chronological sequence in a succession of topographical source areas. The installation of the material is characterized by life-sized reproductions of sections of the digs. In the first section, there are displays of flint and volcanic stone tools, and ceramic materials from necropolises and villages from the Bronze Age. In the section dedicated to Camarina, there is

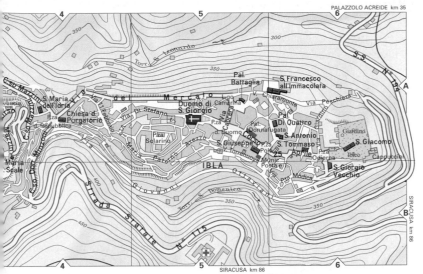

documentation concerning the recent excavations in the city, with terracotta figurines from a sanctuary of Demeter, and the archaic and classical necropolises with Corinthian and Attic ceramics. Of particular interest is the material, especially ceramics, from the archaic and classical Sicilian towns (third section), while among the Hellenistic towns (fourth section), special attention is devoted to the caravan center of Scornavacche and its ceramic manufactory (with a reconstruction of a kiln). There is also material concerning Roman and late-Roman centers (fifth section), and collections (sixth section).

Cattedrale (A2). This Cathedral, the center of the urban renewal of 18th-c. Ragusa, was built between 1706 and 1760, and was dedicated to St. John the Baptist. It stands on a broad terrace supported by a loggia; the façade, which is rendered asymmetrical by the stout bell tower, has a central structure with two orders, and a monumental portal. The *interior* is built to a Latin-cross plan and has a nave and two aisles divided by two orders of columns in a Ragusan asphalt stone.

Palazzo Zacco (B3). The façade overlooking Via S. Vito features harmonious Baroque architecture that is characterized by the carvings that decorate the brackets supporting the balconies. The elegant entrance portal with two columns supporting the central balcony, the aristocratic crest held up by putti, and the grinning mascaron all point to a school of decorative artists that, in this and in other palazzi of

the historic centers of Ragusa, did sublime work carving of white stone.

Palazzo Bertini (A3). This building was erected toward the end of the 18th c., and stands out for its distinctive mascarons set at the keystones of the windows. The most common interpretation is that these are the "three potentates": where the first represents the poor man, powerful because he cares for nothing; the second represents the aristocrat, with the firm gaze of one whose power goes beyond the laws; and the third is the wealthy merchant, powerful with the arrogance of money.

Ragusa: the Cathedral

S. Maria delle Scale (A-B4). Set at the top of the staircases that join the two Ragusas, for centuries this church has marked the boundary of the two towns. Built in the 14th c. on the site of an existing Cistercian monastery dating from Norman times, it was rebuilt following the earthquake of

The façade of S. Giorgio Cathedral

1693. All that survives from the 14th-c. construction is a portal and a Gothic pulpit at the foot of the campanile. The *interior* has three aisles; the left aisle and the nave are rebuilt in a Baroque style, while the right aisle consists of four communicating chapels linked by Catalonian Gothic and Renaissance arches (15th-16th c.). In the third chapel, note the *Dormition of the Virgin Mary*, a polychrome terracotta relief of the Gagini school (1538).

Salita Commendatore (A4). As you climb along the stairs, narrow lanes, arches, and buttresses of this narrow "salita" (literally, in Italian, "climb"), you will pass the Palazzo della Cancelleria, the church of the Idria, and the Palazzo Cosentini. These are three noteworthy works of Baroque architecture. The *Palazzo Nicastro*, built in 1760, was the site of the *Cancelleria Comunale* (town chancery) of Ibla until the 19th c. On its right, a little further down, is the church and the campanile of *S. Maria dell'Idria*, built in 1626 by the Order of the Cavalieri di Malta (Knights of Malta), and rebuilt in 1739. The bell tower is surmounted by a cupola with an octagonal base, sheathed in the bright polychrome tiles of Caltagirone.

Descend even further, and you will find the *Palazzo dei Cosentini*, dating from the early 18th c.

Purgatorio (A4). This beautiful church, founded in the 17th c., dominates Piazza della Repubblica from high atop its staircase. The interior, with a nave and two aisles, features among other things a depiction of *Souls in Purgatory* by Francesco Manno on the main altar. The campanile, set in the rear side and to the left of the church, stands on ancient Byzantine walls, alongside which climbs the *Salita dell'Orologio*.

S. Giorgio* (A5). This Cathedral, designed in 1739 by Rosario Gagliardi, was built at the "center of gravity" of the new urban layout. From high atop a very long stairway, which is off-kilter from the axis of the square, it overlooks the surrounding valleys in a handsome setting emphasized by the sharpness of the slope. The *façade*, articulated in three orders, is convex at the center, and is punctuated by jutting cornices; the cupola is Neoclassical, rises 43 m high, and dates from 1820; the wrought-iron fencework dates from 1880. The *interior* is built to a Latin-cross plan, and is divided into a nave and two aisles. In the nave, 13 polychrome stained glass windows depict the *Martyrdom of St. George* (1926).

S. Giuseppe (A5). The architecture of this church, which overlooks Piazza Pola (called Piazza Maggiore before the earthquake), links it to the Duomo, or Cathedral, in stylistic continuity. The *façade*, attributed to Rosario Gagliardi or his school, is subdivided into three tiers, with Corinthian columns and statues. The interior, with an elliptical plan, is decorated with stucco work; the cupola, frescoed in 1793 by Sebastiano Lo Monaco, depicts the *Glory of St. Benedict*.

S. Francesco all'Immacolata (A5-6). The remains of the bell tower and the Gothic portal derive from an early Franciscan church built in the 13th c. The church that now stands here was built in the 17th c., and was rebuilt in the Baroque style after the earthquake. On the *interior*, it is worth noting the wide use of the local pitch-stone, both in the flooring and in the holy water font and a tomb slab set near the presbytery (1577). In Largo Camarina stands the Baroque Palazzo Battaglia (A5), possibly the work of Rosario Gagliardi.

S. Giorgio Vecchio (B6). The Catalonian-Gothic style portal dating from the 14th c. is the sole surviving relic of the large church dedicated to St. George, destroyed by the earthquake. In the lunette, you should note a bas-relief of St. George on horseback slaying a dragon and, in the rhomboid panels above it, the eagles of Aragon.

Giardino Ibleo (A6). This garden was built in the 19th c. in the area surrounding the churches of S. Giacomo, S. Domenico, and the Cappuccini. Two other churches occupied this location: S. Teodoro, since destroyed, and the first church of S. Giorgio (see above), of which the portal survives. Of the churches that survive, the church of *S. Domenico* (or of the Rosario) is in particu-

larly poor condition due to neglect, though it still has its campanile decorated with colored majolica; *S. Giacomo* (14th c.), originally with three aisles, now features only a central nave dating from the Baroque reconstruction (note the decorated 18th-c. wooden ceiling, and, in the presbytery, a *Crucifix* of the Spanish school of the 17th c.). At the far end of the Giardino Ibleo is the church of the *Cappuccini*, which contains a large altarpiece by Pietro Novelli, known as the Monrealese, of *Our Lady of the Assumption, with Apostles and Angels, and Saint Agatha and Saint Agnes*, as well as a *Nativity* of the southern school, dating from 1520, interesting for its depiction of a medieval village, said by some scholars to be a depiction of Ibla.

5.2 The territory of Ragusa, or Ragusano

This itinerary (route map below) involves two separate routes that cover the two most homogeneous areas. The tour encompasses four main locations, two in each area: Ragusa and Mòdica in the first excursion; Caltagirone and Gela in the second.

For the first route (123 km), starting out from Ragusa, you should take the old road to Mòdica, state road 115, which drops down into the valley or Valle dell'Irminio. The river is crossed by a very high bridge which links state road 514 to Mòdica. You

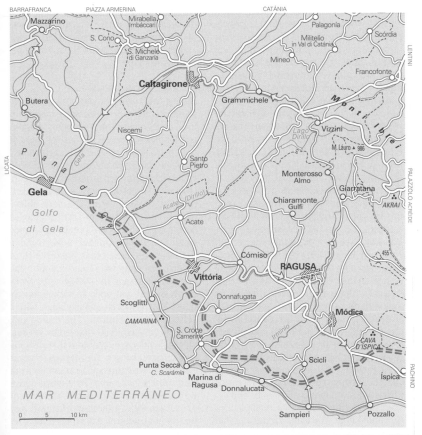

A "masseria iblea" with pastures edged in typical drystone walls in the background

will leave the state road to reach Mòdica, and take it again after the visit, in its southern stretch toward Pozzallo. You then follow the coast in the direction of Marina di Ragusa, leaving behind the detour to Scicli on your right, and driving past a number of tourist accommodations. The landscape of the coast road offers a number of pleasant surprises.

After you reach the last coastal town, Scoglitti, you will follow the local or provincial road to Vittoria, in a territory that alternates farms and huge dry-wall greenhouses. After you leave Vittoria you will travel east along state road 115 as far as Còmiso. The road winds among vineyards and unused watermills that once ran on the flow of the river Ìppari. Before you reach Còmiso, you will note many marble yards, where the traditional working of the local stone, or "pietra di Còmiso," has since been expanded to include imported marble and now constitutes one of the chief industries of the town. Before you enter the straightaway that runs into Ragusa, a road on the right splits off to the Castello di Donnafugata, a lavish 19th-c. residence.

You will leave the city to take the second route (running 111 km) from the easternmost extremity of Ibla, heading north along state road 194 to Giarratana. The road runs parallel with the river Irminio through an area with dense vegetation. Once you pass Giarratana, we advise a detour to Chiaramonte Gulfi, where there are magnificent views. Return to the main route and you will reach Monterosso Almo, the last township in the Provincia di Ragusa, on the boundary with the Provincia di Catania. After a series of twisting switchbacks and climbs and descents, you will reach Vizzini, birthplace of Giovanni Verga. You leave Vizzini and join

the state road 124 heading west toward Grammichele, and from that city with its hexagonal plan you will continue on, crossing the western slopes of the Monti Erei. Once you reach Caltagirone, the third major stopping point on the whole route through the Ragusa territory, after a brief downhill stretch you will cross the Catania-Gela state road, which runs in a southwesterly direction. When you have entered the province of Caltanissetta, the vast plains of Gela and, in the distance, the smokestacks of the petrochemical plant mark an end to the route.

The farms of the Ibla region

Among the green pastures and the dense crosshatching of drystone walls, made with local limestone, in the area around Ragusa and Mòdica it is possible to see clusters of buildings. These are the "masserie iblee," great farmhouse complexes organized into small villages formed around a closed central court of considerable size. In recent periods, some of these "masserie iblee" have become centers for "agriturismo," a sort of agrarian bed and breakfast, or they simply serve unassuming meals. Among the farm complexes that preserve their original structure we should mention the *Masseria Musso* and the *Masseria Rizza*, privately owned, but open to view upon request. The former is a small village, with a little adjoining church. The courtyard, which is quite large, is bounded by low residential buildings; on the sides there are stables and storehouses. The Masseria Rizza is different in structure and in activities from many others in the area. The regular courtyard is defined by the owner's "palazzotto" or mansion with a little church facing it, and two lower structures, set along either side.

Mòdica

The many descriptions that travellers of the past offered of Mòdica (elev. 296 m, pop. 52,464; city map below), tended to describe it as a city torn from the rock, because of its grottoes, which were inhabited until a few decades ago, and its stairways, and its geographic location. As curious as the city's structure may be, it is also renowned for the remarkable sweets that are made here. The city is divided into Mòdica Alta, at the top of the rock, and Mòdica Bassa.

On the edge of the city and within the urban perimeter there are traces of the presence of humans during the period of the Civilization of Castelluccio (20th to 15th c.

B.C.). Documentation shows the existence during Roman times of Motyka, a "civitas decumana." With the Moorish conquest in A.D. 844-45, Mòdica – with its surrounding territory – underwent a profound shift in the way that agricultural resources were used. Under the Normans, the city, with its powerful strategic location, reached its greatest glory. It was the capital of the county ("contea") for Peter I of Aragon, and was later ruled by the Chiaramonte, the Cabrera, and the Henriquez-Cabrera, all families of enormous political influence in Sicily. The concession of emphyteusis, or perpetual lease, from the 15th c. on, introduced a number of privileges that allowed

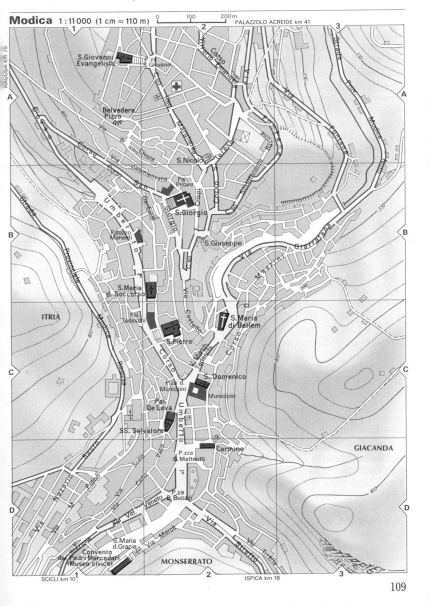

Modica 1 : 11 000 (1 cm = 110 m)

a greater distribution of the wealth that proceeded from agriculture, with the consequential growth of a strong middle class. The medieval city, with its two mountain streams as natural defenses, created the fortification of the castle or Castello on the ridge of the upland where the enclosure wall terminates to the north; not far from the "cave" outside of the walls rise small villages. The earthquake of 1693 caught the city in a period of consolidation around the new settlements founded by the numerous religious Orders. The reconstruction, on the same original site, focused in particular along the axis of Viale Regina Margherita and on either side of what is now Corso Umberto, with the powerful contribution of the new agrarian nobility. The new territorial layout pushed the city downhill, creating a considerable shift in the urban structure during the 19th c.

The tour suggested here touches only the most salient features of a city of easily-overlooked corners full of charm and atmosphere. If you set out from Piazza Buozzi in the southern area of the city, and follow Corso Umberto I you will reach Piazza Matteotti, characterized by the exquisite façade of the church of the Carmine, and then Piazza del Municipio, a nerve center of this city, set at the confluence of the two mountain streams, which were covered over between the 19th c. and the beginning of this century. You may then continue along Corso Umberto I, over the corresponding streambed of the Torrente Janni Mauro, skirting the district known as Cartellone-San Francesco, which was home to a Jewish community until 1474. To the right and to the left of the "corso" there are rows of buildings dating back to the 18th and 19th c. On the "corso" is the Palazzo Manenti; to the right of that building, if you turn into Via Mortillo, you will climb up the spectacular flight of steps that leads up to the Cathedral of S. Giorgio, in the higher part of town. As you enter the district of S. Lucia, one of the town's oldest districts, along Via S. Chiara, you will reach the Belvedere Pizzo, a terrace with a panoramic view, at an elevation of 449 m, from which you can survey most of Mòdica and the hills that surround it. From Via Pizzo, you will reach the church of S. Giovanni Evangelista, and from there you can head back down to the center of town along Corso Regina Margherita, chief thoroughfare of the "città alta," or upper city, lined with 18th- and 19th-c. palazzi. Once you come even with the church of S. Nicolò, you can take Corso Francesco Crispi, and then

it Via del Castello running around the enclosure of the medieval fortress, which was levelled by the earthquake of 1693 and never rebuilt. Follow Via Posterla (on the right, a short detour through Via Sbalzo permits a view of the grottoes that are now used as stables and warehouses, but which until a few centuries ago were used as homes by peasants) and Via S. Maria to head back down to the "città bassa," or lower section of the town; once you pass the church of S. Maria di Betlem you will return along Via Marchesa Tedeschi to Piazza del Municipio.

Convento dei Padri Mercedari (D1). This monastery was built in the 18th c., and now serves as a town library, an auditorium, and a civic museum, or **Museo Civico** (*open 10-1; closed holidays*). The ethnographic section of the museum is, since 1978, the **Museo Ibleo delle Arti e Tradizioni Popolari** (*open 10-1 and 3:30-6:30*); it offers perfect reproductions of the objects and tools of a peasant farmhouse or of the workshop of a master artisan of times gone by, including: the "scarparu" (cobbler), the "firraru e firraschecchi" (blacksmith and farrier), the "mastru ri carretta" (cartwright). Adjoining the monastery, but dating back to an earlier period, is the church of *S. Maria delle Grazie*, which was founded to commemorate the "miraculous" discovery, in 1615, amidst

Mòdica: S. Giorgio

mysteriously burning thorn-bushes, of an image of the *Virgin with Child* painted on a little slab of slate. The image is housed in the main altar of the church.

Carmine (D2). This church was rebuilt after 1693, and of the older structure, all that survives is the pointed-arch portal and a rose-window that surmounts it. On the interior, at the second altar on the left, note the *Annunciation*, a marble group believed to be by Antonello Gagini (1528-30).

Piazza del Municipio (C2). This full-fledged hinge of the city's layout and life, Piazza del Municipio, set at the intersection of Corso Umberto and Via Marchesa Tedeschi – which are the covered-over stream beds of the torrents known as the Janni Mauro and the Pozzo dei Pruni respectively – is surmounted by the crag of the castle (Rupe del Castello), upon which stands an 18th-c. tower with a clock. To the right of the square are the former monastery of the Dominicans, now the town hall or *Municipio* and the adjoining church of *S. Domenico* (14th c.): destroyed by the earthquake of 1613, it was rebuilt in 1678.

Corso Umberto I (B1-C2). On either side of this street, a series of pieces of architecture restore some idea of the enormous importance that this thoroughfare has had over the centuries: on the left is the *former monastery of the Benedictine nuns*, site of the tribunal since 1866; further along, the 19th-c. theater, the *Teatro Garibaldi*; on the right, the spectacular stairway of the Baroque church of *S. Pietro*. As you continue, you will note, again on the right, the *Palazzo Tedeschi* (18th c.), adorned with balconies supported by typical carved brackets, and the 17th-c. church of *S. Maria del Soccorso* adjoining the former Collegio dei Gesuiti; lastly, there is *Palazzo Manenti* with the brackets of its balconies depicting various personages of the period (18th c.).

S. Pietro (C2). This church existed as early as the 14th c., and was rebuilt after 1693. You enter it along a staircase embellished with statues of the twelve Apostles.
The interior has a nave and two aisles: in the second chapel on the right, note the *Madonna dell'Ausilio*, a statue of the Gagini school; in the same aisle, at the second-to-last altar, note the *St. Peter and the Paralytic*, a polychrome group by Benedetto Civiletti (1893).

S. Giorgio* (B2). Rebuilt on the same site in which it was destroyed and rebuilt repeatedly, the Cathedral, or Duomo di S. Giorgio, rises atop a stairway of 250 steps, in a spectacular combination of architecture, stage design, and urban design, the work of Rosario Gagliardi. Inaugurated in 1738, it was completed in a number of stages, and the stairway was finished as late as 1818. The *interior*, with a nave and four aisles, transept, and cupola, abounds in numerous works of art; on the main altar is a *polyptych* attributed to Bernardino Niger (1573); in the chapel to the left of the main altar, note the statue of the *Madonna della Neve* by Giuliano Mancino and Bartolomeo Berrettaro (circa 1510); in the far right aisle, on the second altar, *Our Lady of the Assumption* by Filippo Paladino, signed and dated (1610). You should also note the sundial traced in the floor of the transept (1895).

Alongside the church is the 18th-c. **Palazzo Polara**, an interesting example of an aristocratic residence that still preserves its original structure and part of its furnishings. It houses the *Pinacoteca Comunale* or civic art gallery, with 18th and 19th-c. Sicilian paintings (*open 9-1; closed Sun.*).

S. Giovanni Evangelista (A1). Destroyed by the earthquakes of the 17th c., this church was rebuilt in 1839. The campanile is the highest point in all Mòdica (elev. 449 m); from the top of the stairway a road leads off to the left, to the *Belvedere Pizzo**, a spectacular panoramic overlook with a view of the whole city. A detour on the right of the square leads to the church of *S. Maria del Gesù*, built in the 15th c.: with the adjoining monastery, or Convento dei Minori Osservanti, it features a Catalonian Gothic portal, as well as a cloister with double orders of arches. The building, in a poor state of conservation, is now being used as a prison.

S. Maria di Betlem (C2). This church, built in the 15th c. on a site in that once hosted the structures of four smaller churches, was damaged by the earthquakes of the 17th c., and was rebuilt in the 18th c. The *interior* has a nave and two aisles, with a truss roof and marble flooring. At the end of the right aisle, a magnificent 15th-c. portal leads into the chapel, or **Cappella del Sacramento***, a rare example of late-Gothic-Renaissance architecture; at the altar, a 16th-c. *Virgin with Child* in painted stone.

Pozzallo

This is the only maritime township in the province, or Provincia di Ragusa; the history of Pozzallo (elev. 20 m, pop. 18,035) began

with the construction (14th c.) of loading facilities for the exportation of wheat, which
gave this town considerable importance in
the economy of the county or Contea di
Mòdica. Traffic was directed by the "maestro portolano," the sole official responsible
for the proper operation of the loading facilities. The tower or Torre Cabrera (*open 9-
12; closed Sun.*), which still stands, was built
to protect the storehouses from frequent
raids by pirates; later, it was one of the few
private towers to form part of the overall
systems of defenses along the Sicilian
coasts, undertaken at the end of the 16th c.
Pozzallo developed a regular grid network
with straight roads. Behind the *Torre Cabrera*
is Piazza Rimembranza, overlooked by the
Palazzo Musso (1926), which is characterized by ornamental features in the Liberty,
or Art-Nouveau, style. From the square, if
you continue along Corso Vittorio Veneto,
the city's main thoroughfare, you will reach
the seafront promenade, or Lungomare,
surrounding the large port. Pozzallo is
linked to the nearby island of Malta through
a regular hydrofoil service.

Scicli

This little Baroque jewel is off the beaten
tourist track; Scicli (elev. 106 m, pop. 25,886)
can be reached along a series of roads
arranged radially. Conquered by the Moors
in A.D. 864, it became a royal city under the
Normans, who are said to have fought a
fierce battle with the Moors who had landed along the coast, perhaps in an attempt to
win back lost territory. The battle went in favor of the troops of Roger the Norman, and
it is commemorated, in accordance with
local tradition, by the presence of the sanctuary, or *Santuario della Madonna dei Milici*,
a hermitage founded in 1093, in a scenic location, 1.5 km from Scicli. In further commemoration of the event, each year, on the
last Sunday in May, there is a festival known
as the Sagra dei Milici.

The tour begins from Piazza Italia, where
you can admire the church of *S. Ignazio*,
which became the Chiesa Matrice in 1874,
replacing the church of S. Matteo; the
church dates back prior to the earthquake,
and it was rebuilt in 1751. On the interior is
the *Madonna dei Milici*, a papier-mâché depiction of the Virgin Mary on a white horse
with a drawn sword in hand, in the act of
fighting the Saracens, two of which lie under
the hooves of her horse. From the square,
you can climb up to the church of *S. Bartolomeo* (15th c.), among the few buildings
that were spared by the great earthquake:
inside there is a handsome *crèche* made of

linden wood, dating from 1573, and renovated by the Neapolitan craftsman Pietro
Padula (1773-76). Of the 65 original statues, only 29 survive. You will return to Piazza Italia along Via Nazionale, a 19th-c.
thoroughfare; branching off from this street
are, Via Duca d'Aosta, with the *Palazzo Beneventano*, noteworthy for its unusual
Baroque decorations, and then Via Mormino Penna, marked by a succession of
Baroque aristocratic palazzi and monumental churches, culminating in the church
of *S. Teresa*, no longer used as a place of worship but now serving as a concert and lec-
ture hall. In Piazza Busacca note the
Carmelite monastery, or *Complesso Mona-
stico dei Carmelitani*, founded in 1386, destroyed in 1693, and rebuilt between 1775
and 1778; the church was built in 1769.
From the square, you can walk to the
church of *S. Maria la Nova*, at the foot of the
two hills of the Rosario and of the S. Cassa,
in one of the oldest districts in the city;
the imposing façade of this church, in Neoclassical style, is a reconstruction and enlargement of the earlier, 15th-/17th-c. structures, done in 1816. The interior, decorated
with stuccoes, features these works: on the
3rd altar in the right aisle, *Resurrection of
Christ*, a wooden statue attributed to
Benedetto Civiletti; on the main altar, *Nativity of the Virgin*, by Sebastiano Conca; on
the 3rd altar in the left aisle, *Madonna della
Neve*, a marble statue of the Gagini school
(1496); on the 2nd altar, *Madonna della Pietà*,
a statue made of cypress wood, probably of
Byzantine origin.

Marina di Ragusa

This is a village that is linked to the capital,
some 20 km away; Marina di Ragusa (elev. 6
m) grew around the maritime roadstead
protected by the tower built at the behest of
the Conte Cabrera in the 16th c. to defend
the coast. All that survives of the ancient
tower is the square base. The town developed between the end of the 19th c. and
the first few decades of the 20th c., a product of the intense activity of the port. A second wave of development came over the
last few decades in conjunction with the
burgeoning phenomenon of vacation homes.
Not far from the town, a nature preserve
was established in 1985, the *Riserva Naturale Macchia Foresta del Fiume Irminio*, a
coastal area of great interest in naturalistic
terms.

Camarina

The long beach of Cava di Randello, protected by a forest belonging to the Forest De-

partment, lies near the archeological park or **Parco Archeologico di Camarina** (*open 9-sunset*), an ancient Syracusan colony located at the mouth of the river Ìppari, just a few kilometers outside of the town of Scoglitti. The earliest explorations in 1896, and the systematic survey which began in 1958 and is still underway, have brought to light the urban layout of this ancient town. Historical sources (Thucydides, Herodotus, Diodorus) tell of the most important phases in the history of this city founded by the Corinthians of Syracuse in 598 B.C., the third colony after Acre (664 B.C.) and Casmene (644 B.C.). Camarina possessed a vast territory, some 200 hectares, and became a major maritime trading station. Devastated and rebuilt repeatedly until 258 B.C., this town was a major player in controlling this coastline for the three and a half centuries in which it existed. The sights of the visit include the remains of the walls (5-6 m tall in places), some public areas and, most notable, the *Tempio di Athena*, a temple of which only foundations remain. The park contains the building housing the regional museum or *Museo Regionale di Camarina* (*open 9-1 and 3-6:30*), a typical rural 19th-c. farmhouse, where it is possible to see the finds from diving explorations of the sea, among them a bronze *Corinthian helmet*. Of enormous importance for the understanding of the site and value of the material uncovered here is the exploration of the many rich necropolises that surround the settlement.

Between Punta Secca and Casuzze is an archeological site, the *Parco Archeologico di Caucana* (*open by request, tel. 0932916142*) set amid greenery: it contains the ruins of some twenty houses and a church with apse and mosaic floors.

Vittoria

Founded in 1607 by the Contessa Vittoria Colonna, Vittoria (elev. 168 m, pop. 59,775) enjoyed a series of privileges: concessions of land, exemption from tariffs, and a ten-year tax amnesty, immunity for criminals and indemnity for debtors. As a result, the original town grew constantly, with an interruption due to the earthquake of 1693. The layout of the city follows a regular checkerboard pattern oriented around certain piazzas. The most important meeting place is Piazza del Popolo, with the *Teatro Comunale* (1877) and the church of *S. Maria delle Grazie* (1612, rebuilt in 1754).

Còmiso

There is documentation of the settlement of the territory of Còmiso (elev. 209 m, pop.

Còmiso: the Chiesa Madre

28,886) as early as the Roman period, provided by an unearthed mosaic floor (2nd c. B.C.) not far from the Fonte Diana; but the development of the village of Comicio (or Comicini) coincides with the Byzantine period (4th c. A.D.). The earliest documents per se date back to 1125 and 1168 (with a bull from Pope Alexander III), in Norman times, and speak of the growth of the hamlet around the two monastic complexes of S. Nicola (later Santissima Annunziata) and Abbazia (S. Biagio). When the town became part of the county or Contea di Mòdica, in 1393, the city was enclosed in a set of walls with five gates. In 1453 it passed under the rule of the dynasty of the Naselli, and in 1571 it became a county ("contea") in its own right. The development of the new districts to the east and south (S. Crispino, S. Cristoforo, S. Leonardo, and S. Francesco) between the 16th and 17th c. marked the city with a specific type of residence: one-and two-story row houses with exterior staircases to deal with the steep slope of the streets. The reconstruction that followed the earthquake of 1693 give this town its present Baroque appearance. The history of Còmiso in the 1980s was marked by a controversial chapter linked to the installation of an American missile base, which was strongly opposed by the pacifist movement. The dismantling of the base in the early 1990s left open the question of the use to which the buildings could be put.

The tour begins with *Piazza del Municipio*, with a noteworthy fountain, the Fonte Diana, and bounded, in particular, by two buildings of outstanding construction: the

Palazzo Comunale (or city hall) and the 17th-c. *Palazzo Iacono-Ciarcià*, rebuilt with its loggia following the earthquake. Not far away is Piazza S. Biagio: the adoration of Saint Blaise, the patron saint watching over Còmiso, who is venerated in the church of *S. Biagio*, dates back to Byzantine times. The church, which was rebuilt in the 18th c., still boasts the buttresses of the original structure. Facing it is the castle of the Aragonese counts, the *Castello dei Conti Naselli d'Aragona*; it has been modified over the course of the centuries, and comprises an octagonal keep, probably Byzantine in origin, and by a square donjon: of particular interest are the two round-arch portals with iron doors; over one of the portals is a 16th-c. Serlian window. In 1841 it was converted into a Neoclassical city theater. The church courtyard of the *Chiesa Madre* (S. Maria delle Stelle) dominates Piazza delle Erbe: founded in the 15th c. on the site of an earlier Gothic church, it was reconsecrated in 1699. The wooden ceiling of the nave was frescoed in the 17th c. A monumental stairway leads down to the Biblioteca Gesualdo Bufalino, the cultural heart of the city. From Via Papa Giovanni XXIII you can reach both the church of *S. Francesco* (or of the Immacolata, at the end of Via degli Studi), inside of which is the marble mausoleum of Baldassarre II Naselli, attributed to Antonello Gagini, and the church of the *Annunziata*, high atop a stairway at the intersection with Corso Vittorio Emanuele. Built in the 16th c. by enlarging the Byzantine church dedicated to St. Nicholas, later rebuilt to plans by G.B. Cascione-Vaccarini in 1772, it was completed with a Neoclassical cupola and a campanile dating from the end of the 19th c. The interior, decorated with stuccoes, contains a wooden polychrome statue of St. Nicholas (S. Nicola; 15th c.); on the altar of the right transept is a *Crucifix* believed to be the work of Fra Umile da Petralìa.

Castello di Donnafugata

The castle was built at the behest of the baron Corrado Arezzo in the second half of the 19th c. on structures dating back to the 17th c., including the square tower at the center; it has been restored many times. The main façade – remarkably theatrical, with a long avenue running up it, lined with the houses of peasants on either side – was enriched in the early years of the 20th c. with a small loggia in the Venetian Gothic style. The **interior** includes 122 rooms, not all of which can be visited. The rooms that arc open to the public, set on the first floor,

have period furnishings, and preserve intact the charm of an aristocratic home. The **park** (*open Tue.-Fri., 8:30 and 1:30; Sat.-Sun., 9:30-5:30; closed Mon.*) extends over more than eight hectares, with boulevards embellished with a Neoclassical coffee-house, a maze, and a number of "scherzi," surprises powered by hidden mechanisms.

Giarratana

The second section of the route begins from Ragusa, heading toward ancient "Cerretanum," destroyed completely by the earthquake of 1693 and rebuilt at a lower elevation a few kilometers to the south. All that is visible in the old site are remnants of the fortified walls, the ruins of the castle and of a few churches. Giarratana (elev. 520 m, pop. 3386), the new town, has a regular gridwork layout, with a few monumental structures: the Baroque church of *S. Bartolomeo* (18th c.); the church of *S. Antonio Abate* (mid-18th c.), in the highest point in the city; the *Chiesa Madre*, with a broad façade, which contains noteworthy canvases from the 18th c.

If you leave Giarratana in the direction of Palazzolo Acrèide, at 1.5 km from the town, turn to the left along a road that runs up to the Monte Lauro (elev. 986 m), and in about 7 km you will reach Monte Casale not far from the site of *Casmene*, a military colony of Syracuse, founded in 644 B.C.

Chiaramonte Gulfi

This town can be reached via a 15 km detour from the state road. Just before you enter the town itself, you will see, amidst the greenery, the sanctuary or *Santuario della Madonna delle Grazie*. From here you can begin a short hike through the pine forest, equipped by the forest rangers for comfortable use. Gulfi, the original settlement that gave rise to the little city that now stands here (elev. 668 m, pop. 8327) was founded in the 12th-13th c., and was short-lived because of the destruction visited upon it in 1299 by the troops of Anjou. The rebirth of this town took place at the behest of Manfredi I Chiaramonte, who rebuilt the new city, enclosed it in strong walls, built a castle, and then dubbed it with the name of his family. The earthquake of 1693 was followed by a reconstruction in the Baroque style. The historic center is well preserved and maintains an easily recognizable medieval structure. Once you reach Piazza Duomo, with the *Chiesa Madre* (S. Maria la Nova) built in the 15th c. and restored in 1770, you will enter the medieval district by following Via S. Paolo, on the right, and then Via S. Giovanni, on the left. The arch or *Arco dell'Annunziata* is the only surviving gate. In the distance, the church of *S. Giovanni Battista* on the higher level dominates the surrounding landscape. One of the most noteworthy monuments of the area is the sanctuary or **Santuario di Gulfi**, located at the edge of town to the north, at a distance of about 3 km.

Monterosso Almo

This town (elev. 691 m, pop. 3403), which existed in Norman times, when it was known as "Monte Johalmo," owes most of its development to Enrico Rosso, count of Aidone, who in the 14th c. built a castle, not a trace of which remains. Monterosso Almo was destroyed by the earthquake of 1693 and was rebuilt in the higher section of the hill. The center of the town is Piazza S. Giovanni, higher up, where a broad staircase leads to the church of *S. Giovanni Battista*, attributed to Vincenzo Sinatra from the school of Rosario Gagliardi. Lower down, in Piazza S. Antonio, stand the other two main churches: the *Chiesa Madre*, rebuilt in the Neo-Gothic style after the earthquake, containing two beautiful holy-water fonts from the 12th c. and a wooden *Crucifix* from the 15th c., and the church of *S. Antonio*, dating from the 18th c.

Vizzini

First there were prehistoric settlements, and then later, perhaps, the Roman city of Bidis, mentioned by Pliny and Cicero, and and then later traces in the city layout of a Moorish period – these are features of the poorly documented origins of Vizzini (elev. 586 m, pop. 8698). There is a fair amount of information from the 13th c. on concerning the development and history of the medieval city. The castle, the city walls, and the extension to the east of the present town were all destroyed by the earthquake of 1693. The disaster left very few traces of the main architectural structures, some of which can be recognized in the structures of the *Chiesa Madre*, dedicated to the patron saint, St. Gregory; there is a Catalonian Gothic portal that provides evidence of an earlier building, perhaps the ancient Palazzo di Città. The center of the city is the square, Piazza Umberto I, overlooked by the city hall, or *Palazzo Municipale* (19th c.) and an 18th-c. aristocratic palazzo which once belonged to the family of the author Giovanni Verga who, born in Vizzini, set some of his novellas here. From Piazza Umberto I you can easily reach a number of interesting churches. Via S. Giovanni leads to the church of *S. Giovanni Battista*, which was enlarged in the 16th c. and rebuilt in the 18th c.; it has three aisles and stucco decorations. From Via Vittorio Emanuele you can reach the church of the *Minori Osservanti*; of particular note here, on the main altar, is a *Virgin Mary with Christ Child* by Antonello Gagini (1527).

Grammichele

Grammichele (elev. 520 m, pop. 13,609) is a "planned city." It was founded immediately following the violent earthquake of the Val di Noto in order to prevent the scattering of the survivors of Occhiolà, a rural village that was completely destroyed. Carlo Maria Carafa Branciforte, assisted by the monk and architect Michele da Ferla, ordered the complex design. The idea of this

The hexagonal central square of Grammichele with the Chiesa Madre and the city hall

115

learned prince was inspired by the model of of the fortress-city of Palmanova in Friuli, built in 1593; this basic inspiration was enriched by the prince's love for sundials. The result was a design that is still preserved in the city hall, or Palazzo Comunale, where there is a depiction of "Magnus Michael" (which is a version of "Grammichele") carved into a panel of slate. The structure of the city is organized in accordance with a system of concentric hexagons spreading out from the large square, a sort of center of gravity. The original design was abandoned as early as the late 19th c., with a progressive collapse of the radiating lines. In the hexagonal central square stand the city hall or *Palazzo Comunale* designed by the architect Carlo Sa-

da in 1896, which houses the new *Museo Civico (open Tue.-Sat., 9-1; Tue. and Thu. also 4-6; Sun. by request; closed Mon.)* with its funeral collections from the Terravecchia necropolis (6th c. B.C.). Near it is the *Chiesa Madre*, dedicated to St. Michael and built between 1723 and 1765. Take Via Roma to reach *Piazza Alessandro Manzoni*, one of the six outlying square plazas, and from there you can continue in a clockwise direction by following the former Via Settima, now Via Cavour, which runs through all of the squares of the outlying districts.

Caltagirone

When you say the name of Caltagirone (elev. 608 m, pop. 39,225; city map below) to a Sicilian, he or she will immediately

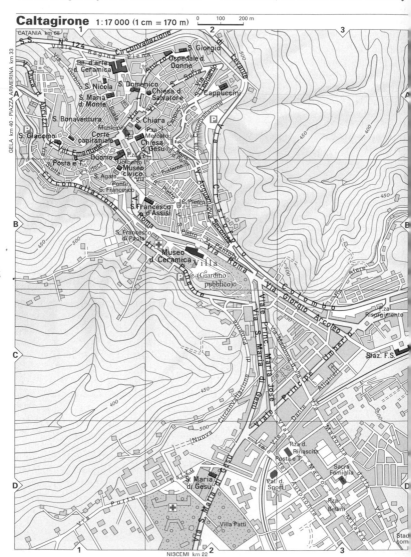

Caltagirone 1 : 17 000 (1 cm = 170 m)

think of a surprising array of colors adorning objects made of terracotta. In Caltagirone, in fact, the tradition of ceramics has very ancient roots. The city has continued this tradition up to the present day, developing new twists to the older ways: among the most recent and most evident new contributions is the facing of the steps of the 17th-c. stairway, the Scala del Monte; the facing was done in 1953. Nowadays this art is in excellent health, and is thriving on the demand of a steady flow of sightseers, as well as the crowds attracted by various cultural sites and activities: a ceramics school and museum, or Istituto d'Arte della Ceramica and Museo della Ceramica; an exhibition of manger scenes (at Christmas) and little terracotta whistles (at Easter).

Numerous archeological finds indicate a continuous human presence here from the Bronze Age to Roman times; one commemoration of the Moors can be seen in the castle to the north of the church of S. Maria del Monte. Roger the Norman conquered it in 1090 with the assistance of a colony of Ligurians who had settled there in 1038-40. Once it had become a state-owned city, protected by walls, Caltagirone began to grow, between the 12th and 17th c., in the form of spread-winged eagle, which is in fact the image that appears in the city coat-of-arms. The crossroads or "croce di strade" made up of Via Principe Amedeo and the stairway or Scala del Monte (north-south) and Corso Vittorio Emanuele and Via S. Sofia (east-west), was established in the 17th c., and it serves to link the main sections of the city's historic growth. These are the castle or Castello, to the north, along with the church of S. Maria del Monte and the monastery, or Convento degli Agostiniani; the church of S. Giorgio to the east; the gate or Porta S. Pietro demolished in the 19th c., and the monastery or Convento dei Francescani, to the south; and the church of S. Giacomo, to the west. In the 17th c., the city's nerve center was the Piano di S. Giuliano. Here, an originally Norman church, the church of S. Giuliano, stands alongside the Casa Senatoria, now the art gallery, or Galleria Luigi Sturzo, and the Corte Capitaniale. Ravaged by the earthquake of 1693, Caltagirone was rebuilt on the ruins of its old self, with the contribution of the most famed architects of Sicily. This route, which follows the main thoroughfares of the urban layout, offers a homogeneous analysis of the development of the city over the course of the centuries. The entrance to the old city can be said to

lie at the intersection between Viale Principessa Maria José and Via Roma. If you continue along Via Roma, you will pass the public park on the left and get your first glimpse of polychrome majolica, and then you will reach the Teatrino, whose steps lead to the ceramics museum or Museo della Ceramica. A little further along,

The tradition of ceramics is visible everywhere in Caltagirone

on the right, there is a splendid 18th-c. balcony by the ceramist Benedetto Ventimiglia. After you pass the "Tondo Vecchio," on the right will be Piazza S. Francesco d'Assisi, with a convent. This square, which was integrated into the walled city in the 16th c., was linked to the Piano di S. Giuliano with a bridge (1626-66), later decorated with majolicas. At the first wide square you will find the Bourbon prison, now a civic museum (Museo Civico), and the little church of S. Agata, site of the confraternity of ceramists. A little further along you will find Piazza Umberto I, with the ancient pawnshop or "Monte delle Prestanze," linked by two streets with Piazza del Municipio, with which it forms the core of the city: Via Duomo, overlooked by the Duomo and the Corte Capitaniale, and Via Principe Amedeo, an extension of the staircase of S. Maria del Monte, the thoroughfare of the ancient city. Once you have passed the city hall, or Municipio, you will see the spectacular stairway of S. Maria del Monte: this route includes the climb up that stairway, tiring but enjoyable due to the decorations of the 142 steps, as well as a descent at the end of the visit to the medieval city. The ancient districts at the summit of the stairway are marked by the presence of numerous churches: S. Maria del Monte, S. Domenico, Santissimo Salvatore, S. Giorgio (this was the church, in the 11th c., of the Ligurian community). If you take Via Luigi Sturzo, the second axis in the crossroads (in an east-west direction), you will return to Piazza del Municipio and you will continue along Corso Vit-

Thanks to tourism, the production of ceramics has become an important source of local income

torio Emanuele, with its numerous aristocratic palazzi; at the end of the "corso" you will see the church of S. Giacomo. It is worth making a special trip to the *monumental cemetery* or Cimitero Monumentale designed by the architect Giambattista Nicastro in 1866.

Giardino Pubblico (B2). The first projects for clearing the hill, which was uncultivated, date back to 1846, and in 1850 the Bourbon governor commissioned the architect Giovanni Battista Filippo Basile to plan how to revamp the hill. His design took its inspiration from the model of the English garden, and was completed in the Liberty style (Art Nouveau) in the early 20th c.

Museo Regionale della Ceramica* (B2; *open 9-6:30*), or regional museum of ceramics. You enter from the so-called *Teatrino*, a scenic overlook of the city, designed in 1792 by the architect Natale Bonaiuto, comprising a network of ramps alternating with steps and benches adorned with panels and reliefs in polychrome majolica. The Museo, established in 1965, contains many examples of the production of ceramics in Sicily from prehistory to the present day.

S. Francesco d'Assisi (B1-2). This convent was founded by the Blessed Richard (Beato Riccardo), a companion of St. Francis himself: the adjoining church was built in 1226

in the Gothic style, and the Gagini family also worked on it beginning in 1592. Rebuilt following the earthquake in the Baroque style, it was completed with a campanile in 1852. In a chapel adjoining the presbytery are the remains of the original Gothic structure. The nearby bridge or *Ponte di S. Francesco* links the hill of this convent with the plain, or Piano di S. Giuliano: built in 1666, it spans some 50 m with a difference in elevation of more than 15 m. From the bridge, on a clear day, you can see as far as the African Sea and the Ionian Sea.

Museo Civico (B1; *open Tue. and Fri.-Sun., 9:30-1:30 and 4-7*) or civic museum. The building that houses it, erected in 1792 and completed in 1799, served as a prison until 1890. It later became a Monte di Pietà (charitable institution) and served other public functions, and was heavily renovated over time, with the destruction of the main chapel and the torture chamber. In the 1960s, the Museo Civico was moved here, with three sections – history, archeology, and the art gallery.

Duomo (A1). When the Senato decided in 1582 to enlárge the Duomo, or Cathedral, giving it a nave and two aisles, it was the reversal of the orientation of this building – founded by the Normans and dedicated to St. Julian (S. Giuliano) – that constituted the largest change; till then it had been facing west. Destroyed by the earthquake of 1693 and rebuilt in the early 18th c. because of the serious damage it had suffered, the Duomo had its façade demolished in 1838; it was replaced in 1909 by the present-day façade in a floral style (the campanile dates from 1954). *Inside* are many paintings by local artists of the 19th c.; in the left transept is a marble statue of the Gagini school. On the right of the Duomo is the *Corte Capitaniale*, a long single-story building dating from the 16th-17th c.

Scala di S. Maria del Monte (A1). With 142 steps, the stairway or Scala del Monte covers a vertical distance of roughly 50 m, and since 1606 it has joined the higher section of the city with the Piano di S. Giuliano. In 1953 the stairway was rebuilt in volcanic stone and the risers embellished with majolica decorations, with patterns that recapitulate the history of local ceramics. For the feast of St. James (24-25 July) the stairway is lit with more than four thousand oil lamps containing a total of more than five quintals (over a thousand pounds) of oil. Along the stairway there are numerous workshops of ceramists, where it is possible to watch various phases of the production and decoration of ceramic products.

S. Maria del Monte (A1). Once the Chiesa Matrice, this church is thought to date back to Norman times. It is believed that it was built in the main square of the old medieval village. Rebuilt immediately following the earthquake, it still has the *Madonna di Conadomini* on its main altar, a panel of the Lucchese school from the 13th c. The treasury includes exquisite gold work and a silver 15th-c. ostensory.

S. Domenico (or church of the Rosario) and **Santissimo Salvatore** (A1-2). These two churches face each other in the Largo S. Domenico: the first dates from 1801 and is currently used as an auditorium; the other dates from the 19th c. and has an interior enriched with fine stucco work as well as a statue of the Virgin Mary believed to be by Antonello Gagini, 1532.
Since 1963, moreover, it has contained the tomb of Don Luigi Sturzo, the illustrious sociologist who was the mayor of the town in the first decade of the 20th c., and the founder of the Partito Popolare Italiano.

S. Giorgio (A2). Local tradition attributes the foundation of this church to the Genoans who were present in the city as early as 1030. Of the original church all that remains are traces of a pointed-arch portal and sharply splayed narrow loopholes. Rebuilt more than once following the earthquake, the façade remains incomplete (designed in 1830). On the interior, in the second altar on the left, a very fine *Trinity* of the Flemish school (attributed to Rogier van der Weyden).

S. Chiara (A1). This little church was built by Rosario Gagliardi between 1743 and 1748, with a polygonal plan and a curvilinear façade. It possess a rich majolica floor, recently redone. Adjoining it on the site of the Clarissan convent is the old plant of the *Officine Elettriche*, built by Ernesto Basile in 1908 in an Art-Nouveau style.

S. Giacomo (A1). This church dedicated to the patron saint of the town, St. James, was built, according to tradition, at the behest of Conte Ruggero (Roger I). Destroyed almost entirely by the earthquake, it was rebuilt immediately and completed in 1700. On the inside were placed a number of works by the Gagini that had been in the church that was destroyed. Above the central portal is the great marble coat-of-arms of the city carved by Gian Domenico Gagini; the portal of the relics in the left transept is by Antonuzzo Gagini. The statue of *St. James* (S. Giacomo) is by Vincenzo Archifel (1518).

Gela*

In a context where archeological relics recall to a rich past, the chaotic urban expansion of Gela (elev. 46 m, pop. 77,562; city

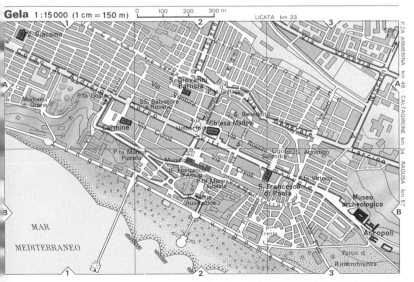

Gela 1:15000 (1 cm = 150 m)

map on p. 119) over the last few decades flies in the face of common sense.

In 668 B.C., colonists from Rhodes and Crete founded the city on the eastern slope of the hill, and they soon dominated coast and plain. The town was destroyed by Carthage in 405 B.C. and was refounded in 338 B.C., only to be razed to the ground in 282 B.C. by the Mamertines and by Phintia, the tyrant of Agrigento, who moved the inhabitants of the city into the town of Phintias, present-day Licata. Scattered to the four winds for more than 1500 years, it was refounded by Frederick II of Swabia in 1230 with the name of Terranova on the site of archaic Gela, between the present-day Piazza Umberto I and Largo Calvario, which are crossed by the perpendicular lines of Corso Vittorio Emanuele and Via G. Marconi. Becoming a feudal holding at the turn of the 15th c., the city was enclosed with walls in 1582. The urban perimeter was thus contained until the 19th c., and the city began to take on structure with a gridwork of streets at right angles. In 1927, Terranova assumed its ancient name of Gela. The development of the city has its negative aspects; one is the huge petrochemical plant run by ANIC, which was built in 1961: this self-contained complex has greatly contributed to the chaotic and jumbled growth of the city, as well as doing overt damage in the form of pollution.

The tour can be broken down into three parts. The first part, dedicated to the medieval layout of the city, begins in Piazza E. Mattei. Once you pass the site of the gate, or Porta Caltagirone (A2), which no longer stands, you will follow Via G. Navarra Bresmes until you reach Piazza Umberto I (A2), where the town's main thoroughfares intersect. Overlooking this square is the main church or *Chiesa Madre*, rebuilt in 1766 with a Neoclassical façade that was completed in 1844. You will turn to the right along Corso Vittorio Emanuele (A-B2-3), the main street of the city, where the townspeople take their evening promenades: around midway, on the right, note

the 18th-c. church of the *Santissimo Salvatore e del Rosario* (A2, 1796). A little further along, Via Trieste on the left leads to the church of the *Carmine* (A1, 1514). At the intersection, with Via G. Matteotti (the intersection corresponds to the site of the gate or Porta Licata demolished in 1860) turn to the left and continue along Via Miramare, skirting the southern walls which still contain two towers built by Frederick II (known as "torri federiciane"). Take Via F. Morello and Via Fratelli Cairoli to reach the church of *S. Francesco d'Assisi* (B2, 17th c.) in Piazza S. Francesco d'Assisi; nearby is the city hall or Municipio. You can then return to Corso Vittorio Emanuele and, turning onto the stretch that runs east toward the Porta Vittoria, you will see on the right the church of *S. Francesco di Paola* (B2-3, 17th c.); on the left, in the Largo Salandra, note the façades of the 15th-c. church of the *Agostiniani* (Augustinians) and the former monastery or *Convento degli Agostiniani* (B3).

The second section of the tour is dedicated to the archeological museum or **Museo Archeologico Regionale***, and to the *Acropolis* (B3; *open 9-1 and 3-7*), which can be reached beyond Porta Vittoria. Established in 1958, the museum has two sections: on the ground floor are finds from the ancient settlement, while the upper floor is devoted to the sanctuaries outside of town, the Greek necropolises, and the territory over which the city had influence. Not far from the museum lies the *acropolis* with the remains of a Doric temple (5th c. B.C.) and of an archaic temple to Athena (6th c. B.C.).

The last part of the tour is of the **archeological area of Capo Soprano*** (A1 off map; *open 9-one hour before sunset*). From Corso S. Aldisio, after you cross the new urban expansion, you will reach Piazza S. Biagio; from there, you can turn off to the left along Via A. Manzoni, reaching Capo Soprano. The high sand dunes have preserved the walls that enclosed the town to the west, which were uncovered between 1948 and 1954.

6 Syracuse and its territory

The special geological structure of eastern Sicily, and its position in the complex interaction of the continental masses and plates in the Mediterranean, has made it a perennial theater of devastating earthquakes as long as it has been an island. The earthquake of 1693, known as the earthquake of the Val di Noto after the area that was particularly hard-hit, was – both because of the historic moment during which it occurred, and because of the consequences that it triggered – an event that provides us with a way of understanding the nature of sites and buildings in the aftermath of that great earthquake. This is true of the entire south-eastern strip of Sicily to the south of the Piana di Catania. This is equally true for cities that

View of the Ortigia promenade at dusk

were wholly destroyed and cities that were only damaged; the ensuing reconstruction offered an excellent opportunity to endow new cities and new buildings with that unique style of Baroque that in Sicily acquired a radically new and diverse character, unlike the style elsewhere, clearly influenced by what had gone before and by outside influences.

6.1 Syracuse / Siracusa**

Situated in one of the loveliest maritime routes of the Mediterranean Sea, Syracuse (elev. 17 m, pop. 126,282; city map on pp. 128-129) is now a modern and dynamic city which proudly displays its great and noble past. The ideal route for a spectacular arrival in Syracuse is by sea, given the beauty of its natural port, with the island of Ortigia jutting into it. The countryside surrounding the port is broad and green with trees, and crossed by the streams of the Ànapo and the Ciane; behind all this is the ledge of the limestone highland of the Epìpoli; in the distance stands Mount Etna.

Syracuse is a central player in the history of the Mediterranean, in part due to the figures that it produced for culture and the arts:

Epicharmus, a Greek poet; Theocritus, a bucolic poet; Archimedes, physicist and mathematician; Ibn Hamdis, an Arab poet; and, more recently, Salvatore Quasimodo and Elio Vittorini.

The most important cultural event, recurring every two years in May and June, is the performance of ancient tragedies in the Greek theater. In July or in September is the Palio, or horse race, and the Festival of the Sea, while on 13 December there is a celebration of the feast day of the patron saint, St. Lucy; on the first Sunday in May, in the context of the adoration of this same saint, a number of quails are freed, and they flock through the sky over the town. The local crafsmen make paper and papyrus parchment, as well as reproductions, in precious and ordinary metals, of ancient Syracusan coins.

The historical background

A reliable historical chronology indicates 734 B.C. as the year of the foundation of Greek Syracuse by a group of Corinthians under the leadership of Archia, though archeological digs have confirmed traces of earlier human settlements. The two core settlements of the first Greek colony were located on the islet of Ortigia and the adjoining mainland (Akradina), in the area of the Foro Siracusano, and were probably linked at first by an earth causeway, and later by a bridge, probably located in the area behind the main post office or Palazzo delle Poste. In the area around Akradina ran a torrential stream of water, the Syrakò; hence the probable derivation of the name Siracusa. The fact that it had an abundant supply of water from the spring or Fonte Aretusa, and that it was well-defended on every side, were the notable advantages of Ortigia.

The political and economic growth of the city as early as the seventh and sixth c. B.C., and above all the transfer en masse of the population of other Sicilian colonies, ordered by Gelon (the tyrant of Gela, who siezed power in Syracuse in 485 B.C.), triggereda sharp increase in population – over the course of the 5th c. B.C. – and a consequential expansion of the city out beyond the original walls, with the creation of two other districts: "Tyche," situated in the area to the east, and so-called because it is close to a temple of the goddess Tyche (Fortuna), and "Neapolis," the new city, where the archeological park or Parco Archeologico now extends. Three other temples were built in the city to commemorate victorious military exploits, and they can be easily found: the temple of Olympian Zeus (Zeus Olimpico), set on a hill overlooking the river Ànapo, near the port; the temple of Apollo, which can be toured in Piazza Pancali; and the temple of Artemis (Artemide). Gelon was responsible for the construction of the temple of Athena, which

can still be identified in the structures of the Cathedral or Cattedrale; he was also responsible for much of the city's growth. Syracuse soon became one of the most important Greek metropolises of the period, and its burgeoning growth raised concern among its neighbors. The war against Carthage caused the city to come under the rule of the tyrant Dionysius I, who found himself forced to undertake major fortifications: he also moved away the population of the island of Ortigia, which he then transformed into a fortress, putting it exclusively to military use; he enlarged the little port and built an enormous circuit of walls that extends some 22 km, and which enclosed the districts and the terrace of Epìpoli (Epipolis, or "city that stands above"), to the west of the settlement; the strongpoint of this location was the castle or Castello Eurialo. The death of Dionysius, which took place around the middle of the 4th c., triggered a long period of transition. Thus, even with the presence of such major figures as Timoleon and Agathocles and with a policy of alliances aimed at preserving the city's role in the Mediterranean basin, there was no way to stave off defeat, which came in 212 B.C. with plunder and sack by the Romans under the Consul Marcellus. But Marcellus was long stymied by the brilliant techniques of defense developed by Archimedes, and only succeeded in conquering Syracuse after two years of siege.

Syracuse in those days must have been spectacular, with its agora, temples, buildings, and walls. Marcellus himself was captivated by the town, and in the plunder that followed the Roman victory he spared all the religious buildings. Though it remained the capital of Sicily and the residence of the Roman praetors, and despite some modest increase in its stock of monuments, Syracuse entered a phase of decline, with the residential section dwindling in size.

As early as the first few centuries of the Roman empire, Christianity had begun to spread through the ties that the city maintained with the major Syrian and

Statue of Venus emerging from the sea (Museo "Paolo Orsi")

Palestinian towns. In the 3rd c. the first community cemeteries were established, such as the catacombs or Catacombe di S. Lucia, Vigna Cassia, and S. Giovanni; early-Christian religious architecture is exemplified by the churches of S. Pietro and of S. Giovanni Evangelista beneath the crypt of the church of S. Marziano. After a long siege, the city was sacked and devastated by the Moors in A.D. 878. But the Moors left a deep sign of their presence: lanes and courtyards enlivened by markets and small shops are especially typical of the island districts of Graziella and Sperduta. The most significant factor in terms of the city structure, in any case, was the shrinkage of Syracuse, beginning during the last twenty years of the 9th c. and extending to the end of the 19th c. – for an entire millennium, in other words . It dwindled to only the island of Ortigia, which had long been separated from the mainland by a channel. In the definitive expulsion of the Moors from the island, the Normans completed the project that had been begun by the Byzantines under George Maniace: the rebuilding of the ancient fortifications and the construction, at the southernmost tip of Ortigia, of a castle (Castello Maniace).

After a brief period of Angevin rule, Syracuse received enormous economic benefits from the rule of the House of Aragon, especially in its trade with the rest of Europe, trade that left its mark in the great architectural development of the city: the bastions that guard the island and a great many palazzi date from this period. The Black Death of 1348 and the feudal conflicts brought Syracuse under Spanish rule for a long period; during that time great fortifications were built and very fine architectural projects were completed. The famines of the 15th c., the earthquake of 1542, and the crushing taxes imposed on the citizenry to pay for the construction of the fortifications, together with the gradual decline in trade, led to the flight of the great families of town, to the degree that by the end of the 16th c., the population of Syracuse was no more than 14,000. One crucial event in the city's history was the terrible earthquake of 11 January 1693. It did not, generally speaking, cause irreparable damage to the buildings of Syracuse, nor did it leave marks in the fabric of the city, but it did offer an occasion for renovations in the style typical of that period. Restorations of damaged buildings were undertaken, in some cases through partial demolition, and often the interiors and the façades were modified, giving the city an 18th-c. appearance, and concealing its ancient aspect.

In 1865 Syracuse was made provincial capital again, and this date was an important one for its future growth. The establishment here of government offices and the considerable growth in population caught the city unprepared, enclosed as it still was within the walls of Ortigia. There was a rush to build upwards, filling in every empty lot; the height of feverish construction madness followed the law suppressing the convents and monasteries (1866) and the demolition, beginning in 1886, of the complex of Spanish fortifications. In urbanistic terms, the most significant projects were the great demolition projects done during the Fascist era, and in particular the construction of Via del Littorio, now Corso Matteotti; while the great boom of the 1950s and the 1960s launched a period of living alongside major industrial plants – however uncomfortable and at times even unprofitable that proved to be. All the same, the city's allure has survived sack, plunder, sieges, earthquakes, rampant development and speculation, industrialization: indeed, it has been this succession of often traumatic events that has triggered an interesting process of stratification and juxtaposition, which can be seen at all and any scale.

The tour of this city can be broken down into two routes starting from the archeological area, one heading toward the mainland and the other toward the island of Ortigia.

The mainland

This mainland route runs through three of the five districts of the pentapolis of Syracuse (Epìpoli, Neàpoli, Tyche) which developed with the growth of the Greek city; several of the districts were abandoned in certain historical periods because of the concentration of population on Ortigia.

The tour, logically enough, begins with the Castello Eurialo, almost a preview of these imposing Greek fortifications on the highland of the Epìpoli.

Castello Eurialo** (plan on page 124; A2, off map, p. 128; *open 9-one hour before sunset*). This castle stands at a distance of roughly 8 km from the center of the city, but it was linked to the city as part of the overall defenses of Greek Syracuse, and is both the most spectacular and historically correct approach to the city. Going up to the highland or Altopiano di Epìpoli means admiring not only Syracuse in its Greek roots, but al-

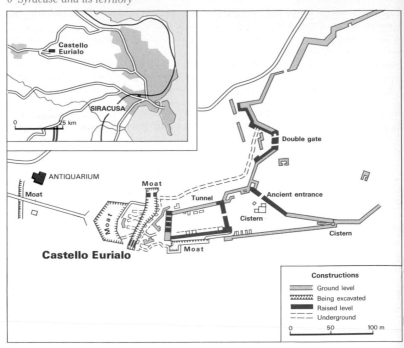

Constructions	
	Ground level
	Being excavated
	Raised level
	Underground

so admiring one of the finest panoramic views of Sicily from a very evocative location. Built at the turn of the 4th c. B.C. by Dionysius, it did its job very well, thanks to the military genius of Archimedes, until the fall of Syracuse to Roman might. Its strategic location and its structure – interior and exterior, built in accordance with new ideas that were innovative at the time – make this a jewel of military engineering; it is however wise to carry a map to find one's way in the vast expanse of ruins extending over one-and-a-half hectares. Today the bulk is divided in two parts – the western is rectangular, the eastern trapezoidal – by a wall into which that has a gate with megalithic archway. The western part features some defensive structures: a *fort*, once linked to the castle through a drawbridge; *five towers* on which were the platforms for the catapults; a series of *moats* which strengthened the defensive system. The eastern part was linked to the walls of Dionysius, and is characterized by three cisterns and a complex network of tunnels, hidden passages, and movable stairways.

Teatro Greco** (A-B1), or Greek theater. The monument that stands here today is the most important structure in the archeological park (*open 9-two hours before sunset*), as well as the greatest expression of theatrical architecture and scenic technology from Greek times to survive to the present day. It is the result of an expansion made at the behest of Hiero II in the 3rd c. B.C. of an existing theater that dated back to the 5th c.: tradition records, with considerable pride, that there were major performances here of tragedies by Aeschylus, but the theater was also used for popular assemblies. Completely carved out of living rock, it is divided into three separate areas: the cavea, the orchestra, and the scaena. The *cavea*, the area reserved for spectators, has a diameter of 138 m, is subdivided into nine sectors, and is marked roughly midway up by a corridor, the diazoma. The northern section of this corridor, or diazoma, is adorned with moldings and has inscriptions of the names of a number of deities and important personalities, after whom various sectors were named. The areas of the *orchestra* and the *scaena*, as we see them today, are the fruit of transformation which the Romans undertook to adapt the theater for their own uses. The abandonment of the monument began with the invasions of the Vandals and the Goths in A.D. 440 and the definitive decline of classical culture and traditions, and culminated with the partial destruction of the building on the orders of Charles V in 1526, who had much marble removed from it to be used in the construction of fortifications. The cavea of the theater is overlooked by a *terrace* carved into the rock; at the center of the northern wall of this terrace you may note a large manmade grotto dedicated to the Muses, in which there was a bubbling fount of water from the Roman aqueduct; the water flowed into a channel cut into the far wall and was then channeled into the theater's hydraulic system. The rock wall to the west is dotted with little niches for votive images linked to the hero cult (pinakes).

To the west of the Theater is **Via dei Sepolcri** (A1), a road carved between two steep walls with a number of votive niches. Further on is the *Santuario di Apollo Termine*.

Ara di Ierone II (B2) or altar of Hiero II. This sacrificial altar must have been truly impressive, to judge from its base, the only part that survives, which measured 198 x 22.80 m. Still visible on the north side are the feet of one of the two telamons that stood at the entrance. Before the altar there was probably a majestic porticoed square at the center of which was a pool, still visible, with a base in the middle on top of which stood a statue of Zeus.

Anfiteatro Romano (B2) or Roman amphitheater. Dating from Roman times, the large elliptical amphitheater, 140 x 119 m, is carved in part out of living rock; the upper section of the cavea, formed of square-hewn blocks, has disappeared, destroyed by plunder and by the elements. The size of this structure is outdone only by the Colosseum and the Arena of Verona. The cavea is subdivided into quadrants by little staircases, and is crossed by two corridors. It is still possible to make out the inscriptions on the stone, which served to identify seating. Under the little nearby church of *S. Nicolò* you can still see the "piscina" or pool used in the cleaning of the arena, which allowed flooding of the arena for the staging of naval battles.

Latomie* (A2) or quarries. These are ancient rock quarries from which, as early as Greek times, large blocks of grey-white limestone were extracted for use in buildings and walls, giving the city its unmistakable and distinctive color. What were once dark grottoes have been opened up by the collapse of the vaults following earthquakes, and strong sunlight and great humidity have caused the growth of luxuriant vegetation in those former quarries. The white limestone walls, eroded into weird shapes of all sorts, are now dotted with citrus trees, immense ficus trees, magnolias, and delicate maidenhair ferns. On the interior of the archeological area is the most famous group of quarries, ranging in height from 25 to 47 m. The group, at the foot of the Greek theater (Teatro Greco), is known as **Latomia del Paradiso** **, and is renowned for the curiosity of the *Ear of Dionysius* (*Orecchio di Dionisio*), a cave which, because of its shape and its remarkable acoustic properties, gave rise to a legend that the tyrant had the place built and used it to listen to the conversations of the prisoners enclosed within. It is far more likely that the Orecchio di Dionisio, originally dug as a rock quarry, later served as a sounding board for the performances of classical theater that were held in the adjoining theater. Near the Orecchio di Dionisio is a huge manmade grotto supported by pillars carved into the rock: this is the remarkable *Grotta dei Cordari**, so called because ropes ("corde") were manufactured here, making use of the humidity that is so

The Orecchio di Dionisio, an old rock quarry

abundant in the grotto, as moisture is required to make good rope.

For years it has been forbidden to enter the **Latomia dei Cappuccini** (A5), which lies at the foot of the Convento dei Cappuccini, for safety reasons; you can, however, see it perfectly from up on Via Acradina. The latomia is quite vast and labyrinthine, and the process of erosion has produced bizarre forms there: enormous caverns, natural bridges, pylons. The odd relationship between nature and man is gently underscored by the little flight of steps created to get over the pits that have been created by the process of excavation in the "latomia."

Piazza S. Lucia (B4). The church of *S. Lucia fuori le Mura*, in popular tradition, was supposedly built on the same site in which the Syracusan virgin, St. Lucy, met her martyrdom in A.D. 303, not far from the catacomb of St. Lucy (Catacombe di S. Lucia). Originally founded in Byzantine times, it now stands as a basilica with nave, aisles and semicircular apses: the oldest part (portal, apses, and the first two orders of the campanile) date back to the 12th c., while the rose window dates from the 14th c. The portico, which extends along the elevation and one of the two sides, was the work of Pompeo Picherali (1727). The famous painting by Caravaggio depicting the *Burial of Saint Lucy* (1609), formerly in the apse of the church, is a work that is stylistically surprising and daring given the artistic culture of the period, and it is now in the Galleria Regionale, in Palazzo Bellomo. Alongside the church, and linked to it by an underground passage, is the octagonal chapel or *Cappella del Sepolcro* built by Giovanni Vermexio in 1630 to contain the tomb of St. Lucy, whose body was however never moved here (it is still in Venice, in the church of S. Geremia).

Museo Archeologico Regionale "Paolo Orsi" ** (A3-4; plan below), the regional archeological museum. Located on the interior of the Villa Landolina, a large park abounding in historical relics (prisons, a cemetery, a number of pagan hypogea or underground chambers), this building, with a triangular shape, fits into the setting as if camouflaging itself. With its exhibition area of 9000 sq. m, the museum, built to plans by Franco Minissi, has since 1988 housed the collections that previously were housed in the historic building in Piazza del Duomo, which had – with the expansion of the collections – become insufficient by this point; it provides a complete presentation of the civilizations that have succeeded one another on this territory. At the center of the building a large circular room is not only the focal and physical point of reference for the museum – in this room one can also find all necessary information concerning the history of the collections and the contents of the three major exhibition areas in which those collections are displayed. *Sector A*, which begins with a closed geological overview of the Ibleo territory, is dedicated to prehistory and early history, from the Paleolithic to the period of Greek colonization. *Sector B* is dedicated to the history of the Greek colonies in Sicily, with special reference to Megara Hyblaea and Syracuse. From Megara Hyblaea we should mention the earliest ceramics and a number of splendid sculptures*, including a funerary statue of the physician Sambrotidas from the middle of the 6th c. B.C. and, from the same era, a

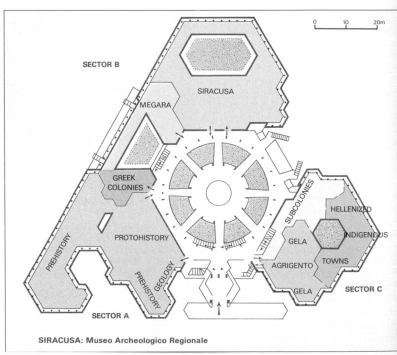

SIRACUSA: Museo Archeologico Regionale

statue depicting a mother nursing twin boys, made of painted limestone. Following these is a series of finds that constitute the funerary furnishing found in the necropolises of the city. The part concerning Syracuse opens with a splendid copy from Roman times of the **Venere Anadiomene**** (meaning "Venus emerging from the sea") found in 1804 by Saverio Landolin; it is also known as the Landolina Venus. Next come collections of statuary and largely ceramic materials from excavations done in the district of the Akradina (Piazza Vittoria) on the sanctuary of Demeter and Kore, and then the funerary furnishings and architectural terracottas from the Temple of Apollo. Lastly, in *Sector C* there are finds from Eloro, a Syracusan outpost along the coast to the south, and from the subcolonies of Akrai, Kasmenai, and Kamarina, including a terracotta group intended for the summit of the roof of a religious building. Furthermore, there is notable material from the Hellenized indigenous towns in the Sicilian hinterland and the major Doric colonies of Gela and Agrigento.

At n. 66 in Viale Teocrito is the **Museo del Papiro** (*open 9-1:30; closed Mon.*) dedicated to the papyrus, a plant that is the symbol of Syracuse. The museum tells the story of the century-old techniques for working the plant. On exhibit are also very rare documents on papyrus scrolls.

Catacombe di S. Giovanni* (A3) or catacombs of St. John. The church of Syracuse has played a major role in the history of Christianity, a clear indicator of the city's importance even in the face of its progressive decline as a result of the Roman conquest. The most important catacombs are the Catacombe di S. Lucia, di Vigna Cassia, and di S. Giovanni (*the only ones that are open to the public; 9-12 and 2:30-5; closed Mon.*). They date back to the 4th c. and present a regular gridwork structure that was built by enlarging an old Greek aqueduct (traces of which can still be seen in the vault of the main corridor). The galleries lead to monumental chapels that, due to their shape, are known as "rotonde" or rotundas: the handsome sarcophagus known as the Sarcofago di Adelfia was found here. Adjoining the catacombs are the remarkable *crypt of S. Marciano* (St. Marcianus, first bish-

op of Syracuse; 6th c.) and, above it, the church of **S. Giovanni Evangelista**, whose altar stands on a line with the tomb beneath it. In the *crypt*, Byzantine in layout, four pillars were built with four capitals

A collection of vases at the Museo "Paolo Orsi"

depicting the four evangelists; these date back to Norman times. The Byzantine church, of which the apse still stands, was the city's first cathedral ("duomo"), and was divided into nave and aisles by columns that still exist. The western façade provides clear evidence of the renovation done during the Norman period, but the harshest blow was that struck by the earthquake of 1693, which caused the collapse of the roof, which was not replaced.

Santuario della Madonna delle Lacrime (B3; *open 7-12 and 4-7*). Built to commemorate the miraculous appearance of tears on an image of the Virgin Mary in 1953, this building, begun in 1966, was completed only much later due to ballooning budgets and to great outcry over its size and height. Designed as an immense cone some 90 m tall, today the sanctuary represents an unmistakable feature on the city's skyline.

The island of Ortigia

The approach to Ortigia best suited to its island nature is of course by sea: the entrance of the Porto Grande consists of a narrow passage emphasized to the left by point, or Punta del Plemmirio and to the right by the towers of the Castello Maniace. Continuing along, you will see a succession of palazzi with a warm golden hue, campaniles, and cupolas of churches, until you reach a broad square in which the eye seeks out the mythical spring, or Fonte Aretusa; and then there is the tree-lined boulevard of the Lungomare, and above it the lovely promenade, or Passeggio Adorno. For those who enter this little islet (the "scoglio," or "shoal" to the people of Syracuse, not even one square kilometer of surface area) from the mainland, on the other hand, there is a different but no less fascinating impression. You leave behind the modern districts and anonymous blocks of buildings, and as soon as you cross the bridge or Ponte Umbertino you are immediately swept up in a world of continuous discoveries, where even the traces of the many eras that followed one on the heels of the other – Greek, Norman, Aragon, Baroque – give a harmonious and unified character to the setting. Every district, historically divided by the main thoroughfares (Via Dione, Via Roma and Via Amalfitania, Via della Maestranza), presents its own characteristics and its own specific qualities, faithfully noted in the place names. Everything tells a story: the temples, the palazzi, the shafts of columns, the courtyards, the façades, the town walls, the portals, the iron work. Setting out from the square that lies before the archeological area and moving along Viale Paolo Orsi, Via Columbia, and Via Elorina, with a stop at the *Ginnasio Romano* (a monumental complex dating from the 1st c. A.D., including a theater, a quadriporticus, and a temple), and the roads that skirt the wharf or Molo S. Antonio, you will find yourself on the bridge or Ponte Nuovo, the only way for cars to get onto Ortigia. We would suggest that you park in this area and continue on foot by one of two routes (or one of three, if you choose also consider the most fascinating of routes, the trip around Ortigia by sea; at the Riva della Posta there are usually plenty of fishing boats that can be hired for this trip). The first route is the trip around the island by land, which emphasizes the relationship between Ortigia and the sea: from Riva Garibaldi and Viale Giuseppe Mazzini you will reach the Largo Porta Marina, and from there you can follow the entire Passeggio Adorno and the Lungomare Alfeo as far as Piazza Federico di Svevia. The Lungomare Ortigia marks the furthest section of the island overlooking the open sea, and by following the successive roads – Via Eolo and Via dei Tolomei – you will hook up with the Lungomare di Levante, which ends at the Riva Nazario Sauro, at the Porto Piccolo. The second route penetrates inland into the center of the island: from Piazza Pancali to the end of the so-called "straightaway" or Rettifilo (Corso Umberto), you will then reach Piazza Archimede via Corso Matteotti, and then by following Via Roma, Via Capodieci, and Via Pompeo Picherali, you will reach Piazza del Duomo. From that square you can enter Via Saverio Landolina and, after returning to Piazza

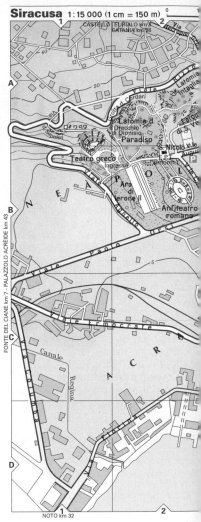

FONTE DEL CIANE km 7 - PALAZZOLO ACRÉIDE km 43

Siracusa 1:15 000 (1 cm = 150 m)

Archimede by Via Amalfitania, you will enter Via della Maestranza, at the end of which, along Via Vittorio Veneto, you can return to the Lungomare di Levante.

The Marina (port) and the Passeggio Adorno (E4-5). The broad waterfront boulevard or Lungomare, a tree-shaded promenade and, above it and running parallel, the promenade or Passeggio Adorno, are ideal places from which to admire the incomparable panoramic view of the Porto Grande, this vast body of water that witnessed many great battles and which in terms of size and shape seems a lake rather than a branch of the sea. The modernization of the jetty of the port did not result in a total demolition of the town walls, and indeed atop the high enclosure wall that formed part of the old Spanish bastions the 19th-c. "hanging"

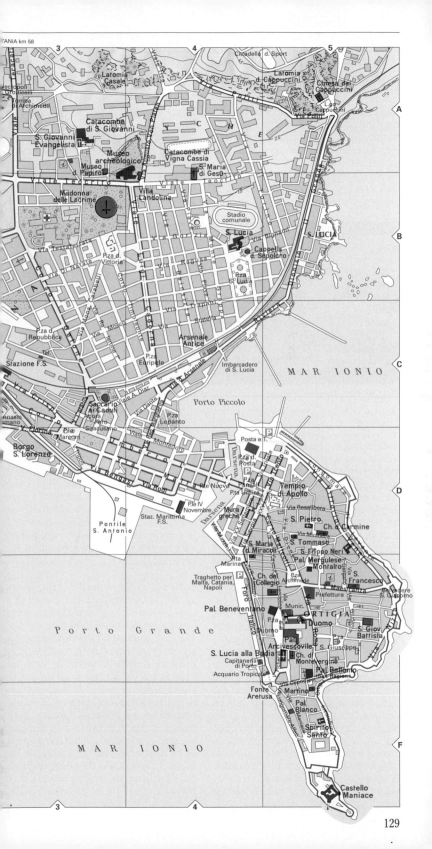

promenade now runs. It is marked by a succession of pink and golden palazzi culminating in two large buildings that stand side by side, the old hotels *Albergo Miramare* and *Hôtel des Etrangères*; the town still hopes that these hotels will be adequately restored. The two points linking the Marina and the Passeggio Adorno are the *Porta Marina*, one of the entrance gates that formed part of the 16th-c. Spanish system of fortifications of the city, and the little villa overlooking the aquarium or Acquario, currently being restored, which leads to the area of the spring or Fonte Aretusa.

each side, and it formed part of the impressive system of structures that included earlier works of fortification. Its name came from the name of the Byzantine general George Maniace who had built a defensive outpost on the same site. The castle stands on the furthest point of the island, atop a rocky promontory, isolated by a manmade channel or moat; the imposing square, enclosed by massive cylindrical corner towers, shows a refined construction technique that made use of three types of stone: limestone and volcanic stone for the square-hewn blocks and sand-

The Castello Maniace situated on the furthest point of the island of Ortigia

Fonte Aretusa* (F5). This thousand-year-old freshwater spring, once enclosed by walls and now populated by ducks, grey mullets, and papyrus plants, is one of the loveliest and most charming places in Syracuse. Legend has it that the nymph Aretusa, a lovely handmaiden of Artemis, was transformed by the goddess into a spring in the forests of the Elide, in order to preserve the nymph from the unwanted attentions of Alpheus, the river god, who had fallen in love with her: fleeing underground across the Ionian Sea, Arethusa emerged on Ortigia. But Alpheus, unwilling to resign himself to the loss, followed her and joined her in the same pool of water. The basin of the spring was created in 1843 and is now populated by ducks and papyrus plants.

Castello Maniace* (F5; *closed for restoration*). From the spring or Fonte Aretusa, if you follow the Lungomare Alfeo you will reach Piazza Federico di Svevia; from here, the tour of the rest of the circuit around the island by land is blocked by an iron gate barring entrance to a military area that is exceedingly difficult to get into; in this area stands the massive structure of the Castello Maniace. This monumental, perfectly square, fortress was built in 1239 by Frederick II with ample dimensions of 51 m on

stone for the fill-rock. Because of the Spanish modifications such as the gate or Porta Vermexiana at the drawbridge, and the changes after the earthquake of 1693 and the great fire caused by the explosion of the powder magazine in 1704, as well as the various uses to which it has been put in more recent years (first as a prison and later as a barracks), the castle has been renovated in many sections with respect to the original plan; that plan can however still be understood clearly.

Lungomare di Levante (D-E5). The history of Ortigia is essentially the history of a fortress-town whose dominant problem was always defending itself from the sea. The cartography that has survived, and a scholarly analysis of the traces of the walls that are still visible, as well as the numerous monuments and structures that survive, allow us now to describe with some certainty the city's complex system of defenses. The entire Lungomare di Levante, even though it was pounded by the open sea and by powerful winds, still preserves most of its military works: the bastion or Bastione S. Giovannello, the platform or Piattaforma Cannella (or Piattaforma di S. Domenico), and the Piattaforma di S. Giacomo stand virtually intact.

To discover another aspect of Ortigia you can venture along *Via Resalibera* into the **Moorish district** (or Quartiere Arabo), where the twisting narrow streets offer protection from the gusts of sea winds and the heat of the sun, creating a cool setting rendered more pleasant by a complex interplay of light and shadow.

Temple of Apollo (D5). The calling card, so to speak, of Ortigia for those who come from the landward side is presented by the ruins of the temple of Apollo in Piazza Pancali, one of the first temples built by the ancient Greeks in Syracuse and one of the oldest temples in Sicily. The fact that it was dedicated to Apollo is shown by an inscription on the stylobate. The ruins that we now admire have withstood the powerful transformations that have affected this structure, located as it is in a strategic point between the older layout and the more recent urban expansion: it was used as a church in the Byzantine period, a mosque in the Moorish period, again as a church under the Normans, and finally it was incorporated into a 16th-c. barracks by the Spaniards. It was not until the turn of the 20th c. that the temple, freed of all its accretions and superstructures, was finally allowed to breathe again.

Piazza Archimede (E5). The long straight thoroughfare of Corso Matteotti was once known as Via del Littorio, and in the stern, square-hewn buildings that line its course, show signs of the brutal demolition done in the heart of the city by the Fascist regime. The street opens out what is considered the warm and welcoming drawing room of Ortigia: Piazza Archimede. Set at the center of the square is a little *fountain*, with burbling jets of water, depicting Diana the Huntress surrounded by handmaidens, sirens and tritons. Overlooking the square is, among other buildings, the *Palazzo Lanza-Bucceri* with its elegant twin-light mullioned windows, along with the *Palazzo Platamone*, also called Casa dell'Orologio or house of the clock; in the courtyard, there is a 15th-c. staircase in the Catalonian Gothic style. At the northeastern corner, is Via Montalto, which gives its name to the **Palazzo Montalto***, a building that may possess the most handsome 14th-c. façade of all Syracuse, punctuated with exquisite twin- and triple-light mullioned windows; an elegant aedicule with a Latin inscription recalls the year of its construction, 1397.

Galleria Regionale* (E5; *open 9-1; Wed. and Fri., also 3-6:30; holidays, 9-1:30; closed Mon. morn.*). This regional art gallery is lo-cated in the former monastery or Monastero di S. Benedetto, which in turn comprises the 14th-c. *Palazzo Parisi* and the 13th-c. *Palazzo Bellomo*. The latter, the larger of the two, is characterized on the ground floor by the distinctive architectural features of the Swabian period (the portal, the masonry structure), while on the upper floor there are clear signs of the renovations made to the structure in the subsequent Catalonian period. Aside from sizable collections of sculpture and painting dating from the high Middle Ages to modern times (the splendid **Annunciation**** by Antonello da Messina, 1474, and the **Burial of St. Lucy**** by Caravaggio from the church of S. Lucia, on the mainland, 1609, and *statues* by the Gagini family and by Francesco Laurana), there are noteworthy collections of the applied arts: silversmith and goldsmith work, ivory, coral work, majolica, religious furnishings, illuminated codices, furniture, ceramics, and terracotta.

Duomo** (E5; plan below). The present-day Cathedral of Syracuse or Duomo di

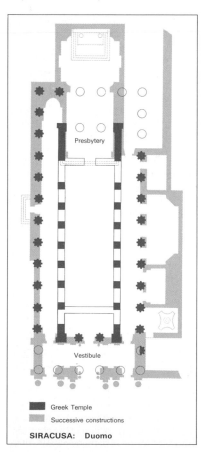

Greek Temple

Successive constructions

SIRACUSA: Duomo

Siracusa, stands on the highest point on the island, a location that has always made this a sacred spot. Here is the most astonishing example of the fascinating accretion and layering and coexistence of styles that is so characteristic of Ortigia: inside of this Cathedral, survive elements of a Doric temple dedicated to Athena dating from the earliest decades of the 5th c. B.C., while below it you see clear signs of Sicilian civilization and what is thought to be an altar ("ara") dating back three centuries earlier. The temple is a hexastyle (with a six-columned front) peripteros, which means a building surrounded by a single row of columns; of the 36 original columns, no fewer than 24 are still in their place, cemented in but perfectly visible in the masonry of the Cathedral. In the central part, of course, stood the cella, on the walls of which were scenes of the battles fought on horseback by Agathocles against the Carthaginians, as Cicero noted admiringly. The transformation into a Christian church was done in the Byzantine era, when a wall was raised, enclosing the columns, and when eight arches were cut in either wall of the cella, thus creating a basilica. Its appearance must have been much more splendid in Norman times, when the church was covered with exquisite mosaics, which, sadly, have since been lost. The earthquakes of 1545 and 1693 caused the façade to collapse ruinously; it was rebuilt in accordance with plans by Andrea Palma in a pure Sicilian Baroque style.

Palazzo Municipale (E5). Formerly the senate building, or Palazzo Senatoriale, this palazzo was built in 1629 on a site in which recent excavations have unearthed relics of an Ionic temple from the 6th c. B.C., dedicated to Artemis but never completed. The work of the Spanish architect Juan Vermexio, nicknamed the lizard, or "Lucertolone," it bears his unmistakable signature: a small lizard carved into the stone at the left corner of the cornice. Facing the town hall or Palazzo Municipale, stands the *Palazzo Beneventano del Bosco*, which still preserves part of its original medieval structure; it was embellished during the Baroque period with lavish decorative elements in the façade and in the courtyard.

Via della Maestranza and Via Vittorio Veneto (E-D5). In architectural terms, these two streets are the richest in the city; they are a succession of Baroque palazzi, their

golden walls adorned with cornices, mascarons, and splendid wrought-iron balconies supported by equally richly-sculpted brackets; inside these palazzi are sometimes hidden far older structures. If you set out from Piazza Archimede you will see the *Palazzo Impellizzeri*, *Palazzo Bonanno* (now housing the tourist office or Azienda Autonoma di Turismo), and *Palazzo Bufardeci* (with its interesting setting on the interior of the courtyard); past here, a lovely little square, or piazzetta, is overlooked by the handsome façade of the church of *S. Francesco* (or church of the Immacolata). If you turn sharply to the right, along Via della Giudecca you will enter the district that housed the large Jewish community; sadly, almost nothing survives of the original rooms. Return along Via della Maestranza, and, as you head down toward the water, you may note other palazzi, among them the *Palazzo Lanza*, the sinuous *Palazzo Rizza*, and a second *Palazzo Impellizzeri*. Also along Via Vittorio Veneto – which meets the end of Via della Maestranza and runs down toward the little marina or Porto Piccolo just inland of the open sea – you may note a line of fine large palazzi or "palazzotti" which still display the graceful style of the Spanish.

Fonte Ciane

The papyrus plant is one of the many treasures that nature has bestowed upon Syracuse, and it has of course been long

The papyrus plant grows wild along the banks of the river Ciane

renowned for its use in the manufacture of paper. Long strips are obtained from the slender stalk of the plant; they are first allowed to soak or steep in a special vegetal solution, then spread out and arranged in a woven crosshatch, first vertically and then horizontally, and are pressed with a roller and joined with a glue made from the stalk of the plant itself. You can watch all the phases of manufacture and the current state of the craft of papermaking with papyrus in various workshops throughout Syracuse, the most noteworthy of which are located in the area around the Museo Archeologico or archeological museum and the gate or Porta Marina a Ortigia. It is also possible to take a boat from the Marina di Siracusa and steam along the banks of the *river Ciane* to the spring or Fonte Ciane, which venerated for the last few millennia, and where it is believed that Pluto plunged downward into the earth following the abduction of Proserpine. This area is protected by a nature preserve or *Riserva Naturale Fiume Ciane e Saline di Siracusa*, established in 1984.

6.2 Noto and the coastline south of Syracuse

The appearance of the southern strip of the Syracuse territory, or Siracusano (route map below), is fairly homogeneous in terms of landscape. Much of the territory, comprising the southeastern extensions of the Iblean massif, is characterized by numerous "cave," deep cuts in the limestone of the highland carved out by streams and rich in luxuriant vegetation. Differing from this typology is the coastal strip, which is flat and sandy and dotted with many marshes. Even more homogeneous is the cultural nature of

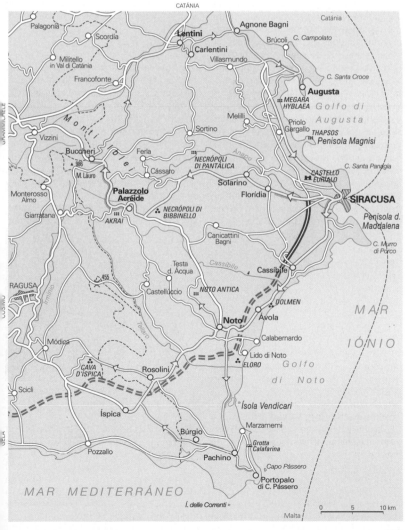

these rural districts or "contrade," marked by a shared historical heritage that dates back as far as prehistoric times, with the spread of the culture of Castelluccio: from the village of that name not far from Noto, it spread over the entire southeastern area of Sicily from the 18th to the 15th c. B.C. The rise of the mighty city of Syracuse in the 8th c. B.C. and its historical and artistic hegemony over the entire territory were two further elements of cultural unification. Nowadays in this area there is an alternation of specialized crops – such as almonds in Àvola and Noto and the vineyards in Pachino – with more traditional uses of the land such as grazing and other sowable crops.

You will leave Syracuse along Via Elorina, and then you will continue south along state road 115, crossing the rivers Ànapo and Ciane. Once you are past Cassìbile you will go through (24 km) Àvola, a large farming town renowned for the production and export of almonds and the distinctive local sweets made from those almonds, and then (after another 8.5 km) you will reach Noto, which is rightly considered to be the capital of Sicilian Baroque. At the crossroads, or Bivio Testa dell'Acqua, near the town, you will find directions to the ruins of ancient Noto, long silenced witnesses of a once-prosperous past. You may then abandon the main route and get onto a provincial road that runs 22 km from Noto to Pachino, in a luminous landscape covered with vineyards and almond groves. A detour not far from the mouth of the river Tellaro will allow you to reach the ruins of the city of Eloro, and in the nearby Contrada Cannedi it is possible to visit the ruins of a Roman villa (the *Villa of the Tellaro*, dating back to the 4th c. A.D.). The charm of the natural setting in this area is protected by a nature preserve, the Riserva Naturale di Vendìcari, which lies just before the township of Pachino. From here you can reach Portopalo, Capo Pàssero, and the island or Isola delle Correnti, the extreme southernmost point of Sicily, which in geographic terms lies further south than Tunis. From Pachino it is just 19.5 km to Ìspica and then, again on state road 115 for another 5.5 km, Rosolini, from which you must go to see the Cava d'Ìspica. Once you pass the Contrada Belliscala with its wine cellar or "Cantina Sociale Elorina," the largest vintner's establishment in eastern Sicily, producing excellent table wines, you will cross the river Tellaro, and in 15 km (95 km from your starting point in Syracuse) you will return to Noto.

Àvola

The busy farming town Àvola (elev. 40 m, pop. 31,816) – foremost in Italy for the production of almonds – has a present refined layout that is the product of the reconstruction that followed the earthquake of 1693, when the inhabitants of ancient Àvola descended from the hill or Colle Aquilone (to the northwest) and took up residence in the feif or Feudo Mutubè overlooking the sea. Designed by the royal architect Frate Angelo Italia, the new city presents a hexagonal plan with a large square in its center from which orthogonal roads spread out

Noto's Duomo and town hall in a spectacularly uniform Baroque setting

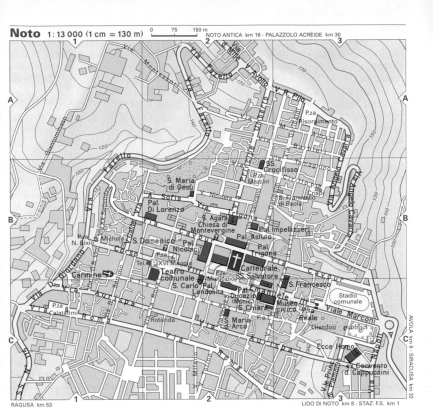

NOTO ANTICA km 16 - PALAZZOLO ACRÉIDE km 30
RAGUSA km 53
LIDO DI NOTO km 8 - STAZ. F.S. km 1
AVOLA km 8 - SIRACUSA km 32

and culminate in four squares that form a cross – along with the central *Piazza Umberto I* – and mark the entrances to the city. This unusual layout is embellished by a number of 18th-c. buildings; the stand-outs, for decorative richness and Baroque sense of space, are the church of the *Annunziata* with its convex front and the *Chiesa Madre* dedicated to St. Nicholas (S. Nicola) with a classic Latin-cross plan, a nave and aisles, and a church courtyard surrounded by pillars with the characteristic figures of saints designed, again, by Angelo Italia. There are also many buildings in the Liberty (Art Nouveau) style with splendid floral decorations carved by master stonecutters to mark the front doors and the windows of the homes, which are also embellished with finely wrought railings.

Noto*

Noto (elev. 152 m, pop. 21,663; city map above) and its history embrace the remarkable features that emerged following the terrible earthquake of 1693, when a new urban plan and an entirely different architectural style erased the memory of an ancient city, long since abandoned. The new layout, in any case, was certainly not created all at once; the first, anonymous plan that was drawn up proved too small, and was poorly laid out. As time went on, a new section was added, based upon a road that divided the city into two parts. This project, which gave substance to the social structure of the community and its economic development, was met with approval by the local aristocracy, which took up residence along the main streets, building their own fine palazzi. The location on a slight incline, the equilibrium shown in the dimensions of the squares, the symmetry of the buildings, the architectural details and the urban furnishings – all these were the features used in the creation of views, perspective, and what we might describe as dynamic articulation, all contributing to the exceptional theatrical and spectacular qualities of this new Baroque city. The exceedingly characteristic and homogeneous physiognomy of Noto, known as the "stone garden," derives as well from the adherence over time to the original techniques of construction and the unbroken use of traditional materials.

The city is laid out in accordance with a checkerboard pattern; the chief thoroughfares are the **Corso Vittorio Emanuele*** and its parallel (higher up), *Via Cavour*, with Piazza del Crocifisso as a sort of urban

135

nexus. Preceded by the imposing gate or *Porta Reale* (C3), the line of the "corso" is broken by three squares overlooked by three churches, each of which has a monumental staircase. The first church that you will see as you head west is the church of *S. Francesco* (B-C3) by Rosario Gagliardi and by Vincenzo Sinatra, one of the moving forces behind the architectural rebirth of Noto. To the left of the square is the Benedictine

Detail of Palazzo Villadorata in Noto

monastery or Monastero del Santissimo Salvatore, which houses the Museo Civico (closed). As you proceed along the "corso" past the square you will see the church of *S. Chiara* by Rosario Gagliardi (another major figure in the history of Sicilian Baroque), with an elliptical interior studded with stuccoes; there is also a *Virgin Mary with Christ Child*, attributed to Antonello Gagini. The second square represents the central space of the city: this is the town square or **Piazza del Municipio*** (B-C2) with the broad and impressive stairway of the Cathedral or *Scalinata del Duomo*. This is an urban space of remarkable charm, a combination of many different presences, each of which is a little masterpiece: the Cathedral or *Duomo* (B2) with its vast façade and its lavish interior (now partially closed, due to the collapse of the cupola and the roof of the nave, which occurred on 13 March 1996), the elegant *Palazzo Ducezio*, now the town hall, the 19th-c. *Palazzo Vescovile* (bishop's palace), and the *Palazzo Landolina*, dating from the 18th c. Between this square and the next one stands the church of *S. Carlo* (or of the Gesuiti). Concluding the architectural progression of Corso Vittorio Emanuele is *Piazza XVI Maggio*, bounded on one side by the convent and church of **S. Domenico***; the façade of the church, like the church itself, is the work of Rosario Gagliardi and is perhaps the most noteworthy work of Noto

Baroque. (The church is currently closed for renovation). On the other side of the square, there is the most significant work of 19th-c. Noto, the *Teatro Comunale* (*open 8:30-1 and 4:6; Sun. 8:30-1*) with the adjoining *Villa d'Ercole*, with a 17th-c. fountain originally from ancient Noto in its center. This is just one of the many tours possible in Baroque Noto, and it is the simplest, as it follows a direct axis; there could be many others, in a voyage of discovery of monumental and vernacular elements, in which Baroque motifs merge with Islamic traces, rich in details of "lesser architecture," which contrasts with the architecture of the "noble city."

A dense blanket of vegetation conceals the ruins of the buildings of **ancient Noto** (Noto Antica, 10 km to the northwest) as if to protect them. Certainly inhabited in prehistoric times, this city had a moment of particular splendor during Greek times; the gymnasium and places of worship of the heroicized dead have been unearthed from that period. Almost nothing remains, on the other hand, from the Moorish period, though Noto was one of the richest strongholds of that time.

Vendìcari

Three marshes – two to the north and one to the south of the lovely tower or *Torre di Vendìcari* overlooking the little islet or Isoletta di Vendìcari – constitute the protected and official nature preserve, or *Riserva Naturale di Vendìcari*. This is an authentic reservoir of nature, with splendid examples of Mediterranean maquis where large populations of birds such as Audouin's gulls, slender-billed gulls, and black-winged stilts find their natural habitat. From the entrance to the preserve or "oasi" you can follow a marked trail through the area of the salinas (salt marshes) of the great marsh or *Pantano Grande* and you will reach the area of the "tonnare" (tunny-fishing nets) and the Swabian tower or Torre Sveva. From here, you can enjoy a vast and sweeping view of the entire preserve set against a lovely marine background, a perfect setting for the little islet mentioned above and, further off, the cape or **Capo Pàssero**. From the tower which marks the center of the preserve, run two trails: one to the north, ending near Eloro, and another to the south, along the beach toward Marzamemi.

Along the northern route, which skirts the

low rocky shoals, there is a predominance of Mediterranean maquis, with bushes of lentisk and thyme and dwarf palms, beyond the small and enchanting bay of Calamosche you will reach the mouth of the river Tellaro, which marks the boundary of the preserve or Oasi di Vendìcari. Further along you will find the ruins of **Eloro**, isolated and looming over the golden sands of the beach: of this town, a Syracusan foundation dating from the end of the 8th c. B.C., there remain stretches of fortifications, fragments of the road system, a theater and religious buildings, and, outside the walls, the sanctuary of Demeter and Kore. The southern route, on the other hand, is entirely different: you climb down into the Pantano Grande, where you tour an old abandoned salina, or saltworks, with its old structures that once surrounded a large windmill and then, walking along the beach, you will reach a dune beyond which is the *Pantano Roveto*. In the summer time, this entirely dry pond is covered with a white crust of salt, a natural habitat for saltwort, a curious reddish succulent plant. The southernmost point of Sicily is to the south of Vendìcari, namely the *Isola delle correnti*.

Ìspica

Set on a hill sloping gently down toward the sea, roughly 6 km away, stands the present-day town of Ìspica (elev. 170 m, pop. 14,629), formed by two separate districts: one district was laid out in the 18th c. and constitutes the present-day settlement, while the other was laid out in the Middle Ages, is now uninhabited, and is part of the archeological park or *Parco Archeologico della Forza* adjoining a rocky spur upon which, along with other ruins, is located the remains of a fortress that was the main core of the city until the earthquake of 1693. In the area of the present-day town, with its regular layout, along the central thoroughfare of Via XX Settembre is the church of *S. Maria Maggiore*, dating from the first half of the 18th c. with a basilican plan and with nave and aisles adorned with frescoes; facing it on the exterior is an elliptical portico. From Via XX Settembre

you can reach Piazza Maria José, which marks the location of the Chiesa Madre and the beginning of Corso Umberto I, along which you may note the *Palazzo Bruno di Belmonte*, now the site of the town hall, or Municipio. Designed by Ernesto Basile in 1906, the parallelepiped bulk of the palazzo is as a latter-day Art-Nouveau (or, in the Italian parlance, Liberty) castle with corner towers, dentelle decorations along the crown of the building, panels of majolica, and elaborate wrought-iron gratework, a distinctive feature of all of the architecture of this town.

Cava d'Ìspica

The limestone highlands of the Iblei are characterized by numerous cuttings eroded by streams and watercourses, here known as "cave," some of them used as far back as prehistoric times. The most important of these is the Cava d'Ìspica (elev. 338 m), which you can easily reach from Rosolini (just a little more than 12 km away along the road to Mòdica). Few other environmental settings in Sicily give so powerful an impression, with the human presence mingling with a natural setting that is perfectly shaped and altered by historical relics and monuments from every era and in every style ranging from the Aeneolithic to the present day. Early Christian catacombs (Larderia, 4th-5th c. A.D.) little Byzantine cliff churches now reduced to ruins (S. Pancrati) or built in caverns (S. Nicola), in some cases with a few fragments of mural paintings; tombs; beehive-style cave dwellings several storys high; cliff dwellings from late antiquity and the Middle Ages (the castle or Castello); homes in caves, used until recently and then abandoned with everything they contained; verdant gardens and rough limestone surfaces; everything seems like a movie in which the soundtrack is provided by the numerous farming activities being done in the area: it is a truly stunning array of stimuli. After much plunder, Cava d'Ìspica is now subject to much closer control, and it is possible to tour it with the accompaniment of local staff and private guides who can be hired on the spot.

6.3 The Ibla highland

The morphology of the northern section of the Syracuse territory is not very different from that to be found in the southern section; we find the same unifying characteristics, both physical and historical. Here too, the territory constituted by the eastern

reliefs of the Monti Iblei is distinguished by the presence of deep hollows ("cave" in Italian) that cut into the limestone ground, a phenomenon that becomes less marked to the north as you descend to the Piana di Catania. Here too the powerful and unifying

The fascinating and suggestive necropolis of Pantàlica

presence of Syracuse and the extensive Baroque reconstruction following the earthquake of 1693 have given the environment a unified appearance. In more recent years, other elements have been added, helping to some extent to diversify the homogeneous cultural and geographic foundations: first of all came the development, beginning in the 1950s, of the industrial zone between Augusta and Syracuse, with the inevitable result being the progressive abandonment of traditional farming activities in favor of industry. This has led to a considerable modification of the landscape and types of settlements; it is only inland that there is an array of mountain towns of feudal origin that are fairly intact.

With this route, which runs a total of 152 km, you will penetrate into the hinterland of Syracuse by following the course of the river Ànapo and the ridges of the Monti Iblei. Moving through a landscape made particularly vivid by little towns with 18th-c. form and image, and with the ruins of Megara Hyblaea and the oil and petrochemical plants serving as a distant backdrop against the sea, you will travel through a territory in which it is possible to directly analyze a cross-section of Sicilian history that has its roots in prehistoric eras. You will leave Syracuse heading west along Viale Paolo Orsi and along state road 124; amidst olive groves and fields, you will drive the lower slopes of the Monti Iblei. After Floridia, the views become broader and, amid handsome olive groves, extend on one side over the valley of the river Ànapo toward Syracuse, and on the other toward the highlands dotted with "cave" and toward the distant Mount Etna. You will pass Solarino at 16 km, a renowned olive-growing town, and then, as you continue along the state road, in Contrada Melilli on the left you will find two very lovely fortified farmhouses ("masserie fortificate"), the first and largest of which is open to visitors. After briefly leaving the state road you will reach Ferla, and from there you will head northeast following the signs for Pantàlica, the largest cliffside necropolis in Sicily.

After you get back onto state road 124, you will continue along the course of the river Ànapo and you will reach Palazzolo Acrèide (26 km from Solarino); then, after you pass through Buscemi and Buccheri, you will turn off toward Francofonte, driving back down along the northern ridge of the Monti Iblei. From Francofonte, a well-known center of citrus farming, located 20 km from Buccheri, passing through Lentini and Carlentini, you will proceed directly to the coast, reaching it at Brùcoli, a lovely little fishing village that stands on a peninsula between the inlet of Brùcoli and the mouth of the mountain stream or Torrente Porcaria. This was the site of the ancient Trotilon, one of the earliest Greek colonies in Sicily; its port has long been used for exporting sea salt. Immediately afterward you will reach Augusta (42 km from Francofonte), a town with a notable historic heritage increasingly swamped by its all-too-modern present. Amid a succession of smokestacks and holding tanks which have a weird charm all their own (especially at night), you will pass through Megara Hyblaea, a major Greek colony, and then, at the turnoff for the station of Priolo, you will take the detour to the left to the peninsula of Magnisi, 2 km long and 700 m wide, jutting out into the Gulf of Augusta and linked to the mainland by a very narrow sandy isthmus. This was the ancient Thapsos, a Bronze-Age and

Iron-Age village, a site that still looks much as it was described by Thucydides. The ridge of the Contrada Targia, marked by a docking structure for oil tankers, is the northern entrance to Syracuse.

Pantàlica*

The site of a warren of cliff tombs overlooking the valley of the river Ànapo, Pantàlica (elev. 425 m) possesses a remarkable charm and allure, surrounded as it is by splendid and uncontaminated nature. There are no houses, there are no trees, and there are no roads; there is only a rocky tableland enclosed by sheer walls carved out over the course of the millennia by the waters of the river and its tributary, the Calcinara, crisscrossed by very few paths or trails: all of these characteristics made this a safe place in antiquity, nicely suited to being easily defended. In a territory covering some 80 hectares, enclosed by a perimeter extending roughly 5 km, there is a vast necropolis comprising more than 5000 tombs in manmade grottoes, with multiple occupation (divided into five main clusters), alongside which stand the few surviving ruins of the early-Sicilian city of Hybla, which flourished between the 13th and the 8th c. B.C. All that survives of this city, which Syracuse was meant to serve as a seaport, is the large rectangular square-block base of the *Anaktoron*, the palace of the prince. Tradition has it that the early Sicilians were known as the People of Bees, and by a noteworthy coincidence the early Sicilian necropolis of Pantàlica is quite reminiscent of a large beehive carved in stone. The site, which was not inhabited throughout the ancient classical age, was newly occupied in the high Middle Ages since as a nearly inaccessible place it offered safe haven from Moorish incursions: from this period a village of cave dwellings and a few small carved-rock churches survive. Nowadays, to enter the necropolis and wander through it freely – especially during periods during which there are not many tourists, when one can fully enjoy the silence broken only by the cawing of crows – is to take a plunge into the earliest history of man. If you are fond of adventure, you may choose to follow – on foot or by the minibus of the local forest rangers or Azienda forestale – the dirt road along the route of the old railroad, now abandoned, which once connected Ferla to Sortino along the banks of the river Ànapo.

Palazzolo Acrèide*

A small city in a 17th-c. style, Palazzolo Acrèide (elev. 670 m, pop. 9097; city map below) is the namesake and heir to the Greek

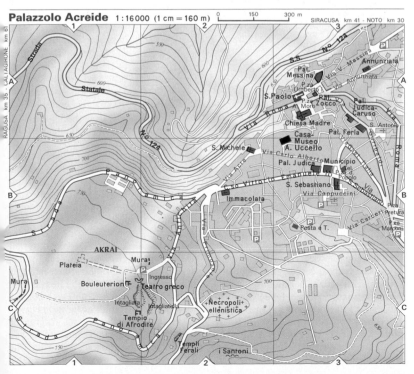

town of Akrai, founded by the Syracusans in 664 B.C. as a fortress overlooking the river Ànapo, fundamental to effective control of the hinterland. The current urban configuration of the town, which dates back to the 17th c., is characterized by a network of thoroughfares that links up the chief points of the urban structure. And within this gridwork is a series of architectural structures from each of the three phases of urban

The traditional procession of Palazzolo Acrèide

growth: the period prior to the earthquake of 1693, the period immediately following that earthquake, and the present day. From the period of its initial formation in the area around the excavations of Akrai, the city still preserves noteworthy monuments, among them the Greek theater or **Teatro Greco*** dating back to the 3rd c. B.C. but heavily renovated in Roman times, quite harmonious in its proportions, even though it was designed to contain only 600 spectators. Behind the theater extends the complex of ancient Greek "latomie," or prisons, named the *Intagliata* and the *Intagliatella*, whose walls, carved into reliefs, are clear evidence of their use as homes and burial grounds during the Byzantine-Christian era; above the "latomie" are the remains of the base of the *temple of Aphrodite* (6th c. B.C.), which can be reached from the archeological zone. To the east of the theater are the *Templi Ferali*, a "latomia" or prison cell whose walls are covered with little votive tablets (pinakes) dedicated to the cult of the heroicized dead; the large relief from the Hellenistic era is also linked to the same cult. You can follow a trail to a little valley where there are so-called **Santoni***, literally holy men, 12 remarkable rock sculptures dating from the 3rd c. B.C. set into the rock, dedicated to the goddess Cybele, who is depicted as standing or seated: this is the largest figurative complex linked to the cult of this Magna Mater, as the ancient Romans called her. Once you leave the archeological area, the tour of the city focuses on the series of Baroque buildings that extend so theatrically along the two main thoroughfares of the city, Corso Vittorio Emanuele and Via Carlo Alberto: these two roads meet on Piazza del Popolo where the massive bulk of the church of *S. Sebastiano* stands, hoisting its spectacular façade on three orders atop a high stairway. The little city features other interesting religious structures such as the church of *S. Paolo*, which dates from the first half of the 18th c., with its imposing and spectacular Baroque tower-like façade, and the church of the *Annunziata*, rebuilt in the 18th c. with a rich Baroque portal with twisted columns; on the interior is a handsome altar with marble inlays. In Via Machiavelli is the *museum-home of Antonino Uccello* with an interesting collection of Sicilian ethnographic material.

Buccheri

This town (elev. 820 m, pop. 2755), which already existed during Norman times, is the highest township in the province or Provincia di Siracusa, and was made a county or "contea" during the war of the Sicilian Vespers or Guerra del Vespro; the original site was further uphill, where you can still see the ruins of the castle. The section of town that was built after 1693 is dominated by the monumental and very tall church of *S. Antonio Abate*, which is certainly the most impressive piece of architecture here, atop its imposing stairway and with its three descending orders. The church of the *Maddalena* also has a rich façade; on the interior is a marble statue by Antonello Gagini (1508).

Carlentini and Lentini

Built in 1551 at the behest of the emperor Charles V, from whom it took its name, for purposes of defense, **Carlentini** (elev. 200 m, pop. 16,946) is set in a site that dominates the surrounding territory, from above the ancient city of Lentini; the strong citadel was meant to defend the hinterland from Turkish raids. Of the entire defensive system, all that remains are a few traces of the walls of the town, which was designed in a checkerboard pattern with a large central square, on one side of which now stands the Chiesa Madre. Following the earthquake of 1693, Carlentini was repopulated thanks to its healthy location. Just to the north of Carlentini, it is possible to visit the archeological zone of *Leontinoi*, a major Greek settlement that existed as early as the 7th c. B.C., as is shown by the perimeter of the first enclosure walls; its history was profoundly and constantly marked by the rivalry with the powerful nearby city of Syracuse, which subjugated it repeatedly. The research done in the area now enclosed by the archeological park or *Parco Archeologico* has made it possible to establish that the city stood on the hill and in the valley, or Colle San Mauro and the Valle San Mauro; excavations have brought to light stretches of three sets of enclosure walls and a gate outside of which extends a necropolis that dates back between the 4th and the end of the 3rd c. B.C.

The city of **Lentini** (elev. 53 m, pop. 27,764), which is the heir to the Greek colony of Leontinoi, dominates a fertile plain known in antiquity by the name of Campi Lestrigoni; partially set below sea level and improved by reclamation projects during the Fascist era, nowadays the area is devoted to intensive cultivation of citrus fruit. A major religious center, Lentini was an episcopal see during the early Christian period. Profoundly marked by various earthquakes (1140, 1169, and 1542), and by the unhealthiness of the site, the decision was made after the great earthquake of 1693 to change the city's location; the selection of the new location and the layout of the settlement were dictated by Angelo Italia, the

architect of Àvola and Noto, but no traces remain of this operation because the inhabitants did not accept the new project and chose to rebuild their city exactly where it had originally stood. In the archeological museum or *Museo Archeologico* there is a collection of antiquities of the territory, with special attention to Leontinoi, but also to the other sites in the area.

Augusta

Set on a peninsula that extends more than 2 km in length, separating two ports (Megarese to the west and Xifonio to the east), Augusta (elev. 15 m, pop. 34,189) was built on a site believed to have been that of the Greek town of Xiphonia at the behest of Frederick II, who wanted to reinforce a strategically fundamental site at the entrance to the enormous inlet that is closed off to the south by the squat promontory or Promontorio di Siracusa. Looming over and protecting the city is the Swabian castle or *Castello Svevo*, which underwent considerable renovation to suit it properly to the defensive needs of the port and the hinterland. Recent restoration work on the structures built by the emperor Frederick have uncovered both military and civil characteristics. The castle has a square plan and four corner towers which are also square, while the interior rooms are partly covered with splendid vaults; under the Spaniards the castle was surrounded by a double enclosure wall with bastions. Later heavily renovated and rebuilt, the castle was converted into a prison beginning in 1890, and it continued to be used as a prison until 1978. What surives of Augusta's original military character is an interesting *Museo della Piazzaforte* or museum of the fortress. Other historical monuments worthy of note include the gate or Porta di Terra, also known as the Porta Spagnola, and the town hall or *Palazzo del Municipio* (1699) decorated with a Swabian imperial eagle grasping the town's coat of arms, and with a sundial to commemorate the eclipse of the sun in 1870. The earthquake of 1990 left evident marks upon Augusta, especially on the interior of the district of Borgata. The entire town of Augusta and the surrounding area inevitably provoke a sense of malaise in any case: a predatory and all-powerful development movement and the false sense of prosperity induced by the presence of large-scale heavy industry have irreparably mangled one of the most splendid, noteworthy and historically rich landscapes in the entire Mediterranean basin.

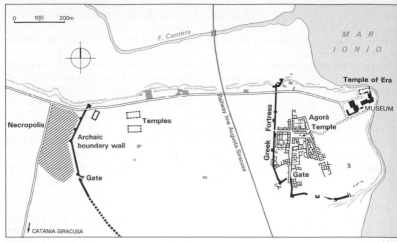

Megara Hyblaea

Megara Hyblaea

From Augusta, skirting the Esso refinery along provincial road 193 in the direction of Syracuse, signs will point the way to Megara Hyblaea (plan above). Surrounded by an industrial zone, to the point that at certain times during the day it is difficult to reach it, the area of the ancient city has however been rescued from the looming presences that surround it on every hand, and represents an oasis of greenery and solitude that is certainly worth a stop. The first explorations were undertaken by Paolo Orsi at the end of the 19th c., and since WWII the city has been the subject of regular excavations, making it one of the best-studied western Greek colonies.

The visitor is almost led by the hand (though we would advise at least a short visit to the little museum on the site) with a series of charts and explanations through the ruins of the ancient city, which was founded in 728 B.C. by Greeks from Megara a few years after the foundation of Syracuse, and which grew thereafter until 483 B.C., when it was razed to the ground by Gelon, the tyrant of Gela, who deported its inhabitants. It was refounded by Timoleon in 340 B.C. on the same site; but this second Megara was also completely destroyed, in 213 B.C., by Marcellus in the operations prior to the conquest of Syracuse and in the context of the Second Punic War. From the 2nd c. B.C. until the 6th c. A.D., however, evidence shows there was a small settlement. The excavations of the city and the adjoining necropolises have unearthed authentic jewels of Greek sculpture, now on display in the archeological museum or Museo Archeologico di Siracusa.

The tour of Megara Hyblaea takes place against the backdrop of the gulf or Golfo di Augusta where there are always oil tankers loading crude oil in the facilities near the port. To walk among the grim industrial structures in search of the relics of ancient Megara, in a chaotic environment and traffic with a savage vitality, provides an experience entirely out of the ordinary with respect to the way that we are accustomed to thinking about the past.

7 Catania and its territory

If you look at a map of Sicily, your attention will immediately be attracted by a large empty space around an elevation that is unusual in this area; the empty spot alters the eastern section of the island to the point of breaking up the logic of morphology and settlement: this is the area surrounding Catania which, for better or worse, has always had Mount Etna as its central point of reference, in visual terms and in ideal and cultural terms, as well as economic terms.

The volcano does not only symbolize the distinctive character of this area; rather, it *is*

A view familiar to travelers in Sicily: Etna in the background

the area, and with respect to the volcano, the renowned and populous towns anchored to its slopes or spread out across the plain – in particular, Catania – wind up as little more than parasitic appendages.

So impressive is this volcano that not even the Greeks dared to contaminate it with their stories of gods and heroes, relegating Vulcan and his forge to the far more accessible depths of the island of Vulcan, in part because of the mining of obsidian and pumice that was done there. The favors of Mount Etna are, on the other hand, much less visible, though they certainly encouraged the endless sequence of human settlements that have taken hold here, at elevations ranging from 500 to 750 m. First of course is the exceedingly fertile earth, the product of the decay of volcanic rock in an eons-long geological process, which, along with the alluvial deposits of the river Simeto, laid the foundation for a very valuable agricultural tradition. This tradition, in its turn, coupled with a coastline rich in anchorage and with at least one major seaport meant that centuries of hard work and enterprise by the inhabitants led to an economic development of great worth and benefit.

7.1 Catania**

A remarkable geographic location, with a setting that includes Mount Etna and the Ionian Sea, has played a major role in the thousands of years of history of this city, a history of light and shadows. The growth of Catania (elev. 7 m, pop. 337,862; map on p. 148) has clearly been affected, for better or worse, by its relationship with the volcano: the volcano made the fields remarkably fertile as it spewed forth its lava, and as the lava cooled it served as a quarry for the volcanic stone with which houses were built. Historic settlement here dates back to the earliest Greek colonization in Sicily, when the Chalcideans founded the earliest core of "Katane" sometime after 729 B.C., according to the documentation provided by Thucydides, in the area that is now occupied by the church of S. Nicolò and the Benedictine monastery of S. Nicolò l'Arena. The traces that still remain of the archaic phase of the settlement find correspondences in the historic sources: they refer to the Catanese origins of the legislator Caronda and the stay in this town of a number of poets, foremost among them Stesicoro, whose tomb gave its name to one of the city gates.

For three centuries it remained in Greek hands, often at war with Syracuse for hegemony over the territory; in 263 B.C. it was conquered by the Romans, who subjected it to the payment of a tribute. Roman domination left a considerable number of buildings and structures that still stand: the Amphitheater (Anfiteatro) in Piazza Stesicoro, the Theater (Teatro) and the Odeon between the lower section of the Via Vittorio Emanuele and the Via Teatro Greco, the ruins of the Forum (Foro) in the Cortile S. Pantaleone, and four thermal complexes (one was transformed during Byzantine rule into the church of S. Maria della Rotonda; the Terme Achilliane lie under the Cathedral; the Terme dell'Indirizzo stand alongside the church of S. Maria dell'Indirizzo; and another structure stands in Piazza Dante).

Early-Christian history is documented in the martyrdom of St. Agatha and St. Euplio prior to the 4th c.; the city was conquered by the Byzantines in A.D. 535, though very few traces now survive of their three centuries of rule. The Saracens conquered Catania in A.D. 875, leaving a strong mark on the countryside, establishing new crops and opening new transportation routes (they created the "trazzere," paths for animals across fields, that crisscross Mount Etna). Under Norman domination, construction began on the Cathedral (1071), which was linked to the town walls and was endowed with parapets that can still be seen in the apses and transept (this is one of the more interesting examples of an "ecclesia munita"); later an earthquake devastated the city (1169), contributing to the economic crisis that continued until the end of Norman rule. In 1239 Frederick II of Swabia ordered the construction of the Castello Ursino at the edge of town, near the sea, in an area that was covered by boiling lava in 1669 (a spectacular image of Catania with lava flows lapping at its edges is preserved in a painting that hangs in the sacristy of the Cathedral).

The few years that separated the eruption and the earthquake of 1693, and, to an even greater degree, the years that followed that date, saw a city on its knees, humbled by the destruction of the countryside, overwhelmed by a mass of penniless refugees. In June of 1694 Giuseppe Lanza, Duke of Camastra and right-hand man of the viceroy Uzeda, assembled the surviving members of the Senate and the clergy and established a plan for a rebirth on the site of the old town. The form of the city showed greater attention to seismic dangers: straight thoroughfares were built on the older tracks of the Via Uzeda (now Via Etnea) and the Via S. Francesco (first stretch of the Via Vittorio Emanuele), which were freed of rubble and rebuilt; the width of the roads was classified into three different orders of magnitude and many large squares were built, offering places of refuge in case of new earthquakes. (The system of squares and roads that now links the old clearing of the Piazza del Duomo to the west with Piazza Mazzini and to the north with Piazza Università is the concrete result of this plan).

In the reconstruction, among the clergy an outstanding effort was made by the Order of the Benedictines who, with their enormous landholdings and new rules concerning purchase and sale of real estate, enlarged old structures (S. Nicolò) and built new ones adjoining the walls (Palazzo del Vescovo, Seminario dei Chierici, church of S. Agata la Vetere), violating the rules of the Duke of Camastra. Of the nobility, only the Prince of Biscari was allowed to build his magnificent palazzo next to the walls, alongside the Palazzo del Vescovo (bishop's palace) and the seaport. Among those who led the reconstruction, particular note should be made of G.B. Vaccarini, who was the city architect from 1730 on; he laid the foundations, shortly before 1750, for an expansion northward as far as the existing settlements of Borgo and Consolazione, founded to house the refugees from the eruption of 1669.

In the early decades of the 19th c., Catania

The fountain of the elephant, symbol of Catania (detail)

Piazza del Duomo, with the Cathedral and the dome of the abbey church of S. Agata

underwent a powerful surge in population, which was not met with careful planning in the inevitable urban expansion that ensued, despite the efforts of Sebastiano Ittar; the expansion that was done in that century did however result in a series of major works: the construction of the railroad, the expansion of the port, the monumental cemetery (Cimitero Monumentale) to the south, as well as the public gardens and a theater, both dedicated to Vincenzo Bellini. The railroad viaduct, whose arches are commonly known as "l'archi da Marina," forever ended the relationship that this city had long had with its view of the sea, and nowadays there is the quiet but continous expansion of the residential buildings of the Italian Navy (Marina Militare) to further seal off that view. Sporadic efforts to recover the historic heritage date from the early years of the 20th c., when the amphitheater (Anfiteatro) was restored in Piazza Stesicoro, and plans were made for the restoration of the Castello Ursino with the allocation of the city museum or Museo Comunale. The chaotic urban development of the past decades allowed the creation of an immense industrial area between the city and the river Simeto and the ravaging of the district of S. Berillo to make way for the creation of a financial center, a project that was however left unfinished.

The urban layout of Catania has developed around the historic center, rebuilt after the earthquake of 1693 in the rich style of the Baroque. Four areas extend outwards from the center: the southern district built between the late 18th and early 18th c. on the lava left by the 1669 eruption; the northern section towards the volcano, marking the architectural evolution from the Baroque to the present day; the western expansion towards Cibali, from the early 20th c.; the 19th-c. eastern expansion, now the prestigious shopping area of the city.

The route, which is a walking tour, runs through the main points of both the older city (the Castello Ursino and the ruins of the Teatro are the most important landmarks) and the post-earthquake section, the most important features of which are the Cathedral (Cattedrale), the Via Crociferi, and the church of S. Nicolò; other interesting walks are along the Via Etnea and the Viale XX Settembre, with a number of examples of 20th-c. construction.

Catania, however, is much more than this; it is also the contrast between the Baroque sumptuousness of Piazza del Duomo and the cries of the street vendors in the nearby fish market, or Pescheria, a concert of aromas and descriptions of wares worthy of the largest and most crowded Moorish souks. Catania is also one of the thousand culinary temptations of its tradition: an almond ice or "granita," or a cup of coffee with cream, or an orange drink – "arancino," ending in "o," because in the rest of Sicily it ends in "a" – or a thirst-quenching "seltz, limone e sale," meaning seltzer, lemon, and salt. Or, to chew on, cookies in the shapes of bones on the Day of the Dead, and rice "crispelle" (rough translation: crêpes) covered with honey on St. Joseph's Day, or almond pastries, or the "crispeddi" with anchovies or ricotta, or pasta asciutta with eggplants and salted ricotta – known as "Pasta alla Norma" in a tribute to the Catanese composer Vincenzo Bellini – or the "sangele" (calf tripe with cooked blood sausage), or "panzerotti," a kind of dumpling filled with chocolate, or the little sweet olives known as the "olivette di S. Agata."

145

Piazza del Duomo* (D3) or cathedral square. The traditional center of Catania was planned immediately following the earthquake of 1693 in place of the medieval "platea magna" or main square, and was selected as the site of civil and ecclesiastical power, in time becoming the point of convergence of the main thoroughfares. The central fulcrum of the space here is the renowned "fountain of the elephant," or *Fontana dell'Elefante*, designed in 1736 by G.B. Vaccarini; in order to create this emblem of the city, Vaccarini used ancient relics (the volcanic-stone elephant dating from Roman times, popularly known as "u liotru," and the Egyptian obelisk with hieroglyphics linked to the worship of the goddess Isis). The whole, set on a pedestal and surmounted by a sphere and the symbols of St. Agatha, expresses a remarkable mixture of Christianity and paganism. The fountain is soon to be restored.

Cattedrale* (D3) or Cathedral. Dedicated to S. Agata (St. Agatha), patron saint of the city, this cathedral was built by Count Ruggero in the years 1078-93 on the ruins of the baths or Terme Achilliane, and rebuilt in 1169 for the first time and again following the earthquake of 1693. The main façade, built by G.B. Vaccarini between 1733 and 1761, has two orders of columns and is adorned on top with a statue of the patron saint, while on the left flank there is a marble *portal* by Giandomenico Mazzola (1577); the rear. Of the original Norman structure, the church preserves the transept, flanked by two towers, and the three semicircular apses. The massive walls in large blocks of volcanic rock and merlons reveal the fortified character of the construction.
The **interior**, with nave and aisles divided by pillars, has modern flooring, while the side altars and the carved and gilt wooden frames date back to the 18th c. Many notables are buried here; we should mention the *tomb of Vincenzo Bellini* and that of the cardinal Giuseppe Benedetto Dusmet. In the right transept, in the center, is a marble *portal* (G.B. Mazzolo, 1545), with bas-reliefs depicting scenes from the life of the Virgin Mary; through this portal you can enter the chapel or *Cappella della Madonna*, on the right wall of which is set the *tomb of Constance of Aragon* (d. 1363), the wife of Frederick III; on the opposite wall is a Roman sarcophagus (3rd c.) which contains the remains of royal members of the House of Aragon who resided in Catania. In the right apse, note the chapel or *Cappella di S. Agata**; here an exceedingly ornate *portal* (1495)

leads into the sacellum containing the relics and part of the immense **Tesoro di S. Agata** (*open during St. Agatha festivities*), the Treasury including a *silver bust* dating from 1373-76 and a *coffer**, a great reliquary case containing the remains of the saint, a fine piece of Gothic work in Sicily. During the St. Agatha festival (2-5 February), the reliquaries are taken in procession on a sort of litter, called the *Vara*, a magnificent silver-plated wooden structure. In the left transept, a marble *portal* (Giandomenico Mazzola, 1563) with Scenes of the Passion marks the entrance to the chapel or *Cappella del Crocifisso* which occupies one of the side donjon towers dating from Norman times. To the left of the transept the *sacristy*, built in 1675, contains a fresco depicting the *Eruption and lava flow of 1669 threatening Catania*, and 17th-/18th-c. carved cabinets; the adjoining Sacrario Capitolare or chapter sacrarium contains a collection of exquisite parchments. The grates in the ground are for the ventilation of the baths or *Terme Achilliane* (entrance on the right side of the façade of the cathedral), which run under the church, the seminary, or "seminario" and the square that lies in front of it.

Porta Uzeda (D-E3). This gate was built in 1696, along a direct line with the Via Etnea, within the fortifications of the city, which in their turn were built between the 14th and the 16th c.; some sections of that enclosure wall can still be seen (outer side of the Duomo). To the east is the *Seminario dei Chierici*, with a complex plan that extends along the 16th-c. walls, runs through the gate, and links up with the cathedral.

Pass through the gate and follow Via Dusmet to the left, and you will come to **Palazzo Biscari*** (D-E4) which overlooks this side with its more lavish façade – pilaster strips in the form of caryatids and balconies framed by scrolls and putti – which was built for the first time in 1707. To enter this building, which was completed in 1763 to plans by Francesco Battaglia and his son Antonino, and which was the site of the museum assembled in 1758 by the prince Ignazio Paternò Castello and eventually donated to the township in 1932 (the material will soon be exhibited in the city museum or Museo Comunale), you must go around to Via Museo Biscari.
The building, made up of structures dating from various eras, is arranged around a large closed courtyard; you can enter the oldest core of the building by climbing a "crossed-tongs" staircase; among the sumptuously decorated halls on the interior are the remarkable *reception hall*, with gilt decorations and mirrors, and the *Gallery*, from which, through a spiral staircase in Rococo style, you can climb to the musicians' floor.

Along the same street (Via Museo Biscari) is the Convento di S. Placido, on the rear wall of which is a 17th-c. aedicula with a relief of St. Agatha. The door beneath the aedicula leads into a number of subterranean chambers dating from Roman times, traditionally said to be the birthplace and home of the saint and now used for temporary exhibitions.

completed in 1250, it was the residence of royalty of the House of Aragon in the 14th c.; it was enclosed by walls in the middle of the 16th c. and, in the centuries that followed, damaged and restored repeatedly. The building has a square plan with walls two meters thick, four cylindrical corner

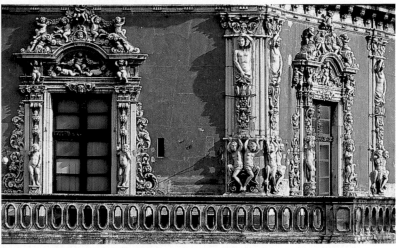

The city center is lined with sumptuous Baroque palazzi

Via Garibaldi (E1-3). This long thoroughfare runs from Piazza del Duomo to the west, and it is lined as far as Piazza Mazzini by 18th-c. palazzi. To the left of the entrance to the street is a fountain, the *Fontana dell'Amenano* (1867), commonly known as "l'acqua a linzolu" (the water sheet) because it gathers up and then pours out the waters of the river Amenano in a great spill; there are traces of this subterranean river both on the hill of the Benedettini and in the Roman theater or Teatro Romano, but its exact course has never been plotted with precision.

S. Maria dell'Indirizzo (E3). This church, rebuilt in 1727-35 on the site of the one destroyed by the earthquake, is part of a monastery complex. It is flanked by the Roman baths known as the *Terme dell'Indirizzo*, that are almost preserved (there are still furnaces, air conduits, and drains for the water).

Castello Ursino* (E3). The oldest documentation concerning the commission given by Frederick II of Swabia for the construction of the castle is a letter of congratulations dating from 1239 for the selection of the site – a promontory surrounded by the sea – addressed to the director of fortifications, Riccardo di Lentini;

towers and two remaining semi-cylindrical towers set midway along the northern and western sides; on the interior, the halls still preserve a number of original structures of considerable interest.

The castle houses the city museum or **Museo Civico*** (*open 9-1 and 3-6; Sun., 9-1*) founded in 1934 with the gathering of much of the material from the Museo Biscari, the collections of the Benedictines, and the material donated by the Baron Zappalà-Asmundo. On the ground floor are the archeological collections including excellent finds such as the *torso of an emperor*, a fragment of a Roman statue taken from a Catanese basilica; the *head of an ephebe**, an Attic sculpture from the 6th c. B.C. which is considered the masterpiece of the museum; and *frescoes* from the catacombs of Domitilla in Rome. Among the other works are medieval and Renaissance sculpture, 18th-c. busts of members of the Paternò Castello family, arms and armor, and numerous paintings. Also worthy of note are the collections of miscellaneous art with majolica and porcelain, goldsmithery, ivory, marble inlay, and 18th-c. crèches.

Casa-Museo di Giovanni Verga (E2; *open 9-1; closed Sun. and holidays*). The late-17th-c. palazzo where the great Italian writer (born in Vizzini in 1840) lived from his early boy-

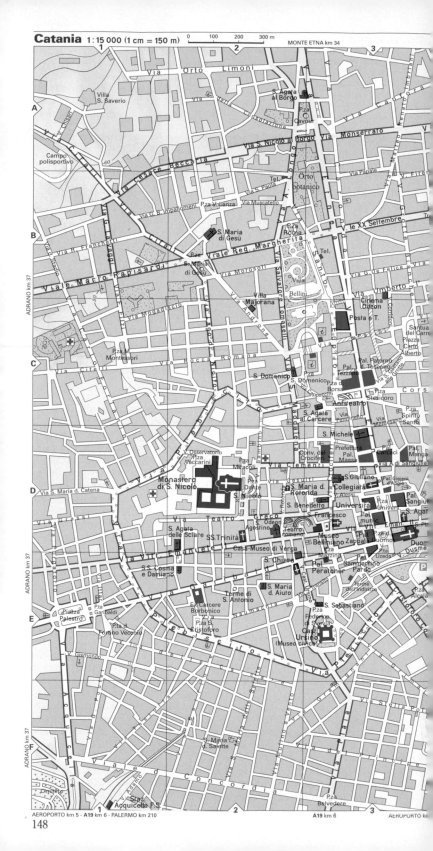

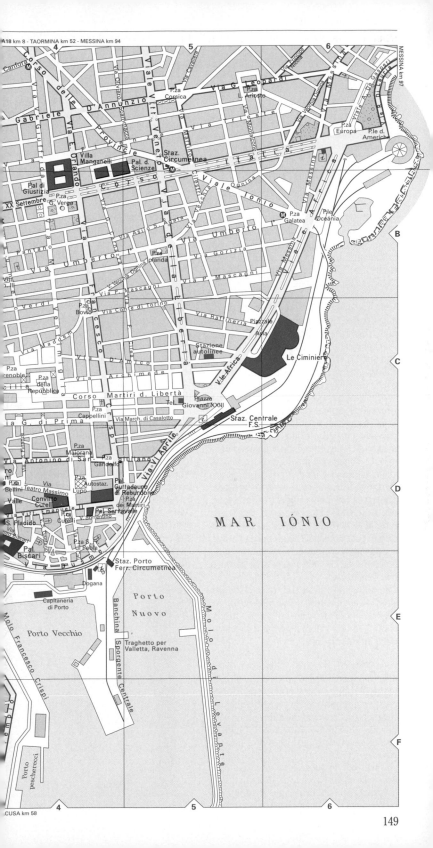

hood was transformed into a *museum* in 1980 (entrance in Via S. Anna, n. 8). The house contains objects, furniture, and portraits which belonged to Verga; the *library* boasts 2000 volumes by Italian and non-Italian authors, some signed.

Nearby in Piazza S. Francesco stands the house of another famous citizen, Vincenzo Bellini, now the headquarters of the **Museo Belliniano*** (E2; *open weekdays, 9-1.20; holidays, 9-12:30*), which exhibits manuscripts and scores by the musician.

Via Vittorio Emanuele (E-D1-3). Running parallel to Via Garibaldi, the "Strada del Corso," as it was called until the Unification of Italy, cuts east and west across the ancient city; framing it on either side are the aristocratic homes and convent buildings that offer such rich examples of the Catanese Baroque style.

Teatro Romano (D2-3; *open 9-sunset*) or Roman theater. Entirely surrounded by buildings, this theater lies between Piazza S. Francesco and Via Vittorio Emanuele (the entrance is in this street, at n. 266). The cavea, which lies athwart the hill upon which the ancient acropolis was built, faced south; it is possible that this structure was Greek in origin – as tradition would have it – but in any case what is certain is that the surviving structures date solely from Roman times. The theater had a diameter of 87 m, and could accommodate as many as 7000 spectators; what survives today are the cavea, the orchestra pit and the stage. The cavea was built of blocks of limestone, divided into nine wedges and two precincts, and was bounded by three corridors, built in volcanic stone and set at various heights, from which the public could reach the various seating sections through the "vomitoria."
The adjoining *Odeon* (D2; *open 9-sunset*), which was smaller and was used for rehearsing choruses and for competitions, is semicircular in form and has a cavea capable of seating 1500.

Via dei Crociferi** (D3). This is one of the most monumental and noteworthy streets of the Baroque section of Catania, though partly compromised by archeological excavations underway at the intersection with the Via Antonino di Sangiuliano (ancient Roman roadways and parts of a mosaic have been unearthed). Take this street and you will see, in succession, the *Arco di S. Benedetto* (D2) or arch of St. Benedict, said to have been built in a single night in 1704 by the powerful Benedictine Order, linking the two buildings of the *Badia Grande* (a fine example of classical style by F. Battaglia) and the *Badia Piccola* (by G.B. Vaccarini); the majestic church of *S. Benedetto* (1704-13), set high on a stairway, with wooden doors depicting scenes from the life of Saint Benedict (the interior is embellished with elegant stucco work and altars with exquisite marble work); the former *Collegio Gesuitico* or Jesuit college, now housing the art institute or Istituto d'Arte, with a plan featuring four courtyards, the first of which is a handsome cloister believed to be in part by G.B. Vaccarini (1742), who certainly did design the other courtyard, with strips of white limestone and black cobbles, inspired by Borromini. (He also designed the *Palazzo Asmundo Francicanava* on the neighboring Piazza Asmundo.) Further along this street are the church of *S. Giuliano* (1739-51), also designed by Vaccarini, with a convex façade in the center and a cupola surrounded by a small loggia; the *convent of the Padri Crociferi* (by Francesco Battaglia; 1771-80) which gave its name to the street, at the crossroads with the Via di Sangiuliano; and the entrance of *Villa Cerami* (from the turn of the 18th c.) at the end of the road.

Via Antonino di Sangiuliano (D2-3). This street was one of the chief thoroughfares of the reconstruction ordered by the Duke of Camastra, and it features a steep ascent which is a considerable obstacle to the bearers of the giant candles and the litter of St. Agatha in the procession of 4 and 5 February in the saint's honor. In the stretch toward the sea you may note the 18th-c. *Palazzo Manganelli* (D3) and, set off to the side in

Baroque façades in Via dei Crociferi

Piazza Bellini, an opera house, the *Teatro Massimo Bellini* (D4), dedicated to the composer and designed by Carlo Sada on the site of an unfinished building dating from the turn of the 19th c. The building, in the Eclectic style, was inaugurated on 31 May 1890 with a performance of "Norma."

S. Nicolò (D2). Work on this church began in 1687, but was interrupted first by the earthquake and later by technical difficulties, probably in connection with the size of the structure, which would have made it the largest church in Sicily (105x48 m in the transept; height of the cupola, 62 m). Because of its incompleteness, the façade – which overlooks the elegant esedra of *Piazza Dante* (Stefano Ittar, 1769) – is quite charming and impressive; note the massive, unfinished columns.

The **interior** features a nave and two aisles set on massive pylons and a cupola; its vastness is astounding: the walls, originally pure white, are interrupted by altars devoid of any furnishings, following the anything-but-liturgical use that has recently been made of the complex (it is now a monument to the war dead, or Sacrario dei Caduti). The pavement of the transept is marked by a marble *meridian* with inlaid signs of the Zodiac, dating from 1841.

Of particular interest is the recently restored organ in the presbytery, with a very tall wooden case, carved and gilded, a masterpiece by Donato Del Piano; the wooden cabinets in the sacristy, in the Rococo style, preserve only a faint hint of their former splendor.

From a niche in the splay of the largest portal it is possible to climb up to the drum of the cupola, and from there the eye can survey everything from Mt. Etna to the Aspromonte in Calabria.

Adjoining the church is the Benedictine monastery of **S. Nicolò l'Arena** (*open 9-1 and 4-8*), now the site of the department of literature and philosophy (Facoltà di Lettere e Filosofia) of the University of Catania. The Benedictines, who had a monastery in the district of S. Nicolò l'Arena at Nicolosi, moved into the city in 1558; the original monastery in Catania, which took its name from its former location and which was almost entirely destroyed by the earthquake of 1693, was replaced, from 1703 on, by a new complex with an even more grandiose structure; among those who worked on it were G.B. Contini and G.B. Vaccarini. In the courtyard to the east, whose walls are splendid testimonials to the culture of the expert stone-cutters of the early 18th c., archeological digs have unearthed remains of buildings from the archaic Greek period.

This former monastery also houses the *Biblioteche Riunite* or united libraries assembled from the original core of the collection of the Benedictines; another addition came with the collection bequeathed by the Baron Ursino Recupero – particularly valuable in terms of Sicilian history – and with the library of the poet Mario Rapisardi. The Vaccarini room is famous for its fine majolica floor.

Anfiteatro* (C3) or amphitheater. This immense elliptical Roman structure (which measures 71 by 51 m, and was second in size only to the Colosseum) probably dates back to the 2nd c. B.C. and could seat 15,000 spectators. What is visible of the structure nowadays, from Piazza Stesicoro, represents only a part of it, with a lava core structure and marble facing, but its foundations extend back as far as the Via Penninello.

Via Etnea (A-D3). This street also dates back to the 18th c., when it was a location of great prestige among the well-to-do in Catania; it now presents a largely 19th-c. style and appearance, because at that time the city grew explosively along this street toward Mt. Etna; much of the urban expansion in the 20th c. took place along this street as well.

If you follow the northern section of this street, and occasionally turn off briefly, you will see the church of *S. Gaetano alla Grotta* (on the Via S. Gaetano alla Grotta, which turns off from the northeastern corner of Piazza Stesicoro), beneath which is an interesting construction from Byzantine times; the *Santuario del Carmine* (1729), a sanctuary overlooking Piazza Carlo Alberto (where a charming market is held); the main entrance of the *Villa Bellini*, now a public park with lavish flowerbeds and old trees; and **Viale XX Settembre**, one of the segments of the longest thoroughfare in the city, which runs straight down to the sea. The section running toward the Ionian Sea, on the other hand, features Piazza Trento and Piazza Giovanni Verga, the *Palazzo di Giustizia* (hall of justice) built by Francesco Fichera in 1937-53, and *Villa Manganelli* by Ernesto Basile, as well as the *Palazzo delle Scienze* (hall of science, 1942), which houses various geological museums (*Museo di Mineralogia, Museo di Paleontologia,* and *Museo di Vulcanologia*); the last of the three museums has interesting collections of material from Mount Etna, the Eolie islands, and other parts of the world.

Collegiata (D3). Also known as the Regia Cappella, this religious building stands along a stretch of the Via Etnea that runs toward the center of town; it is one of the masterpieces of the Catanese late-Baroque, was built in the early 18th c. to plans by Angelo Italia, and the façade was completed by Stefano Ittar (1758); inside, the vaults are frescoed by Giuseppe Sciuti (late 19th c.).

Piazza dell'Università (D3). This square was built at the behest of the Duke of Camastra; it is hemmed in on the left by the *Palazzo Sangiuliano* by G.B. Vaccarini (1745), and on the right by the main university building, or *Palazzo dell'Università*, which was completed at the end of the 18th c., with a square courtyard with two orders of loggias, also built by G.B. Vaccarini in 1730. The Università degli Studi di Catania (the "Siculorum Gymnasium" founded by Alphonse of Aragon in 1434) has an exquisite *library*, one of the richest in all Sicily.

Palazzo Municipale (D3) or Town Hall. Nowadays also known as the Palazzo degli Elefanti, this building was erected following the earthquake of 1696 on an existing loggia, even though its current form was given it by G.B. Vaccarini, who worked on it from 1732 on. Fire broke out in 1944 during a popular revolt and destroyed the furnishings of the interior as well as the historical archives of the city and the Museo del Risorgimento. The building has a rectangular plan with a central courtyard porticoed on two sides; at the entrance are a 15th-c. *bust of St. Agatha*

the so-called *Carrozze del Senato* (carriages of the Senate), used by the Senate members on the occasion of the feast day of the patron saint.

It was for this same patron saint that, in 1735-67, G.B. Vaccarini designed on the Via Vittorio Emanuele, the abbey church of **S. Agata** (Badia di S. Agata, D3), ending in the massive structure of a large cupola set on an octagonal drum. It has a very handsome elevation overlooking Via Raddusa. The interior is designed to a central plan around a regular octagon; there are four chapels with altars that feature, on the right, *statues of St. Euplio and St. Joseph*, and on the left, *Our Lady of the Immaculate Conception* and *St. Benedict*; on the main altar is a *statue of St. Agatha*.

This is only one of the numerous churches dedicated to the patron saint of Catania; among the other churches dedicated to her we should mention *S. Agata alle Sciare* (D2) at the easternmost extremity of the Via Vittorio Emanuele; *S. Agata alla Fornace* (C3) in the Piazza Stesicoro (tradition has it that this was the site of the furnace – "fornace" – where she was martyred); *S. Agata al Carcere* (C3) in the Piazza Santo Carcere – the name "carcere" refers to the belief that the room here dating from Roman times was the cell in which the saint was held prisoner before her execution. There are also numerous relics of the saint; *S. Agata la Vetere* in the Via S. Maddalena, on the site of an early-Christian basilica; and *S. Agata al Borgo* (A2), north of the Piazza Cavour.

7.2 Mount Etna and its slopes

Rising 3323 meters into the sky, this volcano dominates the entire Ionian coast of Sicily, and its mass is so vast that it overshadows all other mountains.

A single and complete description of the cone is practically impossible without slipping into generalizations, so great is the variety of landscapes and vegetation that can be found on the volcano: the maquis of prickly pears of Belpasso; the groves of oak, chestnut, hazelnut, and pistachio trees of Bronte; the birch trees (Betula aetnensis), pines, mushrooms, and vineyards, and the splendid pine forest of Linguaglossa with its rich underbrush. Lastly, as if to join together so many different features, there are the lava deserts, the dry and lifeless flows that punch through the vegetation, creating full-fledged islands of greenery at times surrounded by cooled magma. Currently, the prevailing activity takes the form of lateral flows, while the craters on the summit seem to produce most of the explosions of the Strómboli type; full-fledged eruptions are accompanied by diffuse seismic activity throughout the volcanic struc-

ture. The other notable feature of the area is the sea, which laps at the eastern slope along the renowned "Riviera dei Ciclopi" (literally, the Cyclops Coast), embellished by the rock stacks of Aci Trezza and dotted with an unending succession of towns.

There is a great variety of possible excursions, to all sorts of different places: on Mt. Etna along the trails of the Etna Park (Parco dell'Etna: the administrative headquarters is at Nicolosi, page 159; the map is on page 158), to the 150 volcanic grottoes (Grotta del Gelo, Grotta dei Lamponi, Grotta delle Palombe, and so on) which can be found on the slopes, toward the summit of the volcano; to the renowned "Castagno dei 100 Cavalli" (the 100 Horses' Chestnut Tree) not far from Sant'Alfio, one of the oldest trees in the world; to the snowy ski slopes of the southern flank, which offer the excitement of skiing on the fiery belly of Mount Etna while looking down on Catania and the blue sea glittering far below; to the Ionian Sea for a refreshing swim in the rainbow-hued waters, and to the various towns whose names begin with "Aci."

The automobile tour – which covers a circular route, 141 km long (route map below; the tours of the towns, however, are by foot) – runs (roughly 42 km long) along the coast in the first section, on state road 114 Orientale Sicula through Aci Castello, Aci Trezza, and the largest of the towns, Acireale – whose streets are the site of the finest Sicilian carnival – from which secondary roads lead to Zafferana Etnea. At Fiumefreddo di Sicilia, you leave state road 114 and you skirt the border of the Parco dell'Etna along the state road 120 dell'Etna e delle Madonìe, for roughly 80 km. You will pass through Linguaglossa (another access route to the volcano) and Randazzo, which is marked architecturally by the three ethnic groups that lived together there at some length; then state road 284 Occidentale Etnea leads to Bronte – founded in the 16th c. – Adrano, and Paternò – guarded by an old Norman castle – and from here you can return to Catania along state road 121 Catanese or else you can drive up, on secondary roads, to Nicolosi, the main jump-off point for excursions to the volcano.

Aci Castello and Aci Trezza

The bond linking Aci Castello with Aci Trezza is a long stretch of beachfront, interrupted – as if by a wall – by a bathing establishment that has been the meeting place of high-society Catania for decades.

Aci Castello (elev. 15 m, pop. 19,241), which grew up around a Norman fortress, can no longer be considered a beach resort, as it has been absorbed into the hinterland of Catania. Built in 1076 entirely in volcanic stone, the *castello* fell under the rule of Ruggero di Lauria and then was seized in 1297 by Frederick II of Aragon. It now seems to be an instrinsic part of the natural product of a volcanic eruption upon which it stands. It houses the Museo Civico or City Museum (*open 9-1 and 3-6*) with specimens of undersea archeology. From the square before it, location of the *Chiesa Madre*, also made of volcanic stone, one can admire a superb panoramic view of the "Riviera dei Ciclopi" or Cyclops coast, with the towering silhouettes of the high rocks known as Faraglioni in the distance.

Aci Trezza (elev. 5 m) is a village with a maritime tradition, immortalized in the novel

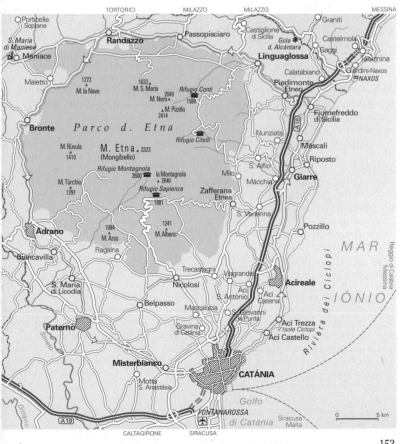

"I Malavoglia" by Giovanni Verga. This is a beach resort but also a town of permanent residents, and it continues to have close ties with the fishing industry. Numerous restaurants cluster around the marina, which has now become a mix of tourist pleasure port and fishing port, where large wooden fishing boats dock and where there is a large and active fish market.

Across the water rise the rock stacks or **Faraglioni dei Ciclopi***, great shoals of basalt rock like the rocks hurled in mythology by Polyphemus, the Cyclops, who was blinded by Ulysses, in a vain raging effort to sink the ships of the escaping Greeks. The largest of them is the *island of Lachea*, now the property of the Università di Catania; on

Acireale: the Duomo with Ss. Pietro e Paolo behind

the island, is a biological-research and hydrophysics station. Since 1989 the Faraglioni have been part of a natural reserve which in 1998 took the name of *Riserva naturale Isola Lachea-Faraglioni dei Ciclopi*.

Acireale*

The prefix "Aci" is joined here to the word "reale" (royal), which indicates that this little town (elev. 161 m, pop. 51,741; map on facing page) is the largest of the seven towns arranged along the eastern slope of Mount Etna whose names bear the same prefix. The origin of the prefix has to do with a stream, wiped out by a series of eruptions, which largely ran underground, and which was linked by tradition to the legend of the loves of the shepherd Aci (in English, Acis) with Galatea, the sea nymph. Polyphemus was in love with the nymph and, in a rage of jealousy, tossed a huge boulder onto Acis, crushing him; the gods, moved by pity, turned the shepherd into a river that, running through subterranean chambers, poured out into the sea to be with his beloved. The tone of this legend is well suited to this little town where the pace of

life is in keeping with the placid nature of the people. Piazza del Duomo, the cathedral square, with its Baroque magnificence, is the fine drawing room of this town – a meeting place where, among the little tables of the elegant "gelaterie" or ice cream shops that surround it, people may seem to be merely eating ice cream, but in fact they are taking part in an old and noble social ritual. The great celebration in Acireale is carnevale, the finest carnival feast in Sicily, with a procession of carri allegorici, or painted carts, and with thousands of tourists attracted by the giddy festival, as well as by the hot springs, first used for baths by the ancient Romans.

The city was built on its current site in 1326 after the destruction of the settlement – originally Roman and later Byzantine ("Aquilia") – first by the earthquake of 1169 and later by sea raiders. It became a feudal holding for three centuries beginning in 1642 by decree of Philip IV of Spain, controlled directly by the crown as a state-owned town under the name of Aci Reale.

The earliest core of the town stands on what is now the Piazza del Duomo or cathedral square, which was finished by the first half of the 17th c. with the completion of the buildings surrounding it (*Duomo*, 1618; *basilica of Ss. Pietro e Paolo*, 1642; *Palazzo Comunale*, 1659). Between the 16th and 17th c., the structure of the city branched out from the thoroughfare consisting of the present-day Corso Vittorio Emanuele and Corso Umberto I, which led respectively to the roads to Catania and Messina; the new settlements of various religious Orders – Dominicans to the west, Capuchins to the northeast, Carmelites to the southeast – that created new poles of urban development, linked in the center and one to the other: Via Cavour joined the monastery of the Dominicans with the Duomo; Via Galatea linked the two convents of the Capuchins and the Carmelites, encouraging the eastward growth of the city.

The earthquake of 1693 caused considerable destruction, though it did not damage the urban structure irreparably. Reconstruction was directed by the Duke of Camastra, and among those responsible we should mention the Aci-born painter Pietro Paolo Vasta. The nobility and the wealthy bourgeois took up residence along the chief thoroughfares; the clergy repaired the damage to the existing churches and built new ones, thus giving a structure to the original center that persists to the present day. Expansion in the 19th c. extended the course of what is now Corso Savoia, which creates a triangle with the Viale Principe Amedeo and the Corso Umberto I.

At the south entrance to the city stand the Baths or *Terme di S. Vénera* (D2), at the very heart of an immense park that was created in 1873. These hot baths take their water from a hot spring (the sulfurous water is 22 °C; it is used in treating certain forms of deafness and is excellent for the skin) which is located in the district or Contrada S. Vénera al Pozzo. Here stood the Terme Xiphonie, possibly Greek in origin, which the Romans enlarged with a construction whose ruins still stand there.

The main thoroughfare of this little city is *Corso Vittorio Emanuele* (C-D2), which intersects with Via Ruggero Settimo on a line with Piazza Vigo. Overlooking this square is the basilica of **S. Sebastiano** (C2), before which stretches a balustrade adorned with ten 18th-c. *statues* with characters from the Old Testament. The 17th-c. architectural structure, restored following the earthquake of 1693, is decorated on the interior by numerous frescoes and canvases by Pietro Paolo Vasta; also note the 18th-c. *litter* used in the procession of the saint.

Walking past 18th-/19th-c. palazzi, we will come to **Piazza del Duomo*** (B2), enlarged in the 17th c., a setting of rare beauty. The *Duomo* (B2) or cathedral dedicated to Our Lady of the Annunciation (Annunziata) and to Saint Vénera was first built in the years 1597-1618 and was renovated in the early 18th c.; the two bell towers, with conical

Acireale 1 : 15 000 (1 cm = 150 m)

cusps sheathed in polychrome ceramics, flank a façade in a pseudo-Gothic style built at the turn of the 20th c. by G.B. Basile, who incorporated a massive marble portal with 17th-c. *statues of the Annunciation and of Saints Vénera and Tecla*; inside, you can admire numerous works by P.P. Vasta and a sundial dating from 1843 set at the intersection of nave and transept.

Completing the setting of this square is the church of the *Ss. Pietro e Paolo*, with an 18th-c. elevation and a façade with two orders, and only one bell tower, on the right, with cusp and pinnacles (perhaps a second bell tower would have blocked the sunlight to the sundial of the Cathedral), and the *Palazzo Comunale* (city hall; B-C2), built in 1659 in the typical flamboyant Baroque of Catania, with balconies supported by carved brackets depicting bizarre figures and surmounted by ornate railings in wrought iron.

The *Biblioteca Zelantea* and the *Pinacoteca Zelantea* (B1) – respectively the library (*open 10-1; closed Sun.*) and art gallery (*open Mon. and Wed., 9-1*) – have been located since 1915 in Via Marchese di S. Giuliano (you can reach it from Piazza del Duomo by following Via Cavour). The library, which dates back to 1671, has one of the largest and richest collections in all of Sicily; in the art gallery, there are canvases by P.P. Vasta and a particularly noteworthy *bust of Julius Caesar**, better known as the Busto di Acireale, a Roman sculpture uncovered in 1676.

Beyond the Piazza del Duomo, the main thoroughfare of Acireale is called *Corso Umberto I* (A-B2), and is lined with boutiques and ice cream shops; these "gelaterie" truly constitute a distinctive feature of the little town. At the end of the "corso" is the *Villa Belvedere*, a public park and garden with a magnificent view of the Ionian Sea and Mount Etna.

If you go from Acireale to **Zafferana Etnea** (elev. 574 m, pop. 8186), on the main square of which stands the Baroque *Chiesa Madre*, you can ascend Mount Etna along the eastern slope; the road is distinguished by the remarkable views and the possibility of looking down over the far edge of Valle del Bove (turn right at the turnoff for Monte Zoccolaro).

From Acireale to Riposto

The secondary road, which runs parallel to state road 114, juts like a broad terrace high over the Timpa and the coast far below, offering a panoramic view that reaches all the way to the coasts of Calabria, and running through orange groves and rebuilt rural farmhouses.

The little hamlet of *Santa Maria la Scala* (elev. 15 m) – which you can reach by walking down a long stairway with spectacular views – is both a fishing village and a beach resort; the little village is clustered around the 17th-c. church and the little marina, in a setting that is still miraculously intact. Rocky beaches of volcanic stone and pleasant little restaurants overlooking the sea characterize the next town, *Santa Tecla* (elev. 365 m), followed by *Pozzillo* (elev. 10 m), set among countless orange groves and a relatively undeveloped coastal area, and *Riposto* (elev. 8 m, pop. 13,775), which until 1841 was part of the adjoining town of Giarre. Its name comes from the original role it played as a storehouse for goods from inland, and it is still possible to see many examples of industrial architecture from the 19th c. linked to the production and sale of wine; nearby there were once famous shipyards, no longer in operation.

Linguaglossa

The name of this town (elev. 550 m, pop. 5437) probably comes from a long bed ("lingua grossa") of lava left after an eruption in 1634 and commemorated by a plaque at the city hall. From here, it is easy to reach the pine forest or *Pineta di Linguaglossa*, and the *Piano Provenzana*, a ski resort on the northeastern slope, a base camp for expeditions to the summit of the volcano, or to walk the trail that leads around Mount Etna.

Randazzo

Located on the northern slopes of Mount Etna, this town (elev. 765 m, pop. 11,566; map on facing page) hearkens back to the Middle Ages, both in terms of the configuration of the center and for the very fact of its existence. The presence of the volcano is a very vivid and keenly felt thing, not only because it bulks so large in the landscape, but also because its products are used in manufactured artifacts of all sorts; volcanic stone is used to build drystone walls in the fields and also to construct buildings in the city, and as the raw material for sculpted and monumental edifices, as well as for the paving of the roads.

Always spared by the magma – even though it was the town located closest to the volcano's main crater – this little city grew in importance during Swabian rule, and it soon became the trading center for the entire range of the Monti Nèbrodi. In 1154, the Arabic geographer al-Idrisi described it as overflowing with merchants. Under the rule of Peter of Aragon the town was fortified and enclosed with walls, some stretches of

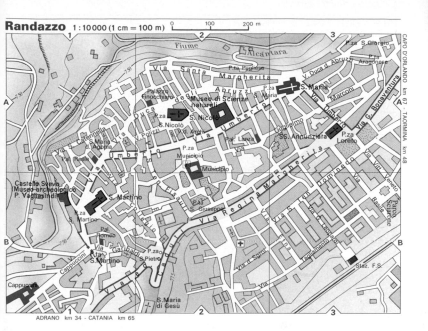

which still stand in an area adjoining the gate or Porta Aragonese. In the 14th c. the population was estimated to be 5000-6000; subsequent growth dwindled only at the end of the 16th c. due to an array of contributing factors: the foundation of the nearby town of Bronte (1535); the damming of the river Piccolo by a lava flow that caused considerable damage to the fields; and the plague, which broke out between 1575 and 1580, raging so fiercely that it forced the abandonment and destruction of entire districts of the city. The reconstruction of a number of buildings and the filling up of the space within the walls were the most notable occurrences of the 17th c.

The town is divided into three main areas, once occupied by three different ethnic communities each gathering around a church: the Latins around the church of S. Maria, the Greeks around the church of S. Nicolò, and the Lombards around the church of S. Martino. The equilibrium of the community was preserved by giving each of these churches the role of Cathedral for a year (it was not until after 1916 that S. Maria was finally named Chiesa Madre). Nowadays, these three churches are still the most significant monuments. Overlooking Piazza Basilica is the church of **S. Maria*** (A3), which was founded by the Swabians (1217-39) and shows very little of its original structure; the façade has a cusped campanile, rebuilt in 1852-63; the apses, shaped like battlemented donjon towers, date from the 13th c.; on the right side, note the splen-

did Catalonian Gothic *portal* (15th c.) complete with an array of triple-, twin-, and single-light mullioned windows. The *interior* has a nave and two aisles, divided by columns made of volcanic stone; the addition of a cupola in the early 19th c. partly undercut the harmony that had been attained with the various modifications done during the 16th and 17th c. The interior boasts numerous frescoes, canvases, and inlaid marble work from various eras: of these, perhaps the most precious piece of iconographic documentation is a painting on panel (*Salvation of Randazzo*), with a view of the 16th-c. town, hanging on the right side door and attributed to Girolamo Alibrandi.

Randazzo: the portal of the Chiesa Madre

157

Parco dell'Etna   1: 300 000 (1 cm = 3 km)

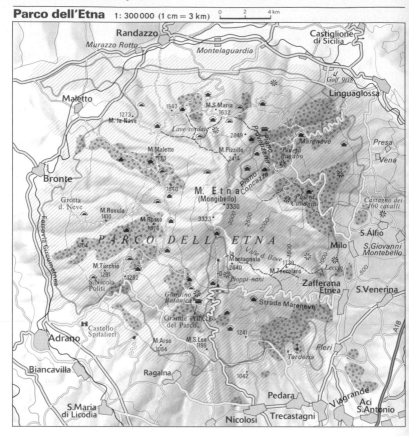

The original structure of the church of **S. Nicolò** (A2), the second basilican church and the largest one in Randazzo (which is why Peter of Aragon accorded it the privilege of holding general civic assemblies), dates back to the 14th c. but was rebuilt in 1583. In the *interior*, with its Latin-cross plan, there are numerous works by the Gagini, including a notable *statue of St. Nicholas* set on the altar of the left arm of the transept and signed by Antonello Gagini (1523).

The church of **S. Martino** (B1) was also founded by the Swabians (13th c.), but the magnificent bell tower on the right dates from the 14th c.; the 15th-c. *interior* contains canvases from the Gagini school and a polyptych (*Virgin Mary with Child, St. Magdalen, and St. Martha, Deposition and Annunciation*) attributed to Antonello de Saliba. Facing the church is the *Swabian castle*, the only surviving structure of the eight towers built along the walls. It houses the civic archeological museum, or *Museo Archeologico "Paolo Vagliasindi" (open 9-6)* with finds ranging from the Neolithic to early Sicilian and Greek times. In the same complex is the *Museo dei Pupi Siciliani (open 9-1 and 4-7; Sun. and holidays, 10-12:30)* with a very fine collection of Sicilian puppets.

In the southern walls, is a remarkable pointed-arch gate, or *Porta Aragonese*, which dates from 1282.

Not far from Randazzo, a short detour toward Cesarò is certainly worth taking to see the Benedictine **abbey of Maniace***, known as Castello, located not far from the place where the Byzantine condottiere George Maniace defeated the Saracens with the assistance of the Normans (1040). It was founded in 1174 by Margaret, the mother of William II, and in 1799 was donated to Admiral Horatio Nelson with the landholding called the Ducea di Bronte; Nelson's descendants lived there almost uninterruptedly until 1981, transforming it into a lavish aristocratic residence with a wonderful garden of exotic plants.

Bronte

Under Spanish rule in the 16th c., the power of the barons had grown out of all proportion, along with the extensive corruption of public officials and outright favoritism on the part of the nobility. The decision of Charles V to reorganize the hamlets of the villages of the Randazzo countryside into a single center was a result of the reorganization of all settlements in administrative and fiscal terms; that decision resulted in the foundation in 1535 of Bronte (elev. 760 m, pop. 19,694) which soon rivaled its neighbor Randazzo, draining it of population and manpower.

Devastated by the eruptions of 1651, 1832, and 1843 whose lava flows, especially those of the eruption of 1832, still lie nearby, this town is now a notable farming center, known in particular for its biennial pistachio harvest. Among the *churches*, the most significant is the church of the *Annunziata* (1535), on the façade of which is a yellow sandstone portal; inside are 17th-c. canvases and a polychrome marble group attributed to Antonello Gagini.

Adrano

Set on a volcanic highland which juts out toward the Valle del Simeto, this farming town (elev. 560 m, pop. 35,604) is particularly devoted to the production and sale of citrus fruit and honey.

Archeological relics of the Greek town of Adranon (5th c. B.C.) have been found in the Contrada Mendolito, not far from which is a bridge, the Ponte dei Saraceni, which spans the river in question; it declined under Roman rule and revived under the Normans with the name of Adernò, a name that it kept until 1929.

Particularly impressive is the **Castello Normanno*** *(open 9-1)* or Norman castle, with a square plan, built in the 11th c. by Count Roger; rebuilt in the 14th c. and recently restored, it contains an archeological museum or *Museo Archeologico* with thousands of finds from excavations in the nearby territory. On the top floor is a museum of crafts

or *Museo dell'Artigianato* and the picture gallery. The nearby *Chiesa Madre*, dedicated to Our Lady of the Assumption (Assunta), is Norman in origin and was enlarged in 1640-56 and restored in 1811; tradition has it that the 16 columns dividing the nave and aisles on the interior come from the ancient temple of Adranon.

Paternò

The little town (elev. 225 m, pop. 48,439) with an economy based on growing, harvesting, and exporting oranges, was founded by the Normans and has a historical center downhill from the basalt crag, atop which looms the castle or *Castello (open Tue.-Fri., 9:15-12:30 and 3:30-6:30; Sat.-Sun., 9:15-12:30)*; this was built by Roger the Norman (1073), but rebuilt after the 14th c., and subjected twice to restorations in the 20th c. The massive cubic structure built of volcanic stone is interrupted along the sides by twin-light mullioned windows which light the armory on the first floor and a gallery on the second.

From the square opposite, also overlooked by the *Chiesa Madre* (or S. Maria dell'Alto), which was rebuilt in 1342 on an existing Norman structure, the development of the city can be recognized in the prevailing colors (the burnt sienna and lava black of the historical center; polychrome hues in the regular urban development to the north; concrete grey and brick red in the settlement – largely in violation of the building codes – to the east and southeast). You can also admire the broad Piana di Catania, the mouth of the valley of the river Simeto, and the spectacular volcano.

Another route providing access to Mt. Etna runs from **Nicolosi** (elev. 700 m, pop. 6163), a town that has been destroyed repeatedly by lava and which has now become a choice summer resort for Catania. Located here are the offices of the **Parco dell'Etna***, where it is possible to get information on the trails running around the volcano (*Gruppo Guide Alpine Etna Sud, tel. 0957914755*).

Of particular note is the route to the hut or *Rifugio Sapienza*; this trail, like many of the trails that wind up to the cone, alternates vast expanses of oak, chestnut, and pine groves with desert-like volcanic lava flows. During the summer, it is possible to continue in off-road vehicles nearly all the way up to the summit of the crater, which is however off limits to visitors.

The incredible volcanic landscape

8 The region of the Monti Peloritani and the Aeolian Islands

Across the Strait of Messina, the continental ridge of the Apennines re-emerges just past the sandy spit of cape or Capo Peloro. The orographic alignment, or mountain range, that takes its name from this remarkable feature of the Sicilian coast is the range of the Monti Peloritani, with more than one summit rising above an altitude of 1000 meters. It extends first to the southwest, and is then blocked by the volcanic mass of Etna, which pushes it sharply west; from this point on the ridge takes the name of Monti Nèbrodi until it reaches the westernmost fringe of the Madonìe. To the east, along the Ioniatn slope, the coast

is steep and rocky, with a littoral strip that leaves little room for farming, manfacturing, and residential communities. The urban settlements from Messina to Taormina are all roughly the same size and equal in importance; they basically revolve around the capital. To the north, on the Tyrrhenian slope, there is a much more gradual grade leading from sea level to the upper ridges, and the slopes of the Monti Peloritani lend themselves perfectly to terrace farming. The dry and arid appearance of the eastern coast is a result of the hot sirocco winds out of Africa, which scald the flora before it can bloom; the northern coast, on the other hand, which receives a "tramontana" wind and is rich in mountain streams, is covered with high-branched forest trees on the middle and upper hills, and by fruit orchards and vineyards at the lower elevations. Milazzo, with its vast harbor in the sheltering lee of the Promontorio di Milazzo, a promontory jutting 6 km out into the Tyrrhenian, and with the fertile rolling hills extending inland, is the second ranking city of the Tyrrhenian area, as far as Sant'Àgata di Militello. Across from Milazzo and across from the entire arch of the coastline of Messina, the volcanic archipelago of the Aeolian Islands constitute one of the greatest tourist attractions of the area.

Home to fire and winds, the Aeolian Islands are set in the midst of a deep blue sea

8.1 Messina, the city on the strait

Any visit to Messina (elev. 3 m, pop. 259,156; city map on page 162) should begin from the sea. From the upper decks of the ferryboats that run across the strait, in fact, you can see a new city; it is fairly evident at a glance just how the urban structure was laid out, punctuated as it is by the transverse axes of the broad river beds or "fiumare" – which have been converted into roads – and organized into long straight avenues running perpendicular to the "fiumare". Old Messina is gone: there is the occasional sculpture or here and there a little architecture in stone, isolated from the original urban context, which only vaguely speaks of the past; these traces are scattered throughout a landscape of reinforced concrete.

Messina has always played a critical role as a point of passage of the chief maritime traffic, between east and west and between north and south. This has been true since the city's foundation, which dates back to before the Greek colonization – which is to say, before the 8th c. B.C. – by early Sicilians, who called it "Zancle," or "sickle"; following its conquest by Dionysius in the 5th c. B.C. its name was changed to "Messana." Between the 3rd c. B.C. and the 5th c. A.D. the city grew in economic power, in part due to the construction of the two Roman consular roads running along the coast: the Via Valeria toward Catania and the Via Pompea toward Palermo. Under the Byzantines, the government was entrusted to the "Stratigoti" (strategists), interesting political figures of Greek influence; it was in this period that the Christianization of the island – already underway in its Latin form – was shifted in the direction of the Greek rite. Following the Arabs came the Normans (1061), who planted the feudal system on the island.

Under the House of Hauteville (11th and 12th c.) and under the dynasty of the Hohenstaufen (12th c.), Messina was girded with a powerful set of walls – not a trace of which is left standing – and numerous monasteries and churches were built as well (Santissima Annunziata dei Catalani), not to mention the foundation of the Duomo or Cathedral and, at the extremity of what is now known as the peninsula of S. Raineri, the titular church of the Greek archimandrite (S. Salvatore dei Greci). The construction of manufacturing infrastructure and improved communications – during the occupation by both Swabians and the House of Anjou – encouraged trade in silk, wool, and leather. The Messina that, in the 16th c., came under the rule of the Spanish viceroys was a wealthy and populous city indeed. Following an initial period of structural renovation, a decisive project was undertaken for the expansion of the city boundaries, with the shift of the enclosure walls; among the many building projects that were completed – many of them long since destroyed – two fortresses still stand: Forte S. Salvatore, at the sickle-hook of the harbor, and the Forte Gonzaga, set high on a mount behind the city center.

A great many of the public and private buildings constructed in this period were destroyed by the brutal earthquake of 1783. In the 19th c., transport links with the capital cities of Catania, Siracusa, and Palermo were improved; a regular ferry boat service was established across the strait, and shortly after the unification of Italy, the first regulatory plan was drawn up, which further extended the boundary of the city, this time toward the south.

The catastrophic earthquake of 1908 once again put a sudden halt to all development, sapping the will of the people of Messina, a determination that had already been sorely tried by centuries of traumatic events. The plan for reconstruction (1911) designed a city in which there is no room left for historic memory, a city with broad boulevards and strong, earthquake-proof buildings organized into blocks on a rigid checkerboard pattern. Although it has been widely discussed and criticized, the "Piano Borzi" – a regulatory plan that was named after its framer – was nonetheless prompted by the harsh necessities of the moment, and it did provide at least a reassuring solidity to the terrorized city that had survived the earthquake. There was also massive damage caused by bombing in 1943, another factor that contributed to the almost totally modern appearance that Messina presents to the visitor: the few pre-earthquake structures that still stand are easily noted in the mass of residential buildings of late-19th-c. appearance. If you have a car, you can drive around the eastern branch of the Punta della Sicilia, or you can venture up into the nearby Peloritani.

Forte S. Salvatore (B-C3). At the farthest tip of the peninsula of S. Raineri, which closes off to the east the natural harbor of Messina, this great fortress was built in the 1540s at the behest of the viceroy Ferrante Gonzaga, to plans by Antonio Ferramolino da Bergamo. The Forte San Salvatore was part of the plan for the fortification of the city made necessary by the incessant raids of the Turks; it constitutes the outlying works of the city defensive apparatus, construction of which began in 1533 and continued until 1686 with the construction of the citadel or Cittadella; the only section of this immense fortification that remains in good condition nowadays is the Forte Gonzaga (see page 166).

Cittadella (C-D3, off map) or citadel. On the central area of the peninsula, now occupied by shipyards and railyards, there still stand, shrouded by many years of neglect, the ruins of the fortress built between 1682 and 1686 following the bloody revolt against Spanish domination in 1678. It was one of the most important coastal fortifications of the time. Justified both for the de-

0   150   300 m

fense of Messina from attacks by outsiders (at the time that Ferramolino was building these fortifications, the peninsula of S. Raineri was unguarded to the south, toward the seafront overlooking the strait), and to keep the city itself under control, in the fear of possible new outbreaks of unrest; the fortress presented a pentagonal plan and was endowed with five projecting bastions, from which to set up a crossfire, giving it the form of a star that was later adopted in other forts under Spanish, French, and Dutch domination, and which still marks the shape of some towns to the present day.

The string of buildings facing the port (D3-C2). These structures were built in the first half of the 20th c., replacing the 19th-c. "Palazzata a Mare," which was destroyed in the earthquake of 1908. The architectural and town-planning invention of the "Palazzata" of the port dates back to the period of the Spanish viceroys (the structures built at that time were first damaged by the insurrection against the Spanish and finally destroyed by the earthquake of 1783) and was also called the "teatro" or front of the city; indeed, the prestigious series of buildings ran unbroken, like a ribbon, along the part of the port's perimeter facing the sickle-shaped area.

Via I Settembre (D2-3, C2). The present-day route of this street dates back to 1911 but retraces the much older Via Austria, built in the 16th c. to link the Palazzo Reale, which stood in the area now occupied by the Dogana or customs office, with the Duomo or Cathedral; the date indicated in the name commemorates the outbreak of the Sicilian uprising of the Risorgimento.

S. Maria degli Alemanni (D2). A rare example of Sicilian Gothic architecture (the interior features a nave, two aisles and three apses), this church was built in the first half of the 13th c., possibly by craftsmen and builders from north of the Alps, at the behest of the Cavalieri Teutonici or Teutonic knights, who abandoned it at the end of the 15th c., causing a steady decline and decay; capitals with all sorts of depictions are the sole surviving decorations.

Santissima Annunziata dei Catalani* (C2). This small church, with a basilican plan with nave and aisles, and cross vaults over the aisles and the transept, was built in the second half of the 12th c. during the wave of Norman foundations. The decoration of both the main façade and the side elevations show clear Moorish influence; surrounding the apse and the drum are smooth, slender columns supporting the little arches that mark the structure, in place of the traditional brick pilaster strips; this differentiates the church from the other churches in the Messina area dating from this same period. The floor is at a much lower level than the level of the modern city, which has been raised considerably due to the accumulation of rubble produced by various earthquakes.

Duomo* (C2) or Cathedral. Built at the behest of the Normans, it was consecrated under the rule of the Swabians (1197) and was partly destroyed a first time by the earthquake of 1783; its current appearance is the result of the reconstruction that was done following the last earthquake and the bombing of 1943: the only parts of the ancient structural elements that survive are the northwestern corner and the room that now contains the crypt. The *façade* is decorated with three marble strips with polychrome bas-reliefs (15th c.) depicting scenes of the fields and of everyday home life. The main portal, a composite work from the late 14th c. and the first half of the 15th c., is flanked by two pillar-bearing lions which date from the 14th c. On the right side is a *portal* by Polidoro da Caravaggio

The Duomo (rebuilt after the earthquake)

and Domenico Vanello (16th c.; the twin portal, set on the opposite side, is now used as an entrance to the modern Baptistery, though this distorts the original composition); in the structure adjoining this side there are Gothic-style twin-light mullioned windows, though only the first of them is original, made of stone and dating from the 15th c. The **interior**, with a Latin-cross basilican plan, is also largely redone: it is divided into a nave and two aisles by columns surmounted by pointed arches, and covered by a roof with painted trusses.

On the first altar in the right aisle, note the *statue of St. John the Baptist*, attributed to Antonello Gagini (16th c.; it is the sole example to survive the fire of 1943, from a series known as the Apostolate). Further along, a stone *portal* from the same period adorns the entrance to the vestibule which leads into the *Tesoro* (Treasury; *open Apr.-Oct., Mon.-Sun., 9-1 and 3:30-6:30; Nov.-Mar., Mon.-Fri., 9-1; Sat.-Sun., 9:30-1:30 and 4-7*), while its twin is located in the left aisle as an entrance to a symmetrical vestibule. On the main altar, in the presbytery, there is an interesting bronze panel depicting the Virgin Mary handing a letter to the ambassadors of Messina. In the left apse, note the chapel or *Cappella del Sacramento*, designed in the last few years of the 16th c. by Jacopo del Duca, a student of Michelangelo; this was the part least badly damaged by the earthquake; it contains the panels depicting the *Supper at Emmaus* and the *Last Supper* and, in the vault of the apse, a 14th-c. mosaic with the *Virgin enthroned*, and surrounded by archangels, female saints, and queens.

Campanile (C2) or bell tower. This tower stands 60 m tall, and it too was rebuilt after 1908; in 1933 the tower was given a large clock with four dials, one on each face of the tower; on the southern face, moreover, there are two other dials, one showing the calendar and the other the system of planets; lastly, there is a globe showing the phases of the moon. On the west side there are niches that contain a number of mechanical figures, which start working every twelve hours of the day or night: if we look from the bottom up, we see: in the first niche, *Allegories of the days of the week*; in the second niche, *Allegories of the ages of man*; in the third niche, the *Santuario di Montalto rises from and then disappears into a small mount*; in the fourth niche, *Characters from four Gospel scenes*; in the fifth niche, the *Delivery of the letter of the Virgin Mary to the ambassadors of Messina*. The first of the two top twin-light mullioned windows, on the same side of the tower, contains two antique bells, and on the external platform, there is a group of mechanical figures including a *rooster* and *Dina* and *Clarenza*, two popular heroines from the Vespri Siciliani or the revolt of the Sicilian Vespers.

Fontana di Orione* (C2). Set in the square facing the cathedral or Duomo, this fountain is one of the few sculptural works that survived the succession of disasters that struck the town; it was built in 1547 by Giovanni Angelo Montorsoli and Domenico Vanello in commemoration of the construction of the city's first aqueduct, which captured water from the mountain streams of Camaro and Bodonaro: the human figures that adorn it represent the rivers Tiber, Nile, Ebro, and Camaro, while a number of verses written by the Messinese mathematician and philosopher Francesco Maurolico, carved into the side of the basin, allude to river-related themes.

The square to the left of the Duomo features a marble *statue of Our Lady of the Immaculate Conception* (Immacolata, 1758).

From Piazza del Duomo, beyond Via Cavour along Via XXIV Maggio you can reach the *Monte di Pietà* (C2), which, of its original structures, preserves the façade by Natale Masuccio (17th c.). The three-arched portico has a 16th-c. fountain; from the atrium, a double-ramp staircase (on the first landing, note the 18th-c. fountain with *a statue of Abundance*) leads up to the church of *S. Maria della Pietà*, of which only the façade now survives.

Via Garibaldi (A-D2). This is the main thoroughfare of the city, extending from Piazza Cairoli (those interested in shopping should explore Viale S. Martino, which runs southward from here) and Piazza Castronuovo. There are few pieces of architecture dating to before the reconstruction of 1911 (the massive classic-style bulk of the city hall or *Municipio* dates back to 1934; C2): the 19th-c. *Teatro Vittorio Emanuele* and, beyond the Piazza Unità d'Italia (where there is a copy of the Neptune by Montorsoli, now in the Museo) note the houses, or *Case Cicala*, built between 1861 and 1864.

S. Giovanni di Malta (B2). Incorporated into the *Palazzo della Prefettura* (1920), this little church with its elegant Mannerist façade was designed in the 16th c. by Jacopo del Duca and is one of the few pieces of religious architecture from that period still to stand in decent condition; on the interior, note the *funerary monument to Francesco Maurolico* as well as 18th- and 19th-c. silverwork on display in little halls, and the sacellum with the tombs of the martyred saints, and large silver reliquary busts.

Museo Regionale* (A3, off map; *Open Tue.-Sat., 9-1:30; Tue., Thu., Sat., also 3-5:30 but Apr.-Sep. 4-6:30; Sun. and holidays, 9-12:30; closed Mon.*) This regional museum was set up in 1914 on the premises of a spinning mill not far from Viale Annunziata, and comprises works taken from the Civico Museo Peloritano, an institution that was located in the former monastery or Monastero di S. Gregorio, since destroyed by the earthquake. The interior halls, the vast area surrounding the old structure and the new museum, under construction, are cluttered with architectural and decorative elements taken from the ruins of buildings destroyed by earthquakes and war; for this reason it is still not possible to admire, among other things, the original of the lovely statue of Neptune by Montorsoli, which stood until recently on the esplanade.

On the left wall of the atrium, 12 18th-c. panels in gilt bronze recount the *legend of the Sacred Letter*: since the people of Messina had long been suffering a great famine, the Virgin Mary, moved to compassion by

Della Robbia, depicting a *Virgin with Child* surrounded by a wreath of fruit and vines (15th c.) and, attributed to Domenico Gagini, a marble bas-relief of *St. George, princess, and dragon* (15th c.).

In the list of works influenced by Antonello da Messina (hall IV), we should note the marble *Virgin and Child*, interesting for the treatment of surfaces with polychrome and gilding, attributed to Francesco Laurana. Antonello da Messina painted a panel oil painting for the chapel of the monastery of S. Gregorio in 1473, a **polyptych**** depicting the Virgin Mary Enthroned between Saint Gregory and Saint Benedict; of the five panels, which are now in relatively poor condition, the two upper panels depict the Archangel of the Annunciation, and Our Lady of the Annunciation (Annunziata). Another panel oil painting (*Pietà and Symbols of*

Messina and the strait which separates Sicily from Calabria

the faith the people had shown, offered her assistance by sending to the port of Messina a ship without a crew, but loaded with wheat and foods of all sorts, along with a letter containing a lock of her hair and a message blessing the city and the people (the words of the letter can be seen on the interior of the Forte S. Salvatore).

Among the objects dating from the Norman-Byzantine period (12th-13th c.), note the three *fragments of trusses* that supported the roof of the cathedral or Duomo, painted by local master craftsmen with themes taken from the Old and the New Testament (hall I); these motifs were probably the inspiration for the recent decoration of the present roof of the church.

In hall III, dating from the early Renaissance in Messina is the splendid two-tone glazed majolica tondo from the workshop of the

the Passion), by an anonymous Flemish painter, also of the 15th c., is a clear indicator of the cultural activity that was in the air in this city during the Antonello da Messina period; a painter of the Neapolitan school, Antonello de Saliba, did the 16th-c. panel of the *Virgin with Child*.

From the fountain or Fontana del Nettuno rebuilt in the Piazza Unità d'Italia comes the marble *Scylla* done by Giovanni Angelo Montorsoli in 1557 (hall VI).

There are two large canvases that Caravaggio painted in 1608 and 1609, during his brief stay in Messina, of the **Adoration of the Shepherds*** (hall X) and the **Resurrection of Lazarus*** (hall X), paintings which were done in his last few years of work (they fit between the Seven Works of Mercy for the Pio Monte di Pietà in Naples and, slightly later, the Beheading of St. John in Malta). The two paintings exerted enormous influence upon the local artistic culture, stimulating works of considerable merit: among these, let us cite the *Supper at Emmaus* (hall X) and the *Disbelief of St. Thomas* (hall X) by the Messinese artist Alonso Rodriguez, in which it is easy to see similarities in composition and style to the work of the master.

In the interior courtyard, the archeological finds from Greek and Roman times are worthy of note.

Circonvallazione a Monte (A2, B-F1-2) or uphill ring road. A long series of boulevards, which you will need a car to explore, mark the urban perimeter of the 1960s and offer lovely views of Messina and the strait. The segment that is known as the Viale Principe Umberto is characterized by the votive church of *Cristo Re* (Christ the King; C2), designed by G.B. Milani in 1937 in a Neo-Baroque style. From the square across from it, the Piazza Montorsoli, there is a fine view of the port and the center of town, with the Duomo and the Via I Settembre in the foreground. Not far away is the sanctuary or *Santuario di Montalto* (C2; you can reach it by following Via Dina e Clarenza to the left), whose façade was rebuilt (1930), replacing the original apses. On the Viale Italia, which comes next, there is an intersection with the Via Montepiselli, which leads up to the 16th-c. fortress, the *Forte Gonzaga* (D1, off map), which can only be viewed from outside.

Continue along Viale Europa until you reach Piazza Zaera and then turn to the right in Via

Catania to visit the monumental cemetery or *Cimitero Monumentale* (1872; F1); inside there are fine works of 19th-c. sculpture and architecture, including successful works from the Art-Nouveau period (Liberty) inaugurated in Sicily by Ernesto Basile.

The easternmost point of Sicily. Handsome views of the Sicilian and Calabrian coastline can be enjoyed by driving the scenic route along the strait as far as the *lakes of Ganzirri*, little brackish ponds linked to the open sea by feeder channels, traditionally used for the breeding and harvesting of mussels. And precisely on the extremity of the point stands the village of *Torre Faro* (elev. 3 m), while *Lido di Mortelle* (elev. 3 m), one of the favorite beach resorts of the Messina territory, is already part of the Tyrrhenian littoral strip.

The hills or Colli San Rizzo. The nearby Monti Peloritani, over which state road 113 Settentrionale Sicula runs toward Palermo, are covered with dense mantles of evergreens. Once you have driven up to the crossroads of the Portella di S. Rizzo, there are three possible routes to follow: turn to the right to reach *Castanèa delle Furie* (elev. 382 m), a hamlet that lies on one of the ridges of the range; turn to the left to climb up to the *Monte Antennamare* (elev. 1127 m), from the summit of which you can see both the Tyrrhenian and the Ionian seas (during migration season, you can see flocks of birds riding the updrafts over the mountains); or turn down toward the sea to reach Gesso (elev. 285 m), a village extending along a hilly crest.

8.2 From the Ionian coast to the Tyrrhenian coast

The route (map on facing page), which runs from Messina to Taormina along the Ionian coast and, after crossing the Monti Peloritani and reaching the Tyrrhenian Sea not far from Tìndari, ends after 155 km at Milazzo, is a succession of remarkably varied landscapes, both in terms of natural environment and in terms of urban and manmade features. The eastern slope of the Monti Peloritani gives way to a very narrow coastal strip with the road to Catania running through the "marinas" of towns that developed high on the slopes during the Middle Ages and then moved down to the coast in the late 18th c. These settlements still preserve their original layout and part of their historic array of religious and public buildings.

Itàla: the Basilian church of S. Pietro

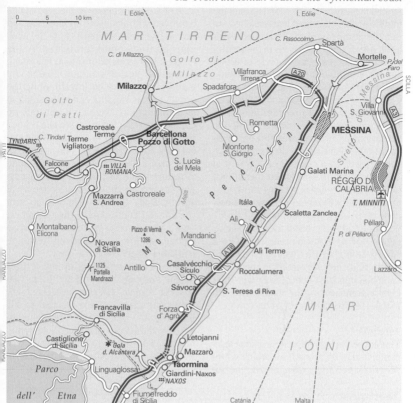

The harsh and almost entirely barren landscape of the southern slopes of the Monti Peloritani is suddenly replaced by another landscape, on the other side of the mountain ridge, a landscape in which dense conifer forests predominate at first, favored by the northwestern exposure of the slopes, and then farmland.

Along the Tyrrhenian Sea there is a strident contrast between the endless succession of little beach towns, devastated over the past few decades by the creeping blight of illegal construction and second homes, and the hilly hinterland, which preserves acceptable conditions of environmental quality.

This route, in the stretch between Messina and Taormina (53 km) follows state road 114 Orientale Sicula. Two brief detours lead to the towns of Itàla and Casalvecchio Siculo, where the Basilian churches are major documents of the civil and architectural history of the province or Provincia di Messina.) As you shift inland, you will follow the length of state road 185 di Sella Mandrazzi (69 km), which, after running through the astonishing canyon or Gola dell'Alcàntara, crosses the Monti

Peloritani at an elevation of 1125 m; having left Castiglione di Sicilia behind you on the left, you will drop down toward the sea and intersect, near Terme Vigliatore, with state road 113 Settentrionale Sicula. Between Tìndari and Milazzo, the terminus of the route, there is a distance of 33 km; this is also the point of departure for the trip to the Aeolian Islands.

Basilian churches

The monasteries founded by the Normans were located in strategic positions (on the banks of mountain streams or on high valley platforms) and were built with a wide variety of techniques and materials; one example, among many, can be seen in the church of *S. Pietro* near Itàla, established in 1093 on the site where, according to tradition, the Normans beat the Moors in battle, and the church of *Ss. Pietro e Paolo**, not far from Casalvecchio Siculo, founded prior to the arrival of the Normans and restored by them.

The history of the Basilian churches is closely bound up with the effort to convert Sicily to Islam; Greek monks, who had escaped iconoclastic persecution, had emigrated to Sicily in the 8th c., and up until the middle of the 9th c. they had remained under the authority of the Byzantine patriarch, organizing themselves in the territory with sites scattered outside of urban centers, constituting a discrete community, apparently no threat whatever to either Catholic or Muslim jurisdictions. The monasteries often provided haven to refugees following the arrival of the Moors, preserving a Christian presence on the island. In the 11th c., Roger (Ruggero I), hearkening back to a clause in the treaty of Melfi, signed in 1059 by his brother Robert Guiscard, succeeded in bringing under Latin jurisdiction the Byzantine dioceses of the reconquered territories. By restoring, founding, and endowing bishoprics, but allowing the abbots of the monasteries of Greek rite to administrate their holdings until death, and then by replacing them with Latin bishops, the Count of Sicily won their loyalty, transforming the monasteries into tools of territorial control, at his service.

Taormina**

This authentic pearl of Sicily is unique in location and in its urban form, which is two wings of a butterfly extending over the ter-race of a crag jutting over the sea, and interwoven with exquisite architecture and thread-like streets. From its high and luminous vantage point, protected by the forthest highlands of the Monti Peloritani, Taormina (elev. 204 m, pop. 10,669; city map below) looks northward along the coast as far as Messina, and to the south as far as Mount Etna. Perhaps it is its intense luminosity, reflected in the sea and echoed by Mount Etna, that makes its setting and scenery so attractive. An obligatory passage on the route between Messina and Syracuse, in the past the city played an important role in the regional economy of eastern Sicily, until the 18th c. when, with the coastal route linking the two cities, Taormina was left to specialize in tourist accommodations, so well suited to the remarkable loveliness of the site.

This site, already populated in archaic times by the early Sicilians and by the inhabitants of "Zancle" (Messina), received new immigrants from nearby "Naxos" in 403 B.C., when the tyrant of Syracuse, Dionysius, destroyed the town, allowing the survivors to occupy the ledge of Monte Tauro that entered the stage of history with the name of "Tauromenion." Near the church of S. Pan-

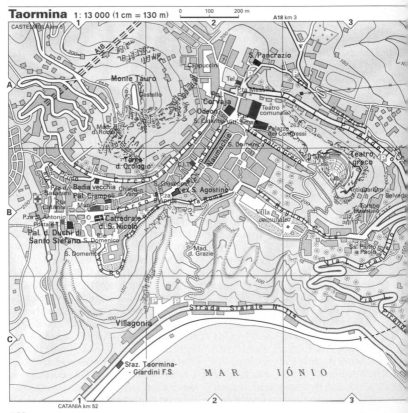

Taormina 1: 13 000 (1 cm = 130 m)

crazio, it is still possible to see ruins of houses that date back to the 3rd c. B.C.: it is believed, therefore, that the residential zone of the Hellenistic city must have been located here, since the acropolis stood on the summit of the mount, where the medieval castle now stands; to the south lay the area of the "polis," with the market square and the agora surrounded by public and religious buildings (the "bouleuterion," the theater, the temples). Monuments that, during the Roman Empire, were all renovated and modified, in form and in function. During the Byzantine era, when Taormina was elevated to the status of episcopal see, it expanded its perimeters, and at the southernmost end of the township, the first cathedral of S. Maria Assunta was built (now the hospital morgue). The Moors, who ruled here from 962 to 1079, enlarged and improved the town's water supply system, leading to improved cultivation of the surrounding land and shifting the urban center toward the earlier Byzantine expansion: around the Cathedral or Cattedrale there are residential districts (Cuseni), clustering around the gate or Porta Saracena – a gate that was cut into existing walls that were consolidated at the time –

Taormina: the Cathedral of S. Nicolò

while in the area of the old Roman Forum, there is a watch tower built to monitor the entrance to the city at the consular road or Consolare Valeria. Taormina became the great trading and caravan station mentioned by the geographer al-Idrisi in the 12th c., and consolidated its urban layout with the construction of the village or "borgo" beyond the Porta di Mezzo, which marked the perimeter of the city's growth in the late Middle Ages. The transfer of the cathedral to its present site dates from this period, while during the centuries that followed there was a great proliferation of palazzi built by the nascent landed aristocracy. Outside of the fortified enclosure, the Franciscan monastery grew up (now a rest home for the aged) as did the convent of S. Maria di Valverde; a 10th-c. watchtower or Torre Saracena, which was integrated in the 12th c. with the addition of a separate structure, attained its final form at the end of the 14th c. in the present-day Palazzo Corvaja.

In the 16th and 17th c. a new expansion affected the city, this time pushing northward; while in the 18th c. the site of the present-day belvedere was completed with the construction of the church of S. Giuseppe, and foreign travelers blazed the path of tourism to this little city, which had monasteries to recycle as tourist accommodations following the suppression of religious Orders in 1866. In the 20th c. the construction of new roads linking up with the ancient Mola (now Castelmola) and the coast encouraged the arrival of tourists, accelerating the growth of the town.

This walking tour runs along the Corso Um-

berto I, the "drawing room" of the city; a stroll along the Via Roma, past the Piazzetta S. Domenico, will allow you to enjoy the many spectacular views that are offered by the coast and Mount Etna; a walk through the dense network of lanes and stairways, interrupted here and there by small squares, winding among the walls of ancient houses and "palazzetti" that are adorned by geraniums and bougainvillea, helps to get into the enchanting atmosphere of this little town.

Corso Umberto I (A-B1-2). This road, whose route follows the ancient consular road, the Consolare Valeria, was the central thoroughfare and, as it were, backbone of the earliest Greco-Roman settlement, which was filled in where there were empty spaces, or more simply recycled into the buildings of later periods. It starts out from the gate or *Porta Messina* (A2), rebuilt in 1808 (immediately outside that gate is the 17th-c. church of *S. Pancrazio*, built on the remains of a temple dedicated to Jove Serapis), and ends at the gate or *Porta Catania* or *Porta del Tocco* (B1;1440), the western boundary of the "borgo."

Palazzo Corvaja (A2). This building on Piazza Vittorio Emanuele, with a central structure of Moorish origins, houses the *Museo delle Arti Figurative Popolari della Sicilia* (*open 9-1 and 4-8; closed Mon.*) with handcarts, puppets, folklore costumes, pottery, crèches and other items of island art.

S. Caterina d'Alessandria (A2). Set to the left of *Palazzo Corvaja*, this church was built in the 17th c. atop the ruins of the Roman *Odeon**, which was in turn built during the Empire through the transformation of an existing building (some think that it was a Hellenistic "bouleuterion," others that it was a Doric temple), uncovered during the excavations of 1893. What can still be seen of the earlier structure, behind the church, are the five wedges, with brick steps, constituting the cavea and a stretch of the original stonework on the "frons scaenae."

Teatro Greco** or Greek theater (B3; *open 9-one hour before sunset*). This construction, which probably dates back to the Hellenistic era, is built to exploit the natural slope of the hill; the cavea, split up into nine wedges with 28 steps each, was crowned at its summit by two porticoes, one on the interior (there are still some traces of it) and another, larger one, on the exterior; the Romans transformed it from a theater for

dramatic performances into an amphitheater for gladiatorial spectacles, replacing the semicircular orchestra with a circular arena set below the level of the foundation of the steps. The far wall of the scaena, in brick, has a large gap in the center which allows a view**, as if it were a perfect theatrical backdrop, of the bay of Schisò and Mount Etna.

Naumachiae (A-B2). The Romans not only "modernized" the city, they also endowed it with the service infrastructures needed for its economic development; among those infrastructures was a system for gathering spring water in large cisterns. The so-called "naumachiae" are the relics of that effort: this massive wall of masonry, exposed for a distance of 122 m, served to consolidate the embankment uphill for the construction of an enormous cistern, from which further hydraulic conduits irrigated of farmlands downhill.
Among the buildings that stand atop Roman structures is the church of *S. Maria del Piliere*, now converted into a shop.

Continue along Corso Umberto I and you will see on the left the former church of *S. Agostino* (1486), and then on the right, atop a staircase, the *Palazzo Ciampoli* (1412; now a hotel), in Catalonian Gothic style, with one floor of lovely small twin-light mullioned windows.

S. Nicolò (B1). Taormina Cathedral, built in the 13th c., has a façade with two 15th-c. single-light mullioned windows and a 17th-c. portal; the portal on the right side dates from the 16th c., while the portal on the left side, adorned with a floral vine motif, dates from the 15th c. In the *interior*, which still preserves the Romanesque basilican layout with evident traces of later renovations, there is a noteworthy *polyptych* on panel by Antonello de Saliba (1504) on the second altar.

Palazzo dei Duchi di S. Stefano (B1). This building, dating back to Norman times, features on its façade splendid twin-light mullioned windows with trilobate arches and a crowning frieze with geometric motifs of clearly Muslim inspiration (the Normans used Moorish craftsmen in construction). The interior is broken up into three stories, the central floor being covered by four cross-vaults with a column in the center; there is a permanent exhibition of the work of the sculptor Giuseppe Mazzullo.

Castelmola* (A1, off map). A scenic route uphill from the city takes you to what is thought to have been the site of the acropolis of "Tauromenion," now occupied by the medieval castle, still in good condition. The village of Castelmola (elev. 529 m, pop. 1080) clearly shows its medieval layout; as you stroll through the little lanes, you may note that the minor adaptations of the buildings have done nothing to alter the original layout; this is because until recent decades the city had attracted little interest from tourism. A number of short stairways lead to the Piazzetta del Duomo; the church of *S. Giorgio*, whose nave has been rotated, now overlooks a narrow terrace from which you can enjoy a fine view of the northern slopes of Mount Etna.

Naxos

On the promontory of the cape or Capo Schisò which closes off to the south the bay of the beach resort of *Giardini Naxos* (elev. 5 m, pop. 9094), excavations begun in the

Thucydides, the construction of Naxos began in 734 B.C., the second year of the eleventh Olympiad, and marked the start of the Greek colonization of Sicily. However, the colony did not have a long existence, as it was attacked and razed to the earth in 403 B.C. by the tyrant of Syracuse Dionysius, who intended to extend his rule over the entire island, and who was hindered in his ambitions by the alliance of Naxos and Athens.

Explorations have shown the existence of two different phases of growth of the city, and have indicated the existence of human settlements from the Bronze Age on the promontory. As of this writing, it is possible to see the walls dating from the 6th c. B.C. which enclosed the settlement in its second configuration, and the layout of the most recent settlement: characterized by a regular orthogonal grid layout, with a clear reference to Ippodamo town-planning, the city

The theater of Taormina with Etna and the bay of Schisò forming a marvelous backdrop

1960s have unearthed the ancient Chalcidian colony. Tradition has it that the Greeks stayed far from the Sicilian coasts because they believed them to be inhabited by monsters and pirates of unheard-of savagery, until the Athenian Theocles was shipwrecked on one of the eastern beaches; he found the Sicilian earth to be fertile, and returned with a contingent of Chalcidians and founded the first colony (the expression "dicerie fenicie," or "Phoenician rumors" indicates the lies that the Phoenicians had spread about the island throughout the Mediterranean, with the goal of preserving their monopoly over the western markets). According to the writings of

had broad roads running lengthwise (plateas) intersecting with other smaller, perpendicular roads bounding the blocks of buildings; the sacred area, enclosed in a further masonry wall, was located at the southernmost end of the promontory of Capo Schisò.

As you enter the boundaries of the excavation area (*open 9-6; summer, until 7*), there is a stretch roughly 300 m long of the massive western *fortification*, in very roughhewn polygonal blocks of volcanic stone; this wall marks the level of the city of the 5th c. B.C.; as you walk along it, you will find the entrance gates and the enclosure wall of the sacred area in which, aside from the sacrificial altars, archeologists found the ruins of a *temple* dating back to the 6th c. B.C., a temple that measured 14.25 x 38.40 m at each front. Near the castle or Castello Paladino to the north are the ruins of an archaic settlement, with an *"a pastas" house* dating back to the 7th c. B.C. At the intersection between the Platea A and the Transverse 11, is a house thought to date back to the earliest settlement 8th c. B.C.), with a square plan and techniques of construction similar to those found in the houses of "Megara Hyblaea," Syracuse, and Eloro.

A view of the enchanting Gola dell'Alcàntara

The furnishings, objects of everyday use, religious paraments and fragments of architectural decorations found in the area of the excavations are preserved in the two stories of the little *museum*, installed in a building dating from the 17th-18th c. at the easternmost point of the cape.

Gola dell'Alcàntara*

The river Alcàntara, which received its names from the Moors because there was a stone bridge over that river near Calatabiano ("al-Qantarah" in fact means "the bridge"), originates on the Monti Nèbrodi and is fed by a spring on the slopes of Mount Etna just over Randazzo, and by the rivers, or "fiumare," of Castiglione and Francavilla; for much of its length it marks the boundary between the provinces of Messina and Catania, and links the great volcanic cone of Mount Etna with the early limestone formations of the Monti Peloritani. In times prior to the Greek colonization, the eruption of the crater or Cratere Moio situated on the northern slope of Mount Etna, formed a cape or Capo Schisò where Naxos was later founded; in time, the river, which the Greeks called "Onobala," dug a deep and lovely canyon into the basalt flow. This canyon or "gola" can be reached on foot or by elevator, and it is pos

sible to walk along the river bed, wearing rubber boots that can be rented on the site, for a distance of roughly 150 m.

Castiglione di Sicilia

Perched high on a hilltop in the valley of the Alcàntara and accessible from Francavilla di Sicilia with a 5.2-km detour, this little town (elev. 621 m, pop. 3880) still preserves the charm of the medieval urban setting, extending around the castle or *Castel Leone* (hence the name) founded by the Normans and Swabians. The fortification, daringly wedged into the crevices of the rocky ridge at the highest place in the town , presents on its façades classic pointed-arch mullioned windows in volcanic rock and brick; these windows were taken as models for the religious and civil architecture of the surrounding area. From here it is possible to get a good idea of the strategic layout of the settlement, as well as to admire the incredible assortment of shapes and colors of the bell towers of the churches, like so many minarets in a casbah. From Piazza Ruggero di Lauria, after you follow a short uphill lane and cross the Piano S. Antonio (the 18th-c. church of *S. Antonio* contains fine marble inlays on the interior), you can observe the Neoclassical church of the *Benedettine* and the Norman-Moorish apse (1105) of the *Chiesa Matrice di S. Pietro*. Embellishing the narrow and charming lanes are balconies and portals made of volcanic stone, which wind and cold have eroded, revealing the porous structure of the material.

Terme Vigliatore

A stop at San Biagio (elev. 24 m), an outlying section of Terme Vigliatore (pop. 6378), offers an opportunity to tour a **Roman villa** unearthed in 1953 (*open 9-one hour before sunset*). It dates back to the 1st c. A.D., which makes it older than the villa of Patti. A part of the *peristyle* survives, with off to the right a small *bath complex*, with typical rooms with floors on hypocaust and surrounded by terracotta tubing for the circulation of steam, and at the center an apsed *tablinum* with a single large exedra, and next to it a slightly smaller room; also in good condition are the black-and-white mosaics in a number of rooms and the hexagonal-tile marble floors of the *tablinum*.

Tindari*

Nowadays a destination for religious pilgrims to with its imposing *sanctuary of the Madonna del Tindari* (1956-79; map below, A-B2), this town owes its historical importance to the role it played in the ancient history of the island. Founded toward the end of the 4th c. B.C. with the name of "Tyndaris," it was – much like "Tauromenion," "Mylai," and "Zancle" – a strongpoint in the possessions of the Syracusan tyrant Dionysius in eastern Sicily; not unlike "Tauromenion," it occupied a crag, high over the sea and protected by the sea, from which one could easily survey the coast from cape or Capo Calavà to the west, to Capo di Milazzo to the east. Like the other Greek cities that were "recycled," it was subjected to considerable renovations by the Romans in its urban layout and in the architectural configuration of its main public buildings; after it partly collapsed into the sea in the 1st c. A.D. following a landslide, it was finally and completely destroyed by the Moors in the 9th-10th c. The archeological digs (*open 9-two hours before sunset*) have unearthed the regular layout of Tindari, with a right-angled grid of *decumani* and *cardines* bounding the blocks of buildings. Of the *walls* that surrounded the hilltop occupied by the city, built in the 3rd c. B.C. and modified by the Romans in correspondence with the theater in the late-Empire, you can see the southernmost stretch, with its towers and main gate, beginning from the point where the road crosses it.

The *basilica** (A1-2), or meeting hall, on the other hand, is a construction from the late Roman Empire, with a barrel-vault roof; it originally extended over three stories, with two staircases set diametrically opposite each other.

Between the upper decumanus and the middle one is an *insula** or block structured with terraces on at least four levels, running down toward the sea: on the first level from the bottom, on the middle decumanus, there are shops and storehouses; on the second level is a little house; on the third level stretches a large residential building, probably dating from the 2nd c. B.C. and successively enriched with mosaic floors (it has an entrance on the western cardo which led to the peristyle, onto which in turn opened the rooms and the tablinum or reception hall); on the fourth level, the hot baths have floors decorated with mosaics in nearly every room (in the dressing rooms on either side of the entrance, *Bull and pilei of the Dioscuri* and *Trinacria*; in the frigidarium to the west, *Struggle between the two athletes Verna and Afer*, signed by "Agathon slave of Dionysius," and, in another panel, a *Marine Centaur*; in the tepidarium, a tondo with *Dionysius and panther*).

The *Museo* (A1) or museum features material from excavations and lavish furnishings found in the Hellenistic and Roman necropolises. A large model reconstructs the "frons scenae" of the theater.

The *theater** (A1), with an originally Greek plan dating from the 3rd c. B.C., has a

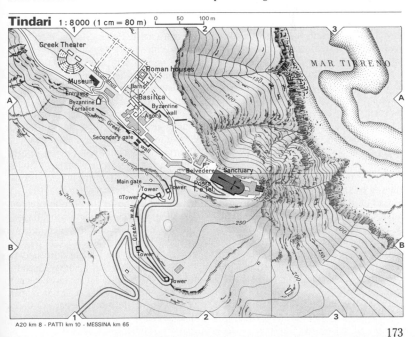

Tindari 1:8 000 (1 cm = 80 m)   0   50   100 m

A20 km 8 - PATTI km 10 - MESSINA km 65

Tindari: Roman ruins

cavea split into 11 wedge segments, with 28 steps; total diameter is 63 m; the circular arena that now exists is the result of a transformation of the orchestra, done in Roman times.

Milazzo

The port, surrounded to the east by smoke-stacks and to the west by a wall of modern buildings, offers an image of an entirely new city: the recent, chaotic expansion inland and the overriding interests of industry are at the root of this appearance. In reality, although the town has certainly undergone considerable environmental decay, it is still possible to admire the physical history of Milazzo (elev. 1 m, pop. 32,459; city map on facing page) so important to the economy of the entire northeastern area of the island: the 18th-c. city, arranged on the plain and overlooking the waterfront at one extremity; the "borgo," with its 16th-/17th-c. monuments, arranged around the castle hill or Collina del Castello, built on the site of the Greek acropolis.

Founded by the inhabitants of "Zancle" in 716 B.C. with the name of "Mylai" and conquered by Dionysius in 392 B.C., Milazzo closes off the easternmost territorial triangle of the landholdings of Syracuse with the contemporary foundation of the bridge-heads of Taormina on the Ionian Sea and of Tindari on the Tyrrhenian Sea. After Hiero II, it became Roman and, in the 7th c., under the Byzantine government, it was made a bishopric.

Between the 9th and 10th c., under the Moors, the city took on new vitality in terms of maritime trade; in 1061 it was returned to the Christian faith by the Normans, and it was fortified at the behest of Frederick II (construction of the earliest core of the Castello), while Alphonse of Aragon built the enclosure walls with circular towers that completed the fortifications in the 15th c.

The 16th and 17th c. were a time in which the present-day layout of this section of the city came into being: during the reign of Charles V, Ferramolino, the same architect who designed the system of fortifications of Messina, and Camillo Camilliani were commissioned to oversee the enlargement of the enclosure walls built during the rule of the House of Aragon, an undertaking that was to make Milazzo one of the six most important strongholds in Sicily. The Spanish enclosure walls, originating from the north and south corners of the Aragonese complex, run with two massive arms in both directions to form a giant pincer that encloses the latest urban expansion: linking up a little lower down from the eastern front of the castle or Castello, the line of bastions of the military quarters marks the perimeter of the walled city. Outside, in the area of the Spanish districts, work began on the restructuring of the leading religious and public buildings. In the meanwhile, the development of commercial activities gave renewed importance to the areas surrounding the port; much of the population moved there, originating the distinction between the lower town, the "città bassa," as opposed to the upper town, the "città alta."

As a confirmation of the new importance of this area in the 18th c., the urban grid was homogenized with the construction of two roads, one running through the center and one running around, the Via Reale (now Via Umberto I) and Via alla Marina (now the Lungomare Garibaldi). The year 1893 marked the advent of the first urban plan, which, in the wake of the radical restructurings that were so popular at the time, cut the road now called Via Cumbo Borgia through the mass of late-medieval buildings, leading to their demolition and replacement.

In your exploration of the historical center, you should pay close attention to the spectacular Baroque architecture, which emerges between crafts workshops and modest homes; the walking tour begins from the old walled city and then descends, through the village, to the more recent lower town or "città bassa," while by car you may drive out along the cape or Capo di Milazzo.

The walled city. At the highest point, enclosed within the Aragon walls with round towers from the 15th c., the castle or *Castello di Federico II* (1237-40; A2; *open Oct.-Mar., 9-12 and 2:30-3:30; Apr.-May, 10-12 and 3-5; Jun.-Sep., 10-12 and 5-7; closed Mon.*) still has, in its center, the Norman keep and, inside, the hall called the Sala del Parlamento. On the lower esplanade, used in recent years for the temporary structure of an open-air theater during the summer, is the façade of the old Cathedral or *Duomo* (A2), dedicated to Our Lady of the Assumption or Vergine Assunta, which constitutes one of the very few examples of 17th-c. Sicilian Baroque; in the vicinity there are the ruins of the 15th-c. *Palazzo dei Giurati*, the site in the 18th and 19th c. of the public council.

The borgo or village. From the walled town, a staircase leads directly to the church of the *Madonna del Rosario* (A2-3), founded by the Dominican Order in 1538 (this was the headquarters of the Holy Office and the tribunal of the Inquisition), which still has a handsome cloister. A little further along a monumental double-ramp stairway runs up to the 18th-c. façade of the sanctuary of *S. Francesco di Paola* (B2), which was founded by St. Francis of Paula in 1464.

The lower city. On the Lungomare Garibaldi is the church of *S. Giacomo Apostolo* (C2), built in 1432 and renovated heavily over the ensuing centuries; on the interior is the *main altar* of the old Cathedral or Duomo, a fine piece of 17th-c. marble intarsia. Also originally founded in the 16th c. were the *church* and the *convent of the Carmine* (C2), whose 17th-c. elevations overlook the Piazza Caio Duilio; in one wing of the convent was built, at the end of the 19th c., the town hall or *Palazzo Municipale* (C2).

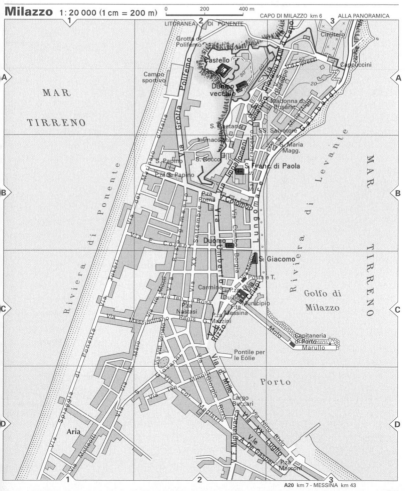

Milazzo 1:20 000 (1 cm = 200 m)

Capo di Milazzo. Two roads which you should plan on driving skirt the promontory: the western one, at sea level, leads to the bay of Tono, where there is an old tuna-fishing station ("tonnara"), now converted into a residence; the eastern one, high over the rocks, leads to the end of the peninsula on which the lighthouse stands amidst bushes of prickly pear; a little before it, a staircase leads down to the cliff sanctuary of *S. Antonio di Padova*. The State road 113 leads to the western cape of Sicily.

8.3 The Aeolian Islands

The seven islands (route map below; inscribed in the World's Heritage List by UNESCO) are all of volcanic origin, though each one is different from the other six, in terms of the colors that make up the natural and manmade landscape. Vulcano is greenish-yellow because of the sulphurous incrustations on its summit, and black because of its beaches of volcanic sand; Lìpari is blindingly bright due to the sharp contrast between the shiny black of the obsidian and the white of the pumice; Strómboli is black by day and incandescent red by night due to the continuous eruptions of lava on the "sciara del fuoco"; Salina is a spectacular green, due to the forests high atop the craters that are long extinct; Filicudi, like Alicudi, is dark green, because of the beautiful caper bushes which burst out of the basaltic rocks; Panarèa has an amber color, dotted with the bright green of vines and the plaster of the local houses, the "dammusi," which are buildings with broad terraces covered with canes, typical in these islands. Set in waters with rocky seabeds, waters of a stunning intense dark blue, all the islands are wrapped in glittering reflections.

The islands were not inhabited continuously as was the mainland, and their soils, which are largely untouched, offer up fragments of

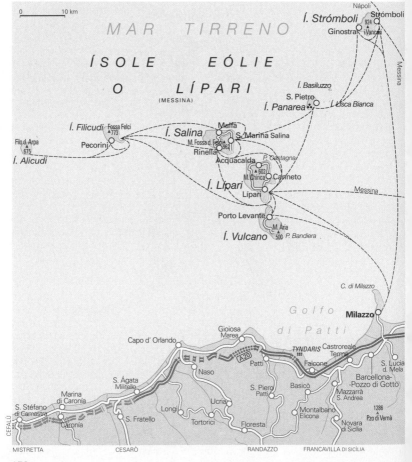

civilizations without historical overlapping, dating back to the 5th millennium B.C. Connections with Milazzo are assured by a service of ferry boats and hydrofoils.

Lìpari*

This is the largest of the seven islands (37.6 sq. km; maximum elevation, 602 m), and the township that includes it and is headquartered here (pop. 11,026) also includes Alicudi, Filicudi, Panarèa, Strómboli, and Vul-

the walled city lost population to the demographic increase of the lower city or "città bassa," and the formation of the villages of Canneto, Acquacalda, Quattropani, and Pianoconte. Along the Via Santo Petro (now the Corso Vittorio Emanuele) the urban expansion of the 19th c. was concentrated; and in 1930 a stairway was built, leading directly to the main portal of the Cathedral or Cattedrale, cutting the 16th-c. enclosure wall.

Lìpari: beyond the ramparts of the boundary wall stands the Cathedral

cano, as well as other smaller islands. Like the others, this island is volcanic in origin. The main center is Lìpari (elev. 44 m; city map on page 178), and its history is entirely concentrated around the narrow platform of the so-called Castello, a fine natural fortress formed by a rhiolytic pedestal, on the flat summit of which there has accumulated a further earth pedestal, carried by the wind.

Lìpari was the site of an early settlement in the 4th millennium B.C., and was selected in 580 B.C. by the Greeks of Rhodes and Cnidus for the foundation of one of the last western colonies. "Lipara," named after the its mythical first king, underwent three phases of expansion under Greek rule, with two resulting shifts of the defensive enclosure walls; beginning in 252 B.C. the acropolis became the first nucleus of the Roman city; it was on the same site that the Normans much later founded the cathedral of S. Bartolomeo (Benedictine Order). After a particularly prosperous period, the result of extensive exploration of the sulphur and alum mines as well as the excavation of pumice, the exportation of these resources to the larger island of Sicily made Lìpari the victim, in 1544, of a raid by the pirate Khair ad-Din, known as Barbarossa, who destroyed the town, killing many of its inhabitants. In a few years, the Spaniards rebuilt an effective system of defensive bastions to protect the port of Marina Corta, the "borgo," and the "civita." In the 18th c.,

Much of the Castello has been transformed into a museum complex; there are prehistoric, classical, epigraphic, and vulcanological sections, along with a section dedicated to the lesser islands; there is also a small archeological park; the tour of the little town is obviously a walking tour, and it passes by the Norman cathedral.

Museo Archeologico Regionale Eoliano* (C2; *open 9-1:30 and 3-7*). This institution, which uses existing buildings, has one of the finest exhibits in Sicily in terms of scholarship and careful exposition of the development of Aeolian culture through documents and souvenirs.

The 18th-c. former *Palazzo Vescovile* (bishop's palace) houses the **Prehistoric Section** (halls I-X), dedicated to materials found in excavations done on the acropolis of Lìpari. In a recently restored building is the *Epigraphic Section* with finds from the Greek-Roman necropolis of Diana. The **Aeolian Section** (halls XI-XV) is housed in the little pavilion facing the Palazzo Vescovile, and features materials from the sites on the other islands of the archipelago. In the pavilion to the north of the Cathedral or Cattedrale (halls XVI-XXVI) are the *Section of Milazzo Archeology*, and the **Section of Marine Archeology**, which contains the relics of about 15 wrecks found in the seabeds of the Aeolian Islands in points that are particularly treacherous for navigation: from the bay of Lìpari comes a prehistoric ship; al-

most 70 vases belong to the cargo of a ship that dates back to roughly 2000 B.C. In a 15th-c. house is the **Vulcanological Section**, which illustrates the formation and geological history of the Aeolian archipelago, as well as the changes that have been introduced by man.

The settlements prior to the Greeks can be broken down into ten periods, six of which are prior to the Bronze Age. The *Neolithic* covers the first few cen-turies of the 4th millennium B.C., the period when people first began to work and export obsidian, a glassy eruptive material that, when reduced to flakes, can be used in manufacturing weapons and cutting or carving tools; these periods are documented by traces of settlements and ceramics decorated in the style of Stentinello, found in Castellaro Vecchio on Lìpari.

Following this, until the middle of the 4th

millennium, was the *middle Neolithic*, the time of the first settlement on the site of the Castello di Lìpari, with ceramics decorated in three colors and characterized by spirals and meanders carved into the surfaces; beginning in the second half of the 4th millennium, it evolved into the refined ceramics of the style of Serra d'Alto (Matera), painted with more complex motifs.

In the 4th period, which includes the end of the 4th and all of the first half of the 3rd millennia, you can find traces of a settlement in Contrada Diana at Lìpari, which has yielded up shiny red tubular or spool-shaped ceramics without designs.

Following this, after the middle of the 3rd millennium, is the period of the *culture of Piano Conte di Lìpari*, during the course of which the beginning of metallurgy caused a crisis in the trade in obsidian, triggering an economic decline.

During the *culture of Piano Quartara di Panarèa*

(last centuries of the 3rd and beginning of the 2nd millenia) the archipelago began to form part of the cultural area of Sicily.

The *Bronze Age* is represented, until the 15th c. B.C., by the *culture of Capo Graziano* on Filicudi: the imported ceramics found there testify to ties with the Aegean Sea. We find the earliest settlements with stone huts, located at first in areas that are poorly protected (Contrada Diana, Piano del Porto and Contrada Fucile on Filicudi, Punta Peppemaria on Panarèa) and later moved to safer locations (Castello di Lìpari, Serro dei Cianfi on Salina, Montagnola di Capo Graziano on Filicudi); this marked the beginning of trade in alum, useful in tanning hides, and in tin, a component in bronze alloys.

Between 1400 and 1270 B.C., Panarèa was the site of the *culture of the Milazzese*: the ceramics took on forms and decorations similar to the contemporary culture of "Thapsos," huts were built on huts from the earlier period, and above all there was a first great destruction, which resulted in the depopulation of the lesser islands for some time.

From the 9th *period*, known as the *Ausonio I* (1270-1125 B.C.), the objects of everday use that have been uncovered indicate contact with the culture of the late Bronze Age on the Italian peninsula, while in the tenth period (*Ausonio II*; late 12th-early 9th c. B.C.) the huts were built with truss roofs and the ceramics were generally thrown on a wheel.

One final destruction put an end to this culture as well, and the islands were left practically uninhabited until the arrival of the Greeks. The earliest tombs, linked to the *Greek period*, were used strictly for burials in conjunction with cremation, and date back to the 8th c. B.C.; they feature cineraria and vases of Aegean importation; by the 6th and 5th c. B.C., simple burial prevailed – at first in stone or brick sarcophagi, and later in sarcophagi made of terracotta – signalled above ground by markers of every sort. Of considerable value are the tomb furnishings, which include finds from the 6th c. B.C. (late-Corinthian ceramics and Attic black-figure ceramics, but also black and striped ceramics of local production) running up through the 5th c. (the subjects consist largely of depictions of the cult of Dionysius, the god of drunkenness and the theater, who offered happiness in the afterlife to his devotees). And on to the 4th c. (four kraters are considered to be youthful works of the artist Asteas of Paestum), during the course of which there was considerable production of tragic, satirical, and comic masks linked to the works of Sophocles, Euripides, and Aristophanes: the examples found on Lìpari – circa 400 – document all the characters of their plays. Dating from the 3rd c. B.C. are masks worn in the New Comedy as well as the innovative work of the Painter of Lìpari, by whom there are some 100 surviving vases.

During the *Roman period*, the tombs with large curved tiles became the only method of burial until 252-251 B.C., while between the 1st c. B.C. and the 1st c. A.D. there is documentation of rough masonry tombs with recycled materials, a trend that in imperial times went so far as to include the reuse of Greek sarcophagi.

Cattedrale (C2) or Cathedral. Dedicated to St. Bartholomew (S. Bartolomeo) and founded by the Normans, this church was destroyed in 1544 by the pirate Barbarossa; the subsequent reconstruction (1654) re-

Typical houses along the coast of the Aeolian Islands

179

sulted in the present-day Baroque style (the façade dates from 1761).

Parco Archeologico (C2) or archeological park. Various digs, since covered up, have been done on the summit of the Castello, in a vast area divided by the modern road. The area that has been thoroughly investigated has yielded – from a depth ranging around 4 m – structures that date from the Bronze Age to Roman times; the lower layers – as much as 9 m deep – date back to the Neolithic and the earliest metal ages, and have

Fumaroles on the island of Vulcano

yielded abundant materials. Special signs, with color-coded indications of the various chronological phases, assist in an understanding of the individual structures.

Salina

This island was called "Dydime" by the Greeks, meaning "double," due to the fact that it was composed of two volcanic cones (Monte Fossa delle Felci, elev. 962 m; Monte dei Porri, elev. 860 m) separated by a saddle; it takes its present name from the salina or salt works of Lingua. It is the second largest in terms of surface area (26.8 sq. km; pop. 2,581, broken up into three townships) and the most lush of all the Aeolian Islands; this latter feature, along with the pleasant environment, still relatively unspoilt thanks to the efforts of a number of groups of dedicated ecologists, make this island one of the favorite resting places of migratory birds.

Vulcano

This island (21 sq. km; 0/500 m) has fallen

victim in the 20th c. to a tourist frenzy which has so damaged the environment that it is hard to imagine how it can recover; all the same, it still preserves the charm of its untamed nature, which can be enjoyed by taking a hike to the craters or by sailing around the island in a boat.

Panarèa

This is the smallest island (3.4 sq. km; elev. 0/421 m); it is also the earliest in terms of geological formation, although there are still secondary volcanic phenomena on the beach of the Calcara. With the islets that surround it (Basiluzzo, Spinazzola, Lisca Bianca, Dattilo, Bottaro, Lisca Nera, the Panarelli, and the Formiche), and which like Panarèa are the tips of a single submerged magmatic basin, it forms a little archipelago in the sea between Lìpari and Strómboli, perfect for exploration by boat. For the past few decades, the three villages of San Pietro, Ditella, and Drauto have been invaded, along with the surrounding territory, by intensive development for holiday homes and second homes.

Strómboli

Set at the northeastern end of the archipelago, this island has the only permanently active volcano in the entire archipelago; the island (12.6 sq. km) is visited especially by tourists interested in the spectacular eruptive phenomena, which can be admired both from the sea and from the summit of the highest cone (elev. 924 m); if you go up to the cone, we strongly recommend that you hire an authorized guide (*for information, tel. 090986315*). The island also offers an interesting *Volcanological Center* with plenty of information on the volcano in the form of maps, guides, videos and a permanent direct link with the crater.

Filicudi and Alicudi

These are the westernmost islands in the archipelago: the first, with a maximum elevation of elev. 774 m, has a total area of 9.5 sq. km; the second, which rises to an elevation of 675 m, has a total surface area of 5.2 sq. km. These are also the islands that are least popular with mass tourism, both because of their out-of-the-way location and because they are not equipped with luxurious accommodations. The islands, however, are ideal for those who want to spend their holidays far from the crowds of tourists, even though they are not furnished with what people call modern comforts.

9 The Tyrrhenian coast of Sicily

The extensive territory bounded to the west by the river Imera and to the east by the river Simeto has been known historically by the name of Val Demone. The name, despite what one might well think, means divine valley: valley in the sense of an expanse of land, and divine in the classical sense, i.e., so beautiful as to be a worthy abode of the gods.

We may consider the area to be divided up into three broad territorial strips, with different environmental qualities that are nicely complementary. The coastal strip can be represented as a long beach periodically punctuated by the mouths of mountain streams and tall rocky promontories. The area beyond the coast appears as a continuous belt of steep and forbidding mountains, rich in spring water and covered with dense forests, the home of the "nebros," meaning "fawn, young of the deer" in Greek. Indeed, it is from this that the Nèbrodi take their name. The territory inland is a vast upland, which – at an elevation of roughly 800-900 m – connects directly into the southern slope of the massif of the Madonìe and the range of the Nèbrodi, characterized by hills and soft rolling lands that are ideal for raising grain and for sheep farming. Though historically the coastal towns all share the crucial phase of re-establishment, and while their hinterlands all share the history of Norman feudalism they still present a wide variety of urban layouts.

The differences between towns become far less marked on the upland. This territory, in fact, was the feudal holding of the family of the Ventimiglia who, from Càccamo to Naso, disseminated towers throughout the towns, rendering development possible, and in some cases, actually presiding at their foundation and reconsolidating the course of the ancient and vital transportation network linking the eastern coast of Sicily and the capital. The natural heritage of the Monti Nèbrodi and the Madonìe, happily, remains virtually intact. Largely overlooked, these are areas of dense forests and silent clearings that offer a spectacular contradiction of the stereotype of Sicily as a land of sun and sea. Both the mountain range of the Nèbrodi and the massif of the Madonìe reach nearly to elevations of 2000 m, and resemble each other in terms of flora and fauna; as low as 1000 m of elevation they are covered with oak forests, and above an elevation of 1400 m there is a dense mantle of beech trees, the southernmost in Europe. The fauna is the same as that of the Apennines: foxes, weasels, and wildcats. Among the birds that nest on the rocky ridges are Bonelli's eagle, the golden eagle, the peregrine falcon, the kite, and the sparrowhawk.

9.1 Cefalù*

On state road 113, from Tusa toward Palermo or from Tèrmini toward Messina, the stunning beauty of a giant rock in the shape of a head, standing out against a blue-green sea, unmistakably marks the site. Protected from northern winds, Cefalù (elev. 16 m, pop. 14,026, city map on p. 183) is cut into the western part of the promontory. Corso

An evocative view of the beach in Cefalù

Ruggero, the chief thoroughfare, divides the town into two sections: one with twisting stepped lanes, ending at the rock wall, another with straight roads running down to the beach, or rather down to the unbroken curtain of small buildings that constitutes the seafront of the walled town. This town was founded in the 5th c. B.C., in a site that was certainly inhabited in prehistoric times, as is indicated by the traces found in the grottoes on the eastern slope of the crag that the Greeks called Kefaloidon. The remains of megalithic walls, on the shore near the Porta Giudecca and at the foot of the crag, as well as the so-called Tempio di Diana (Temple of Diana) on the summit, give a fragmentary image of the settlement's origins. Historians tell us of the important political role that this town played in the Roman Mediterranean between the 3rd c. B.C. and the 2nd c. A.D., of the role that it played in the Byzantine west up to the 9th c., and the even more important role that it played as a stronghold of Islam in Sicily; still, there are no substantial traces of this history in the urban structure. The Normans took it from the Moors in 1064, and destroyed all vestiges of the eastern style – just as they did in Palermo – by rebuilding it completely. With Frederick II of Swabia, nephew of Roger II of Altavilla (Hauteville) and of Frederick I of Hohenstaufen, known as Barbarossa, the privileges that had been handed down by his predecessors were confirmed, but there began a process of division between the Byzantines and the kingdom of Sicily. In the 13th and 14th c., Cefalù was governed by the Ventimiglia, who had their city residence built here, now known as so-called Osterio Magno.

Between the 16th and 17th c., the design of the city center was completed: the monasteries – Convento dei Domenicani, Convento degli Osservanti, and Convento dei Carmelitani – either filled in vacant spaces or were built over existing structures; the perimeter of the Piazza del Duomo was established by the façades of the Palazzo Piraino and the Palazzo Martino-Atanasio; the old enclosure walls with the entry gates to the city were reinforced and the bastion or Bastione di Capo Marchiafava was built. In the 18th c., while the local nobility built its own "palazzetti" (Agnello, Bordonaro, Mandralisca), the bishop's palace ("palazzo vescovile") was rebuilt in its present-day form. With the end of the feudal regime in the 19th c., a profound economic crisis began for Cefalù, as for the rest of southern Italy. The urbanistic consequence was the abandonment, by declining families, of the buildings that they inhabited or patronized. Cefalù fell victim to the building speculation of the last two decades of the 20th c., and now presents an ugly stretch of buildings reaching out into the plain to the west of the old center.

A tour of Cefalù inevitably begins right from the Piazza del Duomo.

Cattedrale** (A2) or Cathedral. Built at the behest of Roger II, according to legend as fulfillment of a vow made when he survived a tempest and landed at Cefalù, construction of this basilica began in 1131. The two towers give the church a look that is both once a fascinating and worrisome. An optical illusion makes them seem to converge, on high, one toward the other, in some sense undercutting the square-hewn and compact shape of the main façade. This façade was embellished in 1472 with the portico that protects the splendid entrance portal, as at Monreale. If you examine the exterior of the monument from the right side (the only side that is unencumbered) you will note the battlements (dates unknown) and the side apses, which present decorative motifs featuring entwined arches, common in the Sicilian architecture of the period, while the central apse has Gothic-style pilaster strips with basket arches.

The **interior** is large and solemn; it has a nave and two aisles, divided by tall columns with figured capitals supporting pointed, double-lintel arches; in the right aisle, note a Romanesque baptismal font. From the end of the central apse the great dark eyes of Christ Pantokrator, the All-Powerful, gaze down at an indefinite point in the unreal mosaic universe. "Glittering old Byzantine gold," to cite an expression of Vincenzo Consolo: from behind his head, the brilliant mosaics** capture the light of the Sicilian sun. And this figure that portrays the Deity even

Cefalù: the Cathedral

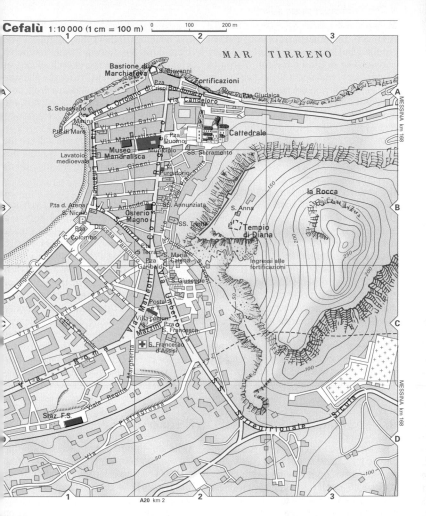

0   100   200 m

MAR   TIRRENO

Bastione di
Marchiafava
Fortificazioni
Pza
di Crispi Bordonaro
P.ta Giudaica
Candeloro
S. Sebastiano
Via C. Ortolano
Via Veterani
Mulini
Via Porto Salvo
P.za di Mare
Via Mandralisca
Pza
Duomo
Cattedrale
Museo
Mandralisca
Municipio
SS. Sacramento
Via Gioeni
Lavatoio
medievale
Via Gioeni
Via Vanni
Purgatorio
Mandralisca
la Rocca
P.ta d. Arena
Via Amendola
SS. Annunziata
S. Nicolò
S. Anna
Osterio
Magno
SS. Trinità
Tempio
di Diana
C. Colombo
Discesa Paramuro
P.za
di Terra
S. Maria
Catena
Ingressi alle
fortificazioni
C. Colombo
Pza
Garibaldi
S. Giuseppe
Via Maestra
Via Umberto
Posta
Via Mazzini
Villa Comun.
Pza
S. Francesco
Via Roma
Via Margherita
S. Francesco
d'Assisi
Piazza Margherita
Viale Regina
SS. Settentrionale
Staz. F.S.
Via
MESSINA km 168
MESSINA km 168
A20 km 2

---

has Sicilian features: blonde hair like the Normans, but dark thick beard and eyebrows, like the Moors; a straight nose and thin lips, like the Greeks. These mosaics in the apse can be dated back to the 12th c., and they have never been altered over their eight centuries of existence. The arches and the walls of the nave and aisles which, with the transept, compose the Latin cross of the church's plan, have been modified more than once, on the other hand. What we see today is the result of a long series of restorations that have not yet been completed. Adjoining the Duomo is a *cloister*, likewise built in the 12th c.; it was partly destroyed by a fire in the 16th c. Overlooking the Piazza del Duomo are a number of small palazzi from the Baroque era, such as the *Seminario* (seminary) and the *Palazzo Vescovile* (bishop's palace), the *Palazzo Maria*, probably a royal residence, and the *Palazzo Piraino* at the southern corner of Corso Ruggero II.

Corso Ruggero (A-B2). Along the "corso," the original architecture alternates with reconstructions: one thing that should be noted is the curious common denominator of the brackets supporting the balconies, all in iron or cast-iron, whether they are applied to medieval or contemporary buildings. The Via Caracciolo, one of the stairways/lanes leading up to the rocky wall, takes one to the church of the *Santissima Trinità*, with the adjoining *convent of the Dominicans* (1521). At the corner of the Via Amendola, one of the perpendicular roads running down toward the sea, you will find the remains of the 14th-c. *Osterio Magno*, heavily renovated over the centuries. The "corso" ends at Piazza Garibaldi, which links the historic center with the new settlement, on the site of the old land gate or Porta di Terra through which people entered the city when arriving along the old consular road or Via Consolare Pompea, and from the interior.

183

Museo Mandralisca (A1; *open 9-12:30 and 3:30-7:30*). This museum is now a public institution, but it was born of the love for art and science of Enrico Piraino, Baron of Mandralisca, who spent his old age in Cefalù, in the years before and after the Unification of Italy. A man of varied interests, Mandralisca collected – for his own intellectual pleasure – ancient marble works, coins, paintings, as well as the seashells which formed the chief focus of his studies – malacological studies, to use the scientific term. Among the works of art collected in this building, once the home of Mandralisca himself, the most famous is certainly the **Ritratto d'Ignoto**** (portrait of an unknown man) by Antonello da Messina. The little "pezzo di legno," or "piece of wood," with the oil painting dated 1465 was the central character in a wonderful novel by Vincenzo Consolo. Interesting items are the Greek ceramics, especially a renowned *krater* with a depiction of a man selling tuna, and the numismatic collection.

Bastione di Marchiafava (A2). If you leave Piazza del Duomo behind you on your right, Corso Ruggero will lead down to Via Carlo Ortolano di Bordonaro, named after a 17th-

c. aristocrat of Cefalù. The road, lined with low buildings, follows the coastline. If you climb down the stairway linking the church of *S. Giovanni* and the church of *Itria*, at Piazzetta Crispi you will reach the platform of the Bastione di Marchiafava; from here you have fine views of the coast, and you can observe a number of ruins of *archaic fortifications* in megalithic structure.

On Via Vittorio Emanuele you will see the Norman church of *S. Giorgio* and the medieval *washhouse*, a structure with a strong Moorish influence.

Rocca (B2-3) or fortress. As tiring as it may be, especially in the month of August, a climb up to the Rocca of Cefalù is a must. Like a relief extracted from the rock through cutting and drilling, Cefalù reveals its urban layout from up here: the red of the roofs and the yellow of the rock of the Duomo or Cathedral, make memorable contrasts with the deep blue of the rocky sea. At the edge of the brink there are are ruins, heavily renovated, of a fortification that probably dates from Byzantine times; further back is the *Temple of Diana* (B2), a massive construction in megalithic stone blocks dating from the archaic Greek period.

9.2 The Madonìe: from Cefalù to Nicosìa

The Tyrrhenian coast, which can be observed from state road 113, is spectacular (route map below); in some sections it is rocky, with a series of stunning views westward from Capo Zafferano and Capo Gallo, two capes that mark the extremities of the Gulf of Palermo. After Campofelice di Roc-

cella and the detour to Collesano, in the area of Buonfornello, at roughly 18 km from Cefalù, you will see on the right the sign for the Tempio della Vittoria (temple of victory; 5th c. B.C.), the monumental ruins of ancient Himera. Just a few meters further along on the left, if you look very carefully, you will

see a sign pointing to the excavations ("scavi") and the Antiquarium. The smokestacks of Tèrmini Imerese appear directly after Buonfornello. Running close around the massif of the Madonìe, green with forests, the road winds over the bare hills of the highland and reaches the Madonìe towns of Polizzi, Petralìa, and Gangi, still immersed in an agrarian and pastoral world of times gone by. Before you come to Nicosìa, you can admire the vertical thrust of Sperlinga high on its point of rock in the middle of the upland. At Nicosìa you will leave state road 120 and you will turn on to 117, skirting the eastern slope of Monte Sambughetti (elev. 1558 m) and leaving to the east the wooded slopes of the Nèbrodi. At roughly 30 km from Nicosìa you will see Mistretta, on the bluff that looks down on the riverbed. You will return to the 113 at Santo Stefano di Camastra, heading toward Cefalù; one can hardly help but notice, on the beach of Villa Margi, the enormous sculpture in the form of a blue window that marks the area of the Fiumara d'Arte: this is a "land art" circuit that links the towns of Tusa, Pettineo, Motta d'Affermo, and Castel di Lucio. Not far from Tusa lie the ruins of ancient Halaesa, with a detour through Castelbuono. From Nicosìa, if you prefer, you can continue along 120, take the provincial or local road to Capizzi and, passing through the handsome forest of Caronìa, reach the sea. In all, the route is 236 km.

Himera

This town was founded in 648 B.C. by the Greeks from Zancle, on a plain midway up the hillside, to the left of the northern branch of the river Imera. The site of combat between Greeks and Carthaginians, it was definitively destroyed by the latter in 409 B.C. The coins minted here bore a rooster, which may hint at the root of the name in "hemera," meaning "day." The excavations have unearthed a few remains of the city, among them a *sacred precinct* with three small archaic sanctuaries, which have yielded important material. To the north of the city is a Doric temple, the Tempio della Vittoria. The archeological site (*open 9-one hour before sunset; holidays, 9-1*) is crossed by the road which leads to the Antiquarium.

Tèrmini Imerese

Set on a hill on the coastline between Capo Zafferano and Cefalù, Tèrmini Imerese (elev. 77 m, pop. 26,571; city map on p. 186) has grown in economic importance in Sicily since WWII due to the establishment of a considerable industrial complex, including the Chimica del Mediterraneo, the power plant that once belonged to TIFEO, and the Sicilfiat. Now, like much of southern Italy, it is plagued with shutdown fever. Atop the hill, ancient Tèrmini still stands, protected perhaps by the steep roads leading up to it. Occupied in prehistoric times, it later fell under the influence of Himera; after the destruction of Himera, it took in the refugees from the town. Conquered in 252 B.C. by the Romans, who renamed it Thermae Himerensis, the town became a thermal spa for the treatment of urological disturbances. Traces of the old Baths remain on the interior of the former Stabilimento Vecchio and the Grande Albergo delle Terme. All that remains of the other Roman public works are a few ruined aqueducts along the road to Càccamo and the memory of the shape of the *amphitheater* in the direction of the block of buildings overlooking the Via Anfiteatro, in the town center, near Villa Palmeri. Fortified twice, in the Middle Ages and in the 16th c., Tèrmini has been inhabited by religious Orders since the 17th c., and until the 19th c. it remained enclosed within its 16th-c. walls. In the present-day urban layout you can make out the path of the old city walls, which have become ring roads, and the locations of the gates, the Porta Messina and the Porta Palermo. From these gates the main thoroughfares ran toward the center of town: from Porta Messina the Corso Umberto and the stepped Via Roma; from Porta Palermo the Via Garibaldi. The civic and religious center is *Piazza del Duomo*, which is overlooked by the 15th-c. Cathedral or *Duomo*, rebuilt in the 17th c., and the city hall, or *Palazzo Comunale* (1610). Nearby, at the mouth of Via Roma, you can tour the *Museo Civico* (*open 9-1:30; Wed.-Thu. and Sat.-Sun., also 3-6:30; closed Mon.*), the municipal museum established in 1873, housed in the halls of the former hospital. It contains three different sections: archeological, with materials dating back to prehistoric times, and as recent as the Late Roman Empire; art historic, with fine artworks from the Moorish-Norman period to as late as the 19th c.; and natural historic, still in progress.

The visit ends with a stroll to the *Belvedere Principe Umberto* (magnificent view of the city and the coast) and the *Villa Palmieri*, passing through the Piazza S. Caterina, where the 15th-c. church of *S. Caterina d'Alessandria* stands.

Càccamo (elev. 521 m, pop. 8618) was a Carthaginian stronghold in the 5th c. B.C. and caused considerable problems for nearby Himera, as well as for other Greek colonies in the area. Documentary sources seem to date the of-

185

Tèrmini Imerese 1:12 000 (1 cm = 120 m)

MAR TIRRENO

Porto

---

ficial foundation of the little town to 1093; the town appears to remain solidly attached to its past, and a tour is quite interesting. You should certainly see the *Duomo* or Cathedral, founded long ago by the Normans but rebuilt in 1614; the medieval church of the **Annunziata**, which was also entirely rebuilt in the 17th c.; it houses a lovely *altarpiece of the Annunciation* by Guglielmo Borremans (1725); the church of *S. Benedetto* dates from 1615, with its splendid pavement in decorated Sicilian majolica. But the monument of which the people of Càccamo are proudest, and rightly so, is their medieval castle, the **Castello***, built into the rocky face that juts over the valley.

Collesano

The ancient center of Collesano is particularly well preserved (elev. 468 m, pop. 4419), which still maintains the medieval layout from its earliest development around the Norman castle, with narrow lanes linked by alleys and stairways all converging upon Piazza Garibaldi. In this area are the ruins of

the castle and the earliest churches: *S. Giacomo*, 1451; *S. Sebastiano*, 1371; and *S. Maria la Vecchia*, founded in the 12th c. and rebuilt in the 15th c., with a marble statue on the interior by Antonello Gagini (1516). On the Corso Vittorio Emanuele, which begins from the Piazza Garibaldi, note the *Chiesa Madre di S. Maria la Nuova*, built at the end of the 15th c., the period of the Catalonian Gothic portal on the right side (the façade dates from the 20th c.): the interior abounds in artworks, including, in the presbytery, 17th-c. frescoes and a wooden choir.

Polizzi Generosa

Polizzi Generosa (elev. 920 m, pop. 4318) has the yellow color of the land in June, and it blends in perfectly with the surrounding landscape, a well-cultivated territory. Its twisting lanes, its lack of space, and the tiny squares all contrast with the immense scope of the view of the valley that separates it from the massif of the Madonìe. The *Chiesa Madre* houses a handsome *triptych** of the 16th-c. Flemish school. The Palazzo Notarbartolo is the seat of the *Museo Ambientalistico Madonita* (*open holidays, 10:30-12:30 and 4:30-6:30; weekdays with reservation*), where some of the natural settings of the Madonìe massif have been recreated. On the 1st Sunday of September is the famous Festa dello Sfoglio, a typical cake with cheese and cinnamon.

Le Petralìe

Set along an ancient roadway that runs east-west across Sicily, Petralìa Soprana (elev. 1147 m, pop. 3802) and Petralìa Sottana (elev. 1000 m, pop. 3479) date back to earliest times. Ancient Petra, now Soprana, is mentioned as early as the 3rd c. B.C., but it took on an administrative role with the arrival of the Moors. The Normans fortified it and endowed it with religious foundations. The halt of urban development around the 17th c. makes it possible now to enjoy the urban structure of these two small towns virtually intact. Petralìa Sottana, today a town in its own right, originally developed as a small dependency of the Norman castle complex atop the hill. The distinction between the two settlements appears in documents only in the 15th c. That both of the settlements were ruled by aristocratic families and were the source of much wealth can be seen in the magnificence of the private and public buildings as well as religious buildings, and in the ostentatious richness of the decorations. This is true of the *Chiesa Madre* of **Petralìa Soprana**, founded long ago, rebuilt by the Ventimiglia family in the 14th c. and subsequently enlarged and adorned with stucco work, gold, and art work of all kinds, including a wooden *Crucifix* by Frate Umile da Petralìa and a statue of the *Madonna della Catena* from the 15th c. Also worthy of note is the church of *S. Maria di Loreto* on the site of the old Norman fortress, with polychrome terracotta cusps of the bell towers on either side of the façade. In **Petralìa Sottana**, on the other hand, we would recommend the interesting 17th-c. *Chiesa Madre*, which includes an earlier building (a late-Gothic portal remains on the right side), and the church of the *Santissima Trinità*, which preserves a marble altarpiece with bas-reliefs by G. Gagini depicting the Life of Jesus.

Parco Regionale delle Madonìe

Instituted in 1989, this natural reserve covers a surface of 40,000 hectares and has its headquarters at Petralìa Sottana. It offers more than 30 paths across the valleys and

mountains of the massif, where the natural setting is almost intact.

Gangi

Gangi (elev. 1011 m, pop. 7812) preserves its original medieval layout unchanged. The buildings cover the sides of the hill like a blanket, and around the *Castello dei Ventimiglia*, they form the first core of the settlement, a compact and minutely articulated urban fabric, marked by the chief thoroughfare of the Corso Umberto and the Via G. Fedele Vitale, crisscrossed by steep and twisting lanes running downhill. As ancient as the castle, the massive tower or *Torre dei Ventimiglia* was the first residence of the lords of the place, and was later adapted for use as a bell tower for the *Chiesa Madre* or Cathedral. It was built in the 18th c. by enlarging a 14th-c. oratory; inside, among other fine art works, is a handsome Gagini statue of the *Virgin with Child*; in contrast you may note, in the presbytery, a canvas depicting the *Last Judgment* clearly emulating the fresco by Michelangelo in the Sistine Chapel. Further down, on the steps of the Via Matrice, the church of the *Santissimo Salvatore* (1612) contains another of the numerous wooden *Crucifixes* by Fra' Umile da Petralìa. And if you descend still further, you will find the church of *S. Maria degli Angeli*, with, adjoining it, the Convento dei Cappuccini, which houses a *museum* with paintings from the 16th and 17th c., and fine decorated 17th-c. terracottas.

Sperlinga

Set on a spur of mossy rock, the battlements and stepped masses of the *Castello** di Sperlinga (elev. 750 m, pop. 1000) seem to provide a perfect setting for a period piece set in the Middle Ages. This too was a castle of Roger's: reinforced by Frederick II in the 12th c., it returned to the Ventimiglia family until the 16th c., when it became the residence of Giovanni Forti Natoli, founder of the town. A sort of cliffside fortress cut into the rock (*open 9:30-1:30 and 3:30-7:30*), it has innumerable chambers (many of them now open to the sky), passageways, courtyards, and corridors distributed over a great many levels, in a mazelike complex of great allure. This was the center of the last, desperate French resistance during the War of the Sicilian Vespers, as the motto reminds us: "What Sicily accepted, only Sperlinga rejected."

Nicosìa

Nicosìa (elev. 724 m, pop. 14,951) is the central hinge of the system of fortified cities

Nicosìa: the Cathedral

along the mountain route running from Messina to Palermo. Set on the site of an existing Byzantine settlement dating from the 7th-8th c., the Islamic city was built in the 9th c; and then destroyed by the Normans. The Normans, with an enormous influx of Franco-Germanic ethnic groups, formed a colony that clustered around the first Norman church of S. Maria. In the 14th c. there was already a considerable class of bourgeois large landowners who, until the 18th c., built their own sumptuous homes along the still medieval lanes of the town. In the 16th and 17th c., the monastic congregations determined, with the buildings they erected, the present-day layout of the historic city. The **Cattedrale** or Cathedral, a 19th-c. reconstruction of a small 14th-c. church of which only the main portal and the campanile survive, preserves a *pulpit*, an *altar frontal*, and a marble *baptismal font* dating from the 16th c.; in the presbytery it is possible to admire handsome carved wooden stalls dating from the 17th c. and an exquisite *altar frontal* made of repoussé and gilt silver. Among the 18th-c. stuccoes of the church of *S. Biagio*, one should note the interesting and unusual composition of the marble *triptych* by Antonello Gagini (1510) with a Christ surrounded by a host of little angels and free-standing statues of the Virgin Mary and St. John the Baptist. A handsome carved *portal* carved with non-religious naturalistic and mythological depictions adorns the main entrance of the **Basilica di S. Maria Maggiore**, built near the end of the 18th c. to replace the old church of the

same name, swallowed up by a landslide in 1757. Like the portal, the works contained inside the church come from religious and civil buildings destroyed by the landslide: among them is the majestic marble *polyptych* in the presbytery by Antonello Gagini. Note the rare 15th-c. *altar frontal* made of painted wood in lively colors, done for a clearly popular audience; lastly, one should note, in the right transept, the wooden 16th-c. throne with an effigy of the Emperor Charles V, who stayed in Nicosìa in 1535.

Mistretta

Thanks to its strategic position on the way between the Tyrrhenian and central Sicily, Mistretta (elev. 900, pop. 5710) was a stronghold for the control of the surrounding territory right up to the end of Spanish rule. The town's churches, nearly all of which were rebuilt during the 17th c., preserve traces of the styles of the earlier versions. The *Chiesa Madre* dating from 1630, for instance, has a marble *altarpiece* by Antonello Gagini, and in the transept has a 14th-c. pointed-arch portal, and on the right side another portal dating from 1494. The *Museo Civico (open 9-1; Tue. and Thu., also 3:30-6:30)* contains canvases from the churches of the town and local archeological finds.

Santo Stefano di Camastra

The state road 113 to Santo Stefano di Camastra (elev. 70 m, pop. 5063) is transformed into an exhibition space of colorful ceramics. The birth and development of this craft are linked to the presence of numerous quarries for excellent clay, and its present survival is perhaps the result of the uncompleted highway from Messina to Palermo. The city, which until 1812 was known as Santo Stefano di Mistretta, was centered in the hills, not far from the town of the same name (Mistretta). Destroyed by a landslide in 1682, it was rebuilt beginning in 1693 in its present site: on a rocky platform high over the sea. It is interesting to observe the layout of the town which, on a much smaller scale, is reminiscent of the layout of the gardens of Versailles: streets fanning out from a central square, set over a comb-like gridwork with an east-west axis. Behind the state road, on the other hand, are urban developments of the 19th and 20th c., with roads running parallel. Located in the 18th-c. section of the city is the *Chiesa Madre* (with a Renaissance portal and a marble Gagini statue), and the ceramics museum or *Museo della Ceramica (open 9-1 and 4-8)* featuring local crafts products.

Fiumara d'Arte is a territorial art museum built on the exposed gravelly river bed and along the banks of the Tusa, with works by major contemporary artists.

Inaugurated in 1986 with an installation by Pietro Consagra in the bed of the river Tusa, this project did not fail to kindle debates and even furious disputes. Next came a project by Tano Festa on the beach of Villa Margi, not far from Santo Stefano di Camastra; one by Antonio Di Palma on the right bank of the river, on a little hill near Motta d'Affermo; another by Hidetoshi Nagasawa in a manmade cave on the road from Motta to Mistretta; one by Paolo Schiavocampo on the road to Castel di Lucio and another by Pietro Dorazio and Graziano Marini in town, in the barracks of the Carabinieri; and lastly a project by Italo Lanfredini in a valley at the foot of Castel di Lucio.

Halaesa

This was an ancient Greek colony founded in 403 B.C.; transformed and enriched in Roman and Byzantine times, it was destroyed by the Moors in the 9th c. Dating back to the 4th or 3rd c. B.C. are walls and towers whose ruins can be seen just before the turnoff that leads to the excavations, while the columbarium made of "opus reticulatum" dates back to Roman times. In the archeological area (*open 9-one hour before sunset*), note the interesting ruins of the acropolis and the agora, with massive rusticated retaining walls from Hellenistic times, and a regular urban layout from the Byzantine period.

9.3 The Monti Nèbrodi

After a short stretch on state road 113 toward Palermo, from Sant'Àgata Militello you will turn off to the left onto state road 289. The road (route map on p. 190), from which you can enjoy splendid panoramic views of the coast as far as Capo d'Orlando, runs through the countryside around San Fratello, and with steep switchbacks reaches Portella Femmina Morta (1524 m). The pullouts, in the points free of forest and rocky outcroppings, offer a view of three different Sicilian volcanoes at once: Etna, Vulcano, and Strómboli. The road drops back down toward the highlands and then, in Cesarò, joins state road 120 which runs west, reaching Troìna (from here, state road 575 leads directly to Catania). After Cesarò, state road 120 crosses the river Simeto. On the left you may note the turnoff to the Ducea dei Nelson, with the abbey or Abbazia di Maniace, directly overlooking the river Saracena. (The road, which follows the course of the Alcàntara, skirts the northern slopes of Mount Etna, and then pours into the Ionian Sea, just past Randazzo, not far from Taormina. In this connection, see chapter 7.) From Randazzo, if instead you take state road 116 you will come, after about 21 km, to Floresta, perched high atop the Monti Nèbrodi (at an elevation of 1275 m: this is the highest township in Sicily). Fine views of the Monti Peloritani and the Tyrrhenian Sea, with the Aeolian islands in the distance, greet you as you drop back down toward Naso and Capo d'Orlando: 175 km total.

Sant'Àgata Militello

Recently founded, Sant'Àgata Militello (elev. 30 m, pop. 12,829) owes its development to its excellent location on the commercial thoroughfare of state road 113, as well as the abundant farming of its hinterland and its proximity to Milazzo. Among its few monumental buildings, we should mention the church of the *Carmelo*, with an 18th-c. bell gable and from, the same period, a castle, the *Castello*. In Via Cosenz is the Museo Etnoantropologico dei Nèbrodi (*open 9-12 and 3-6; Sat., only groups; closed Sun.*) devoted to shepherds' life and work and to folklore.

San Fratello

This town (elev. 675 m, pop. 4665), with a regular grid of streets and houses made of smooth square-hewn stone, was founded in the 18th c. following the transfer of the old city from a location further uphill; it was founded by Adelasia, the wife of Roger I, in the 11th c., and it was destroyed by a landslide in 1754. The Norman queen established a colony of Lombards there, and founded the first church, which was named after the Santi Fratelli or holy brothers (hence the name of the town) Alfio (Alphius), Filadelfo (Philadelphus), and Cirino (Cyrinus). Set on a panoramic point of

Cheesemaking in the Nèbrodi

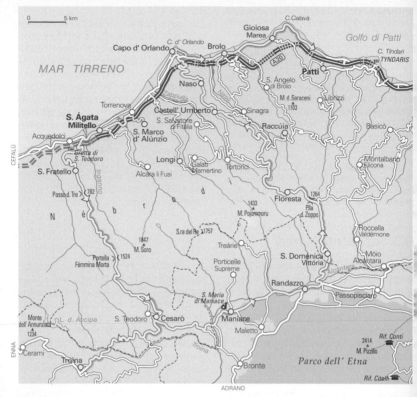

Monte Vecchio, just before the town, accessible by foot from the turnoff to the cemetery or Cimitero, is the sanctuary or *Santuario dei Tre Fratelli* which still preserves, from Norman times, the plan with a single nave and transept, three apses, and a cylindrical cupola base set on a four-sided drum.

Outside of town gentle green hills covered with pasturage and open Mediterranean maquis prepare the traveller for the highlands of the Monti Nèbrodi, covered with dense forests year round. In these areas, it is not uncommon to see pairs or herds of horses, grazing or galloping across the landscape. The horses are bred in this way, in the wild, and have been for centuries; they are a cross between an Arabian breed and a Norman breed that was imported to the island in the 11th c., at the same time that the town was founded.

Cesarò
Situated on the slope of the Monti Nèbrodi that overlooks the northwestern slope of Mount Etna, this town (elev. 1150 m, pop. 2901) has a primarily agrarian economy, with much grazing of sheep. Mentioned in documents dating back to the Swabian era, it was a feudal holding from 1334 of the Romano Colonna family, which built the castle whose ruins still stand not far from the town

itself. The *Chiesa Madre* dates from 1623 and features a *Crucifix* painted on panel.

Before you enter the town, state road 289 runs over the crest of the Monti Nèbrodi near the village of Portella Femmina Morta, at an elevation of 1524 m. From there, two kilometers of dirt road, to be traveled on foot or with an off-road vehicle, lead to *Monte Soro* (elev. 1847 m), the highest peak in the Monti Nèbrodi, and to the lake or *Lago Biviere*. This lake, situated at an elevation of 1274 m, extends over roughly 170 hectares in an area of private property; it is therefore necessary, in order to get to the banks of the lake, to ask permission of the residents in the nearby farm. Near the lake there live many species of animals, including freshwater turtles, coots, mallards, and moorhens. The landscape – verdant, humid, and wild – features a natural environment that, strangely enough, is well preserved, and constitutes a green oasis of great beauty in the heart of Sicily.

Troìna
Set between Nicosìa and Cesarò, well into the Provincia di Enna, Troìna (elev. 1121 m, pop. 10,128) extends over a narrow terrace in the middle of the highland that overlooks Etna from the west. Here, the views are once again the clean, spare panoramas of agrarian Sicily: shallow valleys set amidst smooth hills without trees, lying against

the vast sharp backdrop of the immense volcanic cone that dominates everything here from its distant abode. The territory has been inhabited from prehistoric times, as is indicated by the discovery of underground tombs carved into the rock of the nearby Monte San Pantheon and Monte Muganò. And precisely on the site of present-day Troìna (the Greek Enghion) there are stratifications of various historic eras. On the southeast slopes you can still see remains of Hellenistic fortification in megalithic blocks and part of the structure of a Roman bathhouse. During Byzantine times, Troìna attracted Basilian monks, who built churches and convents around the city. Among these, we should mention the ruins of the monastery or Monastero di S. Michele il Vecchio, set on a nearby highland; the earliest core of it, dating back to before the Moorish conquest, was enlarged during Norman times. In that same period, the city of Troìna was made a bishopric, the first episcopal see in all of post-Islamic Sicily. Of the Cattedrale or Cathedral founded by Roger (the *Chiesa Madre*) the apses still survive, and the bell tower, and a cross-vault that covers the passage through the tower itself. Among the artworks to be found on the interior, we should make special mention of a number of late-Byzantine panels, such as the *Virgin and Child* (15th c.) and the *St. Michael* (1512). The local Archeoclub was recently converted by the young people of Troìna into a museum for the preservation and display of finds from the excavations done in the surrounding territory.

La Ducea Nelson

This landholding covers an area of 6556 hectares which largely belong to the Catanese township of Bronte. It is now public property; its name came from its donation in 1799 to the English admiral Horatio Nelson by Ferdinand III of Bourbon, as a reward for having helped to put down the revolt of Naples. Inside this estate, aside from the 18th-c. family mansion, is the **Abbazia di Maniace** (*open winter, 9-1 and 2:30-5; summer, 9-1:30 and 3-7; closed Mon.*). This abbey stands on the site in which the Greek general George Maniace, leading Byzantine and Norman troops, defeated the Saracens in 1040, well before the landing in Sicily of Roger, which took place in 1061. The church, according to documents, was founded in 1174 by Margaret of Blois, the wife of William I, and was later ceded, along with its territory, to the Benedictine monastery of S. Filippo di Fragalà. This interesting example of late-Norman architecture features a handsome stone portal with figured capitals and a pointed arch, and in the single-nave interior it preserves the original wooden ceiling, a *polyptych* of the Sicilian school of the 13th c., depicting the Virgin Mary and Saints George, Anthony the Abbot, and Lucy, as well as a Byzantine panel, the *Virgin with Child*, which is said to have been brought by George Maniace directly from Greece. The palace, transformed into a sumptuous aristocratic residence by the heirs of Nelson – now it is a *museum* – features English Victorian furniture as well as prints and memorabilia of the famous admiral.

Once you pass *Randazzo* (see page 156), you can take state road 116 through settings of great beauty. On the right, after roughly 35 km, there are markers for the turnoff to *Raccuja* (elev. 640 m, pop. 1692), whose *Chiesa Madre* has handsome 16th-c. marble statues; along with the neighboring towns of San Piero Patti, Patti, Montalbano Elcoma, and Tortorici, this town forms a complete system of settlements that live by growing and harvesting hazelnuts.

Naso

Like other farming towns near the coast, Naso (elev. 490 m, pop. 4420) shows all the signs of the decline of the urban environment that began in the 20th c., including the fringes of residential development behind the center. All the same, there is a lovely view of the broad valley or Valle del Sinagra from the belvedere next to the main square. Hills, which were once cultivated in an orderly manner, and which are now abandoned to wild thorn bushes, run gently down to the river bed; in the distance, there are nothing but mountains framing the view. This city already existed at the time of the Norman conquest: a number of documents state that in 1094 Roger gave half of the lands of Naso to the monastery or Monastero di S. Bartolomeo di Lìpari. From the 16th c. on, it was feudal possession of the Ventimiglia family, who were responsible for its present urban layout and the construction of the main churches and monasteries. These churches and monasteries are known for their remarkable late-Baroque sculptures, with decorations in the styles known as mischio, tramischio, and rabisco, which were quite fashionable in Sicily at the turn of the 18th c. The *Chiesa Madre* dedicated to Saint Philip and Saint James (Ss. Filippo e Giacomo), features – among the Baroque marble curlicues and the minute colorful inlays of the chapel or Cappella del Rosario – a very serious Gagini statue of the *Virgin with Child*. Of greater interest is the *funerary monument* to Artale

Cardona located in the 15th-c. church of *S. Maria di Gesù*, a Renaissance work with four statues of the Virtues supporting the body of the deceased.

Patti

This is the original core of the relatively new settlement down at the marina (elev. 157 m, pop. 13,305); it declined in population as early as the 19th c. due to the shift in economic interest from the countryside as farms to the town as of trading station linking Messina and Palermo. It developed in Hellenistic times as an outgrowth of Tìndari, and grew considerably following the influx of refugees when Tìndari was destroyed. The Normans founded an abbey there and elevated it to the rank of bishopric. Because of its loyalty to the House of Anjou during the War of the Sicilian Vespers it was burned by Frederick II of Aragon and then in 1554 it was plundered and once again burned by the pirate Khair-ed-din Barbarossa (Redbeard). On the summit of the hill that the city stretches over is the complex of religious buildings adjoining the Cathedral or **Cattedrale** (dating from the 18th c.) which stands on the site of the Norman church built by Roger to contain the remains of his mother Adelasia, who died in Patti in 1118: the queen's fine Renaissance *sarcophagus** is located on the left wall of the right transept. On the left wall of the single nave you may also note a panel by Antonello de Saliba depicting a *Virgin with Child* (15th-16th c.).

Facing the mouth of the road that runs from Tìndari into state road 113 you will find the directions for the **Roman villa of Patti***: built during the Roman empire and destroyed in the 5th c. A.D. by an earthquake, the villa of Patti was not unearthed until 1976. It presents similarities of building type with the less well-known villa of Terme Vigliatore: like that one, it has a broad *peristyle*, facing the long sides of which are the private rooms, while on the short side, opposite the vestibule, is the *tablinum*, with the usual three terminal exedrae. A small *thermal complex* is located to the northeast of the peristyle. Unlike the villa of Terme Vigliatore and the large residence of Tìndari, the floor mosaics are polychrome and feature geometric and naturalistic motifs, rather than mythological themes: in the tablinum, for example, we see geometric and animal motifs enclosed in concave-sided octagons, and in the portico, panels bounded by festoons of laurel.

Capo d'Orlando

A major farming and trading town, Capo d'Orlando (elev. 8 m, pop. 12,692), along with Sant'Àgata Militello and Milazzo, plays a leading role in the economy of the Tyrrhenian coast in the province or Provincia di Messina. Its historical origins are ancient and legendary. It is said, in fact, that the promontory upon which the city stands was named Capo Orlando after an officer, called Orlando, serving under Charlemagne, and that this Orlando founded the fortified castle. The ruins of this medieval *castle* preserve traces of ribbing and masonry from the 14th c. Adjoining the castle is the sanctuary or sanctuary of *Maria Santissima di Capo d'Orlando* which dates from 1598.

Between Capo d'Orlando and Sant'Àgata, the first turnoff is an interesting stop among the ruins of the **Convento di S. Filippo di Fragalà**, near Frazzanò (*open Fri.-Sun., 9-1 and 3-6*). Set in a charming location on the highland that overlooks the valley of the river Fitalia, with the Aeolian islands in the distance, this may be considered one of the prototypes of Sicilian religious architecture in the Norman period. In the northern corner stand the ruins of the original Basilian church, dating from the 8th c., around which the monastic complex was built beginning in 1090 with direct funding from Roger I.

Set on a hill just a few kilometers from the coast, *San Marco d'Alunzio* (elev. 540 m, pop. 2212) preserves its original Baroque appearance in its many churches and in its urban layout. The territory of San Marco, between the Torrente Favara, a mountain stream, and the valley of the Rosmarino, was inhabited as early as prehistoric times; on the site of the modern-day settlement stood the Hellenistic city of which only the Temple of Hercules (Tempio di Ercole) survives; it was transformed into a church in the 7th c. Destroyed by Moors, the town was fortified and refounded by the Normans in the 11th c. with the name of San Marco. Still standing on the summit of the hill ("rocca"), are the ruins of the Norman castle (1061) built to dominate the coast from Capo d'Orlando to San Fratello. This was a fief of the Filangieri, princes of Mirto, from the 15th c. until the abolition of feudalism in 1812. The church of the *Santissimo Salvatore* was built in the 17th c. on the foundations of a Roman temple; recently several columns of this temple with their capitals have been found. The Byzantine church of *S. Teodoro*, known as the Badia Piccola, is of note because of its Greek-cross plan, unusual in this area; it has small round cupolas set at the intersection of the arms of the cross. The *Chiesa Madre*, dating from the 17th c., has elegant Baroque portals in its façade, as well as an interior with a single nave and stone walls with Renaissance chapels. The 17th-c. church of the *Aracoeli* stands out for the imaginative composition of its portals and its interior with monolithic columns in Rosso Aluntino, a precious marble that is similar in color and grain to Rosso Veronese.

0 Inland Sicily

ounded by the Monti Nèbrodi to the north and by the Monti Erei to the east, this vast area at slopes down to the Mar d'Africa, with Enna and Caltanissetta in its center, is consid-ed to be an "altopiano" or plateau. The word, which in Italian properly refers to a olling tableland quite high above sea level, is a pale attempt at describing the immense xpanse of rounded hills that intertwine, forming slight depressions and thus restoring the lea of surface not unlike that of a plain.

here is evidence of human settlement scattered all over the area ever since prehistoric mes, but that evidence becomes more common, of course, in the hospitable green val-ys of the rivers Plàtani and Salso. In these areas are located the two most noteworthy istorical and artistic monuments of the area: the little Hellenistic city of Morgantina and

ie Roman villa of Piazza Armerina, a com-ex that is unequalled for the richness of its tosaic floors, preserved perfectly in near-' all of the villa's 40 rooms. The preserva-on, from the 9th c. to the present day, of ie Arabic place names in many of the towns nd villages is a clear indication of the enor-nous role played by the Moors in econom-: and social development, with the im-rovement of systems of irrigation and in-erior transportation routes. The Normans, ho were acclaimed as the rescuers of hristianity from barbarous Islam, were ble to return the cities to Catholic juris-iction, but they could not change their ames. What survives from the Moorish pe-iod are the urban grids of the older towns, rhich can be clearly distinguished, how-ver, from the new cities with their orthog-nal grid, founded between the 16th and 8th c. during the agricultural reclamation f feudal landholdings encouraged by the panish. The inland urban system of Sicily

A fresco in the Roman Villa of Casale

omprises the two cities of Enna and Caltanissetta; the first, which is of ancient origin, al-ays played a major role in the political and military equilibrium of the island, because : was an impregnable stronghold; the second, devoid of natural defenses, had little au-hority in the most important episodes of Sicilian history. Now the situation has been re-ersed: Enna, since it no longer needs to defend its territory, has stopped growing, and ow has half the population of Caltanissetta.

0.1 Enna*

1 the exact center of Sicily, set amongst fer-ile and gently rolling hills, rises a tall peak, imilar in shape to a pyramid whose point ad been lopped off with a gigantic hatch-t. On the plain thus created stands Enna elev. 931 m, pop. 28,424, city map on p. 94), shrouded in fog for much of the year. Jot far from the foot of the mountain, a de-ression that seems to compensate for the levation of the peak, was filled in the dis-ant past and became a lake, elliptical in hape. The mount of Enna projects its own mage in all directions over the entire land-

scape of plateaus and valleys of the Sicilian hinterland, with the only counterpoint, on the other side of the ribbon of highway, being the Rocca di Calascibetta. Given its central location, as against the coastal sit-ing of the maritime cities, and given the multiplicity of convenient points for ob-servation of the surrounding territory, En-na has been called the "the belly button of Sicily." It has not been overlooked, over the centuries, by the interior traffic of the Si-cilian region – indeed, it has become one of the main nexuses in the network of roads,

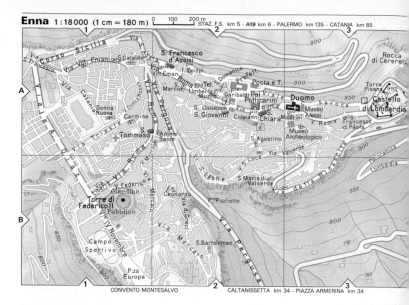

Enna 1:18000 (1 cm = 180 m)   0   100   200 m   STAZ. F.S. km 5 - **A19** km 6 - PALERMO   km 135 - CATANIA   km 85

CONVENTO MONTESALVO   CALTANISSETTA   km 34 - PIAZZA ARMERINA   km 34

like Nicosìa; but Enna still preserves its appearance as a historical city. Unlike Nicosìa, however, the city's settings and its buildings speak a sober medieval language, with little contamination from the flourishes of the Baroque and the 18th c. The preservation of an essentially agrarian economy, which hindered the growth of service industries, has probably contributed to the safeguarding of local historical values. These values constitute a substrate of character and a source of lively and productive pride. The clean streets, the carefully maintained buildings, the absence of neon and banner signs, and even the orderly way in which the excellent pastries are displayed in the elegant "pasticcerie" – all these factors tell us that the city of Enna is not only quite different from the chaotic metropolises on the coast, but also from the cities in the depressed areas of Sicily.

The plateau atop the mountain may have been the site of an early Sicilian city when Siracusa (Syracuse), in 664 B.C. (70 years after its own foundation) established the colony of Henna there for the exploitation of the site's rich agricultural resources. From the archaic Greek period there remain the necropolises, and from the Hellenistic period stretches of the enclosure walls, in the area of Santo Spirito. Conquered by the Romans in the 3rd c. B.C., the town saw an improvement in the road network over the surrounding territory growing grain crops, and the consequential development of the Hellenistic town. Contributing to the consolidation of the city's agricultural production were the technical innovations in irri-

gation introduced by the Moors, who calle the town "Qasr Yannah," from the Lati "Castrum Hennae," which was in time co rupted into Castrogiovanni, a name tha stuck until 1927. The Normans, who, in orde to besiege the invulnerable fortress campe on the peak of Calascibetta, finally storme it in 1088 and reinforced it with the cor struction of a castle to guard the valley be low; the Normans also encouraged the e tablishment of a Lombard colony in th vicinity. At the end of the 14th c., the city ha already acquired its definitive layout. In th 17th c., the initiative of the Spanish crown t found new villages in the vast feudal lanc holdings of the interior tableland, in order t encourage agricultural production, cause the depopulation of the town and an ensuin halt in urban growth.

One characteristic of Enna is the usefu distribution of the ring-roads around th center, all streets cut into terraces in th slope or in some cases perched on viaducts The view that you may enjoy there is uniqu in all of Sicily: it extends 360 degrees, from Mount Etna to Èrice, from the Monti Nèbro di to the hills of the Caltanissetta province Once you have reached the castle or Caste lo di Lombardia at the easternmost point c Enna, you can begin the tour that runs er tirely along the Via Roma, all downhill. Yo can see, in the near distance – protecte behind the entrance gate of the Muse Alessi – the massive apses of the Cathedra or Duomo and, facing the side portal c that church, the entrance to the archec logical museum, or Museo Archeologicc Overlooking the Piazza Colajanni beyon

194

that are the façades of the church of S. Chiara and the handsome Baroque portal of Palazzo Pollicarini. Running past the lovely façades of the city palazzi of the old landed aristocracy, the route continues as far as Piazza Vittorio Emanuele, where the church of S. Francesco stands. A little further along, Via Roma intersects with Via Pergusa and then turns south, crossing the district that was originally built by the Moors; beyond the right side of the street it develops into twisting little stepped lanes and small secluded courtyards. You will reach the more modern section of Enna Alta (upper Enna), and then you may take the Viale 4 Novembre the short distance to the tower or Torre di Federico II.

Castello di Lombardia* (A3; *open 9-1 and 4-7*). This castle stands on the site of an earlier Moorish fortification, and was reinforced by the Normans; in the 12th c. Frederick III of Aragona established a powerful curtain wall with towers distributed on every side. The castle has an irregular plan, since its structures follow the natural morphology of its site. Besides the curtain wall, only six of the 20 original towers still stand, along with the complex internal structure of courtyards which open in a sequence, one gate after the other. The closest courtyard to the entrance is used, during the summer, for remarkable theatrical performances. From

Enna: the castle of Lombardia

the courtyard or Cortile di S. Martino, where it is possible to see the ruins of the little church or Chiesetta di S. Martino, you will reach the entrance to the tower or *Torre Pisana*, from the terrace of which you can admire a splendid panoramic view*, when there is no fog. In the immediate vicinity of the castle, on a rocky crag, you can see the arcaic structure of the *temple of Ceres* (Tempio di Cerere), which Cicero said was filled with statues of the goddess in the 1st c. B.C.

Duomo* (A3) or Cathedral. Originally built as a 14th-c. structure, this cathedral was rebuilt in the 16th c. following a fire. What remains of the ancient structure are the apses and a pointed-arch portal set in the wall of the right transept. The main façade is characterized by the 18th-c. campanile that stands perfectly in the center, directly on the vaulted roof of the portico. The portico itself is closed with fencing made of black iron, with gilded decorations in the form of putti and cornucopias. In the side wall overlooking the Piazza Mazzini is a lovely 16th-c. *portal* which bears a handsome bas-relief, in the upper aedicule, having to do with the legend of St. Martin and the poor man. The Latin-cross basilican **interior** is broken down into a nave and two aisles, with pointed arches on stout columns made of volcanic stone, richly decorated at the bases and capitals. The coffered ceiling of the nave was done in the 17th c.; you should note the odd wooden brackets in the form of winged and remarkably buxom griffins. In the chapel or Cappella della Visitazione there are two tortile columns of intarsia framing the 17th-c. canvas depicting the *Visitation of the Virgin Mary*, which conceals a Golden Nef (*Nave d'Oro*), a very valuable litter upon which the 15th-c. statue of the Virgin Mary is carried in procession every year on 2 July.

Museo Alessi (A3; *open 8-8*). This prestigious institution takes its name from the largest and most important collection it houses, established by the Enna canon Giuseppe Alessi, who lived in the late 18th c. and the early years of the 19th c. Among the many paintings on exhibit on the ground floor of the building there are exquisite Byzantine icons on panels; on the second floor, in the great hall with windows that look out over a lovely view of Calascibetta, it is possible to admire sacred paraments, Renaissance gold and silver work from the *Treasury* of the Cathedral or Duomo. In the smaller hall, glass display cases contain refined jewels, treasures of the goldsmith's art: the crown of the Virgin Mary, in enameled gold studded with precious stones, and a gold pin with an enormous topaz in its center, depicting a pelican that has torn its breast to feed its young, a symbol of the sacrifice of Christ.

In the halls on the last floor there is a *numismatic collection*, almost entirely from the Collezione Alessi; this coin collection is remarkable both because of the great many coins displayed, and because it provides a broad picture of the economic history of Sicily in the earliest times, and because of the presence of fine rare examples of Greek, Roman, and Byzantine coinage.

Museo Archeologico Regionale (A3; *open 9-6:30*) or regional archeological museum. Established in 1985, this museum occupies the elegant halls of the *Palazzo Varisano*. The ground floor halls are of particular interest, with an exhibition of finds from a number of archeological sites under exploration in the Provincia di Enna. The numerous necropolises that have been discovered have yielded an enormous quantity of funerary furnishings, some of which date

The Holy Week procession in Enna

back to the 3rd or 2nd millennium B.C. But the most interesting material is in the third hall, which is entirely dedicated to the areas around the lake or Lago di Pergusa; in particular, the explorations have revealed, in the village of Cozzo Matrice, traces of a settlement from the Copper Age, as well as traces of a Greek town from the 5th to 6th c. B.C., with an area sacred to Demeter and Kore within the enclosure walls.

S. Chiara (A2). This church was originally laid out in the 17th c., and was renovated in the 18th c.; today it is a sacrarium which houses the remains of men who died in the two World Wars. It features a 19th-c. majolica floor with two panels showing unusual subjects: the advent of steam navigation and the triumph of Christianity over Islam. In a courtyard at n. 467 in Via Roma stands the *Palazzo Pollicarini*, with architectural details from the Catalonian Gothic period (15th c.).

S. Francesco d'Assisi (A2). This church, first founded in the 14th c., has undergone extensive transformations over the centuries. The entire building stands on a high stone pedestal with inclined walls, which gives it the appearance of a fortress more than a church. Contributing to this appearance is the massive 15th-c. *bell tower*, lightened up only by the cornices of the upper windows with hanging arches. A stair-

case, recently renovated, leads to the side entrance of the single nave.

Torre di Federico II (B1) or Tower of Frederick II. This remarkable pure geometric shape with an octagonal base rises 24 m atop a little hillock in the center of a park, and can be seen from many places in the town. Built in the 13th c., it clearly shows the stylistic characteristics of Frederick's military architecture. The *interior* (currently being restored) which is reached by a single portal, is subdivided into three stories, the first of which, consisting of a single large hall, has a handsome vaulted ceiling with stone arches. A spiral staircase cut into the thickness of the wall (more than 3 m), leads to the rooms on the upper story, much like the first.

Calascibetta

When seen from Enna, Calascibetta (elev. 681 m, pop. 4925) seems to have been built in the cavea of a natural amphitheater, surrounded by the steep rock walls that embrace it. Nothing at all survives from the Roman period; from the Moorish period the town preserves its distinctive name, which may have referred to a hamlet that existed at the time; but the creation of the medieval "borgo," which still exists in its original urban structure, dates back to the 11th c., when Roger the Norman was forced to camp here, while laying a long siege against Enna. The expansion in the 16th and 17th c., in the form of religious buildings and aristocratic residences, occupied the southwestern area of the slope. The route of the present-day Via Conte Ruggero is that of the original thoroughfare that served all the districts of the little town; in the upper section it ran along the area of the medieval core, abounding in remarkable settings in straitened spaces, overlooked by old working-class houses. The *Chiesa Madre*, a church dedicated to St. Peter (S. Pietro) and Our Lady of the Assumption (S. Maria Assunta), formerly the Palatine Chapel founded back in the 14th c., has undergone a great deal of reconstruction: on the interior, it preserves sculptures dating back to various eras and a rich collection of sacred paraments and liturgical objects. The 18th-c. church of the *Carmine*, with its classical-style façade, also has an *Annunciation* attributed to the Gagini family.

10.2 From Enna to Piazza Armerina

This route (map below) runs through some of the loveliest areas in the provinces of Enna and Caltanissetta, characterized by sunny and neatly cultivated hillsides and vast areas of reforestation; there is an abundance of streams and watercourses. From Enna, if you head south and pass the intersection with state road 117 Bis to Caltanissetta, there is a provincial road that leads, in a few minutes, to the lake or Lago di Pergusa, and, if you continue south, you will join the state road to Gela: at a distance of about 8 km from the intersection, a turnoff to the left leads to Aidone, where you will find directions for the excavations of the Hellenistic Greek city of Morgantina and the Museo Archeologico that houses the finds. Then return to the state road, and at a distance of about 4 km, you will come to Piazza Armerina, not far from which is the Roman Villa del Casale. From Piazza Armerina it is fairly easy to reach the coast to the south, Caltagirone to the east, or Caltanissetta to the west, while passing through the farm towns of Barrafranca and Pietraperzìa, which form part of this route. In all, you will travel 86 km.

Lake or Lago di Pergusa
Set in a broad valley, surrounded by a continuous ridge of hills dense with vegetation some 9 km south of Enna, is the innermost natural basin in Sicily. The Lago di Pergusa is tectonic in origin, full of shallow brackish water, and has neither inflow nor outflow. We have already referred to the function of this place as the site of a myth (the abduction of Kore); but the charm that must have accrued to this place in the past from this connection is nowadays compromised by the presence of a circular automotive racetrack that entirely surrounds it. The lake, moreover, is seriously threatened by worrisome phenomena of drainage and drying up. In the surrounding area, note the *archeological area of Cozzo Matrice*, one of the hills overlooking the northern shore of the lake; here traces have been found of a fortified settlement dating back to the 8th-6th c. B.C., as well as of its necropolis, with chamber tombs carved into the rock. The finds from the excavations, including numerous tomb furnishings, are now in the archeological museum, or Museo Archeologico di Enna.

Morgantina*
This major archeological station now lies on a road of secondary importance which links Aidone to Catania over the plain, but at the time of its greatest prosperity it played a very important role as a commercial city. Built at the center of a gentle valley, surrounded by a ridge of steep hills to the north and the south, Morgantina could be easily defended, and had under its rule enormous productive territories. When the first settlement of the people of Morgantina

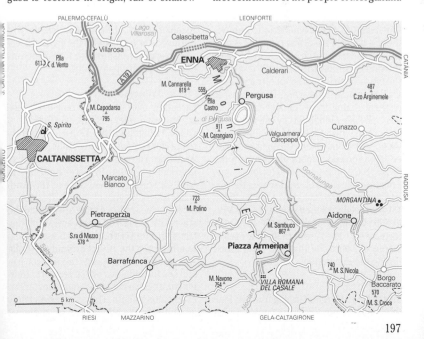

– a tribe from Latium, who migrated here toward the end of the 1st millennium B.C. – was destroyed, the urban center was rebuilt around the 5th c. B.C., and enjoyed its period of greatest growth and prosperity during the Hellenistic era (4th-3rd c. B.C.), under the rule of the tyrant of Syracuse, Agathocles. During that period, the acropolis was built; a few scanty ruins of it survive on the Monte Cittadella, roughly a kilometer-and-a-half from the site of the agora. The city did not live long: in 211 B.C. it was destroyed by hordes of mercenaries at the service of Rome; Rome held the city subject until the 1st c. A.D. The site is particularly charming because it is far from any towns: the excavations (*open winter, 9-5; summer, 9-one hour before sunset*), which were begun in 1955, reveal the interesting layout of the *public square* (agora) set on two different levels, linked by a trapezoidal stairway that also served as seating for public assemblies. On the upper level, the large open square is occupied, at the center, by the quadrangular structure of the *market*, with clear traces of the walls that divided one shop from the next; and it is bounded on the northern and eastern sides respectively by the Roman "*gymnasium*" and by a *portico* (stoa), on the surface of which it is still possible to recognize the bases of the columns. On the lower level is the *theater*, dating from the 4th c. B.C., preserved in excellent condition with most of the stone benches and the scaena; the long building that faces the scaena of the theater must have been used as a grain silo, with kilns for the production of ceramics at the southeastern end. Behind the northeastern portico, mentioned above, there is a paved road, from which it is possible to climb up to the hill on which stands the ruins of one of the *residential districts* of the city, comprising a set of terraces sloping down toward the agora. The houses, all of them dating from the Hellenistic era, were probably inhabited by the well-to-do class of the town, judging from the refined wall decorations and by the figures depicted in the mosaic floors, dating from the 3rd c. B.C., found in the interior rooms. Considerable ruins of another wealthy district can be toured behind the *theater*, in the western section of the excavated area. Morgantina was in the news a few years ago unfortunately, due to the theft of a marble statue of Aphrodite that had been found during the excavations.

Aidone

This is by and large a farming town; Aidone (elev. 800 m, pop. 6409) occupies a high plateau in the eastern slopes of the Monti Erei, in a position overlooking the western wedge of the Piana di Catania. The center has a typical medieval layout, which can be traced back to the original development of the settlement in the 12th c. around the castle built by the Normans, whose ruins can still be seen on the rocky spur at the westernmost end of the hill. The town extended, in the centuries following the 17th c., to the south of the center, in accordance with a regular town plan. In the 18th c., work had to be done on the reconstruction of the civil and religious buildings that were damaged in the earthquake of 1693, which ravaged all of the Val di Noto. The regional archeological museum, or **Museo Archeologico Regionale** (*open 9-7*) is located in the former monastery or Convento dei Cappuccini and in the 17th-c. church of S. Francesco closed to worship and restored overlooking the Largo Torres Trupia. The excellent museum installation makes it possible for the visitor to analyze the historic phases previous to the Hellenistic setlment of Morgantina and to form a complete idea of the development of the territory from prehistory to the Greek period. The hall known as the Sala di Cittadella contains materials from excavations in the Contrada Cittadella of a settlement dating back to the end of the 1st millennium B.C., the tomb furnishings of the indigenous necropolises of the 8th to 7th c. B.C., and those from the Greek necropolises from the same period. The hall or Sala di Serra Orlando contains finds from the area of Morgantina having to do with the period of its reconstruction. In the former refectory of the monastery, a model of the archeological area prepares a visitor for a tour of the various educational halls.

Piazza Armerina

Extending over three adjoining hills, Piazza Armerina (elev. 697 m, pop. 22,382) – called Piazza until the 18th c. – takes its name from one of the three hills, the Colle Armerino. The settlement is surrounded by lands that abound in water and forests with all sorts of trees, making the landscape one of the most fertile in the interior of Sicily. The entrance into the city from the state road is marked by recently built districts with fairly shoddy architecture extending over the plains around the Colle Armerino. On the slopes of this hill, you can still see the old town of Piazza, worth touring for its pleasant streets and most interesting monuments. This site was certainly inhabited in the 8th-7th c. B.C., and must have attracted settlement even in prehistoric times. The Romans settled here, as we can see by the presence of the Villa del Casale, as did the Byzantines and, in the high Middle Ages, the Moors. In the 11th c., the time of the Norman conquest, we learn of conflicts between the Moors and the new conquerors, who, however, built a fortified citadel to the west of Piazza. Dating from the same period is the formation of the earliest inhabited nucleus on the Colle Mira, now known as the Quartiere del Monte. In the 14th and 15th c. a first expansion to the northeast was followed by a second expansion to the east and southeast, and was consolidated, in the course of the 17th c., by a definitive urban layout, the result of the construction and renovation of the monastic complexes of various religious Orders.

Your tour may be limited to the historical center alone, structured around the Piazza Garibaldi; here is a convergence of the main thoroughfares of the town, from which the narrow lanes of the medieval districts of Castelina and Monte branch out. On the north side of the square, separated by the Via Cavour, which leads to the Cathedral or Duomo, stands the 18th-c. *Palazzo di Città*, with its elegant wrought-iron balconies, and the 17th-c. church of *S. Rocco*, with a lavish Baroque portal in carved tufa stone and a large window

standing out against the smooth façade, underscored by heavy corner pilaster strips. The **Duomo**, built in 1604 on the site of an existing church at the behest of a munificent local notable, incorporates – of the various existing structures – only the campanile, with basket-arch windows in the first two orders. The interior, built to a Latin-cross plan, is richly decorated with gilt stucco work; in the chapel to the left of the presbytery, there is a handsome wooden Cross dating from the 15th c., painted on both faces. To the right of the Duomo you can see the long Baroque façade of *Palazzo Trigonia* (18th c.).

The 13 and 14 of August every year there is a festival of local folklore, the Palio dei Normanni, which takes its origin from the historic entrance of Count Roger (Conte Ruggero) into the city of Piazza after liberating Sicily from the Muslims. A procession of characters in period costumes sets out from Piazza Duomo and then moves, on the second day, to the playing fields, where there is an equestrian tournament among the representatives of the districts of Piazza.

Roman Villa of Casale**

Set in the green environment of the area around Piazza Armerina, this villa (plan below; *open 8-6:30*) has magnificent polychrome mosaics in excellent condition; it represents the most important surviving

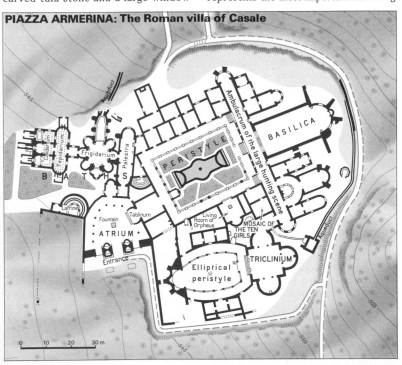

PIAZZA ARMERINA: The Roman villa of Casale

documentation of Roman civilization in Sicily. The excavations, which were undertaken in a systematic manner in 1929, have unearthed a luxurious patrician villa built sometime between the end of the third and the beginning of the 4th c. A.D., extending over three levels with a total surface area of some 3500 sq. m. It comprises more than 40 rooms, almost all them artistically paved with mosaic floors. Moreover, the villa is organized into areas with different functions: the area closest to the entrance contains the baths, the successive

The landscape of inland Sicily

area clusters around a large peristyle, with bedrooms and guest quarters; the area across from the entrance vestibule includes the basilica and the private suites of the owners of the villa; the area to the right of the main entrance comprises a large dining hall with a triclinium. The tour follows an obligatory route over little catwalks suspended above the level of the mosaics.

Just past the entrance, there is a polygonal *atrium* surrounded by a portico with surviving columns topped by Ionic capitals; on the left you may note the large exedra of a collective latrine; from the courtyard, you can pass through two small rooms to enter the large **apsed hall** called the Salone (or *Palestra*) with the mosaic floor depicting a chariot race in the Circus Maximus); adjoining it is an octagonal *frigidarium* with exedrae/dressing rooms and two pools, one facing the other. Next come the *tepidarium* and the *calidarium*, which is a sort of sauna in which you can clearly see the "suspensoria" that support the "hypocaustum," the raised flooring of the baths. In the flooring of the *vestibule* (tablinum) there are depictions of figures welcoming guests, with candelabra and olive branches. Next comes the *rectangular quadriporticus* (peristyle), which features Corinthian marble columns and medallion mosaics with figures of animals. In the rooms of the western

wing you may admire, in two cubicles, the exquisite pirouettes of a *dancing girl** with a fluttering outfit, and the recurring theme of *cupids fishing,* and, in a "diaeta" (living room), the little hunting scene or *Piccola Caccia** with scenes of the sacrifice to Diana in the fields.

The large corridor with thermal apses opening onto the quadriporticus, is separated from the quadriporticus by two little stairways, and serves as a connection to the group of rooms to the left of the basilica and the private apartments to the right: this corridor is called the **ambulacrum of the large hunting scene*** or Grande Caccia because its mosaic floor* depicts an African safari, with the killing, capture, and loading of animals onto ships. In the left apse you can admire the allegory of Armenia flanked by wild beasts; in the right apse is a depiction of Africa, with animals fleeing in terror. Among the *mosaics** of the eastern wing, we should point out the stylistic elegance the mosaic of ten girls, each dressed in a very modern-looking bikini, doing calisthenics in one of the cubicles, and, in the large apsed "diaeta" that opens onto the portico, the mosaic based on the myth of Orpheus, who enchanted animals by playing the lyre.

In order to tour the private apartments, the basilica, and the northern corner, it is necessary to exit and to follow a beaten-earth trail that winds along the rear of the villa. The decoration of the *apsed hall**, preceded by an atrium giving onto the ambulacrum of the large hunting scene, depicts the legend of Arion, who, threatened with death by his sailors, now mutineers, was transported to safety by a dolphin. In the square vestibule of the northern corner there is a *mosaic** depicting Ulysses and Polyphemus, one of the finest mosaics in the villa; it shows powerful naturalism in the representation of the scenic setting, the movements of Ulysses and his companions, and the kid goats in the foreground. Return to the interior of the villa and, along the south side of the quadriporticus, you will reach the little passage that leads into the elliptical peristyle. Lining the curving sides of the portico are two groups of rooms with mosaic floors with naturalistic motifs. On the short side of the portico is the *triclinium**, a large dining hall with three apses, where the mosaic floors depict the mythological subject of the Labors of Hercules, in which the depiction takes on a dramatic tone, especially in the scene of the battle against the Titans.

Barrafranca

Extending over the slopes of a hill at the southern edge of the interior highlands, Barrafranca (elev. 450 m, pop. 13,411) has in the past played the two-fold role of center of strategic control of the region and breadbasket to that same region. Its territory shows traces of settlements dating back to before the arrival of the Greeks, but the origins of the present-day city date back only to the Moorish occuption; the Moors in fact first coined the early name of Convicino. Conquered by the Normans, the city was rebuilt around the Norman castle and, in the 16th c., passed into the hands of Matteo Barresi di Pietraperzìa, who changed its name to Barrafranca. In that same period the *Chiesa Madre* was built, with its slender campanile with corner pilaster strips and a small arabesqued cupola; and in the same era, the orthogonal grid of the center was developed, to continue through all of the following century with the distinctive style of the provincial Baroque of the Val di Noto.

Pietraperzìa

Set on a highland overlooking the verdant valley of the river Salso, Pietraperzìa (elev. 476 m, pop. 7764), which was once in the sphere of influence of the town of Caltanissetta, is predominantly a farming town. Its rich territory has been inhabited ever since prehistoric times, and some people say that the site on which present-day Pietraperzìa now stands is the same as that of the ancient Petra. According to documentary sources, the city originated from a Norman district founded in the 11th c.; dating from the same period is the castle situated on the steepest part of the hill, in a position that dominates and surveys the valley and the city. In the 16th c. it was ruled by Matteo Barresi who, with the aquisition of the feudal landholding of Convicino (Barrafranca), made Pietraperzìa an important farming and administrative center. Barresi himself reinforced the castle, and began the expansion of the medieval "borgo" or village with the usual orthogonal grid. Beyond the *Chiesa Madre*, a project ordered by Barresi in the 16th c. and rebuilt in the 18th c. is the interesting *Palazzo del Governatore*, with its corner balcony with curious brackets carved in the shape of human heads; all that survives of the *castle* are a few ruins clinging to a rocky crag.

10.3 Caltanissetta

Caltanissetta (elev. 568 m, pop. 62,595, city map on p. 203) stands on a site that is easy to reach, a hill that is scarcely 500 m high, with gently sloping sides. There are various hypotheses concerning the origins of the name, which is clearly Arabic in form, and of the present settlement, which developed, according to the documents, beginning in the 11th c. In 1086, in fact, Count Roger (Conte Ruggero), in accordance with his vast plan for the territorial and urbanistic reorganization of Sicily, brought the city back under the jurisdiction of the Latin church, conquering the fortress or Fortezza di Pietrarossa, of which the ruins still stand on a plateau to the southeast of the center, and founding, on another eminence to the northeast, the abbey or Abbazia di S. Spirito, which is still perfectly intact. From these two opposite poles, set up to defend the city, there run two roads which converge in the present-day Via V. Emanuele II, to the south of which it is still possible to recognize the earliest core of the city, contained within enclosure walls that ran down from the castle. From the 15th c., when this feudal landholding became the property of the Moncada family, until the 17th c., the town, which had already extended beyond the medieval enclosure walls, expanded still further, dividing up into four different districts. The 17th-c. urban structure, based on the axes of the present-day Via Vittorio Emanuele and the Corso Umberto, can still be seen clearly. It is also very easy to see the differences in the layout of the three new districts, characterized by straight roads and long blocks, and that of the original district, behind the Cathedral or Cattedrale, with its narrow twisting lanes. Dating from the 19th c. are the reconstructions and restorations of the buildings overlooking the two main thoroughfares, as well as the current appearance of the Piazza Garibaldi, with the construction of the town hall (Municipio) on the site of the ancient church of S. Maria Annunziata, a church that still stood in the 18th c., and the completion of the two façed façades of the Cattedrale, and the church of S. Sebastiano. Following the construction of the Catania-Palermo highway and the main fast road leading to Agrigento, this city replaced Enna as the major inland city. Caltanissetta has been the site of the most important trials for Mafia killings, since this is the headquarters of the Pretura, or magistrate's court, that has jurisdiction for the territory, closest to Palermo. A recent urban expansion created the area that greets the visitor just arriving, while the center of town, clustered around the Piazza Garibaldi, shows clear signs of a complex and even urban history. The 19th-c. Neoclassical style of the main streets, here and there punctuated by a few minor Baroque relics, is set off by the simple and humble image of the districts immediately outside the well-to-do section of town. Relatively unimportant in strategic terms, after a long past as a rural town, this little city enjoyed phases in the 19th c. of great prosperity, from the exploitation of the mineral resources to be found underground in its territory; today its economy is based on the agricultural sector and the service industries.

During Holy Week it is possible to watch a remarkable religious festival with processions and sacred performances, beginning on Palm Sunday and ending on Easter Sunday. On the morning of Holy Wednesday, the procession of the "Real Maestranza," comprising representatives of the various crafts guilds, wends its way through the streets of the city. These guilds are responsible both for maintaining the tradition and preserving the "Vare," papier-mâché simulacra made in the last century, each depicting a different moment of the Passion of Christ. On the evenings of Thursday and Friday, respectively, there are the processions of the "Vare" and of the "Cristo Nero" or "Black Christ," while on the Saturday before Easter, there is a performance of the Passion of Christ.

Starting from Piazza Garibaldi, the route includes the most prestigious architectural elements dating from different historical era. The fragmentary image of the historical city is, however, made up for by the unified appearance of the urban fabric in each of the districts, with their unassuming but dignified architecture. After a stop in Piazza Garibaldi for a tour of the Cattedrale, and of the church of S. Sebastiano, you can climb uphill for a short distance along the Corso Umberto, and you will reach the church of S. Agata; in the surrounding area, behind the town hall or Municipio, is the unfinished Palazzo Moncada, dating from the 17th c. If you veer to the left of the Cattedrale and take the Via S. Domenico, you will reach the church of S. Domenico, set in the heart of the medieval district; from there the steep Via Angeli leads up to the castle or Castello di Pietrarossa. It will also be a pleasure, during the course of the tour,

to see the lively cultural interests of the people here, which is responsible for there being two interesting museums, one of mineralogy, the other of archeology.

Cattedrale (B2) or Cathedral. Commonly known as the church of *S. Maria la Nuova*, this Cathedral is also dedicated to S. Michele Arcangelo (St. Michael Archangel), the early patron saint of the city. Built between the end of the 16th c. and the beginning of the 17th c. in a late-Renaissance style, it underwent considerable transformation in the 19th c., with the reconstruction of the transept and the cupola. *Inside*, in the vault of the nave you may admire 18th-c. frescoes by Gugliemo Borremans, depicting the *Immaculate Conception* and the *Coronation of the Virgin Mary*, as well as the excellent altarpiece on the main altar by the same artist. Facing the Cattedrale is the church of *S. Sebastiano*, originally laid out in the 16th c., but with a high 19th-c. façade in classical style.

Sant'Agata (B2). Also known as the church of *S. Ignazio*, it adjoins the Collegio dei Gesuiti, accessible from the side ramp, and was built in the early years of the 17th c. The elegant Baroque façade, plastered in a warm orange hue, is the work of Natale Masuccio, and closes off the perspective of the Corso Umberto with a fine theatrical effect. The *interior*, with a Greek-cross plan, is richly decorated with stuccoes and polychrome marble work, and preserves masterpieces of religious art, including the interesting marble *altarpiece* on the altar of the left transept, depicting the saint in glory.

S. Domenico (B3). This church, founded in 1480 at the behest of Antonio Moncada, was enlarged and renovated in the 18th c. Dating from that period are the handsome curving façade and the interior stuccoes. Among the art works housed here, we should point out the canvas by Filippo Paladino on the main altar depicting the *Madonna del Rosario* (1614).

Castello di Pietrarossa (C3) or castle of Pietrarossa. Even though there only scattered ruins of this ancient fortress now survive, it is interesting to take a stroll up to the rock on which the castle once stood; from here, you can enjoy a view of the city and the surrounding territory as far as the valley or Valle del Salso. Probably founded by the Moors, it was reinforced, with the addition of three corner towers by the Normans, and then later by the Aragonese. In its halls, the barons of Sicily gathered to pro-

laim Frederick II of Aragon king. The cas-
le and towers are depicted in the town
oat-of-arms.

Museo Archeologico (C1; *open 9-1 and 3-7*)
r archeological museum. Recently rein-
talled with materials from the Museo Civi-
o, this museum features finds from digs
dating back to the 1950s, in various areas of
he territory of Caltanissetta, Gibil Habil,
ambucina, and Capodarso. On exhibit are
bjects from prehistoric times (vases and
ools from the late Bronze Age), furnishings
rom indigenous and Greek necropolises,
decorated terracottas, Greek and early-Si-
ilian ceramics.

Museo Mineralogico (B1, off map; *open 9-1
nd 3-7*) or museum of mineralogy. In the
alls of the Istituto Tecnico Industriale, an in-

teresting collection of minerals from the territory of the capital of Sicilian sulphur has
been on display to the public since 1979.
Outstanding colors and shapes can be seen
in the crystals of sulphur and celestine,
chalks and aragonite, a sulphureous mineral found in abundance in the mines of Aragona. The museum also has minerals found in
other parts of the world, and a section devoted to the machinery used in the extrac-
tion and processing of sulphur, which will
soon become an actual *Sulphur Museum*.

Founded by Roger the Norman in the 11th c. and
consecrated in the 12th c., the abbey or **Abbazia
di S. Spirito** has the typical appearance of Sicilian
religious architecture of the Romanesque period.
The frescoes on the walls inside date back to the
15th c. To the right of the entrance is a Romanesque *baptismal font*, while in the left apse you can
see an epigraph with the date of consecration.

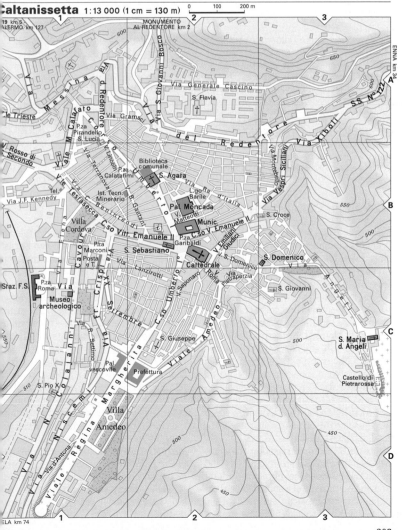

Caltanissetta 1 : 13 000 (1 cm = 130 m)

Caltanissetta: Corso Umberto I, the city's main thoroughfare, leads to the Cathedral

Gibil Habil in Arabic means "mountain of death"; the name was given to this area because of the presence of numerous necropolises carved into the rock cliffs. The fortifications, discovered over the course of the campaigns of excavation, overlook the river Salso and date back to the 6th c. B.C.; they contain an urban layout of the Hippodamean variety, with a regular grid. Finds from the excavations are now in the archeological museum or Museo Archeologico in Caltanissetta.

Archeological excavations carried out on the hill known as the **Sabucina** (*open 9-one hour befor sunset*) reveal the interesting ruins of a Sicilia Greek town that, along with the town of Capc darso, controlled the routes leading up into the valley of the river Salso. Artifacts dating back to the early Bronze Age, found in tombs and within the circular perimeters of the huts, testify to the existence on this site of an indigenous village dating back to the end of the 1st millennium B.C.

10.4 From Caltanissetta to Mussomeli

This route (map on facing page) offers a tour of the mining towns to the west of the river Salso, towns that had the illusion of prosperity based on sulphur mining. You will see farming and mining towns that bear the marks of a bitter history, and villages in which, on the other hand, there is a genuine atmosphere of rural life. As you leave Caltanissetta along state road 122, heading west, you will see San Cataldo and the turnoff for Marianòpoli; after the state road a provincial road, running amid hills that are cultivated in some spots but elsewhere bare and arid, leads to Milena and then joins the fast road 189 to Palermo, along which you will then find the turnoff to Mussomeli. The total distance traveled is 137 km.

In a period of historic transition, the shift – between the end of the 18th c. and the end of the 19th c. – from the rule of the House of Bourbon to the rule of a unified Italian government, we can place the history of sulphur in Sicily. The mining of the mineral was

still a marginal activity at the end of the 18th c., when the nascent French and English manufacturers began to demand more and more sulphuric acid. In a short time, the "solfare" or sulphur mines of central Sicily multiplied in number; in 1834, of the 196 sulphur mines in Sicily, 88 were in the territory of Caltanissetta. The miners, including many boys under the age of 15 (the "carusi"), were forced to work in inhuman conditions, and many died in the dangerous narrow tunnels, without bracing, supported only by plaster. In the second half of the 19th c., Sicily staked its fortunes on the "windfall" of sulphur, which extended until the end of the century, when American sulphur hit the market at cheaper prices. The inevitable crisis hit hard, and the founding, after WWII of the Ente Minerario Siciliano hardly helped. After long and pointless struggles, many sulphur miners, or "zolfari" found themselves forced to choose between a life of misery and emigration.

San Cataldo

San Cataldo (elev. 625 m, pop. 23,487) owes its name to the saint and bishop of Taranto, whose relics were once preserved in the *Chiesa Madre*. Founded in the earliest decades of the 17th c., in the context of a vast agrarian reform of the Sicilian latifundium (large landholding) the town followed a regular grid plan; in the 19th c., after a modest expansion in the 18th c., the town grew still more due to the new prosperity brought by mining. This town grew considerably over the last few decades, especially as a residential center, because of its proximity to the capital. In the surrounding area, it is worth touring the *archeological area of Vassallaggi*, where remains have been found of an early-Sicilian-Greek settlement on five rocky highlands.

Milena

A stop at this little farming town may be of interest, due to the unspoilt atmosphere of the setting, a result of the preservation of old peasant traditions. The township of Milena (elev. 436 m, pop. 3546) was established in the 1920s through the merger of thirteen villages, known as "robbe," which were scattered around the farm, or Masseria di Milocca, now an urban district. The adjoining archeological areas, recently explored, of *Monte Campanella*, *Serra del Palco*, and *Rocca Amorella* have all confirmed the fact that the territory of Milena has been inhabited ever since earliest times, with prehistoric settlements and necropolises dating back to the end of the 1st millennium B.C.

Mussomeli

Mussomeli (elev. 726 m, pop. 11,365) is a major center for the farmers of the area. For centuries, the city lived on an economy based on farming and herding; in the last few years the city has shown a certain vocation for the service industry. The city was founded with the name of Manfreda in the 14th c. by Manfredi III Chiaramonte, lord of the great fief of Mussomeli. The earliest core of the present-day city can still be glimpsed in the district of Terravecchia, in the western section of the historical center. At the same time, Manfredi founded the *Chiesa Matrice*, which was later renovated in the 17th c., and the splendid castle or *Castello**, restored in the 15th c., which now stands on an isolated peak 2 km to the east of the town.

Marianòpoli

The little town of Marianòpoli (elev. 720 m, pop. 2466), founded recently, presents the checkerboard-pattern urban layout that is so typical of new cities of the 18th c. The territory abounds with traces of settlements from a variety of eras, from the third millennium B.C. to the Hellenistic era; you will find archeological zones on the hills of *Mimiani*, *Polizzello*, and *Castelfilici*, but the most important one is in the village of *Castellazzo*, where excavations have revealed the existence of a prehistoric necropolis and a Hellenistic settlement. The ceramic materials and the coins found there are all now in the archeological museum or *Museo Archeologico* di Marianòpoli, in the town hall or Palazzo Comunale.

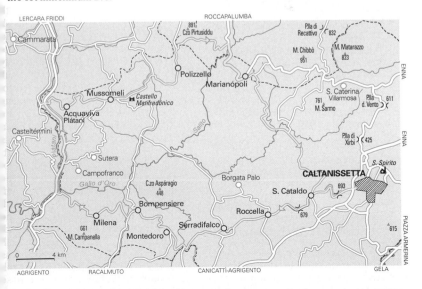

Information for Travelers:
hotels, restaurants, places of interest

Town by town, this list includes the postal code ⊠; the address and telephone numbers of the Tourist Offices ℹ; cafes, shops, cultural institutions; cultural events and natural areas; hotels, camping grounds, and youth hostels, ranked in an official classification expressed by number of stars (from ✱✱✱ to ✱), in accordance with the Italian Tourism Law; restaurants listed according to price category: ⅋ under 23 €; ⅋⅋ between 24 and 34 €; ⅋⅋⅋ between 35 and 44 €; ⅋⅋⅋⅋ between 45 and 54 €; ⅋⅋⅋⅋⅋ over 54 €. The telephone numbers include both local code and subscriber's number. Those calling from abroad must dial Italy's international code (0039), followed by the local code and subscriber's number. The symbols ⒶⒺ American Express, ⓓ Diner's, ⓥⓘⓢⓐ Visa, and ⓜⓒ Master Card indicate which credit cards are accepted. For towns with a map, a site's map coordinates are given by a letter and number. All information has been checked before printing. Changes in the following data may occur at any time.

Aci Castello ⊠ 95021

Page 153

ℹ *Municipio*, tel. 7371208.

Hotels, restaurants, campsites, and vacation villages

✱✱ **President Park.** Via Litteri 88, tel. 095 7116111, fax 095277569; www.president parkhotel.com. Number of rooms: 96. Accessible to the handicapped. Air conditioning, elevator; parking, garden, swimming pool, private beach. ⒶⒺ ⓓ ⓥⓘⓢⓐ ⓜⓒ

at Aci Trezza, km. 2 ⊠ 95026

✱✱✱ **Eden Riviera.** Via Litteri 57, tel. 095277760, fax 095277761; www.herganet.it/eden. Number of rooms: 31. Air conditioning; parking, garden, swimming pool. ⒶⒺ ⓓ ⓥⓘⓢⓐ ⓜⓒ

✱✱✱ **I Malavoglia.** Via Provinciale 3, tel. 095 276711, fax 095276873. Number of rooms: 83. Air conditioning, elevator; parking, parking garage, garden, swimming pool, tennis. ⒶⒺ ⓓ ⓥⓘⓢⓐ ⓜⓒ

⅋⅋ **Cambusa del Capitano.** Via Marina 65, tel. 095276298. Closed Wednesday. Air conditioning. Sicilian cooking – seafood.

⅋⅋ **Galatea.** Via Livorno 146/A, tel. 095277913. Closed Monday, part of November. Air conditioning, parking. Sicilian cooking – seafood. ⒶⒺ ⓓ ⓥⓘⓢⓐ ⓜⓒ

at Cannizzaro, km. 2 ⊠ 95020

✱✱ **Baia Verde.** Via A. Musco 8/10, tel. 095 491522, fax 095494464; www.baiaverde.it. Number of rooms: 158. Accessible to the handicapped. Air conditioning, elevator; parking, parking garage, garden, swimming pool, tennis, private beach. ⒶⒺ ⓓ ⓥⓘⓢⓐ

✱✱ **Sheraton Catania.** Via A. da Messina 45, tel. 095271557, fax 095271380; www.sheraton catania.com. Number of rooms: 170. Accessible to the handicapped. Air conditioning, elevator; parking garage, garden, swimming pool, tennis, private beach. ⓓ ⓥⓘⓢⓐ ⓜⓒ

⅋⅋⅋ **Alioto.** Via Mollica 24/26, tel. 095494444, fax 095492209. Closed Tuesday, August. Air conditioning, parking. Sicilian cooking – seafood. ⒶⒺ ⓓ ⓥⓘⓢⓐ ⓜⓒ

⅋⅋ **Oleandro.** Via A. Musco 8/10, tel. 095 491522; www.baiaverde.it. Air conditioning, parking, garden. Classic Italian and Sicilian cooking. ⒶⒺ ⓓ ⓥⓘⓢⓐ ⓜⓒ

Cafes and pastry shops

Caffè & Dolcezze. Via Re Martino 211, tel. 095 7111540. Specialties: ice creams and cakes.

Museums and cultural institutions

Museo Civico. Castello Normanno, tel. 095 274222. *Closed Monday. Open winter, 9-1 and 3-6.*

Cultural Events

Performances, theatrical, cinema, and artistic, dedicated to Giovanni Verga. Also at Aci Trezza. Fourth week of September.

Natural areas, parks and reserves

at Aci Trezza, km. 2 ⊠ 95026

Area naturale marina and Riserva naturale Isola Lachea-Faraglioni dei Ciclopi. Tel. 095531134.

Acireale ⊠ 95024

Map, page 155

ℹ *Municipio*, tel. 095895111 (A2).

Hotels, restaurants, campsites, and vacation villages

✱✱ **Orizzonte Acireale.** Via C. Colombo, tel. 095886006, fax 0957651607. Number of rooms: 127. Accessible to the handicapped. Elevator; parking, garden, swimming pool. ⒶⒺ ⓓ ⓥⓘⓢⓐ ⓜⓒ; (A1, *off map*).

✱✱✱ **Excelsior Palace Terme.** Via delle Terme 103, tel. 095604444, fax 095605441; excel siorpalace@shr.it. Number of rooms: 229. Accessible to the handicapped. Air conditioning, elevator; swimming pool, private beach. 𝖠𝖤 ⓓ 𝖵𝖨𝖲𝖠 𝖬𝖢; (D2 *off map*).

♨ **Panorama.** Via Santa Caterina 55, tel. 095
★★ 7634124, fax 095608708. Open year-round.

🍴 **La Grotta.** Township of S.M. La Scala, via
Scalo Grande 46, tel. 0957648153. Closed
Tuesday and part of October and November. Air conditioning. Sicilian cooking –
seafood. 𝖠𝖤 ⓓ 𝖵𝖨𝖲𝖠 𝖬𝖢

🍴 **Molino.** Township of S.M. La Sacala, via
Molino 104-110, tel. 0957648116. Closed
Wednesday. Parking. Sicilian cooking –
seafood. 𝖠𝖤 𝖵𝖨𝖲𝖠 𝖬𝖢

at Santa Tecla, km. 4 ✉ 95020

★★★ **Santa Tecla Palace.** Via Balestrate 100, tel.
0957634015, fax 095607705; www.hotelsan
tateclapalace.com. Number of rooms: 215.
Accessible to the handicapped. Air conditioning, elevator; parking, garden, swimming
pool, tennis, private beach. 𝖠𝖤 ⓓ 𝖵𝖨𝖲𝖠 𝖬𝖢

Agriturismo (real Italian country living)

Azienda Agricola Il Limoneto. At Scillichenti; Via
D'Amico 41. A farm with 4 hectares of fruit orchards and olive groves. Guided tours, and tours
of farm. For information: tel. 095886568.

at Giarre, km. 13.5 ✉ 95010

Azienda Agricola Codavolpe. In Trepunti; Strada 87 N°35. This is a fruit and vegetable farm offering accomodation in apartments inside the old
farmstead. Guided tours. For information: tel.
095939802.

Hot springs/Spas

Terme Regionali di Acireale. Via delle Terme,
tel. 095601250-095601508. Hot springs with therapeutic baths, muds, inhalations, and massages.

Cafes and pastry shops

Castorina. Corso Umberto I 63, Corso Savoia 109,
tel. 095601546-095601547. Nougat, stuffed dates.

Castorina al Duomo. Piazza del Duomo 21. Cannoli, ice cream, granita, almond pastries.

Pasticceria Scalia. Via Marchese di Sangiuliano
106, tel. 095601581. Almond biscuits, marzipan
fruit, nougat.

Museums and cultural institutions

Biblioteca and Pinacoteca Zelantea. Via Marchese di S. Giuliano 15, tel. 0957634516. *Open Monday and Wednesday 9-13.*

Cultural Events

Carnevale di Acireale. One of the most beautiful
Sicilian carnivals, with floral and allegorical floats.

Shops, crafts, and curiosities

Lanzafame. Via Vittorio Emanuele 99, tel. 095
606805. Craftsmen making Sicilian "pupi,' or puppets, ceramic, wood sculpture.

Leonardo Barbagallo. Via Nazionale 283, tel.
095809597. Wrought iron.

at Giarre, km. 13.5

Giuseppe Cicala. Via L. Sturzo 59, tel. 095930767.

Craftsmen making Sicilian "pupi," or puppets.
Along the same street are shops of various local
craftsmen, working in wood, iron, copper, and
terracotta.

Aeolian Islands

Map, page 176

at Lìpari ✉ 98055

ℹ️ *Azienda Autonoma*, Corso Vittorio
Emanuele 202, tel. 0909880095 (A1).

Hotels, restaurants, campsites, and vacation villages

at Lìpari

★★★ **Villa Meligunis.** Via Marte 7, tel. 090
9812426, fax 0909880149; villameligunis
@netnet.it. Number of rooms: 37. Accessible to the handicapped. Air conditioning, elevator; garden, private beach. 𝖠𝖤 ⓓ 𝖵𝖨𝖲𝖠 𝖬𝖢;
(D2, *off map*).

★★★ **Augustus.** Vico Ausonia 16, tel. 0909811232,
fax 0909812233; www.netnet.it/villaaugus
tus. Seasonal. Number of rooms: 34. Rooms
only; no dining facilities. Air conditioning;
parking, garden. 𝖠𝖤 ⓓ 𝖵𝖨𝖲𝖠 𝖬𝖢; (A2).

★★★ **Gattopardo Park Hotel.** Via Diana, tel.
0909811035, fax 0909880207; gattopardo
@netnet.it. Number of rooms: 53. Seasonal.
Garden. 𝖠𝖤 𝖵𝖨𝖲𝖠 𝖬𝖢; (C1).

★★★ **Giardino sul Mare.** Via Maddalena 65, tel.
0909811004, fax 0909880150. Number of
rooms: 40. Seasonal. Air conditioning, elevator; garden, swimming pool. 𝖠𝖤 ⓓ 𝖵𝖨𝖲𝖠;
(D2, *off map*).

🍴 **Filippino.** Piazza Municipio, tel. 090
9811002, fax 0909812878; www.filippino.it.
Closed Monday in the low season, 15 No-
vember-Christmas. Air conditioning, garden. The cooking of the Aeolian islands –
seafood. 𝖠𝖤 ⓓ 𝖵𝖨𝖲𝖠 𝖬𝖢; (B2).

🍴 **La Nassa.** Via G. Franza 36, tel. 0909811319;
lanassa@cucinaeoliana.it. Seasonal. Air conditioning. The cooking of the Aeolian islands – seafood. 𝖠𝖤 ⓓ 𝖵𝖨𝖲𝖠 𝖬𝖢; (D2).

△ **Baia Unci.** At Canneto, Via Marina Garibal-
★★ di, tel. 0909811909, fax 0909811715. Seasonal.

at Panarèa ✉ 98055

★★★ **Cincotta.** Contrada S. Pietro, tel. 090983014,
fax 090983211. Seasonal. Number of rooms:
29. Air conditioning; garden, swimming
pool. 𝖠𝖤 ⓓ 𝖵𝖨𝖲𝖠

★★★ **La Piazza.** Via S. Pietro, tel. 090983154, fax
090983003. Seasonal. Number of rooms:
31. Garden; swimming pool. 𝖠𝖤 𝖵𝖨𝖲𝖠

★★★ **Lisca Bianca.** Via Lani 1, tel. 090983004,
fax 090983291; www.liscabianca.it. Seasonal. Number of rooms: 35. Rooms only;
no dining facilities. Air conditioning; garden. 𝖠𝖤 ⓓ 𝖵𝖨𝖲𝖠 𝖬𝖢

at Malfa, on the island, or Isola Salina ✉ 98050

★★★ **Signum.** Via Scalo 15, tel. 0909844222, fax 0909844102; www.netnet.it/salina/signum. Number of rooms: 24. Accessible to the handicapped. Garden. AE ⑩ VISA MC

★★ **Punta Scario.** Near Malfa at Scario, via Scalo 8, tel. 0909844139, fax 0909844077; www.netnet.it/management. Seasonal. Number of rooms: 17. AE ⑩ VISA MC

at Santa Marina Salina ✉ 98050

🍴 **Portobello.** Via Bianchi 1, tel. 0909843125. Closed Wednesday in winter, November. The cooking of the Aeolian islands – seafood. AE ⑩ VISA MC

at Stromboli ✉ 98050

★★★ **La Sciara Residence.** At Piscità, Via Barnao 5, tel. 090986004, fax 090986284; www.lasciara.it. Seasonal. Number of rooms: 62. Parking, parking garage, garden; swimming pool, private beach. AE ⑩ VISA MC

★★★ **La Sirenetta.** At Ficogrande, Via Marina 33, tel. 090986025, fax 090986124; netnet.it/hotel/lasirenetta. Seasonal. Number of rooms: 55. Accessible to the handicapped. Air conditioning; garden, swimming pool, tennis.

🍴 **Locanda del Barbablù.** Via Vittorio Emanuele 17/19, tel. 090986118. Closed 15 January-February and November-15 December. Air Conditioning. Sicilian cooking – seafood. AE ⑩ VISA MC

at Vulcano ✉ 98050

★★★ **Les Sables Noirs.** A Porto Ponente, tel. 0909850, fax 0909852454; www.framon-hotels.com. Seasonal. Number of rooms: 48. Air conditioning; parking, garden, swimming pool, private beach. AE ⑩ VISA MC

★★ **Conti.** A Porto Ponente, tel. and fax 0909852012; www.netnet.it/conti. Seasonal. Number of rooms: 67. Garden. AE ⑩ VISA MC

★★★ **Eolian.** A Porto Ponente, tel. 0909852151, fax 0909852153. Seasonal. Number of rooms: 88. Parking, garden, tennis. AE ⑩ VISA MC

Cafes and pastry shops

at Lipari

Pasticceria del Corso. Corso Vittorio Emanuele 232, tel. 0909812536. Specialties: almond pastries.

Museums and cultural institutions

at Lipari

Museo archeologico regionale eoliano. Via Castello 2, tel. 0909880174. *Open 9-1:30 and 3-7.*

Excursions and organized tours

at Lipari ✉ 98055

Associazione Eolie Ambiente. Tel. 0909811691.

at Panarèa ✉ 98050

Amphibia. Tel. 090983311. Diving.

at Salina ✉ 98050

Cooperativa Salina 80. Tel. 0909843190. Tours for birdwatchers.

at Stromboli ✉ 98050

Associazione Guide Alpine Italiane. Tel. 090 986263-986211. Tours to the volcano.

Agrigento ✉ 92100

Map, pages 89 and 93

ℹ️ *AAPIT*, Viale della Vittoria 255, tel. 0922 401352 (II, B3).
Azienda Autonoma, Via Empedocle 73, tel. 092220391 (II, B3). Information Office, Via Battisti 15, tel. 092220454 (II, B3).

Hotels, restaurants, campsites, and vacation villages

★★★★ **Colleverde Park Hotel.** Strada Panoramica dei Templi, tel. 092229555, fax 092229012. Number of rooms: 48. Accessible to the handicapped. Air conditioning, elevator; parking, garden, private beach. AE ⑩ VISA MC; (I, B3).

★★★★ **Foresteria Baglio della Luna.** Contrada Maddalusa, tel. 0922511061, fax 0922598802; www.esperia.it/pregiohotel/bagliodellaluna.htm. Number of rooms: 24. Air conditioning; parking, garden. AE ⑩ VISA MC; (J, C1).

★★★★ **Jolly Della Valle.** Via U. La Malfa 3, tel. 092226966, fax 092226412. Number of rooms: 120. Air conditioning, elevator; parking. AE ⑩ VISA MC; (J, C1).

★★★ **Kaos.** Villaggio Pirandello, tel. 0922598622, fax 0922598770; www.athenahotels.com. Number of rooms: 105. Air conditioning, elevator; parking, garden, swimming pool, tennis (I, C1).

★★★★ **Villa Athena.** Via Panoramica dei Templi 33, tel. 0922596288, fax 0922402180; www.athenahotels.com. Number of rooms: 40. Air conditioning; parking, swimming pool. AE ⑩ VISA MC; (J, C1).

🍴 **Le Caprice.** Strada Panoramica dei Templi 51, tel. 092226469. Closed Friday and part of July. Air conditioning, parking. The cooking of Agrigento – seafood. AE ⑩ VISA MC; (I, B3).

at Villaggio Mosè, km. 8

★★★★ **G.H. Mosè.** Viale L. Sciascia, tel. 0922608388, fax 0922608377; www.iashotels.com. Number of rooms: 102. Air conditioning, elevator; parking, swimming pool. AE ⑩ VISA MC

★★★ **Tre Torri.** Tel. 0922606733, fax 0922607839; www.mediatel.it/public/tre-torri. Number of rooms: 118. Air conditioning, elevator; parking, indoor and outdoor swimming pools. AE ⑩ VISA MC

at San Leone, km. 7

⛺ **Internazionale San Leone.** Contrada Dune, tel. 0922416121, fax 0922416008. Open year-round.

Cafes and pastry shops

Pasticceria La Promenade. Via Panoramica dei Templi 8, tel. 092223715. Almond specialities.

Bar Sajeva. Viale della Vittoria 61/65, tel. 092220671. Dry pastries, plumcake, "panettoni."

Museums and cultural institutions

Area archeologica. Tel. 0922497226. *Open 9-9.*

Museo Civico. Piazza Pirandello 16, tel. 0922 20722. Closed for restoration. Ethno-anthropological section: Monastero di S. Spirito. *Closed Sunday. Open summer, 9-2, Tuesday and Thursday also 3:30-6:30; winter, 9-1, Tuesday and Thursday also 3:30-6:30.*

Museo Diocesano. c/o Cattedrale, tel. 0922 401352. Closed for restoration.

Museo archeologico regionale. Contrada San Nicola, tel. 0922401565. *Open Tuesday-Sunday, 9-1:30 and 2:30-5:30; Monday 9-1:30.*

Quartiere ellenistico-romano. *Open 8:30-5.*

at Villaseta, Contrada Caos, km. 5.6

Casa Pirandello. Tel. 0922511102. *Open 8-2, 4-6:30.*

Cultural Events

Festa di S. Calogero. An entire week of festivities, from the 1st-2nd Sunday of July.

Sagra del Mandorlo in fiore. In the Valle dei Templi, amid flowering almond trees, celebrations to welcome springtime. On a stage in front of the Temple of Juno, performances by folklore groups from Sicily, other Italian regions, and Europe. First ten days of February.

Shops, crafts, and curiosities

Zambuto Salvatore. Via Saponara 8, tel. 0922 23924. Creations made of cork.

Natural areas, parks and reserves

Giardino della Kolymbetra. Run by FAI, tel. 0246761583. *Closed Monday. Open 1 February-30 April, 9-6; 1 May-31 October, 9-7; 1 November-31 January, 10-5.*

Aidone   ✉ 94010

Page 198

i   *Pro Loco,* Via Mazzini 1, tel. 093586557.

Museums and cultural institutions

Museo Archeologico Regionale. Largo Torres Trupia, tel. 093587307. *Open 9-7.*

at Morgantina, km. 6

Archeological digs. Tel. 093587955. *Open winter, 9-5; summer, 9-1 hour before sunset.*

Cultural Events

at Morgantina, km. 6

Classical performances at the agorà. July and August.

Àlcamo   ✉ 91011

Map, page 84

i   *Ufficio turistico del Comune,* Piazza Ciullo 1, tel. 0924590001 (B2).

Museums and cultural institutions

Castello. *Open 9-12:30, 4-8; Saturday and Sunday 9-12:30, 4-8:30.*

Museo etno-antropologico. Inside the Castle, tel. 0924590270. *Open 9-12:30, 4-8; Saturday and Sunday 9-12:30, 4-8:30.*

Cultural Events

Summertime blues festival. Free concerts in Piazza Ciullo. July.

Aragona   ✉ 92021

Map, page 94

Cultural Events

Incontro dei giganti. Gigantic statues in papier-mâché are moved from the inside by two men and follow the procession; they represent St. Peter and St. Paul. Easter.

Natural areas, parks and reserves

Riserva naturale integrale Macalube. Tel. 0922699210. Guided tours.

Augusta   ✉ 96011

i   *Municipio,* Via Umberto I 104, tel. 0931980111.

Hotels, restaurants, campsites, and vacation villages

at Acquasanta, km. 6

★★   **Europa Club.** Tel. 0931983080, fax 0931978696; www.megara.com/euroclub. Seasonal. Number of rooms: 35. Parking, garden, tennis, private beach.

at Monte Tàuro, km. 6

★★   **Villa dei Cesari.** Tel. 0931983311, fax 0931 983090. Number of rooms: 24. Air conditioning; parking, garden, private beach. ▣ ▣ ▣

at Brùcoli, km. 7   ✉ 96010

🍴   **Fragio.** Via Libertà 56/58, tel. 0931981145; www.augustaintasca.com. Closed Tuesday and part of September and October. Air conditioning, parking. Sicilian cooking – seafood. ▣ ▣ ▣

⛺ ★★   **Baia del Silenzio.** Tel. 0931981881, fax 0931982288. Open year-round.

Cafes and pastry shops

Caprice. Via Turati 81, tel. 0931994363. Pastries and ice cream.

Eurobar. Via Principe Umberto 256, tel. 0931 975652. In summer, a superb breakfast: almond "granita," espresso and cream, with a brioche.

La Creperie. Via Principe Umberto 149, tel. 0931975675. Pastries and ice cream.

Museums and cultural institutions

Archeological digs of Megara Hyblaea. Tel. 0931512364. *Open 9-one hour before sunset.*

Bagherìa   ✉ 90011

Page 52

ℹ️   Tourist information center, Corso Umberto I, tel. 091909020.

Cafes and pastry shops

Gelateria Anni 20. Via Mattarella 13, tel. 091 902140. Fruit "gelati" in the most exotic flavors. Excellent lemon, orange, nectarine, cantaloupe sherbets, and frozen cakes.

Museums and cultural institutions

Villa Cattolica e Galleria Renato Guttuso. State road 113, tel. 091905438. *Closed Monday. Open 10-8.*

Villa Palagonia. Piazza Garibaldi 3, tel. 091 932088. *Open 9-1 and 4-7.*

Shops, crafts, and curiosities

at Casteldaccia, km. 6   ✉ 90014

Casa Vinicola Duca di Salaparuta. State road Nazionale, tel. 091953988.

Barcellona Pozzo di Gotto

✉ 98051

Hotels, restaurants, campsites, and vacation villages

🏕️ **Centro Vacanze Cantoni.** At Cantoni, tel. and fax 0909710165. Seasonal.

Bronte   ✉ 95034

Page 158

ℹ️   *Pro Loco,* Corso Umberto I 22, tel. 0957723040.

Hotels, restaurants, campsites, and vacation villages

★★ **Parco dell'Etna.** Contrada Borgonovo, tel. 095691907, fax 095692678; www.itwg.com/ itw 11551.a99. Number of rooms: 14. Accessible to the handicapped. Air conditioning; parking, parking garage, garden, swimming pool.

Cafes and pastry shops

Conti. Corso Umberto I 275, tel. 095691165. Specialty: pistachio pastries.

Museums and cultural institutions

at Maniace, km. 18   ✉ 95030

Abbazia di Maniace (castello di Nelson). Tel. 095690018. *Open winter, 9-1 and 2:30-5; summer, 9-1:30 and 3-7.*

at Adrano, km. 14   ✉ 95031

Museo regionale del castello normanno. Tel. 0957692660. *Open 9-1.*

Cultural Events

at Adrano, km. 14   ✉ 95031

Diavolata. Mystery play symbolizing the struggle between Good and Evil. Easter.

Caltagirone   ✉ 95041

Map, page 116

ℹ️   *Azienda autonoma,* Via Volta Libertini 3, tel. 093353809 (A1).

Hotels, restaurants, campsites, and vacation villages

★★★ **G.H. Villa San Mauro.** Via Porto Salvo 10, tel. 093326500, fax 093331661; www.fra mon-hotels.com. Number of rooms: 91. Accessible to the handicapped. Air conditioning, elevator; parking, swimming pool. ⒶⒺ ⓪ 𝚅𝙸𝚂𝙰 ᴍᴄ; (D1).

🍴 **La Scala.** Scala S. Maria del Monte 8, tel. 093357781. Air conditioning; garden. Classic Italian and Sicilian cooking. ⒶⒺ ⓪ 𝚅𝙸𝚂𝙰 ᴍᴄ; (A1).

Agriturismo (real Italian country living)

La Casa degli Angeli. Contrada Angeli, S.P. 39 al km 9. This is a hillside working farm with citrus grove, olive grove, and vegetable garden. Mountain bike rental, cooking courses, guided tours. For information: tel. 093325317.

Museums and cultural institutions

Museo Civico and Pinacoteca Sturzo. Bourbon prison, Via Roma 10, tel. 093341812. *Open Tuesday and Friday-Sunday 9:30-1:30 and 4-7.*

Museo dei Pupi Siciliani. Via Roma 65, tel. 0933 54085. *Open 9-1 and 3-7.*

Museo Regionale della Ceramica. Viale Giardini pubblici, tel. 093321680. *Open 9-6:30.*

Cultural Events

Festa di S. Giacomo. Historical procession on the 142 steps of the stairway of S. Maria del Monte. 24-25 July.

Shops, crafts, and curiosities

Ceramiche di Caltagirone. Via Roma 49, tel. 093354217.

Maria Morales. Via Stazione Isolamento 82, tel. 093358398. Ceramics and terracotta.

Riccardo Varsallona. Via Colombo 33, tel. 0933 40531.

Caltanissetta   ✉ 93100

Map, page 203

ℹ️   *AAPIT,* Corso Vittorio Emanuele 109, tel. 0934530411 (B2).

Hotels, restaurants, campsites, and vacation villages

✦✦ **San Michele.** Via Fasci Siciliani, tel. 0934553750, fax 0934598791; inzoli@techma.it. Number of rooms: 136. Accessible to the handicapped. Air conditioning, elevator; parking, garden, swimming pool. ᴀᴇ ⑩ ᴠɪsᴀ; (A1, *off map*).

✦✦ **Plaza.** Via B. Gaetani 5, tel. 0934583877, fax 0934583877. Number of rooms: 33. Rooms only. Accessible to the handicapped. Air conditioning, elevator; parking garage. ᴀᴇ ⑩ ᴠɪsᴀ ᴍᴄ; (B2).

Cortese. Viale Sicilia 166, tel. 0934591686. Closed Monday, and part of August. Air conditioning. Sicilian cooking – seafood and mushrooms. ᴠɪsᴀ ᴍᴄ; (B1, *off map*).

Cafes and pastry shops

Bar pasticceria Fiorino. Viale Candura 4/F, tel. 0934583109. Excellent glazed cream puffs filled with cream, coffee, "gianduia," or chocolate.

Caffè Pasticceria Rair. Corso Umberto I 163, tel. 093421402. Cannoli and "cannolicchi alla ricotta," dusted with cinnamon, with ground hazelnuts and almonds.

Museums and cultural institutions

Museo Archeologico. Via Colajanni 3, tel. 093425936. *Open 9-1 and 3-7.*

Museo Mineralogico. Istituto Tecnico Industriale, Viale della Regione 73, tel. 0934591280. *Open 9-1.*

at Gibil Habil, km. 5

Zona archeologica. Tel. 0934566982. *Open 9-ne hour before sunset.*

at Sabucina, km. 7

Zona archeologica. Tel. 0934566982. *Open 9-ne hour before sunset.*

Cultural Events

Easter celebrations. Holy week. From Wednesday to Holy Friday, processions and religious events.

Campofelice di Roccella
✉ 90010

Hotels, restaurants, campsites, and vacation villages

✦✦ **Plaia d'Himera Park Hotel.** Contrada Pistavecchia, tel. 0921933815, fax 0921933843. Number of rooms: 139. Air conditioning, elevator; parking, garden, swimming pool, tennis, private beach. ᴀᴇ ᴠɪsᴀ ᴍᴄ

Canicattì
✉ 92024

Hotels, restaurants, campsites, and vacation villages

✦✦ **Collina al Faro.** Via Puccini 29, tel. 0922 853062, fax 0922851160. Number of rooms: 28. Rooms only. Accessible to the handi-

capped. Air conditioning; parking. ᴀᴇ ᴠɪsᴀ ᴍᴄ

Capo d'Orlando
✉ 98071

Page 192

ℹ️ *Azienda Autonoma*, Via Piave 67, tel. 0941 912517.

Hotels, restaurants, campsites, and vacation villages

★★★ **Il Mulino.** Via A. Doria 46, tel. 0941902431, fax 0941911614; mulino@netpoint.locnet.it. Number of rooms: 85. Accessible to the handicapped. Air conditioning, elevator; parking, parking garage. ᴀᴇ ⑩ ᴠɪsᴀ ᴍᴄ

★★★ **La Meridiana.** At Piana, tel. and fax 0941957713. Number of rooms: 45. Air conditioning, elevator; parking, garden, swimming pool. ᴀᴇ ⑩ ᴠɪsᴀ ᴍᴄ

★★★ **La Tartaruga.** At Lido San Gregorio, tel. 0941955012, fax 0941955056; enterprisenet.it/tartaruga. Number of rooms: 38. Accessible to the handicapped. Air conditioning, elevator; parking, swimming pool, private beach. ᴀᴇ ⑩ ᴠɪsᴀ ᴍᴄ

🍴🍴 **La Tartaruga.** At Lido San Gregorio, tel. 0941955012, fax 0941955056; enterprise net.it/tartaruga. Closed November. Air conditioning, parking. Classic Italian cooking and the cooking of Messina – seafood. ᴀᴇ ⑩ ᴠɪsᴀ ᴍᴄ

⚠ **Santarosa.** At Tavola Grande, Via Trazzera Marina, tel. 0941901723, fax 0941 912384. Seasonal.

at Fiumara di Naso, km. 10   ✉ 98074

🍴 **Bontempo.** Tel. 0941961188. Closed Monday. Air conditioning, parking, garden. The cooking of Messina. ᴀᴇ ⑩ ᴠɪsᴀ.

Agriturismo (real Italian country living)

at San Gregorio, km. 2

Milio. This working farm has 150 hectares of olive trees and fruit orchards, just 500 m. from the sea. Walks are organized to the Parco dei Nebrodi. For information: tel. 955008.

Carini
✉ 90044

Page 48

ℹ️ Ufficio Turistico. Piazza Duomo, tel. 091 8611339.

Hotels, restaurants, campsites, and vacation villages

at Villa Grazia di Carini, km. 6   ✉ 90040

★★★ **Porto Rais.** Via Piraineto 125, tel. 091 8693481, fax 0918693458; www.sicilyok.com/portorais. Number of rooms: 43. Air conditioning; parking, garden, tennis, private beach. ᴀᴇ ⑩ ᴠɪsᴀ ᴍᴄ

★★★ **Residence Hotel Azzolini.** State road 113 at km. 286.600, tel. 0918674755, fax 091 8675747; neomedia.it/azzolini. Number of rooms: 66. Air conditioning, elevator; parking, swimming pool, tennis, private beach. Æ Ⓞ 𝗩𝗜𝗦𝗔 MC

Museums and cultural institutions

Castle. *Open 9-1 and 4-8.* For guided visits, tel. 0918611339.

Carlentini ✉ 96013

Page 141

ℹ️ *Pro Loco*, Via Porta Siracusa 85, tel. 095 991108.

Agriturismo (real Italian country living)

Casa dello Scirocco. Contrada Piscitello. Comfortable lodgings built inside prehistoric grottoes, in an estate surrounded by orange groves. Swimming pool, horse riding, cooking courses. For information: tel. 095447709.

Tenuta di Roccadia. Contrada Roccadia. Accommodations in independent rooms, on a farm growing citrus, olives, and almond trees; swimming pool, horseback riding; guided excursions. For information: tel. 095990362.

Terias. Contrada Corridore del Pero. 19th-century farm in an estate of citrus groves, with vegetable garden, and other crops, along the river S. Leonardo and near the sea. Mountain bike and canoe rental. For information: tel. 095997212.

Cafes and pastry shops

Laboratorio di pasticceria Lazzara. Via Tivoli 5, tel. 095992597. Cannoli and other sweets.

Museums and cultural institutions

Parco archeologico di Leontinoi. Tel. 0931 481111. *Open Monday-Friday 9-1.*

Castelbuono ✉ 90013

ℹ️ *Ufficio Turistico*, Corso Umberto I 79, tel. 0921671124.

Hotels, restaurants, campsites, and vacation villages

🍴 **Vecchio Palmento.** Via Failla 4, tel. 0921 672099. Closed Monday and part of September. Garden. Sicilian cooking and pizza. Æ 𝗩𝗜𝗦𝗔.

at San Guglielmo, km. 5

🍴 **Romitaggio.** Tel. 0921671323. Closed Wednesday, 15 June-15 July. Parking. Sicilian cooking.

Castellammare del Golfo ✉ 91014

Page 85

ℹ️ *Ufficio Turistico Comunale*, Viale Umberto 1, tel. 092431320.

Hotels, restaurants, campsites, and vacation villages

★★★ **Al Madarig.** Piazza Petrolo 7, tel. 0924

33533, fax 092433790. Number of rooms: 3. Air conditioning, elevator; parking garage Æ Ⓞ 𝗩𝗜𝗦𝗔.

🔺 **Nausicaa.** At Forgia, tel. 092433030, fa 092435173. Seasonal.

at Scopello, km. 10 ✉ 9101

🍴 **Torre Bennistra.** Via Natale di Roma 19, te 0924541128. The cooking of Trapani seafood.

🔺 **Baia di Guidaloca.** Contrada Guidaloc tel. 0924541262, fax 092435100. Seasonal

🏕 **Lu Baruni.** Contrada Barone 27, tel. and fa 092439133. Seasonal.

Agriturismo (real Italian country living

Camillo Finazzo. Contrada Baida Molinazzo. farm surrounded by a 10-hectare estate, wit horses and other animals, olive groves and vine yards. Fine view. For information: tel. 09243805

Marmora. Contrada Marmora 22. High qualit horse riding in a splendid estate. Other inte esting activities. For information: tel. 09243925-

Cultural Events

Festa di Maria SS. del Soccorso. Folkloristi shows and famous nocturnal sea procession From 19-21 August.

Hot springs/Spas

at Ponte Bagni, km. 7

Terme Segestane. Tel. 0924530057. Hot spring with therapeutic baths in natural and manmad pools, grottoes, muds, inhalations, and ma sages.

Natural areas, parks and reserves

Riserva naturale dello Zingaro. Tel. 0924541142 For tours, tel. 0924541197.

Catania ✉ 9510

Map, page 148

ℹ️ *AAPIT*, Center city, Via Cimarosa 12, te 0957306222 (C3); Airport, tel. 0957306260 Train station, tel. 0957306255 (C5); Port, te 0957 306209; Etna North, Piano Proven zana, tel. 095 647352; Etna South, Piazza Rifugio Sapienza, tel. 095916356.
Azienda Autonoma, Corso Italia 302, te 095373084.

Hotels, restaurants, campsites, and vaca tion villages

★★★ **Excelsior Grand Hotel.** Piazza Verga 3 tel. 0957476111, fax 095537015; www.thi.i Number of rooms: 176. Accessible to th handicapped. Air conditioning, elevator. Æ Ⓞ 𝗩𝗜𝗦𝗔 MC; (B4).

★★★ **Central Palace.** Via Etnea 218, tel. 09 325344, fax 0957158939. Number of room 99. Air conditioning, elevator; parkin garage. Æ Ⓞ 𝗩𝗜𝗦𝗔; (C3).

★★★ **Jolly Bellini.** Piazza Trento 13, tel. 09

316933, fax 095316832. Number of rooms: 159. Air conditioning, elevator; parking. ☒ ☑ ☑ ☑; (B3).

★★★ **Jolly Hotel Ognina.** Via Messina 628, tel. 0957528111, fax 0957121856. Number of rooms: 56. Rooms only. Air conditioning, elevator; parking. ☒ ☑ ☑; (A6, *off map*).

★★★ **Poggio Ducale.** Via Paolo Gaifami 5, tel. 095330016, fax 095580103; www.poggioducale.it. Number of rooms: 28. Accessible to the handicapped. Air conditioning, elevator; parking. ☒ ☑ ☑ ☑; (A4, *off map*).

🍴🍴🍴 **I Tre Bicchieri.** Via S. Giuseppe al Duomo 31, tel. 0957153540, fax 0952500712; www.osteriaitrebicchieri.it. Closed Sunday, Monday at midday, August. Air conditioning; parking. Mediterranean and fine cuisine – seafood. ☒ ☑ ☑ ☑; (D3).

🍴🍴 **Cantine del Cugno Mezzano.** Via Museo Biscari 8, tel. 0957158710; cantinecugno @tin.it. Closed Sunday, Monday at midday, and part of August. Air conditioning. Wine bar, Mediterranean cooking – seafood. ☒ ☑ ☑; (D4).

🍴🍴 **Il Carato.** Via Vittorio Emanuele II 81, tel. 0957159247; ilcarato@libero.it. Closed Sunday, August. Air conditioning. Sicilian and vegetarian cooking. ☒ ☑ ☑ ☑; (D5).

🍴🍴 **La Siciliana.** Viale Marco Polo 52/A, tel. 095376400, fax 0957221300; www.lasiciliana.it. Closed evenings on holidays, Monday. Air conditioning; garden. Sicilian cooking. ☒ ☑ ☑; (A5, *off map*).

🍴 **Da Rinaldo.** Via Simili 59, tel. 095532312. Closed August. Air conditioning. Cooking of Sicily and other regions. ☒ ☑ ☑; (B5).

🏠 **Europeo.** At La Plaia, Viale Kennedy 91, tel. 095591026, fax 095591911. Seasonal.

🏠 **Jonio.** At Ognina, Via Villini a Mare 2, tel. 095491139, fax 095492277. Open year-round.

Agriturismo (real Italian country living)

Bagnara. Contrada Cardinale. Rural lodgings in an estate with orange and olive groves, peach and prickly pear trees. Horse riding. For information: tel. 095336407.

Fondo 23. Via San Giuseppe La Rena. 19th-century farm of lava stone, surrounded by bouganvilleas and oleanders. Bicycles, horse riding at 1 km. For information: tel. 095592521.

Cafes and pastry shops

Caprice. Via Etnea 30, tel. 095320555. Torroncini nougat, cassata, ice cream; and restaurant.

Mantegna. Via Etnea 350, tel. 095311918. A century-old shop sign.

Nuovo Caffè Italia. Corso Italia 247, tel. 095 388807.

Privitera. Piazza S. Maria del Gesù 1-2, tel. 095 325403. Home-made pastries.

Savia. Via Etnea 302, tel. 095322335. Home-made almond pastries, cassata and pinoli.

St. Moritz. Via Etnea 198 and 206, tel. 095320936. Home made pastries and ice cream.

Museums and cultural institutions

Casa-Museo di Giovanni Verga. Via S. Anna 8, tel. 0957150598. *Closed Sunday and holidays. Open 9-1.*

Complesso monumentale del monastero benedettino di S. Nicolò l'Arena. Piazza Dante. *Open 9-1 and 4-8.*

Musei di Mineralogia, di Paleontologia e di Vulcanologia. Corso Italia 55, tel. 0957195764. Open by appointment.

Museo Belliniano. Piazza S. Francesco 3, tel. 0957150535. *Open weekdays 9-1:30, holidays 9-12:30.*

Museo Civico di Castello Ursino. Piazza Federico di Svevia, tel. 095345830. *Open 9-1 and 3-6; Sunday 9-1.*

Museo di Botanica e Orto Botanico. Via A. Longo 19, tel. 095430901. Guided tours to be booked.

Museo Emilio Greco. Piazza S. Francesco d'Assisi 3, tel. 095317654. *Open 9-1:30; 9:12.*

Teatro Romano. Via Vittorio Emanuele 266. *Open 9-one hour before sunset.*

Cultural Events

Bellini d'oro. At Teatro Massimo Bellini, tel. 095312020, music award dedicated to the famous musician, with a concert. October.

Catania Musica Estate. Classical music festival with concerts by European artists, at the Centro Culturale "Le Ciminiere," tel. 0957349911.

Estate catanese. Theatrical and music performances in the historic center. From the end of June to the end of August.

Festa di S. Agata. Processions and festivals dedicated to the patron saint. From 3 to 5 February.

Excursions and organized tours

CAI (Club Alpino Italiano). Piazza Scamacca 1, tel. 0957153515.

Excursion to Etna. Bus service from the Central Station to the Sapienza Refuge. AST: 095347330-0957461096.

Tour Etna da vedere in treno. Ferrovia Circumetnea, tel. 095541250-095431002.

Sports

Centro Equitazione La Plàia (riding). Viale Kennedy 52, tel. 095281826.

Tennis Club Umberto. Via Monsignor Orlando 6, tel. 095497191.

Piscina Comunale Plàia (pool). Viale Kennedy 20, tel. 095340362.

Scuola di sub (diving). Viale Africa 186, tel. 095539905.

Shops, crafts, and curiosities

Giuseppe Ferilli. Viale Regione 7, tel. 095204598. Baskets of handwoven willow.

Armando Gelsomino. Via Fondo Romeo 15/H, tel. 095206334. Works in lava stone.

Motta Sant'Anastasia. Via Nizeti 16, tel. 095 494148. Wrought iron.

Natural areas, parks and reserves

Riserva naturale Oasi del Simeto. Tel. 095 388227; for guided tours, tel. 0955349351.

Cattolica Eraclea   ☒ 92011

Page 98

Museums and cultural institutions

at Eraclèa Minoa, km. 13

Antiquarium and Zona Archeologica. *Open 9-one hour before sunset.*

Cefalù   ☒ 90015

Map, page 183

i   *Azienda Autonoma*, Corso Ruggero 77, tel. 0921421050; www.cefalu-tour.pa.it (B2).

    Presidio turistico, Corso Ruggero 113, tel. 0921923327 (B2).

Hotels, restaurants, campsites, and vacation villages

★★★ **Kalura.** At Caldura, Via V. Cavallaro 13, tel. 0921421354, fax 0921423122. Number of rooms: 75. Air conditioning, elevator; parking, garden, swimming pool, tennis, private beach. ᴀᴇ ⓪ 🆅🅸🆂🅰 ᴍᴄ; (D3, *off map*).

★★★ **Le Calette.** At Caldura, Via V. Cavallaro 12, tel. 0921424144, fax 0921423688; www.ke fa.it/hotel_lecalette. Seasonal. Number of rooms: 50. Accessible to the handicapped. Air conditioning; parking, garden, swimming pool, private beach. ᴀᴇ ⓪ 🆅🅸🆂🅰 ᴍᴄ; (D3, *off map*).

❙❙ **Ostaria del Duomo.** Via Seminario 5, tel. 0921421838. Seasonal. Closed Monday in the off season. Sicilian cooking. ᴀᴇ ⓪ 🆅🅸🆂🅰 ᴍᴄ; (A-B2).

❙ **Gabbiano-Da Saro.** Lungomare Giardina 17, tel. 0921421495. Closed Wednesday (except in summer), Christmas. Garden. Classic Italian and Sicilian cooking – seafood, pizza. ᴀᴇ ⓪ 🆅🅸🆂🅰 ᴍᴄ; (B1).

❙ **La Brace.** Via XXV Novembre 10, tel. 0921423570. Closed Monday, 15 December-15 January. Air conditioning. Classic cooking. ᴀᴇ ⓪ 🆅🅸🆂🅰 ᴍᴄ; (B1).

at Capo Plàia, km. 8

★★★ **Carlton Hotel Riviera.** Tel. 0921420200, fax 0921420264; www.carltonhotelriviera.it. Seasonal. Number of rooms: 144. Air conditioning, elevator; parking, garden, swimming pool, tennis, private beach. ᴀᴇ 🆅🅸🆂🅰.

at Sant'Ambrogio, km. 7   ☒ 90010

⚑★★ **Plaja degli Uccelli.** State road 113 at km. 180.4, tel. and fax 0921999068. Seasonal.

Museums and cultural institutions

Museo Mandralisca. Via Mandralisca 13, tel. 0921421547. *Open 9-6.*

Cultural Events

Cefalù Incontri. Music, folklore, cabaret, theatre. From July to September.

Chiaramonte Gulfi   ☒ 97012

Page 114

i   *Pro Loco*, tel. 928087.

Hotels, restaurants, campsites, and vacation villages

❙ **Majore.** Via Martiri Ungheresi 12, tel. 0932 928019; www.ibla.net.majore. Closed Monday, July. Air conditioning. Sicilian cooking from Ragusa. ᴀᴇ ⓪ 🆅🅸🆂🅰 ᴍᴄ

Còmiso   ☒ 97013

Page 113

i   *Pro Loco*, Via Di Vita 6, tel. 0932961586.

Museums and cultural institutions

Biblioteca Gesualdo Bufalino. Piazza delle Erbe, tel. 0932962617. *Closed Monday. Open 9-1 and 3-6; Saturday 9-1.*

Museo di Storia naturale. Piazza delle Erbe, tel. 0932722521. *Closed Monday. Open 9-1 and 4-7:30; Sunday 9-1.*

Corleone   ☒ 90034

Page 56

i   *Ufficio Turistico.* C/o Museo civico, tel. 0918464907.

Museums and cultural institutions

Museo Civico di Palazzo Provenzano. Tel. 0918464907. *Open 9-1 and 4-8; Sunday 9-1.*

at Bisacquino, km. 21.7

Museo Civico. Via Orsini, tel. 0918351111. Presently closed.

Ègadi Islands

Map, page 69

i   *Pro Loco* at Favignana, Piazza Matrice 8, tel. 0923921647.

Hotels, restaurants, campsites, and vacation villages

at Favignana   ☒ 91023

★★★ **L'Approdo di Ulisse.** At Calagrande, tel. 0923922525, fax 0923921511. Seasonal. Number of rooms: 126. Parking, garden, swimming pool, tennis, private beach. ᴀᴇ ⓪ 🆅🅸🆂🅰

★★ **Aegusa.** Via Garibaldi 11, tel. 0923922430, fax 0923922440; www.egadi.com/aegusa. Number of rooms: 28. Accessible to the handicapped. Air conditioning; garden. ᴀᴇ ⓪ 🆅🅸🆂🅰 ᴍᴄ

★★ **Egadi.** Via Colombo 17, tel. 0923921232, fax 0923921232. Seasonal. Number of rooms: 11. Air conditioning. ⒜Ⓔ ⓞⒹ ⓥⓘⓢⓐ

¶| **Sorelle Guccione.** Via Colombo 17, tel. 0923921232; pngsgu@tin.it. Seasonal, closed at midday. Sicilian cooking – seafood. ⒜Ⓔ ⓞⒹ ⓥⓘⓢⓐ ⓜⒸ

¶ **Trattoria El Pescador.** Piazza Europa 43, tel. 0923921035. Closed Wednesday, February. Sicilian cooking – seafood. ⒜Ⓔ ⓞⒹ

𝔸 ⓥⓘⓢⓐ ⓜⒸ
★★★ **Miramare.** Contrada Costicella, tel. 0923 921330, fax 922200. Seasonal.

𝔸
★★★ **Egad.** Contrada Arena, tel. 0923921555, fax 0923539370. Seasonal.

at Lèvanzo ✉ 91010

[i] *Delegazione del Municipio*, tel. 0923924089.

★★ **Pensione dei Fenici.** Via Lungomare, tel. and fax 0923924083; www.emmeti.it. Number of rooms: 10. Air conditioning.

Natural areas, parks and reserves

Area marina protetta Isole Ègadi. Tel. 0923 328900.

Excursions and organized tours

at Favignana ✉ 91023

Vitalba Patti. Tel. 0923921411. Visit to the archeological sites and the tuna fish works.

Enna ✉ 94100

Map, page 194

[i] *APT*, Via Roma 411, tel. 0935528228 (A2). *Azienda Autonoma*, Piazza Colajanni 6, tel. 09355500875 (A2).

Hotels, restaurants, campsites, and vacation villages

★★★ **Demetra.** Contrada Misericordia, state road 121, tel. 0935502300, fax 0935502166; hoteldemetra@tin.it. Number of rooms: 30. Accessible to the handicapped. Air conditioning, elevator; parking, garden. ⒜Ⓔ ⓞⒹ ⓥⓘⓢⓐ ⓜⒸ; (A2, *off map*).

★★★ **G.A. Sicilia.** Piazza Colajanni 7, tel. 0935 500850, fax 0935500488. Number of rooms: 76. Rooms only; no dining facilities. Accessible to the handicapped. Elevator; parking garage, garden. ⒜Ⓔ ⓞⒹ ⓥⓘⓢⓐ ⓜⒸ; (A2).

¶| **Centrale.** Piazza VI Dicembre 9, tel. 0935 500963; centraleristorante@usa.net. Closed Saturday (except in high season). Air conditioning. Classic Italian and Sicilian cooking. ⒜Ⓔ ⓞⒹ ⓥⓘⓢⓐ ⓜⒸ; (A2).

¶| **Liolà.** Via Duca d'Aosta 2, tel. 093537706. Closed Tuesday (except in high season). Air conditioning. Sicilian cooking. ⒜Ⓔ ⓞⒹ ⓥⓘⓢⓐ ⓜⒸ; (A2).

at Pergusa, km. 10 ✉ 94010

★★★ **Riviera.** Via Autodromo di Pergusa, tel. 0935 541267, fax 541260; www.rivierahtl.it. Number of rooms: 26. Air conditioning; parking, garden, swimming pool. ⒜Ⓔ ⓞⒹ ⓥⓘⓢⓐ ⓜⒸ

Cafes and pastry shops

Pasticceria Il Dolce. Piazza Sant'Agostino 40, tel. 093524018. Excellent cannoli, "sfogliatine alla ricotta," and almond cookies.

Bar Pasticceria Caprice. Via Firenze 17, tel. 0935 25281. Fruit ice creams, cakes, and ricotta "cassatelle."

Museums and cultural institutions

Museo Alessi. Via Roma 326, tel. 0935503165. *Open 8-8.*

Museo Archeologico (Palazzo Varisano). Piazza Mazzini 5, tel. 093524720. *Open 9-6:30.*

Castello di Lombardia. Piazzale Lombardia. *Open 9-1 and 4-7.*

Shops, crafts, and curiosities

Fornasier Mosaicista. Via Michelangelo 61, tel. 093529425. Painted mosaics, stained-glass windows.

Natural areas, parks and reserves

Riserva naturale Lago di Pergusa. Tel. 0935 521111.

Excursions and organized tours

Scarlat Travel Service. Via Roma 137, tel. 0935 500101. Tours of the area and of Enna archeological sites.

Èrice ✉ 91016

Map, page 67

[i] *Azienda Autonoma*, Viale Conte Pepoli 56, tel. 0923869388 (B1).

Hotels, restaurants, campsites, and vacation villages

★★★ **Elimo.** Via Vittorio Emanuele 73, tel. 0923 869377, fax 0923869252; elimoh@ comeg.it. Number of rooms: 21. Air conditioning, elevator; parking, parking garage, garden. ⒜Ⓔ ⓞⒹ ⓥⓘⓢⓐ ⓜⒸ; (B2).

★★★ **La Pineta.** Viale N. Nasi, tel. 0923869783, fax 0923869786. Number of rooms: 23. Parking. ⒜Ⓔ ⓞⒹ ⓥⓘⓢⓐ ⓜⒸ; (A2).

★★★ **Moderno.** Via Vittorio Emanuele 63, tel. 0923869300, fax 0923869139; www.pippo catalano.it. Number of rooms: 40. Air conditioning, elevator; parking garage. ⒜Ⓔ ⓞⒹ ⓥⓘⓢⓐ ⓜⒸ; (B2).

¶| **Moderno.** Via Vittorio Emanuele 63, tel. 0923869300; www.pippocatalano.it. Closed Monday in low season. Air conditioning. Classic Italian and Sicilian cooking. ⒜Ⓔ ⓞⒹ ⓥⓘⓢⓐ ⓜⒸ; (B2).

¶| **Monte San Giuliano.** Vicolo S. Rocco 7, tel. 0923869595; www.montesangiuliano.it. Closed Monday, part of November and in January. Air conditioning; garden. Sicilian cooking. ⒜Ⓔ ⓞⒹ ⓥⓘⓢⓐ ⓜⒸ; (B2).

Agriturismo (real Italian country living)

Pizzolungo. Contrada San Cusumano. Accomodation in the main villa of a citrus fruit and vegetable farm. Bicycles and canoes for rent. Accessible to the handicapped. For information: tel. 0923563710.

G. Amodeo. Ostello per la Gioventù (youth hostel). Strada Provinciale Trapani-Erice, tel. 0923552964. Posti letto 52. Open year-round.

Centro internazionale di cultura scientifica "Ettore Majorana." Via G. Guarnotti 26, tel. 0923 869133.

Museo Civico "A. Cordici." Piazza Umberto I, tel. 0923869172. *Open 8-2; Monday and Thusday also 2:30-5:30; holidays 9-1.*

Seven-day Festival of Medieval and Renaissance Music. August.

Antonino Catalano. Via G.F. Guarnotta 15, tel. 0923869126.

Ceramica Ericina. Contrada Fontanarossa, tel. 0923869040.

Falconara ✉ 93011

★★★ **Stella del Mediterraneo.** State road 115 at km. 243.4, tel. and fax 0934349004; www. stelladelmediterraneo.it. Number of rooms: 17. Air conditioning; parking, garden, swimming pool, private beach. A̲E̲ ⓪ V̲I̲S̲A̲ M̲C̲

Favara ✉ 92026

Page 94

ℹ Municipio, tel. 092234233.

Caffè Patti. Via Vittorio Emanuele, tel. 092231023. "Latte di mandorla" and a vast assortment of "pasticcini."

Museo Civico A. Mendola. Piazza Cavour 56, tel. 092234233. *Closed Sunday. Open 9-1 and 4-6; Saturday 9-1.*

Forza Agrò Mare ✉ 98030

★☆★ **Baia Taormina.** Via Nazionale at km. 39 tel. 0942756292, fax 0942756603; www.baia taormina.com. Number of rooms: 60. Accessible to the handicapped. Air conditioning, elevator; parking, garden, swimming pool, private beach. A̲E̲ ⓪ V̲I̲S̲A̲ M̲C̲

Furci Sìculo ✉ 98023

★★ **Foti.** Via Milano 34, tel. 0942791815, fax 0942793203. Number of rooms: 27. Air conditioning, elevator; private beach. A̲E̲ V̲I̲S̲A̲ M̲C̲

Gangi ✉ 90024

ℹ *Ufficio turistico*, Palazzo Bongiorno, Corso Umberto I, tel. 0921502017.

Museo civico. Corso Vitale 54, tel. 0921689907. *Closed Monday. Open 9-1 and 3-6/30; Saturday and holidays 9-1 and 3-7.*

Celebrazioni pasquali. Procession with large decorated palm leaves.

Sagra della spiga. Ancient rite dedicated to Ceres. Second Sunday of August.

Gela ✉ 93012

Map, page 119

ℹ *Azienda Autonoma*, Via Navarra Bresmes 104, tel. 0933913788 (B2).

Bar Pasticceria Incardona. Via Navarra 98, tel. 0933924496. Home made pastries, especially ricotta "pasticcini."

Acropoli. Contrada Molino a Vento. *Open 9-one hour before sunset.*

Museo Archeologico Regionale. Corso Vittorio Emanuele 1, tel. 0933912626. *Closed the last Monday of each month. Open 9-1 and 3-7.*

Archeological digs of Capo Soprano. Viale Indipendenza, tel. 0933930975. *Open 9-one hour before sunset.*

Giardini Naxos ✉ 98035

Page 171

ℹ *Azienda Autonoma*, Via Tysandros 54, tel. 094251010.

★☆★ **Hellenia Yachting.** Via Jannuzzo 41, tel. 094251737, fax 094254310; www.hotel-helle nia.it. Number of rooms: 112. Air conditioning, elevator; parking, parking garage, garden, swimming pool, private beach. A̲E̲ ⓪ V̲I̲S̲A̲ M̲C̲

★☆★ **Ramada Hotel.** Via Jannuzzo 47, tel. 0942 51931, fax 094256128; www.ramadaho tels.com. Number of rooms: 298. Accessible to the handicapped. Air conditioning, clevator; parking, garden, swimming pools, tennis, private beach. ☒ ⌾ ☒ MC

★★ Arathena Rocks. Via Calcide Eubea 55, tel. 094251349, fax 094251690; arathena@taormina-ol.it. Seasonal. Number of rooms: 49. Air conditioning, elevator; parking, garden, swimming pool. ☒ ⌾ ☒ MC

★★ Cundari Inn. At Trappitello, Via Francavilla 6, tel. 0942578238, fax 0942578268. Number of rooms: 36. Rooms only, no dining facilities. Accessible to the handicapped. Air conditioning, elevator; parking, parking garage, tennis. ☒ ⌾ ☒ MC

★★ Nike Hotel. Via Calcide Eubea 27, tel. 094251207, fax 094256315; www.tao.it/niks. Number of rooms: 50. Parking, garden, private beach. ☒ ⌾ ☒ MC

★ Palladio. Via IV Novembre 269, tel. and fax 094252267; palladio@tao.it. Number of rooms: 16. Rooms only; no dining facilities. Elevator; parking, private beach. ☒ ⌾ ☒ MC

afes and pastry shops

affè Cavallaro. Via Umberto 165, tel. 094251259. ounded in 1937, this cafe offers excellent ri-otta flaky pastries for breakfast, a white buttery ollò di crema" or its chocolate counterpart, a etta moka super," an excellent dessert, the azed lemon "cassatelle," and other fine hand-ade pastries.

ar Pasticceria Salamone. Via Vittorio Emanuele 36, tel. 094251398. Excellent lemon, coffee, mul-erry, and almond granita, and brioches and uit ice cream cakes.

Museums and cultural institutions

arco Archeologico e Museo. Capo Schisò, tel. 04251001. *Open 9-6; summer, 9-7.*

rcheological digs of Naxos. Capo Schisò, tel. 04251001. *Open 9-one hour before sunset.*

hops, crafts, and curiosities

a Fauci Gaetano. Via Vittorio Emanuele 204, tel. 04251254. Wrought iron objects.

atané. Via Regina Margherita 111, tel. 04251149. Wrought iron objects.

---

ioiosa Marèa   ✉ 98063

otels, restaurants, campsites, and acation villages

Cicero. At San Giorgio, Contrada Cicero, tel. 094139551, fax 094139295. Seasonal.

---

nello   ✉ 90010

otels, restaurants, campsites, and acation villages

t Piano Torre, km. 8

★ Piano Torre Park Hotel. Tel. 0921662671, fax 0921662672; pianotorre@libero.it. Number of rooms: 27. Air conditioning; park-

ing, garden, swimming pool, tennis. ☒ ⌾ ☒ MC

¶¶ Ristorante del Piano Torre Park Hotel. Tel. 0921662671, fax 0921662672; pianotorre@libero.it. Closed Tuesday. Air conditioning, parking, garden. Sicilian cooking. ☒ ⌾ ☒ MC

Isola delle Femmine   ✉ 90040

Hotels, restaurants, campsites, and vacation villages

★★★ Eufemia. Via Nazionale 28, tel. 0918677800, fax 0918678002. Number of rooms: 54. Air conditioning, elevator; parking. ☒ ⌾ ☒ MC

¶ Cutino. Via Palermo 10, tel. 0918677062. Closed Tuesday. Air conditioning. Sicilian cooking – seafood. ☒ ⌾ ☒ MC

⚑ La Playa. Viale Marino 55, tel. and fax ★★ 0918677001. Seasonal.

Natural areas, parks and reserves

Riserva naturale Isola delle Femmine. Tel. 0918616167.

Excursions and organized tours

Cooperativa Ss. Cosma e Damiano. Tel. 091338704745. Boat tours of the Grotta dell'Oglio, Capo Gallo, Isola delle Femmine.

Lipu. Tel. 0918616167. Tours of the island and diving excursions.

Ìspica   ✉ 97014

Page 137

ℹ *Pro Loco*, Via dello Stadio 20, tel. 0932 3351224962.

Museums and cultural institutions

Cava d'Ìspica. Tel. 951133. *Open 1 November-31 March, Monday-Saturday, 9-1:15; 1 April-31 October, 9-7.*

Parco Archeologico della Forza. Tel. 0932951133. *Open 1 November-31 March, 9-5:30; 1 April-31 October, 9-7.*

Shops, crafts, and curiosities

Salvatore Giunta. Via Doria 1, tel. 368426005. Artistic glass.

Lentini   ✉ 96016

Page 141

ℹ *Municipio*, Piazza Duomo, tel. 095941008.

Cafes and pastry shops

Navarria. Via Conte Alaimo 12, tel. 095941045. The ricotta pastries and the excellent fruit ice creams are not to be missed.

Museums and cultural institutions

Museo Archeologico. Piazza degli Studi, tel. 0957832962. Closed for restoration.

Shops, crafts, and curiosities

Crisci. Via Vittorio Emanuele 76, tel. 095902764. Oranges and wine sent all over the world.

Francesco Pulvirenti. Via Conte Alaimo 37, tel. 095941658. Meat and hams from local producers.

Letojanni   ✉ 98037

Hotels, restaurants, campsites, and vacation villages

★★★ **Park Hotel Silemi.** Via Silemi 1, tel. 0942 36228, fax 0942652094. Seasonal. Number of rooms: 49. Air conditioning, elevator; parking, garden, swimming pool, private beach. Æ ₩ MC

¶¶ **Da Nino.** Via L. Rizzo 29, tel. 094236147. Seasonal. Closed Tuesday, except from June to September. Air conditioning. Sicilian cooking – seafood. Æ ⓪ ₩ MC

▲★★★ **Eurocamping Marmaruca.** Contrada Marmaruca, Via Leto, tel. and fax 094236676. Open year-round.

Licata   ✉ 92027

Page 96

ℹ️ *Municipio*, Piazza Progresso 10, tel. 0922 774378.

Museums and cultural institutions

Museo Archeologico della Badia. Via Dante 12. *Open weekdays 9-1:30 and 4-7:30.*

Cultural events

Festa di S. Angelo. Procession with the relics of the saint, which are carried by runners and are followed by 4 candle-shaped structures placed on 4 high towers. From 3 to 6 May.

Linguaglossa   ✉ 95015

Page 156

ℹ️ *Pro Loco*, Piazza Annunziata, tel. 095647352.

Museums

Museo delle Genti dell'Etna. Piazza Annunziata 8, c/o Pro Loco, tel. 095643094. *Open 9-1 and 3:30-7.*

Shops, crafts, and curiosities

Pino Azzurro. Piazza Matrice 10, tel. 095643843. Marzipan fruit.

Excursions and organized tours

Rifugio Brunek. T. 095643015. Tours of the Grotta del Gelo.

Marina di Ragusa   ✉ 97010

Page 112

Hotels, restaurants, campsites, and vacation villages

★★★ **Terraqua.** Via delle Sirene 35, tel. 0932

615600, fax 0932615580. Number of room 77. Air conditiong, elevator; parking, garden, tennis, private beach. Æ ⓪ ₩

¶¶ **Alberto.** Lungomare A. Doria 48, tel. 093 239023. Closed Wednesday, for a period November. Sicilian cooking – seafood. Æ ▮

▲★★★ **Baia del Sole.** Lungomare Andrea Doria, te 0932239844, fax 0932230344. Open yea round.

at Camarina, km. 16.5

Club Méditerranée Kamarina. In th Scoglitti area, tel. 0932919111, fax 093 825156. Seasonal.

Natural areas, parks and reserves

Riserva naturale Macchia Foresta del fiun Irminio. Tel. 0932675525. Guided tours, te 0932675526.

Museums and cultural institutions

at Camarina, km. 16.5

Museo Regionale di Camarina. Tel. 093282600(*Open 9-1 and 3-6:30.*

Parco Archeologico di Camarina. Tel. 093 826004. *Open 9-sunset.*

Parco Archeologico di Caucana. Tel. 093 916142. *Open only by appointment.*

Marsala   ✉ 9102

Map, page 75

ℹ️ *Ufficio informazioni turistiche*, Via XI Magg 100, tel. 0923714097 (B2).

Hotels, restaurants, campsites, and vacation villages

★★★ **Delfino Beach.** Lungomare Mediterrane 672, tel. 0923751076, fax 092375130. www.delfinobeach.com. Number of room 91. Accessible to the handicapped. Air co ditioning, elevator; parking, garden, swir ming pool, private beach. Æ ⓪ ₩ M (C3, *off map*).

★★ **Villa Favorita.** Via Favorita 27, tel. 092 989100, fax 0923980264. Number of room 29. Parking, garden, swimming pool, tenni Æ ⓪ ₩ MC; (A3, *off map*).

¶¶ **Delfino.** Lungomare Mediterraneo 672, te 0923969565; delfino@delfinobeach.cor Closed Tuesday from November to Apr Air conditioning, parking, garden. The coo ing of Trapani – seafood. Æ ⓪ ₩ MC; (C *off map*).

¶ **Volpara.** Contrada Volpara Digerbato, te 0923984588; delfino@delfinobeach.cor Closed Monday. Air conditioning, parkin garden. Sicilian cooking; also pizza. Æ ⓪ ₩ MC

Agriturismo (real Italian country living

Baglio Vajarassa. At Spagnola, Via Vajarassa 17 Accommodations in an old restored farmhous exhibition of objects from the old peasant cultur archery. For information: tcl. 0923968628.

Cafes and pastry shops

Dolci sapori. Corso Calatafimi 29, tel. 0923981404. Locally-produced sweets.

Lilibeo. Via Salemi 5, tel. 0923952844. Sicilian sweets.

Museums and cultural institutions

Enomuseum. Contrada Berbano 388. State road 115, tel. 0923969667. *Open 9-1 and 3-6; Sunday, 8:30-1.*

Insula romana. Viale Piave, tel. 0923952535. *Closed Sunday. Open 9-1 and 3-one hour before sunset.*

Museo Archeologico. Baglio Anselmi, Lungomare Bozo, tel. 0923952535. *Open 9-1:30, Friday, Saturday and Sunday also 4-7.*

Museo Civico. Monastero di S. Pietro, Via L. Anselmi Correale, tel. 0923716298. *Open 8:30-1:30 and 3:30-8:30.*

Museo degli Arazzi. Via Garraffa 57, tel. 0923 712903. *Closed Monday. Open 9-1 and 4-6.*

Museo Nazionale di Pittura Contemporanea. Convento del Carmine, tel. 0923718822. *Closed Monday. Open 10-1 and 6-8.*

on the Island of Mozia

Archeological digs of Mozia and Museum. Tel. 0923712598. *Open 9-1 and 3-6:30.*

Cultural events

Easter celebrations. Procession with stage and costume theatrical performances. Good Thursday.

Sports

Circolo Velico Marsala (sailing). Vicolo Saline 5, tel. 0923951162.

Shops, crafts, and curiosities

Baglio antico. Via dei Gasperi 11, tel. 0923761343. Wine, oil and local cheese production, typical Sicilian almond sweets, hand-decorated pottery.

Enoteca Gran Galà. Via Mazara 253/B, tel. 0923721485. This wine cellar features fine wines of the Marsala region, with tastings. *Open 9-1, by appointment.*

Natural areas, parks and reserves

Riserva naturale Isole dello Stagnone di Marsala. Visitors center, tel. 0923967897.

Màscali   ✉ 95016

Hotels, restaurants, campsites, and vacation villages

⚠ ** Mokambo.** At Fondachello, Via Spiaggia
★★ 211, tel. and fax 095938731. Seasonal.

Mazara del Vallo   ✉ 91026

Page 77

i   *Ufficio informazioni turistiche*, Piazza S. Veneranda, tel. 0923941727.

Hotels, restaurants, campsites, and vacation villages

★★★ **Hopps.** Via Hopps 29, tel. 0923946133, fax 0923946075. Number of rooms: 240. Air conditioning, elevator; parking, garden, swimming pool, private beach. ᴀᴇ ⓪ ᴠɪsᴀ ᴍᴄ; (D3).

❙❙ **Pescatore.** Via Castelvetrano 191, tel. 0923947580. Closed Monday; annual closure dates. Air conditioning, parking. Sicilian cooking – seafood. ᴀᴇ ⓪ ᴠɪsᴀ ᴍᴄ; (D3, *off map*).

⚠ **Sporting Camping Club.** Contrada Bocca
★★★ Arena, tel. and fax 0923947230. Open year-round.

Museums and cultural institutions

Museo Civico. Piazza del Plebiscito, tel. 0923 940266. *Closed Saturday and Sunday. Open 9-1; Tuesday and Thursday also 3:30-5:30.*

Museo Diocesano. Piazza della Repubblica, tel. 0923909431. *Closed Sunday. Open 8:30-12:30.*

at Castelvetrano, km. 21.5

✉ 91022

Museo Civico. Via Garibaldi 50, tel. 0924904932. *Open 9:30-1:30 and 3:30-7:30.*

Cultural events

Festa di S. Vito. Procession with 17th-century costumes, allegorical chariots and a silver reliquary. Last two Sundays of August.

Natural areas, parks and reserves

at Castelvetrano, km. 21.5

✉ 91022

Riserva naturale Foce del fiume Bèlice. Via Antonio Vivaldi 100, tel. 092446042.

Messina   ✉ 98100

Map, page 162

i   *AAPIT*, Via Calabria is. 301/bis, tel. 090 675356 (D3). Information office: Via Calabria corner of Via Capra, tel. 090674236; highway to Tremestieri, tel. 090730713.
Azienda Autonoma, Piazza Cairoli, tel. 090694780 (D2).

Hotels, restaurants, campsites, and vacation villages

★★★ **Jolly dello Stretto.** Via Garibaldi 126, tel. 090363860, fax 0905902526. Number of rooms: 96. Air conditioning, elevator; parking. ᴀᴇ ⓪ ᴠɪsᴀ; (C2).

★★★ **Royal Palace Hotel.** Via T. Cannizzaro 224, tel. 0906503, fax 0902921075; royalpalace@framon-hotels.com. Number of rooms: 106. Air conditioning, elevator; parking garage. ᴀᴇ ⓪ ᴠɪsᴀ ᴍᴄ; (D-E3).

★★★ **Giardino delle Palme.** At Lido di Mortelle, state road 113, tel. 090321017, fax 090 321666; www.giardinodellepalme.it. Number of rooms: 25. Air conditioning, elevator;

swimming pool, private beach. ⒶⒺ ⓌⒹ 🆅🆂🅰.

🍴 **Alberto.** Via Ghibellina 95, tel. 090710711; sporting3@tiscali.it. Closed Sunday evening and Monday, August. Air conditioning. Sicilian cooking – seafood. ⒶⒺ ⓌⒹ 🆅🆂🅰 🅼🅲; (D2).

🍴 **Casa Savoia.** Via XXVII Luglio 36/38, tel. 090 2934865; www.ristorantecasasavoia.it. Closed Sunday evening. Air conditioning. The cooking of Messina. ⒶⒺ ⓌⒹ 🆅🆂🅰 🅼🅲; (D-E2).

🍴 **Piero.** Via Ghibellina 121, tel. 090718365. Closed Sunday, August. Air conditioning. The cooking of Messina – seafood. ⒶⒺ ⓌⒹ 🆅🆂🅰 🅼🅲; (D2).

🍴 **Le Due Sorelle.** Piazza Municipio 4, tel. 09044720. Closed Monday, August. Parking. Sicilian cooking – seafood. (C2).

⛺ **Il Peloritano.** At Rodìa, contrada Taranto-
✴✴ nio, tel. and fax 090348496. Open year-round.

at Pistunina, km. 6

✶✶✶ **Europa Palace Hotel.** State road 114 at km. 5.4, tel. 090621601, fax 090621768. Number of rooms: 115. Air conditioning, elevator; parking, garden, indoor swimming pool, tennis. ⒶⒺ ⓌⒹ 🆅🆂🅰 🅼🅲

Cafes and pastry shops

Pasticceria Irrera. Via Boccetta 4, tel. 090344209. Black and the white "pignolata," glazed egg-white pastries.

Bar Pasticceria Pisani. Via T. Cannizzaro 45, tel. 0902938158. The "cannolata" is a special "pignolata" enclosed in an enormous cannolo that is sheathed in chocolate. "Arancini" of rice in ragu or butter, or meatless.

Pasticceria La Spada. Via Natoli 19, tel. 090 674655. Fruit ice creams, granita, and "cassate" in the finest tradition.

Museums and cultural institutions

Acquario comunale. Villa Mazzini, Piazza Unità d'Italia, tel. 09048897. *Open Tuesday-Saturday 10-12; Friday 4:30-6:30; Sunday 9-1.*

Museo Regionale. Via della Libertà 465, tel. 090361292. *Open Tuesday-Saturday 9-1:30; Tuesday, Thursday and Saturday also 3-5:30 (1 April-30 September, 4-6:30); Sunday and holidays, 9-12:30.*

Tesoro del Duomo. Cattedrale, Piazza del Duomo, tel. 09048897. *Open April-October daily 9-1 and 3:30-6:30; November-March 9-1; Sunday and holidays 9:30-1:30 and 4-7.*

Cultural Events

Madonna della Lettera. On 14 August two gigantic wood and papier-mâché statues are towed by two groups of people along the city streets. On 15 August is the carrying of the "Vara," a devotional structure with the statue of Our Lady of the Assumption.

Shops, crafts, and curiosities

Mario Ruggeri. Via Fabrizi 90, tel. 090675682. Ceramics.

Il Telaio. Viale S. Martino, tel. 0902930969. Fabrics and embroidery.

Milazzo ✉ 98057

Map, page 175

ℹ️ *Azienda Autonoma*, Piazza Duilio 10, tel. 0909222865 (C2).

Hotels, restaurants, campsites, and vacation villages

✶✶✶ **Eolian Inn.** Via Cappuccini 21, tel. 090 9286133, fax 0909282855; eolianinn@tin.it. Number of rooms: 250. Air conditioning, elevator; parking, garden, swimming pool, tennis, private beach. ⒶⒺ ⓌⒹ 🆅🆂🅰; (A3).

✶✶✶ **Riviera Lido.** Strada Panoramica, tel. 090 9283457, fax 0909287835; www.milazzo line.it/ rivieralido. Number of rooms: 43. Accessible to the handicapped. Elevator; parking, garden, private beach. ⒶⒺ ⓌⒹ 🆅🆂🅰; (A3).

🍴 **Covo del Pirata.** Via Marina Garibaldi 2, tel. 0909284437. Closed Wednesday. Air conditioning. The cooking of Messina. ⒶⒺ ⓌⒹ 🆅🆂🅰 🅼🅲; (B2).

🍴 **Salamone a Mare.** Strada Panoramica 36, tel. 0909281233. Closed Monday and part of January. Parking. Sicilian cooking – seafood. ⒶⒺ ⓌⒹ 🆅🆂🅰 🅼🅲; (A3, *off map*).

⛺ **Cirucco.** At Capo di Milazzo, Strada Pano-
✴ ramica 66, tel. 0909284746, fax 0909227384. Seasonal.

Museums and cultural institutions

Castello di Milazzo. Via del Castello, tel. 090 9221291. *Closed Monday. Open 9-12 and 2:30-3:30; 1 April-30 September, 10-12 and 3-5 (1 June-31 August, 5-7).*

Museo enologico Grasso. (Wines) Via Albero 5, tel. 0909281082. *Closed Sunday. Open 8-1 and 3:30-7:30; Saturday, 8-1.*

Mistretta ✉ 98073

Page 188

ℹ️ *Municipio*, Piazza V. Veneto, tel. 0921382053

Cafes and pastry shops

Extra di Lo Jacono. Piazza Marconi 3, tel. 0921381006. Specialty: "pasta reale."

Pasticceria Rosticceria Testa. Via Monte 2, tel. 0921382580. Specialties: "pasta reale" and typical pastries of Mistretta.

Museums and cultural institutions

Museo Civico. Via Libertà, tel. 0921382499. *Open 9-1.*

Cultural events

I giganti. Two men dance inside gigantic statues in papier-mâché. 8 September.

Shops, crafts, and curiosities

Antonino Tamburello. Via S. Giovanni 10, tel. 0921383209. Ceramics.

Mòdica ✉ 97015

Map, page 109

i Pro Loco, Via I. Galfo 7, tel. 093253377 (C2).

Hotels, restaurants, campsites, and vacation villages

★★★ **Motel di Modica.** Corso Umberto I, tel. 0932941022, fax 0932941077. Number of rooms: 36. Rooms only; no dining facilities. Parking, parking garage. AE ⊙ VISA; (A1, *off map*).

¶¶ **Fattoria delle Torri.** Vico Napolitano 14, tel. 0932751286; zelia@tin.it. Closed Monday. Garden. Sicilian cooking. AE ⊙ VISA MC; (A2).

Agriturismo (real Italian country living)

Villa Teresa. Contrada Bugilfezza, Via Crocevia Cava d'Ispica. Rooms with private little gardens in an 18th-century farm. For information: tel. 0932 771690.

Cafes and pastry shops

Antica Dolceria Bonaiuto. Corso Umberto I 159, tel. 0932941225. Specialty: "i'mpanatigghi," pastries made of meat and chocolate.

Caffè Fratelli Ciacera. Corso Umberto I 28, tel. 0932752746.

Museums and cultural institutions

Casa Museo Quasimodo. Via Posterla 5, tel. 0932752747. *Open 10-1 and 3:30-6:30.*

Museo Civico. Convento dei Padri Mercedari, Via Mercé, tel. 0932945081. *Closed Sunday and holidays. Open 9-1.*

Museo Ibleo delle Arti e Tradizioni Popolari. Convento dei Padri Mercedari, Via Mercé, tel. 0932752897. *Open 10-1 and 3:30-6:30.*

Pinacoteca Comunale. Corso S. Giorgio (Palazzo Polara), tel. 0932330377837. *Closed Sunday. Open 9-1.*

Shops, crafts, and curiosities

Pietro Casiraro. Via Tirella 30, tel. 0932946355. Marzipan fruit.

Monreale ✉ 90046

Map, page 50

i Ufficio informazioni, Piazza Vittorio Emanuele, tel. 0916564501 (B3).

Hotels, restaurants, campsites, and vacation villages

¶ **Taverna del Pavone.** Vicolo Pensato 18, tel. 0916406209. Closed Monday, for a period between September and October. Sicilian cooking. AE ⊙ VISA MC; (B3).

Museums and cultural institutions

Chiostro del Convento dei Benedettini. *Open 9-7; holidays 9-1.*

Civica galleria d'arte moderna Giuseppe Sciortino. Tel. 0916405443. *Closed holidays. Open 9-1 and 2:30-6:30.*

San Martino delle Scale, km. 9.5
✉ 90040

Benedictine abbey and cloister. *Open 9-6; holidays 9:30-11:30 and 5-9.*

Nicolosi ✉ 95030

Page 159

i Azienda Soggiorno e Turismo, Via Garibaldi 63, tel. 095911505.

Hotels, restaurants, campsites, and vacation villages

★★★ **Biancaneve.** Via Etnea 163, tel. 095914139, fax 095911194; www.hotel.biancaneve.com. Number of rooms: 83. Air conditioning, elevator; parking, garden, swimming pool. AE ⊙ VISA MC

★★★ **Gemmellaro.** Via Etnea 160, tel. 095911060, fax 095911071. Number of rooms: 56. Accessible to the handicapped. Elevator; parking. AE ⊙ VISA MC

¶¶ **Grotta del Gallo.** Via Madonna delle Grazie 40, tel. 095911301. Closed Monday in the low season. Air conditioning, parking, garden. Sicilian and Italian classic cooking. AE ⊙ VISA MC

△★★ **Etna.** Via Goethe, tel. 095914309, fax 095 7915186. Open year-round.

Hostels

△ **Etna.** Via della Quercia 7, tel. 0957914686. Posti letto 50. Open year-round.

Natural areas, parks and reserves

Ente parco dell'Etna. Via Etnea 107/A, tel. 0958211111; www.parcoetna.ct.it; Centro di Educazione Ambientale a Formazzo di Milo, tel. 33829930077.

Excursions and organized tours

Gruppo Guide Alpine Etna Sud. Tel. 0957914755. Excursions on Mount Etna.

Nicosìa ✉ 94014

Page 187

i Municipio, Piazza Garibaldi, tel. 0935638139.

Hotels, restaurants, campsites, and vacation villages

★★★ **Pineta.** Via S. Paolo 35/A, tel. 0935647002, fax 0935646927. Number of rooms: 43. Elevator; parking, garden. AE ⊙ VISA

¶ **Vigneta.** Contrada S. Basile, tel. 0935638940; www.grafinetweb.com/vigneta. Closed Tuesday. Garden. Sicilian cooking; also pizza. VISA MC

Agriturismo (real Italian country living)

Masseria Mercadante. Contrada Mercadante. Rural construction from the 17th c. Olive groves and vegetables. For information: tel. 0935 640771.

Cafes and pastry shops

Pasticceria Al Bocconcino. Via Roma 8, tel. 0935 638894. Specialty: "nocatele" (almonds and nuts).

Noto ✉ 96017

Map, page 135

ℹ️ *APT,* Piazza XVI Maggio, tel. 0931836744 (B2).

Hotels, restaurants, campsites, and vacation villages

at Lido di Noto, km. 8

★★★ **Eloro Hotel Club.** Tel. 0931812244, fax 0931812200. Seasonal. Number of rooms: 222. Air conditioning, elevator; parking, garden, swimming pool, tennis, private beach. 🆎 🆅🆂🅰

★★ **Villa Mediterranea.** Viale Lido, tel. and fax 0931812330. Number of rooms: 15. Rooms only; no dining facilities. Accessible to the handicapped. Parking, garden, swimming pool.

Agriturismo (real Italian country living)

at Vendìcari, km. 10

Il Roveto. 18th-century farm near the sea in the protected area of Vendìcari, with orange and olive groves and vineyard. Birdwatching. For information: tel. 093166024.

Cafes and pastry shops

Caffè Sicilia. Corso Vittorio Emanuele 125, tel. 0931835013. Famous pastry shop with traditional sweets. Orange jams with biological fruit. Ice cream and Sicilian, Italian and foreign wines.

Costanzo. Via Spaventa 7, tel. 0931835243. High quality Sicilian pastry. Interesting ice cream flavored with roses and jasmine.

Museums and cultural institutions

Museo Civico. Corso Vittorio Emanuele II 134, tel. 0931836462. Closed for restoration.

Teatro comunale. Piazza XVI Maggio 1, tel. 0931835073. *Open 8:30-1 and 4-8; Sunday 8:30-1.*

at Eloro, km. 10

Scavi di Eloro. *Open 9-one hour before sunset.*

Villa romana del Tellaro. Tel. 0931573883. *Open 8-7:30.*

Cultural Events

Festival delle arti barocche. Concert of classical music and other entertainment. August.

Infiorata or Primavera Barocca. Every year, on the third Sunday of May, Via Nicolaci is covered with religious images composed of flower petals.

La notte di Giufà. Ethnical music festival with Mediterranean artists.

Shops, crafts, and curiosities

Francesco Tomasi. Via Tofaro 8, tel. 0931893082. Wrought Iron workshop.

Azienda Nieli Brugaletta. Contrada Sparano. Tel. 0931872285. Cheese from local producers.

Natural areas, parks and reserves

Riserva naturale Pantani di Vendìcari. Tel. 0931571457. *Open 7-one hour before sunset.*

Excursions and organized tours

Allakatalla. Lago Porta Nazionale 10, tel. 0931 835005. Guided tours of the city, archeological and natural excursions, bike andmountain bike rentals.

Palazzolo Acrèide ✉ 96010

Map, page 139

ℹ️ *Ufficio Turistico Comunale* Piazza del Popolo, tel. 0931882000 (B3).

Cafes and pastry shops

Antica Pasticceria Corsino. Via Nazionale 2, tel. 0931875533. This pastry shop is always open. They prepare ice cream, wonderful "pasticcini alla crema," and almond pastries.

Museums and cultural institutions

Scavi di Akrai. Tel. 0931881499. *Open 9-12:30 and 3-one hour and a half before sunset.*

Home-museum of Antonino Uccello. Via Machiavelli, tel. 0931881499. *Open 9-1.*

at Pantàlica, km. 31

Necropolis of Pantàlica. Tel. 0931953695. *Open 7-one hour before sunset.*

Cultural Events

Festa di S. Paolo. Evenings at the Villa Comunale, with processions. 27-29 June.

Rassegna di spettacoli al teatro greco di Akrai. From July to Sptember.

Natural areas, parks and reserves

at Pantàlica, km. 31

Riserva naturale di Pantàlica, Valle dell'Anapo e Torrente Cavagrande. Tel. 0931462452.

Palermo ✉ 90100

Maps, pages 28-29 and pages 32-33

ℹ️ *AAPIT,* Piazza Castelnuovo 35, tel. 091 6058111 (II, C3); City center, Piazza Castelnuovo 34, tel. 091583847; Train station, Piazza Giulio Cesare, tel. 091 6165914; Airport Falcone Borsellino, tel. 091591698; www.aapit.pa.it.

Azienda Autonoma Turismo Palermo e Monreale, Salita Belmonte 1, tel. 091540122 (I, C4).

Hotels, restaurants, campsites, and vacation villages

★★★ **Villa Igiea Grand Hotel.** Salita Belmonte 43, tel. 0916312111, fax 091547654; www.thi.it. Number of rooms: 115. Accessible to the handicapped. Air conditioning, elevator; parking, garden, swimming pool, tennis. AE OD VISA; (I, C4).

★★ **Astoria Palace.** Via Monte Pellegrino 62, tel. 0916281111, fax 0916372178; www.astoria palace.com. Number of rooms: 326. Air conditioning, elevator; parking. AE OD VISA MC; (I, D4).

★★ **Baglio Conca d'Oro.** Via Aquino 19/C-D, tel. 0916406286, fax 0916408742; www.pagi negialle.it/baglioconcadoro. Number of rooms: 27. Accessible to the handicapped. Air conditioning, elevator; parking. AE OD VISA MC; (I, F2).

★★ **Centrale Palace Hotel.** Corso Vittorio Emanuele 327, tel. 091336666, fax 091334881. Number of rooms: 63. Accessible to the handicapped. Air conditioning, elevator; parking, parking garage. AE OD VISA MC; (II, E4).

★★ **Holiday Inn Palermo.** Viale Regione Siciliana 2620, tel. 0916983111, fax 091408198; www.holiday-inn.com/palermoitaly. Number of rooms: 95. Accessible to the handicapped. Air conditioning, elevator; parking. AE OD VISA MC; (I, D3).

★★ **Jolly del Foro Italico.** Foro Italico 22, tel. 0916165090, fax 0916161441; www.jollyho tels.it. Number of rooms: 277. Air conditioning, elevator; parking, garden, swimming pool. AE OD VISA MC; (II, E6).

★★ **Principe di Villafranca.** Via Giuseppina Turrisi Colonna 4, tel. 0916118523, fax 091588705; www.principedivillafranca.it. Number of rooms: 34. Air conditioning, elevator; parking, parking garage. AE OD VISA MC; (II, B2-3).

★★★ **Massimo Plaza.** Via Maqueda 437, tel. 091325657, fax 091325711; www.massimo plazahotel.com. Number of rooms: 15. Rooms only; no dining facilities. Private beach. AE OD VISA MC; (II, D4).

★★★ **Mediterraneo.** Via Rosolino Pilo 43, tel. 091581133, fax 091586974; hmedpa@tin.it. Number of rooms: 106. Air conditioning, elevator; parking garage. AE OD VISA MC; (II, C4).

★★★ **San Paolo Palace.** Via Messina Marine 91, tel. 0916211112, fax 0916215300; www.san paolopalace.it. Number of rooms: 290. Air conditioning, elevator; parking, swimming pool, tennis. AE OD VISA; (I, E5).

★★ **Villa Archirafi.** Via Lincoln 30, tel. 091 6168827, fax 0916168631. Number of rooms: 40. Rooms only. Accessible to the handicapped. Air conditioning, elevator; parking, garden, private beach. AE OD VISA MC; (II, E-F6).

❙❙ **Cedro.** Via Monte Pellegrino 62, tel. 0916281111, fax 0916372178; www.astoria palace.com. Air conditioning; parking. Classic Italiana and Sicilian cooking. AE OD VISA MC; (I, D4).

❙❙ **Il Ristorantino.** Piazzale A. De Gasperi 19, tel. 091512861, fax 0916702999. Closed Mon-

day and part of August. Air conditioning, garden. Sicilian cooking. AE OD VISA MC; (I, C3).

❙❙❙ **Scuderia.** Viale del Fante 9, tel. 091520323, fax 091520467. Closed Sunday and part of August. Air conditioning, parking, garden. Classic Italian and Sicilian cooking – seafood. AE OD VISA MC; (I, C3).

❙❙ **'A Cuccagna.** Via Principe Granatelli 21/A, tel. 091587267; www.acuccagna.com. Annual closure dates. Air conditioning, parking. Classic Italian and Sicilian cooking – seafood. AE OD VISA MC; (II, C4).

❙❙ **Friend's Bar.** Via Brunelleschi 138, tel. 091201401; catering@friendsbarsrl. Closed Monday and part of August. Air conditioning. Classic Italian and Sicilian cooking – seafood, pizza. AE OD VISA; (I, D3).

❙❙ **Regine.** Via Trapani 4/A, tel. 091586566; www.cd-net.it/ristoranteregine. Closed Sunday, August. Air conditioning. Classic Italian and Sicilian cooking – seafood. AE OD VISA; (II, B3).

❙❙ **Santandrea.** Piazza S. Andrea 4, tel. 091 334999. Closed Tuesday (Sunday from 1 July to 30 September) and part of January. Air conditioning; garden. Sicilian cooking – fish. AE OD VISA MC; (II, D4-5).

❙ **Palazzo Trabucco.** Via dei Bottai 24/28, tel. 091326123. Closed Monday. Air conditioning. Sicilian cooking – seafood. AE OD VISA MC; (II, D5).

❙ **Piccolo Napoli.** Piazzetta Mulino a Vento 4, tel. 091320431. Closed Sunday and part of August. Air conditioning. Sicilian cooking – seafood. AE OD VISA MC; (II, B4).

at Mondello, km. 10 ✉ 90151

★★ **Mondello Palace.** Viale Principe di Scalea 2, tel. 091450001, fax 091450657. Number of rooms: 83. Air conditioning, elevator; parking, garden, swimming pool, private beach. AE OD VISA MC; (I, A3).

★★★ **Addáura Hotel Residence.** Lungomare Cristoforo Colombo 4452, tel. 0916842222, fax 0916842255; www.addaurahotel.it. Number of rooms: 50. Accessible to the handicapped. Air conditioning, elevator; parking, parking garage, garden, swimming pool, private beach. AE OD VISA MC; (I, B3-4).

★★★ **Splendid Hotel la Torre.** Via Piano Gallo 11, tel. 091450222, fax 091450033; www.lator re.com. Number of rooms: 179. Air conditioning, elevator; parking, garden, swimming pool, tennis, private beach. AE OD VISA; (I, A3).

❙❙❙ **Charleston-Le Terrazze.** Viale Regina Elena, tel. 091450171. Closed Wednesday. Classic Italian and Sicilian cooking – seafood. AE OD VISA MC; (I, A3).

❙❙ **Bye Bye Blues.** Via del Garofalo 23, tel. 0916841415; www.byebyeblues.it. Closed Tuesday, November. Air conditioning, garden. Sicilian haute cuisine. AE OD VISA MC; (I, A3).

223

at Sferracavallo, km. 13   ✉ 90148

🏛 **Degli Ulivi.** Via Pegaso 25, tel. and fax
★ 091533021. Open year-round.

Cafes and pastry shops

Bar Pasticceria La Cubana. Via G. Pitré 141, tel.
091213410. Pastries ice cream, and pizza and
delicatessen.

Bar Pasticceria Alba. Piazza San Giovanni Bosco
7/C, tel. 091309016/0916256390. "Arancini" of
rice, ice cream and ricotta cannoli.

I Peccatucci di Mamma Andrea. Via Principe di
Scordia 67, tel. 091334835. This shop offers tra-
ditional Sicilian pastries in elegant packages.
For connoisseurs, strawberry or herb "rosolio."

Bar Stancapiano. Via Notarbartolo 51, tel.
0916817244. Also serves hot meals, in one of
the more elegant neighborhoods in Palermo.

Pasticceria Costa. Via D'Annunzio 15, tel.
091345652. It produces "cassate" in the finest
Palermitan tradition.

at Mondello, km. 10

Caflisch. Viale Regina Margherita di Savoia, tel.
0916840444. Ricotta cannoli and the traditional
"testa di turco," a special kind of blancmange
with thin layers of flaky pastry dusted with fine
colorful sugar.

at Sferracavallo, km. 13   ✉ 90148

Pasticceria Gianfranco Graziano. Via dei Bar-
caioli 42, tel. 091530125. Handmade and traditional Sicilian pastries, breads, and breadsticks.

Museums and cultural institutions

Cappella Palatina. Palazzo dei Normanni, tel.
0917054879. *Open 9-11:45 and 3-4:45; Saturday 9-
11:45; Sunday 9-9:45 and 12-12:45.*

Castello a mare. Piazza XIII vittime, tel.
0916961319. Visit by reservation only.

Cantieri Culturali alla Zisa. Via Paolo Gilli 4, tel
0916524942.

Catacombe dei Cappuccini. Via Cappuccini 1, tel.
091212117. *Open 9-12 and 3-5.*

Cuba. Corso Calatafini 100, tel. 091590299. *Open
9-7; holidays 9-1.*

Galleria d'Arte Moderna E. Restivo. Via Turati
10, tel. 091588951. *Closed Monday. Open 9-8; holidays 9-1.*

Galleria Regionale della Sicilia. Palazzo Abatellis,
Via Alloro 4, tel. 0916230011. *Open 9-1:30; Tuesday
and Thursday also 3-7:30; holidays 9-1.*

Lo Spasimo. Permanent exhibitions. Via Spasimo,
tel. 0916161486.

Museo Archeologico Regionale. Piazza Olivella,
tel. 0916116805. *Open 8:30-1:30; Tuesday-Friday also 3-6:30; holidays 9-1.*

Museo Diocesano. Via Bonello, tel. 0916077111.
Closed for a new installation.

Museo Etnografico Siciliano G. Pitrè. Palazzina
Cinese, Via Duca Abruzzi 1, tel. 0917404893.
Closed Friday. Open 8:30-7:30.

Museo Internazionale delle Marionette. Via

Butera 1, tel. 091328060. *Open Monday-Friday 9-
1 and 4-7.*

Museo del Risorgimento. Piazza San Domenico
1, tel. 091582774. *Open Monday, Wednesday and
Friday 9-1.*

Museo Mormino. Viale della Libertà 52, tel
0916259519. *Closed Saturday and Sunday. Open 9-
1 and 3-5.*

Oratorio di S. Cita. Via Valverde 3, tel. 091332779.
Open Monday-Friday 8-12; Saturday 9-1.

Oratorio del Rosario. Via dei Bambinai. *Open
Monday-Friday 8-12; Saturday 9-1.*

Oratorio di S. Lorenzo. Via del'Immacolatella,
tel. 091332779. *Open Monday-Friday 8-12.*

Orto Botanico. Via Lincoln 2B, tel. 0916238241.
*Open 9-5, Saturday and holidays 9-1; summer, 9-6;
Saturday and Sunday 9-1.*

Palazzo Comitini. Via Maqueda 100, tel. 091
6628368. Guided tours: *Monday-Friday 9:30-1:30;
Saturday and Sunday by appointment.*

Palazzo dei Normanni. Piazza Indipendenza,
tel. 0917057003. Guided tours: *Monday, Friday and
Saturday 9-12; by appointment on the other days.*

Santuario di S. Rosalia. Monte Pellegrino, tel
091540326. *Open 7-7.*

Tesoro e Cripta della Cattedrale. Corso Vittorio
Emanuele, tel. 091334376. *Open 9:30-5:30; Sunday
groups only.*

Zisa. Piazza Guglielmo il Buono, tel. 0916520269.
Open 9-7; Sunday and holidays 9-1.

Natural areas, parks and reserves

Riserva naturale Monte Pellegrino. Tel
0916716066. Visits by reservation only.

Excursions and organized tours

Excursions in the Palermo hinterland. Guided
visit with reservation. AAPIT, tel. 091583847.

Palermo Sightseeing Tour. Seven bus tours
around the city. AAPIT and AMAT; tel. 0913501450

Palermo Sottosopra. Guided tours of the city's
evocative underground areas. Tours: *9-1.* For
information: tel. 091580433.

Progetto carrozze. Five itineraries by horse and
cart around the city. Palermo City Council, tel
0916112285.

Sicilia Excursions. Guided tours all over the is
land. Via Emerico Amari 124, tel. 091582294.

Viaggi in Sicilia. Interesting guided tours around
Sicily to discover villas and private houses not usu
ally open to the public. Via delle Croci 2, tel
091308721.

Theater and music

Teatro Biondo. Via Teatro Biondo 258, tel. 091
582364.

Teatro Golden. Ente Autonomo Orchestra Sin
fonica Siciliana. Via Terra Santa 60, tel. 091
305217.

Teatro al Massimo. Piazza Verdi 9, tel. 091589575.
Prose and melodrama season from November to
May.

Teatro della Verdura. Parco di Villa Castelnuo-vo, Viale del Fante 70/b, tel. 0916053301.

Teatro dei Pupi di Mimmo Cuticchio. Via Bara 52, tel. 091323400.

Teatro Massimo. Piazza Verdi, tel. 0916053515. *Open Tuesday-Sunday 10-3:30.*

Teatro Politeama. Piazza Politeama at the corner of Via Turati, tel. 0916053315.

Festino di S. Rosalia. From 10-16th July every year, one week of festivities in honor of the pa-tron saint.

Palermo di Scena. Theatre, dance, music and cinema. Every year in August.

Ippodromo della Favorita. Viale del Fante 9, tel. 0916703462.

Mediterraneo Club. Via Imperatore Federico 70, tel. 0916372444. Tennis courts.

Piscina Polisportiva. Via Belgio 2, tel. 091 6703078.

Antonio Amato. Piazza Meli 5, tel. 091580287.

Il Dodo. Via Notarbartolo 46, tel. 091347966. Wrought iron workshop.

Giorgio Comandé. Via Ciraulo, tel. 0916631147. Glassware workshop.

Salvatore Andò. Vc. Pino 4, tel. 091587124. Mar-ble items.

Sicily's Folk. Corso Vittorio Emanuele 450, tel. 0916512787. Ceramic crèches.

Pantelleria   ✉ 91017

Map, page 71

ℹ️ *Pro Loco*, Piazza Cavour, tel. 0923911838.

★★★ **Port Hotel.** Via Borgo Italia 6, tel. 0923 911299, fax 0923912203. Number of rooms: 43. Accessible to the handicapped. Air con-ditioning, elevator. ᴀᴇ ⓓ ᴠɪsᴀ

★★ **Miryam.** Corso Umberto I 1, tel. 0923911374, fax 0923911777. Number of rooms: 29. Air conditioning, elevator. ᴀᴇ ⓓ ᴠɪsᴀ

🍴🍴🍴 **I Mulini.** Contrada Tracino, tel. 0923915398; imulini@galactica.it. Closed Tuesday in winter, January/February. Parking. Mediter-ranean cooking. ᴀᴇ ⓓ ᴠɪsᴀ ᴍᴄ

🍴 **La Nicchia.** Contrada Scauri Basso, tel. 0923916342. Closed Wednesday, 15 Janu-ary-15 February. Garden. Fish and pizza.

at Mursia, km. 4

★★★ **Cossyra.** At Cuddie Rosse, tel. 0923 911154, fax 911026; www.mursia.pantelleria.it. Sea-sonal. Number of rooms: 80. Parking, gar-den, swimming pool, tennis, private beach. ᴀᴇ ⓓ ᴠɪsᴀ ᴍᴄ

★★★ **Mursia.** Tel. 0923911217, fax 0923911026;

www.mursia.pantelleria.it. Seasonal. Num-ber of rooms: 74. Air conditioning; parking, swimming pool, tennis, private beach. ᴀᴇ ⓓ ᴠɪsᴀ ᴍᴄ

Cooperativa Panturistica Escursionismo. Ex-cursions by boat or horse or on foot, tel. 0923 911272.

Fabio Chiolo. Excursions by boat, tel. 0923 918170.

Quelli di Pantelleria. Excursions by sailboat, by horse or on foot, tel. 0923918306.

Cantina Agricoltori Associati. Tel. 0923911253. Passito Doc Tanit and spumante Doc Solimano.

Cooperativa Produttori Capperi. Contrada Scau-ri, tel. 0923916079.

Lele e Peter. Contrada Bugeber 50, tel. 0923 914061. Handcraft ceramics.

Paternò   ✉ 95047

Page 159

ℹ️ *Pro Loco*, Piazza Indipendenza, tel. 095 7970111.

Gran Caffè Italia. Piazza Regina Margherita 12, tel. 095854379. Almond pastries and torroncini.

Castello normanno. Tel. 095621109. *Closed Mon-day. Open Tuesday-Friday 9:15-12:30 and 3:30-6:30, Saterday and Sunday 9:15-12:30.*

Festival di Rocca normanna. Concert, dance and theatre festival. August.

Le Nid. Via F. Maimonide 89, tel. 095621081. Ce-ramics.

Patti   ✉ 98066

Page 192

ℹ️ *Azienda Autonoma*, Piazza Marconi 11, tel. 0941241136.

at Marina di Patti, km. 2   ✉ 98060

★★★ **Park Philip Hotel.** Via Lungomare 57, tel. 0941361332, fax 0941361184; parkhotel@tiscali.it. Seasonal. Number of rooms: 43. El-evator; swimming pool, private beach. ᴀᴇ ⓓ ᴠɪsᴀ ᴍᴄ

Bar Pasticceria Jolie. Via Trieste 20, tel. 0941

22102. Ricotta "cardinali" and "pasticciotti" stuffed with meat.

Laboratorio Pasticceria Praticò. Via Vittorio Emanuele 10, tel. 094121818. Fruit baskets with short pastry, chocolate, and pastry cream.

Pasticceria del Bignè. Via XX Settembre, tel. 094121959. Exquisite almond pastries and typical Sicilian pastries.

Museums and cultural institutions

Villa Romana. At Patti Marina, along state road 113. *Open 9-one hour before sunset.*

at Tìndari, km. 10; map, page 173

Archeological digs of Tìndari. Via Teatro Greco. Tel. 0941369023. *Open 9-two hours before sunset.*

Shops, crafts, and curiosities

Filippo Melita. Via Orti 19/A, tel. 0941367724. Ceramics.

at Marina di Patti, km. 2

Ceramiche Caleca. Via Giovanni XXIII, tel. 0941361346. Full sets of dishes with hand painted decorations, and other objects.

Pedara ✉ 95030

Hotels, restaurants, campsites, and vacation villages

🍴 **La Bussola.** Piazza Don Bosco, tel. 095 7800250. Closed Monday in winter and part of November. Sicilian cooking – mushrooms. ⒶⒺ ⓪ ⓋⒾⓈⒶ ⓂⒸ

Pelagie Islands

Page 101

at Lampedusa ✉ 92010

ⓘ *Pro Loco*, Via Vittorio Emanuele 89, tel. 0922971390.

Hotels, restaurants, campsites, and vacation villages

★★★ **Medusa.** Via Rialto Medusa 3, tel. 0922 970126, fax 09229700023; www.emme ti.it/Hmedusa. Number of rooms: 20. Air conditioning, elevator. ⒶⒺ ⓪ ⓋⒾⓈⒶ

★★★ **Guitgia Tommasino.** Via Lido Azzurro 13, tel. 0922970879, fax 0922970316; www.trav el.to/ lampedusa. Number of rooms: 35. Accessible to the handicapped. Air conditioning; parking, garden. ⒶⒺ ⓪ ⓋⒾⓈⒶ ⓂⒸ

🍴🍴🍴 **Gemelli.** Via Cala Pisana 2, tel. 0922970699. Seasonal. Air conditioning. Sicilian cooking. ⒶⒺ ⓪ ⓋⒾⓈⒶ

★★ **La Roccia.** At Cala Greca or Cala Stretta, tel. 0922970964, fax 0922973377. Open year-round.

Cafes and pastry shops

at Lampedusa

Gran Caffè Royal. Via Roma 58, tel. 0922971032. Granite and ice cream.

Shops, crafts, and curiosities

at Lampedusa

Conservicio Ittico Pelagico. Via F. Riso 7, tel. 0922970536. Fish preserved in oil.

Titino Sanguedolce. Via Roma. Sponges worked according to local tradition.

Natural areas, parks and reserves

at Lampedusa

Riserva naturale orientata Isola di Lampedusa. Tel. 0922971611.

Excursions and organized tours

at Linosa

Massimo Errera. Tel. 0922972082. Tour of the island by boat, trekking at the craters, and excursions inland.

Petralìa Sottana ✉ 90027

Page 187

ⓘ *Pro Loco*, Corso P. Agliata 16, tel. 0921 641451.

Agriturismo (real Italian country living)

Azienda Agricola Monaco di Mezzo. Contrada Monaco di Mezzo. Accommodations in an old restored farmhouse, on an estate that grows forage and has olive groves, with livestock. Swimming pool, tennis, archery, horse riding. For information: tel. 0934673949.

Piana degli Albanesi ✉ 90037

Page 55

ⓘ *Ufficio turistico*, Via Kastriota 207, tel. 0918571787.

Cafes and pastry shops

Pasticceria Di Noto. Via Portella della Ginestra 79, tel. 0918571195. Specialties: ricotta cannoli and ricotta ravioli.

Museums and cultural institutions

Museo antropologico. Corso Kastriota 213, tel. 0918571787. *Closed Monday. Open 9-1; Tuesday, Thursday, Saturday and Monday also 3-7.*

at San Cipirello, km. 10 ✉ 90040

Museo civico. Via Roma 320, tel. 0918573083. *Open 9-1; Sunday 9-12:15 and 4-6:15.*

Parco archeologico dell'antica Ietas. Monte lato. *Open 9-1.*

Theater, music and cultural events

Epifania and Easter at Piana degli Albanesi. On 6 January, ceremony at the Fonte dei Tre Cannoli. From the Thursday before Easter to Easter Sunday, numerous folkloristic events. Sunday's procession of old Albanese costumes is particularly picturesque. For information: Municipio, tel. 0918571787.

Shops, crafts, and curiosities

Five artists in this town create, in their home studios, icons, stone and wooden sculptures, and mosaics. For information, ask at the Pasticceria Di Noto.

Piazza Armerina   ✉ 94015

Page 198

📋   *Azienda Autonoma*, Via Cavour 15, tel. 0935680201.

Hotels, restaurants, campsites, and vacation villages

★★★   **Park Hotel Paradiso.** Contrada Ramaldo, tel. 0935680841, fax 0935683391. Number of rooms: 65. Air conditioning, elevator; parking, swimming pool, tennis. A͞E ⓪ V͞I͞S͞A M͞C

★★★   **Villa Romana.** Piazza A. De Gasperi 18, tel. 0935682911, fax 0935682911. Number of rooms: 55. Air conditioning, elevator; parking.

★★   **Mosaici-da Battiato.** Contrada Paratore Casale 11, tel. 0935685453, fax 0935685453. Number of rooms: 23. Accessible to the handicapped. Parking, parking garage, garden.

🍽   **Al Fogher.** Contrada Bellia 1, tel. 0935 684123. Closed Sunday evening and Monday and part of January. Parking, garden. Sicilian cooking – grilled meats. A͞E V͞I͞S͞A

Agriturismo (real Italian country living)

Azienda Agricola Savoca. Loc. Polleri, 13. Accommodations in a restructured nineteenth-century farmhouse, in an estate of 170 hectares with a stream. Bicycling, fishing, guide to farming activities. For information: tel. 0935683078.

Museums and cultural institutions

Villa Romana del Casale, tel. 0935680036. Open *8-6:30.*

Cultural events

Palio dei normanni. Famous historic celebration with costume parades. 13 and 14 August.

Portopalo di Capo Pàssero

                      ✉ 96010

📋   *Municipio*, Via Lucio Tasca 1, tel. 0931 842687.

Hotels, restaurants, campsites, and vacation villages

🍽   **Da Maurizio.** Via Tagliamento 22, tel. 0931 842644; www.damaurizio.it. Closed Tuesday, November/mid-December. Air conditioning. Sicilian cooking. A͞E ⓪ V͞I͞S͞A M͞C

⚑ ★★   **Capo Passero.** Contrada Vigne Vecchie, tel. 0931842333, fax 0931842333. Seasonal.

Theater, music and cultural events

Sagra del pesce e del vino. August.

Natural areas, parks and reserves

Riserva naturale Isola di Capo Pàssero. Tel. 0931813273.

Pozzallo   ✉ 97016

Page 111

📋   *Pro Loco*, Piazza Studi, tel. 0932954572.

Hotels, restaurants, campsites, and vacation villages

★★   **Villa Ada.** Corso Vittorio Veneto 3, tel. 0932954022, fax 0932954022. Number of rooms: 21. Air conditioning, elevator; parking. A͞E ⓪ V͞I͞S͞A M͞C

Cafes and pastry shops

Pasticceria F.lli Sciuto. Via Mazzini 31, tel. 0932953022. Marzipan fruit.

Museums and cultural institutions

Torre Cabrera. Piazza Rimembranza, tel. 0932794641. *Closed Sunday. Open 9-12.*

Ragusa   ✉ 97100

Map, page 104

📋   *AAPIT*, Via Bócchieri 33, tel. 0932621421.

Hotels, restaurants, campsites, and vacation villages

★★★★   **Eremo Giubiliana.** Contrada Giubiliana, tel. 0932669119, fax 0932623891; www.ere modellagiubiliana.it, tel. 0932654080, fax 0932653418. Number of rooms: 10. Accessible to the handicapped. Parking, garden, private beach. A͞E ⓪ V͞I͞S͞A M͞C.

★★★★   **Mediterraneo Palace.** Via Roma 189, tel. 0932621944, fax 0932623799; www.mediter raneo palace.it. Number of rooms: 92. Accessible to the handicapped. Air conditioning, elevator; parking garage. A͞E ⓪ V͞I͞S͞A; (B2).

★★★   **Montreal.** Corso Italia 70, tel. and fax 0932 621133; hotelmontreal@sprintnet.it. Number of rooms: 50. Accessible to the handicapped. Air conditioning, elevator; parking garage. A͞E ⓪ V͞I͞S͞A M͞C; (A-B3).

🍽   **Baglio La Pergola.** Contrada Selvaggio, Piazza Luigi Sturzo 6/7, tel. 0932686430; www.lapergolarg.it. Closed Tuesday, August. Air conditioning, parking, garden. Sicilian cooking – seafood. A͞E ⓪ V͞I͞S͞A M͞C; (A1, *off map*).

🍽   **Duomo.** Via Capitano Boccheri 31, tel. 0932651265; ristorante_duomo@inwind.it. Closed Monday (from October to April, also Sunday evening), and from mid-October to mid-November. Air conditioning. Sicilian cooking – seafood. A͞E ⓪ V͞I͞S͞A M͞C; (A5).

🍽   **Il Barocco.** Via Orfanotrofio 29, tel. 0932 652397; www.ilbarocco.it. Closed Wednesday and part of August. Air conditioning. Sicilian cooking. A͞E ⓪ V͞I͞S͞A M͞C; (A5).

Monna Lisa. Via Ettore Fieramosca, tel. 0932642250. Closed Monday. Parking, garden. Classic Italian and Sicilian cooking; also pizza. ▣ ▣ ▣ ▣; (C1, *off map*).

Cafes and pastry shops

Caffè Pasticceria Ambassador. Via Archimede 6, tel. 0932624701. Also Enoteca.

Pasticceria Di Pasquale. Corso V. Veneto 104, tel. 0932624635. Almond biscuits.

Museums and cultural institutions

Museo Archeologico Ibleo. Via Natalelli, tel. 0932622963. *Open 9-1:30 and 4-7:30.*

Museo Diocesano. Sagrestia della Cattedrale, Via Roma, tel. 0932621658. *Closed Saturday and Sunday. Open 10-1 and 5-8.*

Sports

Palestre Comunali (gyms). Via S. Roberto Bellarmino, tel. 0932643553; Via Sirene, tel. 0932 615574; Via Moro, tel. 643342; Via Marsala, tel. 0932653954.

Shops, crafts, and curiosities

Nunzio di Pasquale. Contrada Cisternazzi, tel. 0932255043. Artistic sculptures.

Excursions and organized tours

CAI (Club Alpino Italiano). Sezione di Ragusa, Via Diodoro Siculo 23.

Randazzo ▣ 95036

Map, page 157

ℹ️ *Pro Loco*, Piazza Municipio, tel. 095921028.

Hotels, restaurants, campsites, and vacation villages

★★ **Scrivano.** Via Bonaventura, tel. and fax 095921126; www.mediterraneo palace.it. Number of rooms: 30. Accessible to the handicapped. Air conditioning, elevator; parking, garden. ▣ ▣ ▣ ▣; (A3, *off map*).

🍴 **Trattoria Veneziano.** Via dei Romano 8, tel. 0957991353. Closed Monday and evenings on Sunday, Christmas holidays. Air conditioning. Sicilian cooking – mushrooms. ▣ ▣ ▣ ▣; (A3).

Agriturismo (real Italian country living)

L'Antica Vigna. At Montelaguardia. On the border with the Parco dell'Etna, and near the Parco dei Nèbrodi and Riserva naturale della valle dell'Àlcantara. For information: tel. 095924003.

Cafes and pastry shops

Musumeci. Piazza S. Maria 5, tel. 095921196. Pinoli, pistachios, nut-based pastries.

Museums and cultural institutions

Museo Archeologico "Paolo Vagliasindi." Castello Svevo, tel. 0957990064. *Open 9-6.*

Museo dei Pupi Siciliani. Castello Svevo, tel.

0957991214. *Open 9-1 and 4-7; Sunday and holidays 10-12:30.*

Shops, crafts, and curiosities

Local crafts and artisan market. Every Sunday morning. Clothing, tools, wooden and metal products typical of the Etna region.

Salemi ▣ 91018

Page 81

ℹ️ *Pro Loco*. Tel. 0924982197.

Hotels, restaurants, campsites, and vacation villages

🍴 **La Giummara.** Via Favara 214, tel. 0924 983398. Closed Wednesday. Air conditioning; parking. Classic Italian and Sicilian cooking; also pizza.

Museums and cultural institutions

Museo Civico di Arte Sacra. Via F. d'Aguirre, 0924982248. *Open 8-2 and 4-6; Sunday and holidays 11-1 and 4-6.*

Museo dei Cimeli del Risorgimento. Piazza I Lampiasi 4, 0924982248. *Open 8-2 and 4-6; Sunday and holidays by appointment only.*

Cultural Events

Festa di S. Giuseppe. On 19 March each year, sumptuos tables are laid in the village lanes and decorated with bread sculptures.

San Cataldo ▣ 93017

Page 205

ℹ️ *Pro Loco*. Tel. 3683515670.

Hotels, restaurants, campsites, and vacation villages

★★★ **Helios.** Contrada Zubbi S. Leonardo, tel. 0934573000, fax 0934574500. Number of rooms: 40. Air conditioning; parking, garden, swimming pool. ▣ ▣.

Museums and cultural institutions

Zona archeologica di Vassallaggi. Tel. 0934525936. *Open 9-1.*

Santa Flavia ▣ 90017

ℹ️ *Municipio*. Tel. 091932148.

Hotels, restaurants, campsites, and vacation villages

★★★ **Kafara.** At Sant'Elia, litoranea Mongerbino, tel. 091957377, fax 091957021; www.kafarahotel.it. Number of rooms: 63. Air conditioning, elevator; parking, garden, swimming pool, tennis, private beach. ▣ ▣ ▣ ▣

★★★ **Zagarella and Sea Palace.** At Sòlanto, Via

Nazionale 77, tel. 091903077, fax 091901422; www.shr.it/zagarella.html. Number of rooms: 360. Accessible to the handicapped. Air conditioning, elevator; parking, garden, swimming pool, tennis. AE ⑩ VISA MC

¶¶¶ Muciara-Nello El Greco. At Porticello, Via Roma 105, tel. 091957868, fax 091957271. Closed Monday. Air conditioning. Sicilian cooking – seafood. AE ⑩ VISA

at Sòlunto, km. 1

Archeological digs and Antiquarium. Tel. 091904557. *Open 9-one hour before sunset; Sunday 9-1.*

Sant'Àgata Militello ✉ 98076

Page 189

ℹ️ *Municipio.* Tel. 0941701992.

*** Roma Palace Hotel. Via Nazionale, tel. 0941703516, fax 0941703519. Number of rooms: 48. Air conditioning, elevator; parking, garden. AE ⑩ VISA MC

Museo Etno-Antropologico dei Nèbrodi. Via Cosenz (lungomare), tel. 0941722308. *Closed Sunday. Open 9-12 and 3-6; Saturday groups only, by reservation.*

Castello. Piazza F. Crispi, tel. 0941701000. *Closed Sunday. Open 9-12 and 3-6; Saturday groups only, by reservation.*

Santo Stefano di Camastra ✉ 98077

Page 188

ℹ️ *Municipio.* Tel. 0921331110.

Museo della ceramica. Via Palazzo, Biblioteca Comunale, tel. 0921331110. *Open 9-1 and 4-8.*

Fratelli Fratantoni. State road 113 94, tel. 0921331833. Ceramics workshop. Always open in the summer. By request, it is possible to tour the workshop, with the stone kiln and the potting wheel, and watch the decorators at work.

Sebastiano Insana. Via Vittoria 1/A, tel. 0921337223. Majolica crockery and objects.

San Vito Lo Capo ✉ 91010

Page 86

ℹ️ *Ufficio di informazione turistica*, Via Savoia 74, tel. 0923972160.

*** Capo San Vito. Via Principe Tommaso 29, tel. 0923972122, fax 0923972559. Number of rooms: 35. Air conditioning, elevator; private beach. AE ⑩ VISA MC

** Riva del Sole. Via G. Arimondi 11, tel. and fax 0923972629, fax 0923972621; hotel rds@tin.it. Number of rooms: 9. Air conditioning; private beach. AE ⑩ VISA MC

¶¶ Alfredo. At Valanga, tel. 0923972366. Closed Monday in the low season and part of October and November. Parking, garden. Seafood. AE ⑩ VISA MC.

¶ Tha'am. Via Abruzzi 32, tel. 0923972836. Closed Wednesday from October to June. Air conditioning. Tunisian cooking and the cooking of Trapani – seafood. AE ⑩ VISA

⛺ *** El Bahira. At Salinella, tel. 0923972577, fax 0923972552. Seasonal.

⛺ *** Pineta. Via del Secco 88, tel. 0923972818, fax 0923974070. Open year-round.

⛺ *** La Fata. Via Mattarella 68, tel. 0923972133, fax 0923972133. Open year-round.

Ceramiche Bik Bak. Via Farini 20, tel. 0923 972753. Hand painted ceramic vases and tiles.

Sagra del cuscus. Festival devoted to the culture and cooking of the Mediterranean, with permanent exhibition of Sicilian products and items linked to tuna fishing. September.

Circolo Nautico. Via Faro, tel. 0923972999.

Sciacca ✉ 92019

Map, page 99

ℹ️ *Azienda Autonoma*, Corso Vittorio Emanuele 84, tel. 092521182 (B2).

*** G.H. delle Terme. Viale Nuove Terme 1, tel. 092523133, fax 87002; www.termehotel.com. Number of rooms: 77. Accessible to the handicapped. Air conditioning, elevator; parking, garden, indoor and outdoor swimming pools, private beach. AE ⑩ VISA MC (C3).

¶¶ Hostaria del Vicolo. Vicolo Sammaritano 10, tel. 092523071. Closed Monday and part of October. Air conditioning. Sicilian cooking – fish. AE ⑩ VISA MC; (B2)

¶ Le Gourmet. Toward San Calogero, Via Monte Kronio 7, tel. 092526460; legourmet@tin.it. Closed Tuesday in winter, November. Air conditioning, parking, garden. Classic Italian and Sicilian cooking – seafood. AE ⑩ VISA; (A2, *off map*).

229

on the state road, toward Agrigento, km. 8

★★★ Torre Macauda. Tel. 0925968500, fax 0925 997007; www.torremacauda.com. Seasonal. Number of rooms: 297. Air conditioning, elevator; parking, garden, indoor and outdoor swimming pools, tennis, private beach. AE ⊙ VISA MC

Agriturismo (real Italian country living)

Montalbano. At Scunchipani. Accommodation in a delightful, and modern rural house surrounded by olive and citrus groves. For information: tel. 092580154.

Hot springs/Spas

Nuove Terme. Via Agatocle, tel. 0925961111. Hot springs, with therapeutic baths, mudbaths, inhalations, and massages.

at San Calogero, km. 7

Stufe Vaporose Naturali di S. Calogero. Tel. 092526153. Natural grottoes with steam vents; therapeutic baths, mudbaths.

Cafes and pastry shops

Bar Gelateria La Favola. Corso Vittorio Emanuele 234, tel. 092582777. Ice cream and frozen cakes with fruit.

Pasticceria Pierrot. Via Licata 6, tel. 092526466. Specialties: almond and ricotta. Exquisite pastries served with granita for breakfast in the summer.

Museums and cultural institutions

Museo Scaglione. Piazza Duomo, tel. 092583089. *Open Monday 9-1; Tuesday and Thursday 9-1 and 3-7.*

Castello incantato. State road 115, km. 1.5 east of town, tel. 0925993044. *Closed Monday. Open 1 May-30 September, 10-12 and 4-8; 1 October-30 April, 9-1 and 3-5.*

Shops, crafts, and curiosities

Cantina Sociale Enocarboj (wines). Via Lioni 2/4, tel. 092521992.

Cascio ceramiche. Corso Vittorio Emanuele 115, tel. 092582829.

Marchese ceramica. Via Ghezzi 19, tel. 0925 993227.

Perconte Ceramiche. Contrada Stancapadrone and Via Marco Polo, tel. 0925994005.

Segesta ⊠ 91013

Page 83

Museums and cultural institutions
Tempio. *Open 8:30-one hour before sunset.*

Selinunte ⊠ 91022

Map, page 80

ℹ️ *Parco Archeologico*, tel. 092446251.

Hotels, restaurants, campsites, and vacation villages

at Marinella, km. 1

★★★ Alceste. Via Alceste 21, tel. 092446184, fax 092446143; www.hotelalceste.it. Number of rooms: 26. Air conditioning, elevator; parking, garden. AE ⊙ VISA MC

Ⅱ **Pierrot.** Via Marco Polo 108, tel. 092446205. Closed Tuesday in winter, and from mid-January to February. Parking. Traditional cooking of Trapani. AE ⊙ VISA MC

Museums and cultural institutions

Area archeologica and Antiquarium. Tel. 0924 46251. *Open 9-one hour before sunset.*

Siracusa (Syracuse) ⊠ 96100

Map, page 128-129

ℹ️ *AAPIT*, Via S. Sebastiano 43, tel. 0931481232 (A3).

Azienda Autonoma, Via Maestranza 33, tel. 093165201.

Hotels, restaurants, campsites, and vacation villages

★★★ G.H. Villa Politi. Via Politi Laudien 2, tel. 0931412121, fax 093136061; www.villapoliti.com. Number of rooms: 100. Air conditioning, elevator; parking, garden, swimming pool. AE ⊙ VISA MC; (A5).

★★★ Grand Hotel. Viale Mazzini 12, tel. 0931 464600, fax 0931464611. Number of rooms: 58. Accessible to the handicapped. Air conditioning, elevator; parking, parking garage, private beach. AE ⊙ VISA MC; (D4).

★★★ Jolly. Corso Gelone 43/45, tel. 0931461111, fax 0931461126; www.jollyhotels.it. Number of rooms: 100. Air conditioning, elevator; parking. AE ⊙ VISA MC; (C3).

★★★ Relax. Viale Epipoli 159, tel. 0931740122, fax 0931740933; www.sistema.it/relax. Number of rooms: 42. Air conditioning, elevator; parking, swimming pool, tennis, private beach. AE ⊙ VISA MC; (A2, *off map*).

Ⅱ **Archimede.** Via Gemmellaro 8, tel. 0931 69701; www.trattoriaarchimede.it. Closed Sunday except summer annual closure dates. Air conditioning, garden. Sicilian cooking – seafood. AE ⊙ VISA MC; (E5).

Ⅱ **Darsena-da Iannuzzo.** Riva Garibaldi 6, tel. 093161522. Closed Wednesday. Air conditioning. Sicilian cooking – seafood. AE ⊙ VISA MC; (D4).

Ⅱ **Don Camillo.** Via Maestranza 92/100, tel. 093167133; doncamillo@estranet.it. Closed Sunday, November and Christmas. Air conditioning. Sicilian cooking – fish. AE ⊙ VISA MC; (E5).

Ⅱ **Jonico-'a Rutta 'e Ciauli.** Riviera Dionisio il Grande 194, tel. 093165540. Closed Tuesday, Christmas. Garden. Sicilian cooking – seafood. AE ⊙ VISA MC; (A-B5).

Cantinaccia. Via XX Settembre 13, tel. 093165945. Closed Tuesday except high season, and part of November. Garden. Sicilian cooking – seafood. ⊙ 𝗩𝗜𝗦𝗔 𝗠𝗖; (D4).

Cenacolo. Via del Consiglio Regionale 10, tel. 093165099. Closed Wednesday except summer, from mid-January to mid-February. Sicilian cooking – seafood. 𝗔𝗘 ⊙ 𝗩𝗜𝗦𝗔; (E5).

Medusa. Via S. Teresa 21/23, tel. 093161403. Closed Monday and part of August and September. Air conditioning. Tunisina and Sicilian cooking – seafood. 𝗔𝗘 𝗩𝗜𝗦𝗔 𝗠𝗖; (F5).

Rinaura. Contrada Rinaura, state road 115 at km. 4, tel. and fax 0931721224. Open year-round.

at Fontane Bianche, km. 15 ✉ 96010

★★★ **Fontane Bianche.** Via Mazzarò 1, tel. 0931790611, fax 0931790571. Seasonal. Number of rooms: 164. Accessible to the handicapped. Air conditioning, elevator; parking, swimming pool, tennis, private beach. 𝗔𝗘 ⊙ 𝗩𝗜𝗦𝗔 𝗠𝗖

Spiaggetta. Viale dei Lidi 473, tel. 0931 790334. Closed Tuesday in winter. Air conditioning, parking. Sicilian cooking – seafood; also pizza. 𝗔𝗘 ⊙ 𝗩𝗜𝗦𝗔 𝗠𝗖

Agriturismo (real Italian country living)

La Perciata. Via Spinagallo 77. A 10 km. Reached along the Mare-Monti road, this well-equipped lodging has a swimming pool, tennis court, horse riding. For information: tel. 0931717366.

Limoneto. Provincial road 14 to Canicattini. A farm amid lemon, olive and fruit groves, at 9 km. from Siracusa on the Mare-Monti road. For information: tel. 0931717352.

Villa Lucia. At Isola, traversa Mondello 1. Only 5 km. from downtown, near the sea, a building from the early 20th century. For information: tel. 0931721007.

Cafes and pastry shops

Antico Caffè Minerva. Via Minerva 15, tel. 093122606. One of the oldest cafes in the city. Tea parlor and open-air tables.

Dolcidea. Viale Regina Margherita 23, tel. 093122920. Production and sale (also abroad) of typical sweets and ice cream.

Gran Caffè del Duomo. Piazza Duomo 18, tel. 093121544. Try the "buccellati," the ricotta cannoli, the "frutta martorana," and the tiramisù.

Museums and cultural institutions

Acquario Tropicale (aquarium). Villetta della Marina (accanto alla Fonte Aretusa), tel. 0931 483375. *Open 9-1 and 4-8.*

Castello Eurialo. Tel. 711773. *Open 9-one hour and a half before sunset.*

Castello Maniace. Temporarily closed for renovation.

Catacombe di S. Giovanni. Via S. Giovanni alle Catacombe. *Closed Monday. Open 9-12 and 2:30-5.*

Cripta di S. Marciano. Basilica di S. Giovanni Evangelista. *Closed Tuesday. Open 9-12:30 and 2:30-5:30.*

Galleria Regionale. Via Capodieci 14, tel. 0931 69617. *Closed Monday morning. Open 9-1; Wednesday and Friday also 3-6:30; holidays 9-1:30.*

Ginnasio romano. Via Elorina 7, tel. 093148111. *Closed holidays. Open 9-1.*

Museo Archeologico Regionale Paolo Orsi. Villa Landolina, Viale Teocrito 66, tel. 0931 464022. *Closed Monday morning. Open Tuesday-Saturday 9-1; afternoons and holidays by appointment.*

Museo del Papiro. Via Teocrito 66, tel. 0931 61616. *Closed Monday. Open 9-1:30.*

Parco Archeologico della Neàpoli. (archeological site: Greek theater, altar of Hiero II, Roman amphitheater, latomie or prisons). Viale Rizzo, tel. 093166206. *Open 9-two hours before sunset.*

Santuario della Madonna delle Lacrime. Via del Santuario, tel. 093121446. *Open 7-12:30 and 4-7.*

Excursions and organized tours

Excursions at the Porto Grande and the island Ortigia. On board the Selene. For information: tel. 093162776-093139889.

Excursions on the river Ciane. For information: tel. 093169076-093139889.

Cultural events

Estate Siracusana. Music and theatrical performances in the historic center of Ortigia and at the sea resorts.

Festa del mare - Regata dell'Assunta nel Porto Grande. Tel. 0931481232. 15 August.

Festa di S. Lucia. Celebrations for the patron saint of the city. First Sunday of May and 13-20 December.

Rappresentazioni classiche al teatro Greco (Greek theater). Biennial cycle organized in May and June by Istituto Nazionale del Dramma Antico. For information: tel. 093167415.

Shops, crafts, and curiosities

Azienda Agricola Pupillo. Contrada Targia (Provincial road Siracusa-Priolo), tel. 0931492701. Moscato DOC of Siracusa.

Dieci e lode. Viale Zecchino 165, tel. 0931442655. A selection of regional products.

Fabbrica del Papiro. Via Capodieci 46, tel. 0931703572. Handmade items of papyrus paper.

Flavia Massara. Via Capodieci 15, tel. 093161340. Items and decorations of papyrus paper.

Quadrifoglio. Via SS. Coronati 13, tel. 0931 463649. Artistic glass items.

Natural areas, parks and reserves

Riserva naturale fiume Ciane e Saline di Siracusa. Tel. 09317079262. *Open 7-one hour before sunset.*

Taormina ☒ 98039

Map, page 168

ℹ️ *Azienda Autonoma*, Piazza S. Caterina, tel. 094223243 (A2).

Hotels, restaurants, campsites, and vacation villages

★★★ **San Domenico Palace.** Piazza S. Domenico 5, tel. 0942613111, fax 0942625506; www.thi.it. Number of rooms: 108. Accessible to the handicapped. Air conditioning, elevator; parking, parking garage, garden, swimming pool, private beach. ⏣ ⓐ 𝖵𝖨𝖲𝖠 𝖬𝖢; (B1).

★★★ **G.H. Timeo.** Via Teatro Greco 59, tel. 0942 23801, fax 0942628501; www.framon-hotels.com. Number of rooms: 56. Air conditioning, elevator; parking, garden, private beach. ⏣ ⓐ 𝖵𝖨𝖲𝖠 𝖬𝖢; (B3).

★★★ **Excelsior Palace.** Via Toselli 6, tel. 0942 23975, fax 094223978. Number of rooms: 88. Air conditioning, elevator; parking, garden, swimming pool. ⏣ ⓐ 𝖵𝖨𝖲𝖠 𝖬𝖢; (B1).

★★★ **G.H. Miramare.** Via Guardiola Vecchia 27, tel. 094223401, fax 0942626223. Seasonal. Number of rooms: 68. Air conditioning, elevator; parking, garden, swimming pool, private beach. ⏣ ⓐ 𝖵𝖨𝖲𝖠 𝖬𝖢; (B3).

★★★ **Villa Diodoro.** Via Bagnoli Croce 75, tel. 094223312, fax 094223391; www.gaishotels.com. Number of rooms: 102. Accessible to the handicapped. Air conditioning, elevator; parking, garden, swimming pool, private beach. ⏣ ⓐ 𝖵𝖨𝖲𝖠 𝖬𝖢; (B3).

★★★ **Villa Fabbiano.** Via Pirandello 81, corner of Via Bagnoli Croci, tel. 0942626058, fax 094223732. Seasonal. Number of rooms: 27. Rooms only; no dining facilities. Air conditioning, elevator; parking, garden, swimming pool, private beach. ⏣ ⓐ 𝖵𝖨𝖲𝖠 𝖬𝖢; (A3).

★★★ **Bel Soggiorno.** Via Pirandello 60, tel. 094223342, fax 0942626298. Number of rooms: 18 – 17 of them with bath or shower. Rooms only; no dining facilities. Parking, garden. ⏣ ⓐ 𝖵𝖨𝖲𝖠 𝖬𝖢; (B-C3).

★★★ **Isabella.** Corso Umberto 58, tel. 0942 23153, fax 094223155; www.gaishotels.com. Number of rooms: 32. Air conditioning, elevator; private beach. ⏣ ⓐ 𝖵𝖨𝖲𝖠 𝖬𝖢; (B1-2).

★★★ **Villa Belvedere.** Via Bagnoli Croce 79, tel. 094223791, fax 0942625830; www.villabelvedere.it. Seasonal. Number of rooms: 47. Elevator; parking, garden, swimming pool. ⏣ 𝖵𝖨𝖲𝖠 𝖬𝖢; (B3).

★★★ **Villa Fiorita.** Via Pirandello 39, tel. 094224122, fax 0942625967. Number of rooms: 24. Rooms only, no dining facilities. Air conditioning, elevator; parking garage, garden, swimming pool. ⏣ ⓐ 𝖵𝖨𝖲𝖠 𝖬𝖢; (A3).

★★ **Condor.** Via Dietro Cappuccini 25, tel. 0942 23124, fax 0942625726; www.logis.it. Seasonal. Number of rooms: 12. Rooms only, no dining facilities. Air conditioning; parking, private beach. ⏣ ⓐ 𝖵𝖨𝖲𝖠 𝖬𝖢; (A2).

★★ **Villa Ducale.** Via L. da Vinci 60, tel. 0942 28153, fax 094228710; www.hotelvilladucale.it. Number of rooms: 12. Rooms only, no dining facilities. Accessible to the handicapped. Air conditioning; parking, garden, private beach. ⏣ ⓐ 𝖵𝖨𝖲𝖠 𝖬𝖢; (A1).

★★ **Villa Schuler.** Piazzetta Bastione, corner of Via Roma, tel. 094223481, fax 094223522; www.villaschuler.com. Seasonal. Number of rooms: 26 (22 with bath or shower). Rooms only, no dining facilities. Accessible to the handicapped. Air conditioning, elevator, parking garage, garden, tennis, private beach. ⏣ ⓐ 𝖵𝖨𝖲𝖠 𝖬𝖢; (B2).

🍴🍴🍴 **La Giara.** Vico La Floresta 1, tel. 094223360, fax 094223233. Closed at midday and Monday (except August), November and from 1 January to 28 February. Air conditioning. Refined Sicilian cooking – seafood. ⏣ ⓐ 𝖵𝖨𝖲𝖠; (B2).

🍴🍴🍴 **Casa Grugno.** Via S. Maria de' Greci, tel. 094221208; www.casagrugno.it. Closed Sunday, February. Air conditioning, garden. Classic Italian cooking – seafood. ⏣ ⓐ 𝖵𝖨𝖲𝖠 𝖬𝖢; (B1).

🍴🍴🍴 **Maffei's.** Via S. Domenico de Guzman 1, tel. 094224055. Closed Tuesday in winter, and part of January and February. Garden. Sicilian cooking – seafood. ⏣ ⓐ 𝖵𝖨𝖲𝖠 𝖬𝖢; (B1).

🍴🍴 **Al Duomo.** Vico Ebrei 11, tel. 0942625656. Closed Sunday in low season, February. Air conditioning. Sicilian cooking – fish. ⏣ ⓐ 𝖵𝖨𝖲𝖠 𝖬𝖢; (B1).

🍴🍴 **Griglia.** Corso Umberto 54, tel. 094223980; www.tao.it/intelisano. Closed Tuesday, from mid-November to mid-December. Air conditioning. The cooking of Messina – seafood. ⏣ ⓐ 𝖵𝖨𝖲𝖠; (A2).

🍴 **Il Ciclope.** Corso Umberto, tel. 094223263; ristoranteilciclope@tiscali.it. Closed Wednesday, from mid-January to mid-February. Air conditioning. Cooking of Messina – seafood. ⏣ ⓐ 𝖵𝖨𝖲𝖠 𝖬𝖢; (B1).

at Capo Taormina, km. 3 ☒ 98030

★★★ **G.A. Capotaormina.** Via Nazionale 105, tel. 0942572111, fax 0942625467; www.capotaorminahotel.com. Seasonal. Number of rooms: 202. Air conditioning, elevator; parking, parking garage, garden, swimming pool, private beach. ⏣ ⓐ 𝖵𝖨𝖲𝖠 𝖬𝖢; (C4).

at Mazzarò, km. 4 ☒ 98030

★★★ **G.H. Mazzarò Sea Palace.** Via Nazionale 147, tel. 0942612111, fax 0942626237; www.mazzaroseapalace.it. Seasonal. Number of rooms: 88. Air conditioning, elevator; swimming pool, private beach. ⏣ ⓐ 𝖵𝖨𝖲𝖠 𝖬𝖢; (A5).

★☆☆ **Villa Sant'Andrea.** Via Nazionale 137, tel. 094223125, fax 094224838; santandrea@fra mon-hotels.com. Number of rooms: 67. Air conditioning, elevator; parking, garden, private beach. $\overline{AE}$ $\overline{OD}$ $\overline{VISA}$ $\overline{MC}$; (A5).

❙❙ **Delfino-da Angelo.** Via Nazionale, tel. 094223004. Seasonal. The cooking of Messina – seafood. $\overline{AE}$ $\overline{OD}$ $\overline{VISA}$ $\overline{MC}$; (A5).

Cafes and pastry shops

Pasticceria Gilda. Corso Umberto I 208, tel. 0942 24877. Jasmine ice cream, almond paste, and "torrone," a kind of nougat, with aroma of orange.

Pasticceria Vasta. Via Giardinazzo 18/A, tel. 0942 625567. Aside from the confectionery specialties, they offer fine pasta dishes, such as Pasta alla Norma, or Pasta alle sarde, to eat at the counter.

at Castelmola, km. 5

Caffè San Giorgio. Piazza San'Antonio 1, tel. 094228228. A cafe with a long tradition, where you can enjoy sweet almond wine, sitting on distinctive "scanni," or stools.

Museums and cultural institutions

Museo delle Arti figurative popolari della Sicilia. Palazzo Corvaja. Piazza S. Caterina. *Open 9-1 and 4-8.*

Teatro Greco (Greek theater). Via Teatro Greco 40, tel. 094223220. *Open 9-one hour before sunset.*

Cultural Events

Taormina Arte. In summer there is a revue of film, theater, dance, and music. For information: tel. 094221142.

Villa Comunale e Palazzo Corvaja. Series of musical and theatrical performances organized by the Azienda di Soggiorno e Turismo, tel. 094223243.

Tèrmini Imerese ✉ 90018

Map, page 186

🛈 *Municipio*, tel. 0918128253.

Hotels, restaurants, campsites, and vacation villages

★☆☆ **G.H. delle Terme.** Piazza delle Terme 2, tel. 0918113557, fax 0918113107. Number of rooms: 69. Air conditioning, elevator; parking, parking garage, garden, swimming pool. $\overline{AE}$ $\overline{OD}$ $\overline{VISA}$ $\overline{MC}$; (B-C2).

★☆☆ **Himera Polis Hotel.** State road 113, near Buonfornello, tel. 0918140566, fax 091 8140567. Number of rooms: 55. Air conditioning, elevator; parking, private beach. $\overline{AE}$ $\overline{OD}$ $\overline{VISA}$ $\overline{MC}$; (D3, *off map*).

Hot springs/Spas

Stabilimento Termale. Piazza delle Terme 2, tel. 0918113557. Hot springs, with therapeutic baths, mudbaths, inhalations, grottoes, mists, and massages.

Cafes and pastry shops

Pasticceria del Vicolo. Via Mazzarino 100, tel. 0918114052.

Museums and cultural institutions

Museo Civico. Via del Museo, tel. 0918128279. *Closed Monday. Open 9-1 and 3:30-5:30.*

Cultural Events

Il Carnevale di Tèrmini. Impressive procession of allegorical floats in February. For information: tel. 0918128253.

at Buonfornello, km. 13

Archeological digs of Himera and antiquarium. Tel. 0918140128. *Open 9-6; holidays 9-1.*

Terrasini ✉ 90049

Page 48

🛈 *Presidio turistico*, Piazza Duomo, tel. 091 8686733.

Hotels, restaurants, campsites, and vacation villages

★★★ **Azzolini Palm Beach.** Via Ciucca, tel. 0918682033, fax 0918682618; www.neome dia.it/azzolini. Number of rooms: 38. Air conditioning, elevator; parking, garden, private beach. $\overline{AE}$ $\overline{OD}$ $\overline{VISA}$ $\overline{MC}$

❙❙❙ **Primafila.** Via Saputo 8, tel. 0918684422; www.sicilian.net/primafila. Closed Monday, for a period in November. Air conditioning. Sicilian cooking – seafood. $\overline{AE}$ $\overline{OD}$ $\overline{VISA}$ $\overline{MC}$

Museums and cultural institutions

Museo Civico. Palazzo Daumale, lungomare P. Impastato, tel. 0918619000.

Cultural events

Festa de li schietti. At Easter eve, the unmarried men of the city cut an orange tree which they set in front of the church the next day then, decorated with ribbons and other objects. They compete in having the tree balanced on their palm as long as possible. Great feast with goat meat.

Trapani ✉ 91100

Map, page 64-65

🛈 *AAPIT*, Via San Francesco d'Assisi 27, tel. 0923545511 (B2).

Hotels, restaurants, campsites, and vacation villages

★☆☆ **Crystal.** Via S. Giovanni Bosco 12, tel. 092320000, fax 092325555. Number of rooms: 70. Accessible to the handicapped. Air conditioning, elevator; parking garage. $\overline{AE}$ $\overline{OD}$ $\overline{VISA}$ $\overline{MC}$; (A-B3).

★★★ **Nuovo Albergo Russo.** Via Tintori 4, tel. 092322166, fax 092326623. Number of rooms: 36 – 31 of them with bath or show-

233

er. Rooms only; no dining facilities. Elevator; parking, parking garage. $\overline{VISA}$ $\overline{MC}$ (B2).

★★★ **Vittoria.** Via Crispi 4, tel. 0923873044, fax 092329870; www.hotelvittoriatrapani.it. Number of rooms: 65. Rooms only; no dining facilities. Air conditioning, elevator. $\overline{AE}$ $\overline{OD}$ $\overline{VISA}$ $\overline{MC}$ (A3).

¶¶ **P. e G.** Via Spalti 1, tel. 0923547701. Closed Sunday, from 1 August to mid-September. Air conditioning. The cooking of Trapani. $\overline{AE}$ $\overline{OD}$ $\overline{VISA}$; (A-B3).

¶¶ **Taverna Paradiso.** Lungomare D. Alighieri 22, tel. 092322303. Closed Sunday, August. Air conditioning. Seafood. $\overline{AE}$ $\overline{OD}$ $\overline{VISA}$ $\overline{MC}$; (A4, *off map*).

¶ **Ai Lumi.** Corso Vittorio Emanuele 75, tel. 0923872418; www.ailumi.it. Closed Sunday. Air conditioning. Seafood. $\overline{AE}$ $\overline{OD}$ $\overline{MC}$; (B2).

Agriturismo (real Italian country living)

Duca di Castelmonte. At Xitta, Via Salvatore Motisi 3. Comfortable apartments. Bicycles and cooking courses, excursions. For information: tel. 0923526139.

Cafes and pastry shops

Colicchia. Via delle Arti 6, tel. 0923547612. Ice cream and typical pastries.

Novecento. Via G.B. Fardella 88, tel. 092322502. Home-made pastries and ice cream.

Museums and cultural institutions

Museo della Preistoria. Torre di Ligny, tel. 0923 22300. *Open 9:30-12:30 and 4:30-7.*

Museo Regionale Pepoli. Via Conte Agostino Pepoli 200, tel. 0923553269. *Open 9-1:30; Tuesday and Thursday also 3-6; Sunday and holidays 9-12:30.*

at Paceco, km. 5

Museo del Sale (salt museum). Contrada Nùbia, tel. 0923867442. *Closed Saturday and holidays. Open 9-1.*

Theater, music and cultural events

Luglio Musicale Trapanese. Villa Margherita, Concerts in July and August. For information: tel. 092321454.

Processione dei Misteri. Procession of 20 artistic groups representing the Passion. Good Friday and Saturday.

Sports

Circolo Canottieri (rowing). Viale Regina Elena 94, tel. 092328084.

Circolo Tennis. Contrada Milo, tel. 0923532488.

Shops, crafts, and curiosities

Ditta Poma. Via del Legno 22, tel. 092328682. Production of coral objects.

Natural areas, parks and reserves

Riserva naturale Saline di Trapani e Paceco. Run by: WWF Italia, Via Garibaldi 138, Paceco, tel. 0923867700.

Trecastagni ✉ 95039

Hotels, restaurants, campsites, and vacation villages

¶ **Villa Taverna.** Corso Colombo 42, tel. 095 806458. Closed Sunday evening and Monday and part of January and September. Parking, garden. Sicilian cooking. $\overline{VISA}$

Ùstica ✉ 90010

Page 54

🛈 *Ufficio informazioni*, Piazza Umberto I, tel. 0918449456.

Hotels, restaurants, campsites, and vacation villages

★★★ **Grotta Azzurra.** Contrada San Ferlicchio, tel. 0918449048, fax 0918449396; ricevimento.hga@framon-hotels.it. Seasonal. Number of rooms: 51. Swimming pool, private beach. $\overline{AE}$ $\overline{OD}$ $\overline{VISA}$ $\overline{MC}$

¶¶ **Mamma Lia.** Via S. Giacomo 1, tel. 091 8449594. Seasonal. Parking, garden. Seafood. $\overline{AE}$ $\overline{VISA}$

Museums and cultural institutions

Acquario. Punta Spalmatore, tel. 0918449456. *Open summer 10-1 and 3-6; winter 10-1.*

Museo Archeologico. Torre di S. Maria, tel. 0918449456. *Open only by appointment.*

Cultural events

Festa di S. Bartolo. Folklore performances. 24 August.

Natural areas, parks and reserves

Area naturale marina e Riserva naturale Isola di Ùstica. Visitors center, tel. 0918449456; free call 091848207926.

Valdérice ✉ 91019

Hotels, restaurants, campsites, and vacation villages

★★★ **Tonnara di Bonagia.** At Tonnara di Bonagia, Piazza Tonnara, tel. 0923431111, fax 0923592177. Seasonal. Number of rooms: 46. Accessible to the handicapped. Air conditioning, elevator; parking, garden, swimming pool, tennis, private beach. $\overline{AE}$ $\overline{OD}$ $\overline{VISA}$ $\overline{MC}$

▲★ **Lido Valderice.** At Sant'Andrea Bonagia, Via del Dentice 15, tel. 0923573477. Seasonal.

Vittoria ✉ 97019

Page 113

i   *Pro Loco*, Via Cavour 53, tel. 0932510140.

Hotels, restaurants, campsites, and vacation villages

★★★ **Grand Hotel.** Vico III C. Pisacane 53/B, tel. 0932863888, fax 0932863888. Number of rooms: 27 – 26 with shower or bath. Rooms only; no dining facilities. Air conditioning, elevator; parking garage. ⒜Ⓔ ⓞⒹ ⓥⒾⓈⒶ

at Scoglitti, km. 13 ✉ 97010

★★★ **Agathae.** Via Montale 33, tel. 0932980730, fax 0932871500; www.agathaehotel.it. Number of rooms: 27. Air conditioning; parking, parking garage, garden, swimming pool, private beach. ⒜Ⓔ ⓞⒹ ⓥⒾⓈⒶ Ⓜ Ⓒ

¶¶ **Sakalleo.** Piazza Cavour 12, tel. 0932871688. Closed from mid-November to mid-December. Air conditioning. Seafood. ⒜Ⓔ ⓞⒹ ⓥⒾⓈⒶ

¶ **Maria Tindara.** Provincial road 38, tel. 0932853004; mariatindara@ciaoweb.it. Seasonal. Parking, garden. Aeolian cuisine.

Zafferana Etnea ✉ 95019

Page 156

i   *Pro Loco*, Piazza Luigi Sturzo 1, tel. 095 7082825.

Hotels, restaurants, campsites, and vacation villages

★★★ **Airone.** At Airone, Via Cassone 67, tel. 0957081819, fax 0957082142; www.hotel-airone.it. Number of rooms: 60. Accessible to the handicapped. Air conditioning, elevator, parking, parking garage, garden. ⒜Ⓔ ⓞⒹ ⓥⒾⓈⒶ Ⓜ Ⓒ

★★★ **Primavera dell'Etna.** At Airone, Via Cassone 86, tel. 0957082348, fax 0957081695; www.hotel-primavera.it. Number of rooms: 57. Accessible to the handicapped. Air conditioning, elevator; parking, parking garage, garden, tennis. ⒜Ⓔ ⓞⒹ ⓥⒾⓈⒶ Ⓜ Ⓒ

¶¶ **Parco dei Principi.** Via delle Ginestre 1, tel. 0957082335; www.paginegialle.it/parcodeiprin cipi. Closed Tuesday. Air conditioning, parking. Classic Italian and Sicilian cooking. ⒜Ⓔ ⓞⒹ ⓥⒾⓈⒶ Ⓜ Ⓒ

Index of places and monuments

Index of places and monuments

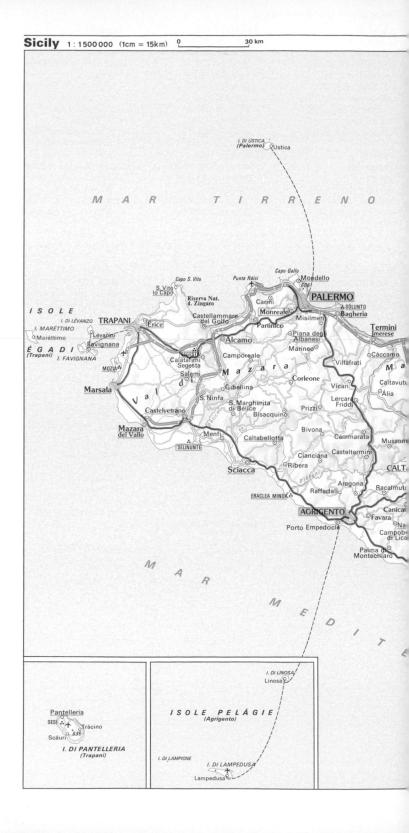

Sicily

1 : 1 500 000 (1cm = 15km)   0 _____ 30 km

MAR TIRRENO

I. DI ÚSTICA
(Palermo) ○ Ustica

Capo S. Vito   *Punta Ráisi*   *Capo Gallo*   ○ Mondello
                                                806I
S. Vito   Carini   **PALERMO**
lo Capo   ⚓SOLUNTO
        Riserva Nat.   Castellammare   Monreale ○   ○Bagheria
ISOLE   d. Zíngaro   del Golfo   Misilmeri   **Termini**
I. DI LÉVANZO **TRAPANI** ○ Erice   Alcamo   Partinico   *Imerese*
I. MARÉTTIMO   Piana degli   **M a**
○Maréttimo   Lévanzo   Albanesi   ○Cáccamo
ÉGADI   ○Favignana   Camporeale   Marineo○
(Trapani) *I. FAVIGNANA*   ○Villafrati   **M a**
        MOZIA⚬   SEGESTA   **M a z a r a**   Caltavutu
                        Calatafimi   Vicari
                         Segesta   Corleone○   ○Ália
Marsala   Salemi   Lercara
                          d i   S. Margherita   Friddi
        V a l   S. Ninfa   di Bélice   Prizzi○
        Castelvetrano   Bisacquino
Mazara   Bivona○   Cammarata
del Vallo   Menfi   Caltabellotta   Casteltermini Mussom
                     SELINUNTE   Cianciana
                                                  ○Ribera   **CALT**
                             Scíacca   Aragona   Racalmuto
                  ERACLEA MINOA⚬   Raffadali○   Canicat
                                      AGRIGENTO   ○Favara
                                   Porto Empédocle   ○Na
                                                              Campobe
                                                              di Lica
                                                        Palma di○
                                                        Montechiaro

MAR

MEDITE

Pantelleria   *I. DI LINOSA*
SESI⚬   Linosa ◦
    ○Trácino   **ISOLE PELÁGIE**
    836   **(Agrigento)**
Scáuri
I. DI PANTELLERIA
(Trapani)   *I. DI LAMPIONE*   *I. DI LAMPEDUSA*
                                      Lampedusa ◦

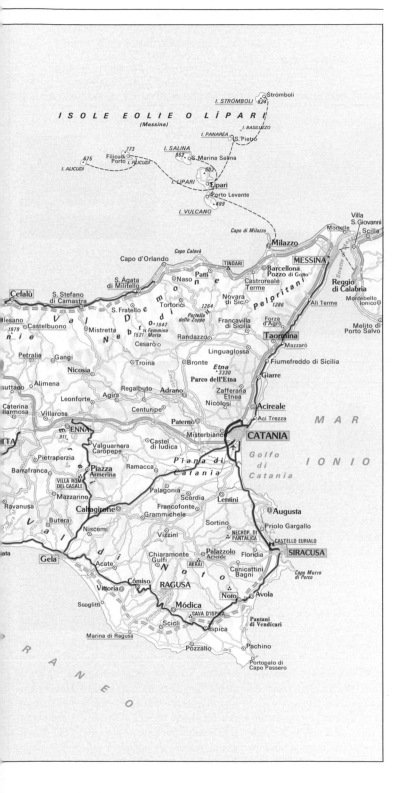

HOTEL ALOHA D'ORO

★ ★ ★ ★

The Aloha D'Oro Hotel is adjacent to the city centre of Acireale and, in the mean time, at a stone throw from the sea. It is located within a park gradually descending to our private beach below, made of lava stones, and to our outfitted platforms, reached by a private 500 Mt long road. The hotel also disposes two swimming pools, one of which is heated from 21st March until 31st October. Unusual for a modern hotel, it is characterized by a main area called "Il Castello" (The Castle). It is build with materials and techniques ty-

pical of this area, enriched with wooden windows and window frames, red tiles, arches, towers and wrought iron decorations. As for the architecture, our cuisine is highly influenced by local traditions of good food; our restaurant "Le Torri" (The Towers) displays every evening on its menu at least one main course and one second course, both based on fresh Mediterranean fish.

De Gasperi rd, 10 - 95024 Acireale
Tel. +39 095 7687001 - Fax +39 095 606984
info@hotel-aloha.it - www.hotel-aloha.com

CALTAGIRONE TOURIST BOARD

Caltagirone

Lady of colours UNESCO'S world heritage list

IN THE HEART OF SICILY, THE CITY OF CERAMICS

Information Azienda Turismo - Volta Libertini, 3 - 95041 Caltagirone (Italia) - Tel. 339 933 53809

In purezza

The "**Aziende Vitivinicole Donnafugata**" are located in Sicily. They were born thanks to the enterprise of a family who have been working for 150 years in the production of quality wines.

Giacomo Rallo, the forth-generation child of the oldest Sicilian family engaged in viniculture, together with his wife Gabriella Anca and their two children José and Antonio, have started a modern wine firm.

Donnafugata and its wines are the result of an efficient équipe research work aiming at the recovery of vine tradition and at a new development of production techniques in wine making for a better exploitation of Nature.

The production process goes from the growing of the vines up to the harvesting, fermentation and ageing. The vineyards and cellars are located on the Belice hills in Contessa Entellina area and in the island of Pantelleria. Out of these vineyards as well as other neighbouring ones, thanks to their climatic and soil characteristics, is produced a great range of top quality wines. Donnafugata wines are aged and bottled in the ancient cellars of the Rallo family in Marsala

Today Giacomo and Gabriella, together with their son Antonio and daughter José open the ancient cellars in Marsala, to all winelovers, offering them the chance of guided tours, professional wine tastings and sought after Sicilian culinary specialities.

DONNAFUGATA

Vineyards and Cellars: Contessa Entellina (PA) - Pantelleria (TP)
Historical Cellars and Administration: Via S. Lipari, 18 - 91025 Marsala (TP) - Italy

Tel. +39.0923.724200 - Fax +39.0923.722042
www.donnafugata.it • info@donnafugata.it

Hotel Raya

The hotel complex is made up of three separate bodies each 200 metres from each other:

Raya® Hotel: situated 400 mtrs from the port on a hillside in gardens of luxurious Mediterranean flora. A pyramid shaped structure which includes 30 rooms that look out over the sourranding islets and the volcano Stromboli. Each room, all with air conditioning, with its own terrace differs from the other in design but are linked by a similar style. A small bar is on hand for a continental breakfast, wich can also be served on your terrace(for a small surcharge).

Raya® Boutique: descending the narrow streets from Raya® Hotel one passes the boutique where Myriam Beltrami design a wide range of clothes, sarong and bathing suits of natural fibres ideal for Panarea. A vast selection of gifths, and wooden Indonesian furniture can be found in the antique section. Above the boutique are situated the six rooms which make up the dependence, all with air conditioning and bathrooms with sauna-shower.

Raya® Porto: a few moments walk from boutiques overlooking the sea, holds the reception, bar, restaurant, disco (opening hight season) and solarium terrace. Here guestes are served a buffet-brunch till midday; our restaurant is open for dinner (menu à la carte). You can eat in the relaxing light of oil lamps while watching the eruptions of the volcano Stromboli. We suggest you to reserve it.

Raya® Hotel has double rooms, doubles use for single, triple rooms and suites; due to the many steps and low walls this property is suitable neither to guests with walking difficulties nor to childreen under 12 years og age.

Airport nearest: Reggio Calabria – Catania – Palermo – Naples
Hydrofoil (double the time for ferries) crossing from Milazzo approx. 2hrs
From Naples by ship 12h (Siremar) by hydrofoil 4h 30m (Snav only in summer)

Via San Pietro - 98050 Panarea Messina
Tel. 0039 090 983013 - Fax 0039 090 983103
E-mail: info@hotelraya.it

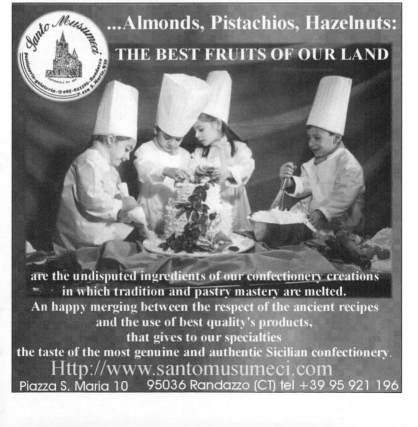

HOTEL

VILLA PARADISO DELL'ETNA
★★★★

Via per Viagrande, 37 - S.G. La Punta
95030 Catania
Tel. 0957512409 pbx - Fax 0957413861
E-mail: hotelvilla@paradisoetna.it
Internet: http//www.paradisoetna.it

The Hotel built in 1927 was for many years the haunt of artists, travelers and notables of the time. It has been completely restructured. Surrounded by

a magnificent garden, situated at the foothill of Etna it is only a short distance from Catania, Taormina and the most popular tourist sites in Sicily. The Hotel is provided with all modern amenities. Guests are greeted with the warmth of our hospitality in an old style atmosphere of antiques and romantic fire places. Al 30 rooms and 4 suites have a panoramic view of Etna or the garden and are furnished with sicilian antiques, old style uphol-

stery and antique prints and paintings. Inlayed floors of old marble "graniglie", afrescoed waals decorated with trompe l'oeil and plaster mouldings created by experienced craftsmen come together to create a very refined environment. The culinary delights of our restaurant "La Pigna" complete your stay. You may try typical sicilian cooking or have a taste of traditional italian or international dishes. All of which are prepared with the freshest ingredients, great care and a touch of class. Those with particular tastes have the pleasure of choosing their favorite wines from our cellar. In our 3 conference

rooms we are able to offer the most sophisticated technical equipment for buisness meeting or conferences, confortably seating up to 180 people. The Cosmo Mollica room with its old "lava stone" wall, the "boiseries" and liberty glass windows create a warm atmosphere for selected

groups, working breakfasts and pleasurable private meetings.

A warm
Sicilian Welcome

Excelsior Palace Terme
(Acireale - CT)

Hotel Zagarella & Sea Palace
(S. Flavia - PA)

Hotel Biancaneve
(Nicolosi - CT)

Hotel Airone
(Zafferana Etnea - CT)

Hotel Club Eolian Inn
(Milazzo Mare - ME)

Cristal Palace Hotel
(Palermo)

december 2002	*february 2003*	*june 2003*
Casale Mongibello (Zafferana Etnea - CT)	Hotel Selene (Piazza Armerina - EN)	Hotel Kore (Agrigento)

next opening

Sales Office:
Via delle Terme, 103
95024 Acireale (CT)

phone +39.095.7688508-056
fax +39.095.7688014
Internet: www.shr.it
E-mail: info@shr.it

grafica **tml** +39.095.370120